POLITICAL MEMOIR:
ESSAYS ON THE POLITICS OF MEMORY

Political Memoir

Essays on the Politics of Memory

edited by
GEORGE EGERTON

FRANK CASS

First published in 1994 in Great Britain by
FRANK CASS & CO. LTD.
Gainsborough House, Gainsborough Road,
London E11 1RS, England

and in the United States of America by
FRANK CASS
c/o International Specialized Book Services, Inc.
5804 N.E. Hassalo Street, Portland, Oregon 97213-3644

Transferred to Digital Printing 2004

British Library Cataloguing in Publication Data

Political Memoir: Essays on the Politics of Memory
I. Egerton, George
320.9

ISBN 0-7146-3471-9 (cased)
ISBN 0-7146-4093-X (paperback)

Library of Congress Cataloging-in-Publication Data

Political memoir : essays on the politics of memory
/edited by George Egerton
    p.   cm.
    Papers presented at the Conference on Political Memoirs, held at
the University of British Columbia, Sept. 22–24, 1989.
    Includes bibliographical references.
    ISBN 0-7146-3471-9 (cased) — ISBN 0-7146-4093-X
(pbk.)
    1. Politics and literature—Congresses. 2. Politics in
literature—Congresses. 3. Biography as a literary form—
Congresses. 4. Autobiography—Congresses. 5. Historiography—
Congresses. I. Egerton, George W. II. Conference on Political
Memoirs (1989 : University of British Columbia)
PN51.P556 1994
920.02—dc20   93-30585
                                                  CIP

Typeset by Vitaset, Paddock Wood, Kent

Contents

Preface

The essays included in this volume represent the collaboration of participants in the Conference on Political Memoirs which convened at the University of British Columbia, 22–24 September 1989. The Conference, in turn, had its origins in the Political Memoirs Project, a multi-disciplinary project initiated in 1987 within the History Department at the University of British Columbia and designed to study the nature and functions of the genre of political memoir. The Project and its Conference have attracted the participation of some 25 scholars from Britain, Europe, Canada and the United States, chosen because of their interests and publications relating to selected political memoirists and themes in the production of memoir literature.

The editor of the present volume has served as the Director of the Political Memoirs Project and Chairman of the Conference on Political Memoirs. He would like to acknowledge the support received from colleagues in the History Department and the Office of the Dean of Arts, from the students of the International Relations Students Association and History Students Association, and from International House which hosted the Conference.

Financial assistance for the Project and the Conference on Political Memoirs has come from the Social Science and Humanities Research Council of Canada and is gratefully acknowledged. A special debt of gratitude is owed to Professor Mark Zacher, past Director of the Institute of International Relations at the University of British Columbia, who extended the Institute's financial support for the Conference on Political Memoirs and the subsequent editorial expenses leading to publication of this volume.

Notes on Contributors

Stephen Ambrose Alumni Distinguished Professor, University of New Orleans; biographer of Eisenhower and Nixon; author of *Rise to Globalism: American Foreign Policy since 1938* (1991).

János Bak Professor Emeritus of History, University of British Columbia; co-editor of *Socialism and Social Science: Selected Writings of Irvin Szabo* (1983); co-author of *Religion and Rural Revolt* (1984).

Robert Bothwell Professor of History, University of Toronto; author of *Nucleus: The History of Atomic Energy of Canada, Ltd.* (1988); co-author of *Canada: 1900–1945* (1987).

Valerie Cromwell Reader in History, University of Sussex; member of the Lord Chancellor's Advisory Council on the Public Records; a Vice-President of the Royal Historical Society; author of *Revolution or Evolution: British Government in the Nineteenth Century* (1977); Director, History of Parliament.

George Egerton Associate Professor of History, University of British Columbia; author of *The British Government and the Creation of the League of Nations* (1979); 'The Lloyd George *War Memoirs*: a Study in the Politics of Memory', *Journal of Modern History* (March 1988); Director, Political Memoirs Project.

Robert H. Ferrell Professor of History, Indiana University; editor of *Eisenhower Diaries* (1981); *Off the Record: The Private Papers of Harry S. Truman* (1980); author of *Harry S. Truman and the Modern American Presidency* (1983) and *Woodrow Wilson and World War I* (1985).

Barry Gough Professor of History, Wilfred Laurier University; editor of *To the Pacific and Arctic with Beechey* (1973); author of *The Royal Navy and the Northwest Coast of North America, 1810–1914* (1971) and *Gunboat Frontier: British Maritime Authority and Northwest Coast Indians, 1846–90* (1984).

Francis H. Heller Roy A. Roberts Distinguished Professor of Law and Political Science, University of Kansas (ret. 1988); author of *The Truman White House* (1980). Assisted President Truman with his memoirs.

Leonidas E. Hill Professor of History, University of British Columbia; editor of *Die Weiszäcker Papiere* (1974, 1982); articles on modern German history.

Milton Israel Associate Professor of History, University of Toronto; co-editor of *City, Country, and Society in Maharashtra* (1988); *Sikh History and Religion in the Twentieth Century* (1988).

B.J.C. McKercher Associate Professor, Royal Military College of Canada; author of *Esme Howard: A Diplomatic Biography* (1988); editor of *Anglo-American Relations in the 1920s: The Struggle for Supremacy* (1990).

Joshua Mostow Assistant Professor, Department of Asian Studies, University of British Columbia.

John A. Munro Professional writer; researcher, Diefenbaker memoirs; co-editor of *The Memoirs of the Rt. Hon. Lester B. Pearson* (1973, 1975); editor of *The China Diaries of Margaret Outerbridge* (1989).

John F. Naylor Professor of History, State University of New York at Buffalo; author of *Labour's International Policy: The Labour Party in the 1930s* (1969), *A Man and an Institution: Sir Maurice Hankey, the Cabinet Secretariat, and the Custody of Cabinet Secrecy* (1984).

Otto Pflanze Charles P. Stevenson Professor of History, Bard College, New York; former editor of *American Historical Review*; author of *Bismarck and the Development of Germany* (1990).

Zara Steiner Fellow and Lecturer in History, New Hall, Cambridge; author of *The Foreign Office and Foreign Policy, 1889–1914* (1986); *Britain and the Origins of the First World War* (1978).

Tim Travers Professor of History, University of Calgary; author of *The Killing Ground: The British Army, the Western Front and the Emergence of Modern Warfare* (1987) and *How the War Was Won: Command and Technology in the British Army on the Western Front, 1917–1918* (1992).

Wesley K. Wark Assistant Professor of History, University of Toronto; author of *The Ultimate Enemy: British Intelligence and Nazi Germany, 1933–1939* (1986); articles on intelligence and co-editor of *Security and Intelligence in a Changing World* (1991).

Robert Young Professor of History, University of Winnipeg; author of *In Command of France: French Foreign Policy and Military Planning, 1933–1940* (1978) and *Power and Pleasure: Louis Barthou and the Third French Republic* (1991).

Introduction

GEORGE EGERTON

From the ancients to the moderns, those engaged in political leadership have endeavoured to leave some sign or record of their deeds, *res gestae*, that would make future ages remember their names and accomplishments. Whether verbalized in story or song, chiselled in stone, carved on totem pole, woven in tapestry or, most effectively if less durably, written on papyrus, parchment or paper, with audio/ video tape and computer disk now offering yet other media, generations of leaders from nearly every age and culture have attempted to transmit to the future an account of their lives and achievements. The late British historian, G.P. Gooch, spoke of the mixture of vanity and pathos displayed in this quest to surmount the bounds of mortality.[1] It is from this tradition that the modern political memoir has derived, in all its diverse forms.

If the impulse to generate political memoirs has seldom abated throughout the course of human civilization, so also the attraction of readers to this type of literature, where history and politics are narrated in personalized form, has remained powerful. In the contemporary world, readership surveys and best-seller listings indicate that, along with political biography, political memoir constitutes the most popular form of historical literature. Understandably this is not a condition universally applauded by professional historians or political scientists, whose scholarly monographs seldom match the excitement generated in the book industry by a political memoir promising major revelations, insight and high-class gossip.

Despite its antiquity, durability and ubiquity, political memoir has attracted little in the way of systematic critical analysis as a distinct form of historical and political literature. The essays in this symposium endeavour to address this lacuna in presenting a historical, political and literary critique of the 'genre' of political memoir, while analysing specific aspects of the production and reception of select memoirs in the context of their political and literary cultures.

In these essays, political memoir is studied from a variety of perspectives and with complementary methodologies. Since most of the participants in the original Conference on Political Memoirs are practising historians, analysis and criticism are predominantly historical; but the perspectives come also from a political scientist, a biographer, an Asianist, a medievalist and a professional writer. An early finding of any study of political memoir would conclude that it is a problematic genre – if indeed it can claim status as a genre at all. Certainly its severest critics would dismiss any such claim, asserting that writings by politicians justifying their careers are inherently flawed, and seldom likely to produce accurate history, convincing political analysis or literature of enduring merit. Moreover, the parameters marking off political memoir from other genres or types of writing often appear indistinct as it appropriates autobiography, biography, diary, history, political science, journalism and pamphleteering, to name only its nearest literary neighbours. For every Cellini who considered it a duty that great men record their accomplishments, there have been critics ranging from Cicero, who contended it was ill-judged for a man to write his own life, to John Charnock who in the late eighteenth century berated memoirs as 'this monster in literature'.[2] Modern literary theorists are, for the most part, sceptical that autobiographical writing can ever reconstitute the past with accuracy; rather it should be reviewed and valued in poetic and fictive categories.[3] On the other hand, the literature of nearly every human culture contains superlative records by politicians of their lives and times that have fascinated contemporaries, instructed subsequent generations and contributed immeasurably to our knowledge and understanding of the past.

The editor's opening essay attempts the formidable tasks of defining the nature of this complex genre and surveying the historical development of political memoir from its origins in antiquity until the eighteenth century, when the genre emerged in its modern variations. A review of the origins of this type of literature and the etymology of the term illustrates clearly the polymorphous forms and diverse elements which have constituted memoir-type writings in different eras and cultures. The elements that figure most prominently include: contemporary descriptive recording of political events and impressions in diaries or journals, where one has been a participant in or observer of the events; retrospective narration of political engagements together with explanatory and interpretive reflections; autobiographical portrayal of one's life in politics, with childhood, education and personal development given full treatment; biographical depiction of political contemporaries from personal knowledge; revelation of the inner working of a political system based on personal acquaintance with 'the hidden springs of power'; and, in its most ambitious mode, portrayal not only of one's political life but also of the times in which this career occurred – in other words, contemporary history. It is perhaps the very diversity of the elements constituting political memoir that has impeded the development of an effective criticism. Such diversity, and the tendency of political memoir to invade the neighbouring territories of autobiography, political science and historiography, suggest that it might best be termed a 'polygenre' – a designation which concedes the difficulty in classifying this literary chameleon. The editor's essay argues that it was in the context of Enlightenment thought and historiography that the long-term hegemony of memoirists in the writing of contemporary history came to an end; historiography and political memoir would be differentiated as the new 'scientific' history led to the establishment of a professionalized discipline which, in turn, subordinated memoir to the category of personal narrative source. While the political memoir would undergo further development in the contexts of the nineteenth and twentieth centuries, as several of the essays indicate, the differentiation from historiography, accepted consciously if regretfully by such eighteenth-century memoirists as Hervey and Walpole, marks the seminal departure in the evolution of the genre.

In the modern period the most common usage of the term political memoirs denotes the endeavour by a retired politician to recount the important political engagements of his or her career, to explain and interpret the choices made and forces encountered, to portray the relationships experienced in the course of political activity and perhaps to offer some precepts or wisdom to assist political successors. It is this type of political memoir that served as the principal focus for this symposium. But our studies show that there are many unconventional memoirs to be encountered, and the adjective 'political' is used in a broad sense to encompass military, naval, diplomatic and bureaucratic memoirs. Memoirs by those who were political observers more than participants also merit treatment as, in many instances, they have composed the most valuable memoirs of their eras. Political memoir represents a complex and predatory polygenre; as is seen in many of the following essays, it is perhaps the very unconventionality and polymorphous composition of political memoir that contributes most to its enduring appeal while troubling its critics.

By the time Bismarck composed his three volumes of memoirs in the 1890s, the genre of political memoir in its many variations had been fully developed. The essay by Otto Pflanze turns the critical focus of a political biographer and historian on the process and purpose which generated the memoirs of this modern political colossus. We are shown both the immediate political ammunition assembled in his memoirs by Bismarck against Kaiser Wilhelm II, who had dismissed him and departed from his policies, and the lessons in statecraft which the Chancellor drew from his major policies and now wished to stand as his memorial. Published after his death (and a third volume being delayed until 1921 because of its criticisms of the kaiser), Bismarck's memoirs enjoyed vast sales of approximately 300,000. Lauded by many historians at the time and subsequently, Bismarck's memoirs are shown to illustrate clearly the fundamental tension between the political and personal objectives which animated the author and the accuracy of the resulting historical narrative. If the former heavily condition the latter, as with many memoirists, Professor Pflanze makes the vital point that the very distortions of the memoirs give telling evidence about the character of their author.

The next four essays locate their analyses of political memoirs, biography and diaries within the national political contexts of France, India, Japan and Canada, respectively. While Robert Young and Robert Bothwell (along with the later essay by Professor Hill) present the harsh critiques of these genres, pointing out the many temptations and vagaries to which they are prone, both scholars recognize their value to the historian when approached with appropriate reserves of scepticism. Milton Israel, by contrast, shows a more attractive aspect in his portrayal of the ancient Hindu and Muslim traditions of memoir in India. His essay illustrates the potent political functions of memoirs by modern nationalist leaders in forging a collective national tradition and a 'literature of challenge', while effectively communicating the charisma of indigenous leaders to a mass readership ripe for mobilization. For the later historian, Indian nationalist memoirs offer prolific and rich sources for the study of divided mentalities struggling for new identity, and present an intimate human record where the vast dramas of modern Indian history were played out in the lives of a handful of leaders who made the decisions. Despite the antiquity of the Indian memoir tradition, Professor Israel shows how some of the nationalists viewed the genre as alien and western; Gandhi attempted to transcend such cultural imperialism by presenting his record as *Experiments With Truth* in the form of highly personalized philosophic and religious discourse. Joshua Mostow in his analysis of Japanese court records, especially the *nikki* composed by female witnesses of court life and politics, contests the thesis that autobiography has an exclusive western derivation. His essay adds further testimony to the cultural ubiquity of memoir-type literature, while illustrating the diversity of its forms.

The production of memoir literature throughout history has regularly been stimulated when three conditions are present: the occurrence of dramatic events such as war or revolution; the desire of participants or witnesses to record their observations on these events; and the provision of necessary leisure time for the memoirist to write the narrative. It is the combination of these conditions which perhaps best explains the ubiquity and prolixity of naval and military memoirs, where intense bursts of dramatic engagement in international tensions, wars and their aftermath, are often followed by relative leisure and the provocations of public controversy. Barry Gough's essay on British naval memoirs traces the development of this literature from its early eighteenth-century origins, through its proliferation after Trafalgar in the era of *pax Britannica*, to its apogee in the wake of the First World War. Of particular interest here is the role of the Navy Records Society in promoting a corporate memory through the publication of memoir literature, while also advancing the institutional interests of the Royal Navy. Professor Gough illustrates both the weaknesses and strengths of memoirs as sources for understanding the operation of the Navy and the nature of its social structure. The essay by Tim Travers portrays the evolution of British military memoirs through several distinct phases and forms, demonstrating how a close reading of military memoirs can serve as a major corrective to such fascinating but largely ahistorical literary studies as Paul Fussell's *The Great War In Modern Memory*[4] and Modris Eksteins' *Rites of Spring*.[5]

If, fortunately, the diplomatic career does not always involve the dramas of war and peace-making, it does usually afford the leisure to reflect, while the profession itself entails regular practice in the arts of recording and writing. This, as well as background and training, accounts for the literary quality which often distinguishes diplomatic memoirs and diaries, in contrast to the more elementary style of most generals and politicians. Zara Steiner's essay portrays the types of information which can be gleaned from diplomatic memoirs and which serve to supplement the historian's concentration on the more impersonal official records. It is from these personal sources that we can obtain insight into the nature of daily life in both the Foreign Office and the diplomatic service, the social origins and habits of the diplomatic élite, their educational background and economic standing, their relationships and opinions of each other, and sometimes their political attitudes – when the ingrained veil of discretion is briefly lifted. From the testimony of memoirs, it is Dr Steiner's conclusion that the class structure, routines and attitudes of the 'old' Foreign Office and diplomatic service persisted through repeated reforms and the upheavals of two world wars, until the radical readjustments of the 1950s and 1960s. Brian McKercher is more optimistic than Dr Steiner that the historian can use memoirs to learn about the substance of policy-making as well as the background of British diplomacy. Professor McKercher's essay addresses memoirs published during the inter-war period, focusing on the shifts in mentalities and morale of the policy-making élite as the confidence of the Locarno era gave way to the foreboding and despair of the late 1930s. Of all the authors, Professor McKercher shows greatest empathy with the policy-makers' apologetic impulse to present their justifications and defend their memory.

Leisure no doubt has facilitated the production of many diplomatic memoirs. This factor perhaps also helps account for the particular affinity of women for memoir literature, both as readers and as writers. Given the near-exclusion of women from formal political power in most political cultures until recent decades, the writing of memoirs of social and political observance has provided an attractive outlet for critical and creative energies. Often such writing, as in the memoirs of Mesdames Campan, Roland, de Staël and Récamier, utilizes brilliantly the perspective of personal intimacy combined with political exclusion to portray the conventions, manners and relationships which constitute the background to the formal political process. This theme figures prominently, as noted, in Joshua Mostow's essay on Japanese *nikki*. Valerie Cromwell illustrates the valuable insight into the informal operation of British diplomatic establishments abroad through the modern period that can be drawn from the memoirs of wives and daughters of ambassadors. These memoirs not only cast light on the significant status and influence accorded a 'diplomatic wife' in her role as 'ambassadress' within the embassy family, but also demonstrate the decline of this standing as the post-1945 British diplomatic establishment gradually opened professional diplomatic careers to women.

Professor Hill's essay on Nazi memoirs illustrates powerfully both the weaknesses endemic to the genre, and the capacity of the historian to exploit such sources critically and open a window into the Nazi mentality.

Three of the participants in the Political Memoirs Project have written of their direct experience in the production of memoirs or the editing of political autobiography. John Munro speaks from the unique vantage point of having served as historical researcher and writing assistant for two Canadian prime ministers, Lester Pearson and John Diefenbaker. The concurrent attractions, dilemmas and hazards of the 'devil', 'ghost' or 'negre' engaged to assist in the writing of political memoir are portrayed with candour and due warnings for those tempted to such an undertaking. If the essay by Francis Heller pays tribute to the courtesy with which he was treated by Truman during the production of the *official* memoirs of the President, Robert Ferrell shows the many impediments which marred the process of drafting these memoirs and severely reduced their quality despite Professor Heller's best efforts. By contrast, Professor Ferrell's essay conveys a historian's excitement in first discovering the amazingly rich personal records generated by Truman throughout his career, more revealing by far than the official memoirs and containing unique detail on the life and political career of this seminally important American president.

If Truman spoke with increasing frankness and prolixity in retirement, and finally with near-unrestrained candour for Merle Miller in *Plain Speaking*,[6] Stephen Ambrose notes that Richard Nixon holds the record as the most prolific president. Professor Ambrose reviews the many purposes and functions served by the seemingly endless volumes issued by the disgraced ex-President: therapy, public rehabilitation, vindication, vengeance, statecraft, maintenance of the Watergate cover-up, royalties to pay off enormous debts to lawyers – all have driven the Nixon memoirs industry. And if Professor Ambrose points to the extremely functional nature of historical truth under Nixon's hand, he rightly argues that the memoirs are, not least because of this, utterly revealing of the man's character.

János Bak, in analysing the memoir literature of communist eastern European regimes through the eyes of a medievalist, draws telling parallels between the political functions and control of personal narratives, biographies and memoirs under cultures dominated by medieval church dogma or modern party ideology. As Professor Bak demonstrates, the popularity of personal narrative and religious or ideological hagiography and their effectiveness as tools of socialization made them both useful and potentially dangerous forms of literature. If autobiographies by Bolsheviks are rare, indeed viewed as almost heretical according to Professor Bak, Khrushchev's memoirs stand as both a uniquely valuable window into the Soviet system and an early herald of glasnost-to-come. The rapid and radical changes now transforming the formerly closed political cultures of Stalinist Russia and its satellites are being accompanied by the publication of a surge of previously suppressed memoirs, as well as those recently written. After decades of enforced silence, the Russian memory shows every sign of speaking anew with many voices.

Wesley Wark's essay on memoirs from the United States intelligence community emphasizes the paradox of clandestinity and revelation inherent to literature of the 'spy house'. If publishers have been eager to exploit the public's fascination with the role of intelligence in the wars – hot, cold and covert – of the modern era, it is Professor Wark's principal concern to explicate the ways in which spy memoirs have evolved as a distinct form, often subverting the formulaic rules of autobiography in pursuing personal and institutional causes relating to the role of intelligence in American politics.

The potency of memoir as a carrier of political messages and an enemy of official silence or secrecy has invoked attempted governmental control not just in the totalitarian societies of Professor Bak's essay, but also in western democracies. The essay by John Naylor analyses recent challenges to the conventions and laws governing Cabinet secrecy in Britain, notably with the publication of Richard Crossman's diaries, and reviews the efforts by subsequent governments to regulate the published disclosures of eager ministerial diarists and memoirists. Given the prolixity and import of political memoirs in modern Britain, the attempts by governments to assess this genre of political literature, and to control publication, merit special attention.

It is clear from this study that political memoir remains a dynamic and controversial form of historical and political literature in contemporary political cultures. While the essays comprising these volumes necessarily touch only on a selection of the many facets and dimensions of political memoir, the authors, in their studies of specific memoirists and particular themes related to the genre, have nevertheless offered rich material for general critical discourse. A concluding chapter addresses the broader critical issues raised in the essays and in the discussions generated by the Conference on Political Memoirs.

NOTES

1. George Peabody Gooch, *Studies in Diplomacy and Statecraft* (London, 1942), Ch. 4, 'Political Autobiography', p. 227.
2. On Cellini and Charnock see the essays below by Robert Young and Barry Gough. Cicero's views on autobiography are treated in Georg Misch, *A History of Autobiography in Antiquity* (2 vols.) (London, 1950), Vol. I, pp. 187–8.
3. This position, common to much contemporary criticism, is presented powerfully in Susanna Egan, *Patterns of Experience in Autobiography* (Chapel Hill, 1984), Ch. 1, 'The Inevitability of Fiction'.
4. Paul Fussell, *The Great War In Modern Memory* (New York, 1975).
5. Modris Eksteins, *Rites of Spring: The Great War and the Birth of the Modern Age* (Toronto, 1989).
6. Merle Miller, *Plain Speaking: An Oral Biography of Harry S. Truman* (New York, 1974).

POLITICAL MEMOIR:
ESSAYS ON THE POLITICS OF MEMORY

1

The Politics of Memory: Form and Function in the History of Political Memoir from Antiquity to Modernity

GEORGE EGERTON

Former President Ronald Reagan's announcement upon leaving office that he intended to publish memoirs evoked little surprise among political commentators.[1] Indeed it is now expected that major political figures of modern countries, if they survive their years in power, will publish an account of their leadership. All retired German Chancellors, British Prime Ministers, and French and American Presidents since the Second World War have published memoirs, or have announced their intention to do so.[2] It is now customary for such leaders while in power to arrange the record-keeping of their offices so that the documentation will be at hand when it comes time to write the memoirs. Mrs Thatcher is reported to have kept a careful personal record of facets of her administration, despite strictures to her Cabinet ministers against emulating Richard Crossman and other Labour Cabinet diarists, and her retirement sparked anticipation that she would soon turn to the rewarding task of writing memoirs.[3] Elsewhere in the world, the replacement of communist regimes will generate a new wave of memoir literature, written by communists, former communists, their victims, their antagonists, and previously suppressed authors. Third World leaders have also shown increasing attraction to political autobiography, especially as a vehicle for projecting a political agenda and mobilizing mass support.[4]

If Mr Reagan's intention to write memoirs caused little surprise, at the same time there were few signs of enthusiasm or anticipation from historians, political scientists, or literary critics that his book would offer major revelations to contemporary history, penetrating insight into the processes of decision-making, or an elevating style to evoke the remembrance of politics past. Publication of Mr Reagan's memoirs in late 1990 would do little to confound the scepticism of the critics. That Mr Reagan's agent arranged a figure estimated at between five and seven million US dollars for the memoirs did nothing to enhance the expectations of academics regarding these transactions.[5] Indeed, the lucrative contracts which many former political leaders arrange for the sale of their privileged memories tend to elicit sulphurous ruminations from historians and political analysts, not all drawn from the acid of envy: are not politicians uniquely disqualified, by years of habit-forming professional obfuscation, from telling the truth about what they have done and why they did it? Did they, or could they, understand what they were doing? If their memoirs do convey such an understanding, and engage us in their vindications, is not this perhaps an even more seductive substitution of illusion for historical truth? Furthermore, does not a political career necessarily focus one's energies, time, and attention so absorbingly on the externals of life that little is left for the type of introspection vital to the autobiographical sensibility? And finally, after years of manipulative use of language in political combat, can the politician's verbal instincts be translated into 'literature'?

Such queries begin to suggest the problematic status of political memoir as a genre of historical, political, or autobiographical literature. There are powerful temptations to relegate political memoirs beyond the pale of scholarly attention, leaving such offerings to the more ephemeral ministrations of journalists. Further consideration, however, would suggest persuasive reasons against dismissing political memoir as an inherently flawed category of writing. For one thing, we know that the desire of political leaders to record their deeds constitutes one of the most ancient and enduring forms of historical documentation. From the inscriptions in the burial chambers of the Pharaohs' pyramids, the court diaries of Alexander the Great, the *commentarii* and *res gestae* of the Roman Caesars, the personal narratives of Byzantine leaders, the Norse sagas, the *recordanzi* of Renaissance Italian city state patricians, the seventeenth- and eighteenth-century memoirs of monarchs and courtiers, to the 'best-seller' memoir in contemporary mass markets, the desire of politicians to place before their contemporaries or posterity a record of their deeds has shown a remarkable constancy. While much of such self-recording serves only the cause of vanity or apologia, it is nevertheless true that our knowledge of many facets of human history, ancient and modern, would be massively impoverished without the memoirs generated by the political actors themselves. Memoirists, in any case, have seldom shown much concern for the critiques of academics; they know that what they write will often reach a far wider market than the books of the scholars. Mr Reagan expressed some initial consternation in beginning his story, facing the daunting challenge of so many blank pages. There was little need for worry; with ample help at hand the pages would soon fill up, and the Reagan memoirs would find the usual serialization in mass circulation magazines, occupy the windows of bookstores around the world, form the subject of reviews in the weekend newspapers, attract the attention of television talk shows, enjoy rebirth in paperback format, and thereby leave a cumulative imprint on the political and historical perceptions of contemporary and future readers.[6] It is the ubiquity of political memoir in modern mass cultures which contributes the most compelling reason for paying critical attention to this pervasive form of popular history.

The scope of the political and historical imprint of political memoirs depends of course on many factors beyond the marketing efforts of publishers and booksellers. And if the immediate popular interest often derives from the fame and power of the memoirist, the drama inherent to the events being narrated, and the entertainment of secrets revealed and gossip about cohorts, the longer-term importance will depend primarily on such qualities as the political insight, historical accuracy and perspective, autobiographical candour and literary skill which go into the portrayal of character, circumstance and behaviour. It is this amalgam of political, historical, autobiographical, bio-graphical and literary elements which generates the multifaceted and ubiquitous appeal of political memoir; it is also this diffuse quality which challenges the aspiring memoirist to fashion diverse elements of this 'polygenre' into a literary unity of enduring appeal and value. If few political memoirists excel in this quest, there are the towering classics of Thucydides, Caesar, Clarendon, Saint-Simon, Hervey, Grant, Bismarck, Lloyd George and Churchill to exemplify the fascination of political memoir and its power to draw the reader into the dramas of history as remembered and recounted by the leading actors themselves.

The constituent elements of memoir have attracted critical attention in greater or lesser degree on their own: historical criticism has refined the methodology of using memoir as documentation; literary criticism has recently focused much attention on autobiography; and political science has produced many studies on the nature of leadership. But one searches in vain for sustained critical analysis of political memoir as a genre of writing *in itself*, with a concern not only for the constituent elements as they have been expressed over time but also for how they interact dynamically, and function in the context of their political cultures. It is the purpose of this essay to provide such a study by analysing the history, forms and functions of political memoir and its emergence as a genre with distinct historical, autobiographical and political dynamics. The focus will be on those eras where the genre of memoir was cultivated with particular intensity and genius – notably the Classical Age, the Renaissance, and the eighteenth century. The essay will conclude with an analysis of the differentiation of political memoir from historiography by the new 'scientific' historians of the early nineteenth century which, it is argued, marks the vital point of departure in the development of the modern political memoir.

The production of personal accounts of their deeds by political and military leaders has occurred, in varying forms and intensity, throughout most periods of recorded history. While such records are now usually classified as 'narrative sources' in modern methodological classifications of historiography, the traditional and popular term in English is 'memoir' or 'memoirs'. It quickly becomes apparent to the student of memoir literature that the vast corpus of such writing is distinguished by both its variability of form and its fluidity of parameters.

A review of the lexicography and etymology of the term 'memoir' can serve as a first step in suggesting its meanings and usages over time, as well as its defiance of neat categorization. The English *memoir* has a mid-seventeenth-century derivation from the French, *mémoire*, which in turn has its root in the Latin, *memoria*, for memory.[7] In modern dictionaries, the term connotes the following: a note, memorandum or record; a specifically diplomatic memorandum or record of business done; an essay or dissertation on a learned subject; a biography or bibliographical notice; 'a record of events, not purporting to be a complete history, but treating of such matters as come within the personal knowledge of the writer, or are obtained from certain particular sources of information'; and finally, 'a person's written account of incidents in his own life, of the persons he has known, and the transactions or movements in which he has been concerned; an autobiographical record'.[8] If the first three of these definitions are obsolete or rare in modern usage, the others encompass elements of memoir which pertain directly to our subject: recording of events from a privileged vantage point; and reflective narration of events and relationships based on personal engagement, with the record therefore appropriating biographical and autobiographical elements.

Georg Misch, in his classic *History of Autobiography in Antiquity*, demonstrates how both psychological and formal factors led to the distinctions between memoirs on the one hand and historiography and studies of lives on the other in the literary classifications of the Graeco-Roman world – distinctions which illuminate more clearly the problematic etymology of the term memoir. The conflicts between historical truth and personal apologia, with the latter's inherent biases of memory, interest and pride, were apparent to those ancients who had absorbed the ethical precepts of Greek philosophy. Cicero, for one, thought it more seemly that one's life and deeds be recorded by someone other than oneself.[9] Most of the self-portrayals that abounded in the writing of this period were therefore categorized as '*hypomnemata*', in the Greek, or its Latin equivalent, '*commentarii*', denoting, as Misch explains, a class of writings associated with memory but eschewing claim to literary form:

the word itself simply means that something has been 'noted down as an aid to the memory' – a conception indefinite in itself, simply expressing the absence of artistic elaboration; it served . . . to indicate all the manifold documents in which the writers were concerned only with the contents, and not with any use of rhetorical style; it was the usual name for the autobiographical works, in addition to *bios* in the sense of 'way of life' or 'career'.[10]

While Misch's distinction is generally useful, the case of Caesar's *Commentarii* illustrates that the use of these terms did not always exclude works of great literary and historical artistry. The term *mémoire*, derived from these Greek and Latin roots, would encompass a broad reach of personal records in subsequent European history, with the expression 'autobiography' not being used commonly until the early nineteenth century. Our primary concern here, however, is neither with the vast corpus of memoir-as-record, nor with the focus on development of the self which Roy Pascal in his seminal study of autobiography presents as the defining characteristic of that genre,[11] but rather with the history and variety of memoirs where authorship and political engagement are dynamically fused.

Misch reviews a broad sweep of such accounts, many of them fragmentary, surviving from the earliest civilizations of Egypt, Babylon, Persia and especially classical Greece and Rome. While Misch's concern is to chart the origins and development of autobiography, because the remaining records of antiquity mainly originate from, or deal with, the political/military élites, the records which they generated tell much about the derivations and functions of political memoir. Indeed, many of the constituent elements of what would later be recognized as political memoir can be seen operating in the political and historical literature of antiquity. With the Egyptian, Babylonian, and Assyrian inscriptions of the third and second millennia BC accompanying the pictorial representation of their leaders' conquests, we meet, according to Misch, 'the motive which is a special point of departure for historical literature – the great erect lasting monuments to themselves to proclaim the glory of their names and of their deeds to their contemporaries and to posterity'.[12] The Egyptian Pharaohs, with the construction of pyramids, excelled all cultures – previous and subsequent – in the erection of lasting monuments to themselves. Darius, the great fifth-century BC Persian conqueror, had his likeness carved on the 1,500-foot-high sheer face of Mount Behistun, his defeated enemy Gaumata underfoot, where all eyes passing on the main military road from Babylon to the east could peruse the cuneiform inscriptions 300 feet up, in Persian and the languages of Susa and Assyria, which described his ancestors, rulers for nine generations, the lands he had subjected, the might and justice of his rule – beyond all the works of other kings – and his favour by the great god Ahuramazda, whose carving crowned the monument.[13] The uninhibited quest for self-glorification typical of the earliest leaders of antiquity would take more literary form with the next world conqueror, Alexander the Great, who arranged to have his triumphs recorded in the diaries of his generals and chronicled by court scribes.

Apart from the desire to imprint one's name on the memory of future generations, the Jewish religious and literary tradition of antiquity left a legacy which would be paradigmatic in prefiguring many elements of future political literature: the narration of a people's historical experience through the voice of charismatic leaders – notably Moses and David; the chosen form of personal narrative – autobiographical and biographical – to convey religious and social teaching; and the highly personalized depiction of a seminal collective experience – the Exodus – with the intent that its meaning be recounted and remembered from generation to generation.

The practice of historiography would advance dramatically under Greek civilization; the works of the greatest of Greek historians – Thucydides and Polybius – reflected their personal engagement in the events they narrated, Thucydides as a general in the Peloponnesian war and Polybius as a leader of the mid-second-century BC Achaean League, anxious to account for the rise of Rome. Autobiographical writings by Greek political leaders would proliferate through this period; Aratus of Sicyon, head of the Achaean League, composed an apologia of some 30 books of over 10,000 words each, in which he vindicated his own deeds while pouring malevolence on his critics and enemies.[14]

It would be Roman leaders, however – republican and imperial, senators and emperors – who would excel all previous cultures in both the quantity and power of their political testaments. Of the many familial histories transmitted from generation to generation, the innumerable biographical funereal eulogies, burial epitaphs, rhetorical self-projections and self-written lives of statesmen, two Roman political memoirs stand above all others – Julius Caesar's *Commentaries on the Gallic War*, and Augustus Caesar's *Res Gestae*. The narrative skill of Caesar's *Commentaries*, recording his military leadership with clarity, precision and brevity, impressed his contemporaries and posterity alike as both a masterful record of seminal historical events and a classic of Latin literature. Augustus, whose extensive political apologia remains only in sparse and fragmentary references, ensured a durable record of his political achievements by building an enormous family mausoleum in Rome, and in his last year, at the age of 76, composing his incisive *Res Gestae* for inscription on the inner face of the grand bronze doors of his shrine. In the testaments of both Caesar and Augustus, what leaves an indelible impression on the reader is the projection of political will and the exercise of power. While the focus of both rulers is external, on actions, challenges and events, leaving little scope for introspective analysis, the dominant personal charac-teristics of each are conveyed in the style of their writing – resolution, commanding authority and personal mastery. In each case, the imperative of adding written justification to the triumph of the sword serves as an early illustration of the powerful function of political apologia in the legitimation of leadership – for Caesar the establishment of his dictatorship, and for Augustus the initiation of rule by emperor.

It is clear from the records of Graeco-Roman civilization that political apologia was a prolific form of political literature. The dependence of the literature of this period on the labours of pro-fessional scribes did not prevent the wide circulation of the most important and popular writing through the social élites of Greece and Rome. Roman culture especially exhibited an insatiable curiosity for writings by, or dealing with, its leaders. And not all Roman political apologias exhibited the austere grandeur of Caesar and Augustus. Indeed, contemporary references to the lost political autobiography of Augustus himself illustrate another, more usual, trait of apologia – vindication of behaviour which had resulted in controversy or criticism. The manoeuvring, ambition and violence of the young Octavian in grasping the mantle of Caesar is translated by Augustus, in his political apologia, into the disinterested restitution of constitutional authority in the face of the treachery of others.[15]

That the Greeks and Romans developed no specific term for autobiography, despite Hellenist philosophical consciousness of the individual as an ethical entity, is perhaps a telling signal of their latent conceptualization of the self in relational categories – notably to the *gens*, and the polity. A radically different conceptualization of the self would be generated in the religion of the Christians, itself rooted in the monotheistic tradition of Israel, whose understanding of God was narrated and recorded in the Scriptures in highly personal as well as tribal categories. With the dissolution of Roman imperial power in the fifth century, it would be St Augustine who would express the first great religious conceptualization of the self in literary terms, in his *Confessions*.

Augustine's distinction between the divine and earthly cities heralded the development of a religious culture – medieval Christianity – which would prove inhospitable to the production of secular political memoir. The fall of Rome marked the attenuation of secular political literature for nearly eight centuries. In the interim, while history took the form of annals, chronicle and hagiography during the medieval period, intimations of memoir can be seen in the Byzantine court records of Procopius, Michael Psellus and Emperor John VI,[16] the vernacular narratives by such crusaders as Geoffrey of Villehardouin,[17] and in the Scandinavian–Icelandic sagas recounting the rule not only of legendary figures but of historic kings as well.[18] The fourteenth-century Holy Roman Emperor Charles IV produced perhaps the richest personal narrative by a ruler from this era.[19] As in the classical age, the finest medieval historiography was written by those who were witnesses to, or participants in, the events which they describe.

With the coming of the Renaissance, European thought after the fourteenth century would witness a new focus on the individual and the dramas of secular life. The cultural and political environments of many areas of Europe, infused with the rediscovered models of classical Greece and Rome, would generate major advances in historical, biographical and autobiographical literature, together with a greatly enhanced capacity for political analysis. In Italy the histories of Leonardo Bruni and Francesco Guicciardini, the biographies of Petrarch, the autobiographies of Cellini and Cardano, together with the masterful political analysis of Machiavelli's *The Prince*, all signify the scale of creativity marking this era of European development. If the 58 volumes of Marino Sanuto's *Diarii*[20] point to the new scope of the memoirist's impulse, the recently discovered *ricordi* of Marco Parenti serve to illustrate the qualities of political insight and literary skill focused by a participant-observer on the politics of mid-fifteenth-century Florence under the Medici.[21] So, too, in the autobiographical records of Aeneas Sylvius Piccolomini (Pius II), the encounters of an adventure-filled life, together with the diplomacy and internal politics of the papacy, are presented with a dramatic flair and candour unsurpassed by any subsequent Vatican author.[22]

More than the city-states of Italy, it would be the consolidating European monarchies of the fourteenth and fifteenth centuries, with their increasingly centralized courts and dynastic rivalries, that would provide the environment conducive to the production of memoirs by courtiers. Early versions of the courtier memoir can be seen in the *Chronicle* of Jean Le Bel, a Canon of Liège, who narrated his experiences from 1326 to 1361 as a soldier and courtier. The courtier's perspective also informs the popular chivalrous *Chronicle* of Jean Froissart, whose accounts of the deeds of the courtly and military élites set a pattern continued by his fifteenth-century French successors. The latter, mainly laymen, wrote in the vernacular, and were usually participants in the events they recorded.[23] The *Memoirs* of Philippe de Commynes present a rich record of a statesman's service during the years 1468–98 in Burgundy and France under Charles the Bold and Louis XI. With his exile by Louis and later imprisonment upon the advent of Louis XII, we also have an early instance of embittered loss of power affording the time and motive to animate the memoirist's pen. Commynes' memoirs are filled with penetrating insight into the leading actors and institutions of his time and, in their focus on personal political experience, they advanced beyond the medieval pattern of chronicle. Written with impressive literary style, even though the author claimed they were but a vernacular prelude to their translation by another hand into polished Latin, Commynes' *Memoirs* stand as the most impressive early example of the fusion of political, historical and autobiographical sensibilities awakened by Renaissance learning and exercised in the political context of the new secular administrations.[24]

Commynes' writing would powerfully influence subsequent historical literature, as memoirs by French and Italian soldiers, diplomats and courtiers emulated his approach if failing to match his quality. The increasing use of the vernacular of course made such writings more accessible. In addition, after the mid-fifteenth century the new technology of printing from movable type facilitated the production and circulation of literature, including memoirs. The reach of such literature, however, remained confined to the relatively small literate circles centred on the courts.

While a courtly tradition of memoirs was developing in Europe, the early sixteenth-century autobiography of Babur, founder of the Mughal empire in India, represents an indigenous rich development of personal narrative in a wholly different cultural context.[25] Babur recorded in great detail the vicissitudes of his dramatic life as it unfolded, the immediacy of the diarist mingling often with the reflection of reminiscence. With only 18 of his 47 years available to us in what has survived of his writings, Babur nevertheless left a unique imprint on historical memory in vivid portrayals of his family relations, life and death victories over enemies, romantic adventures and the places and circumstances he encountered in an eventful life. His son and successor, Humayun, would also compose memoirs; but Akbar, his grandson and greatest of the Mughal rulers of India, although a generous patron of the artists and scholars attracted to his sumptuous court, was himself illiterate.

In sixteenth-century England, while cultural energies would concentrate with unsurpassing genius on the production of drama for the stage, the Elizabethan court would also generate several notable memoirs. It is from the personal narratives of such courtiers as Robert Cary, Earl of Monmouth, and Sir Robert Naunton[26] that unique information on the personalities and inner politics of the Elizabethan period come to us, complementing the rich and skilful new historiography of William Camden.

The monarchies of Europe, however, with their religious and dynastic warring, provide the seed-bed for the unprecedented outpouring of memoir literature of the seventeenth century which, in compass as well as quantity, surpassed all previous eras in the production of political memoirs. It would be France under the Bourbons that would lead Europe in both the proliferation of political memoirs and the construction of a memoir tradition which would be emulated throughout European courts. The memoirs of Sully, Richelieu and de Retz exercised skilfully the varied functions of what was now perceived with increasing clarity as a distinct genre of contemporary historiography. Indeed, both the volume and the quality of French political memoirs produced during the seventeenth century make this genre the period's leading form of historiography. All of these memoirs are, of course, repositories of vital information for subsequent historians of seventeenth-century France and the making of the absolutist monarchies. There is not space here even to begin to survey the contents of such memoirs; what is notable for the purposes of our study is the richness of documentation which these leaders include in their writings, the passionate determination to commemorate their personal roles in the building of the new national monarchy, the candour of self-revelation and the commitment to ensure that what they wrote would be published, if not while they were alive, then after they had gone. Not since the days of the Roman Caesars had the impact of personality on politics been portrayed with such monumental vanity (as in the case of Sully), such wilfulness (as with Richelieu), and such sensational self-exposure (as in the revelations of de Retz). The Sun King himself, Louis XIV, would compose a memoir of the early part of his reign, allegedly as instruction for the dauphin, but in reality an apologia for absolutism and a monument to the glory of his kingship.[27]

The memoirists of the absolutist monarchies in France and elsewhere would dominate the writing of contemporary history, despite historians such as William Camden in Britain and Jacques-Auguste de Thou in France, whose work, increasingly steeped in the empiricism of the new science, exhibited growing sophistication in methodology and analysis. Camden would defend the competence of the historian as compared with the memoirist who could claim personal knowledge of events; describing his methods and sources, Camden asserted that he had attained 'no less knowledge of those affairs than some others who have been long and deeply versed in state-matters'.[28] However, Camden's contemporary, Francis Bacon, author of *The Life of Henry VII* and certainly versed in state matters, affirmed the prevailing wisdom as to the superiority of history written by the statesman-participant:

But it is not to monks or closet penmen that we are to look for guidance in such a case [as that of Queen Elizabeth]; for men of that order, being keen in style, poor in judgment, and partial in feeling, are no faithful witnesses as to the real passages of business. It is for ministers and great officers to judge of these things, and those who have handled the helm of government, and been acquainted with the difficulties and mysteries of state business.[29]

As with the wars of religion in France and the challenge of the Fronde, so too in England's bitter Civil War it would be leading participants who first produced powerful and influential accounts. Edmund Ludlow's *Memoirs of the Lieutenant General Ludlow* recount the experience of a leading Parliamentarian and regicide.[30] And in Clarendon's *History of the Rebellion and Civil Wars in England* the elements of personal narrative, political analysis and history were fused into a classic political memoir of both high literary quality and major historical influence.

Edward Hyde, First Earl of Clarendon, lived at the centre of English politics from his initial parliamentary opposition to Charles I, his conversion to the Royalist cause in response to Parliament's growing radicalism, his service after the outbreak of the Civil War as the King's Chancellor of the Exchequer and representative in the failed Uxbridge negotiations to end the war, to his exile after the victory of the Roundheads and execution of the King, his service as chief adviser to Charles II, his return to office at the time of the Restoration and his final embittered exile in France after dismissal by his ungrateful master in 1667. Clarendon had both cause and leisure to write. Trained in the law, and widely read in the historians of classical Greece and Rome as well as contemporary European writers, Clarendon composed the first draft of his 'History' in the years 1646–48, after the defeat of the Royalist forces and his flight first to the Isles of Scilly and then to Jersey. With a supply of state and personal papers to supplement his memory of recent events, Clarendon recounted the story from the beginning of Charles I's reign, through the struggles with Parliament, and up to the campaign of 1644. The 'History' was intended as a defence of the King and the Royalist cause, but its production was interrupted when the author was drawn back into the service of Prince Charles in his exile in Europe. The 'History' would remain dormant as Clarendon was pre-occupied with the politics of exile and as the king's leading minister after the Restoration, until his impeachment and flight to France in 1667.

The second exile soon propelled Clarendon into another vindication, this time of his own career. Without his papers, and lacking the draft 'History', Clarendon was forced to rely largely on memory in preparing a lengthy study of his 'Life'. What was here sacrificed in accuracy of factual detail, given the absence of documentary records, was compensated for in the intensified analysis and personal interpretation of the events and relationships of Clarendon's career. As the work on the 'Life' reached the point of the Restoration of 1660, and when his son was able to bring his manuscript and other papers from England in

1670, Clarendon turned to complete his 'History of the Rebellion', grafting in much of the material from the 'Life', especially from the period 1644 to 1660, and also revising the history in light of new information and memoirs culled from helpful donors. The result of this composite effort was a classic political memoir, which, published first in 1702–4, also marked a major advance over previous British historiography.[31]

Clarendon's *History of the Rebellion and Civil Wars in England*, despite its obvious political animus, has justly achieved enduring fame for its many qualities: the grandeur with which the seminal dramas of the Civil War are staged, the analytic skill shown in presenting the interaction of personality and circumstance, the array of penetrating character portrayals and assessments, and the conviction with which the cause of the monarchy and the political precepts of the author are presented. As historian, Clarendon had surpassed by far the conventional annals-type historiography of his predecessors, his organization drawing its unity from his engagement with the convulsive events which the nation had experienced rather than from a strict adherence to chronology. After publication, the *History* became a best-seller of its time, going through 20 printings and establishing the economic underpinnings of Oxford University Press before Macray's edition was published in 1888.[32]

Clarendon's mining of his manuscript 'Life' to serve the purposes of the *History* illustrated clearly his own preference for history over autobiography. In his commitment to write history, and with the classical models of Thucydides, Plutarch, Livy, Tacitus and Cicero very much in mind, it was equally Clarendon's contention that history could best be written by those whose qualifications had been 'contracted by the Knowledge and Course and Method of Business, and by the Conversation and Familiarity in the Inside of Courts, and the most active and eminent Persons in the Government'.[33]

The continuing fascination with political memoir and its high valuation as the most useful form of history can be seen in the publisher's commentary prefaced to the 1683 (first) edition of *The Memoirs of Sir James Melvil*, Privy Councillor and Gentleman of the Chamber to Mary, Queen of Scots, and her son James VI of Scotland, who succeeded Elizabeth as James I:

As there is scarce any kind of civil knowledge more necessary and profitable than history; (which is therefore very aptly styled by the ancients, the mistress of life,) so of all sorts of history there is none so useful as that which unlocking the cabinet, brings forth the letters, private instructions, consultations and negotiations of ministers of state; for then we see things in a clear light, stripped of all their paints and disguisings, and discover those hidden springs of affairs, which give motion to all the vast machines and stupendous revolutions of princes and kingdoms, that make such a noise on the theatre of the world, and amaze us with unexpected shiftings of scenes and daily vicissitudes.

Of this latter kind are those Memoirs wherewith we here oblige the world, being the many years transactions and experiences of an eminent public minister in his long and faithful services under and negotiations with several princes, and at as ticklish a juncture and important crisis of affairs as could almost happen in any age . . .[34]

The publisher, George Scott, continued by outlining the three things 'essential to any history': first, the subject matter 'must be real, and of considerable moment'; second, the author must 'be capable of knowing what he speaks, and have opportunities to discover the certainty, and full circumstances of those affairs, whereof he undertakes to treat'; and third, the writer must be a man of 'honesty, of impartial veracity, and firm resolution to observe that prime law of history, . . . not to dare deliver any falsehood, nor to conceal any truth'. While Scott commended Melvil's *Memoirs* as having 'happily met' all such essentials of history, it was clearly asking too much that statesmen who might qualify under Scott's first two counts would also fully meet the third canon of historical truth with any regularity. Indeed, the seventeenth-century vogue for political memoirs would soon come under a critique which reflected both the growing sophistication of contemporary historiography itself and the continuing legacy of Renaissance re-engagement with classic Greek and Roman historio-graphy. The editor of the *Memorials* of Bulstrode Whitelock, first published in 1682, referring to the recent publication of prominent French, Italian and British diaries and memoirs, recalled that the Roman historian Suetonius had discussed the 'ephemerises' or diaries of several of the first Caesars, and that other princes and ministers in subsequent years had taken time to note down the 'memorials of daily passages'. However, these sorts of commentaries 'were rather accounted proper to furnish materials for other men of leisure and capacity, than to pass for history themselves'. Even Julius Caesar, who wrote so well as to discourage historians from writing after him, designed his com-mentaries 'for the world' and therefore failed to keep faith with the truth: 'wheresoever his or his justice might be arraigned, all is slurred over in silence, as they who confront him with Plutarch, Dion Cassius,

Ammianus, Lucan, etc. may observe; so that he composed his Commentaries with great elegancy of style, but not with much reputation to his integrity.'[35] The editor clearly wished to assert the distinctions between memoirs as personal recording and apologia, and the domain of history proper.

It would take another century, however, before the methods, forms and sources of the modern historian would have developed sufficiently to make it possible to surmount the memoirists' natural advantages of immediate access to the inner political life of courts and a personal narrative style which, although generally following a yearly structure, had greater freedom than the annals-chronicle form which still constrained historiography. In these circumstances, the period of the late seventeenth century and the eighteenth century, rich in satirists, diarists and biographers (Dryden, Pope, Swift, Pepys, Johnson and Boswell, to name but a few of the leading British writers), would also be an age of political memoir *par excellence*. This is true in terms of not only the numbers of memoirs written, but also the popular reception of what was now recognized by political élites as a distinct and appealing vehicle of personal, political and historical discourse.

The abundance of political memoirs written in the eighteenth century or, in the case of many seventeenth-century authors, now published for the first time, serves to illustrate the manifold varieties of form and function which this genre presented.[36] There were still instances where the memoirist assumed the role of historian; Bishop Burnet was most notable in this category with his account of the later Stuarts, the Glorious Revolution and the reign of William and Mary, based on long years of intimate acquaintance with the principals involved and his central role in the events of 1688–89.[37] Burnet would emulate Clarendon in aspiring to historical scope in preference to the autobiographical form he had initially adopted.[38] Frederick the Great of Prussia represents the most extensive effort by an eighteenth-century statesman to encompass his deeds in history, even if he failed to match the grandeur, unity and sustained literary power of Clarendon. A friend of Voltaire, and as interested in the writings of the *philosophes* as he was in the military expansion of his state, Frederick composed a *Histoire de Brandebourg* for publication in his own lifetime.[39] Not surprisingly, it was a highly selective account, with a very different rendering of his father, Frederick William, from those which would be given by his sister Wilhelmina in her memoir. Frederick, moreover, was determined to render an account of his series of wars not, as he claimed, for publication, but for his successors. The literary care that

Frederick devoted to his *Histoire de Mon Temps* perhaps discounts these professions. The Prussian monarch tells us of the therapeutic pleasure he found in writing up the events of his time, how it 'occupies me, diverts me, and makes me fitter for work'.[40] The result was Frederick's accounts of the first and second Silesian wars, the Seven Years War, the partition of Poland and the war of the Bavarian succession which, after much revision by the author, would fill the first seven volumes, the *Oeuvres Historiques*, of his collected works.[41] Catherine the Great of Russia, sharing Frederick's attraction to Voltaire, would also write a memoir; but here the focus was more narrow and inwardly directed, with Catherine telling as much about her sexual liaisons as about her steely ambition to wield power as ruler of Russia.[42]

More usual than the ruler-memoirist in the eighteenth century were those who wrote primarily as witnesses, well placed to observe the political élites and their behaviour but seldom playing leading political roles themselves. This category now included several perceptive women who portrayed with penetrating insight the personalities and relationships of European courts. From the pen of Madame Motteville we have a sympathetic study of her confidante, Anne of Austria, and the latter's regency during the minority of her son, the future Louis XIV, with the dramas of the Fronde being presented in the same vivid detail as in the memoirs of the Frondeur, de Retz.[43] Wilhelmina of Prussia, sister of Frederick the Great, composed a memoir of Prussian court life which gives invaluable information on the brutal childhood to which she and her brother were subjected by Frederick William I, the latter forcing the young Frederick to watch the beheading of his attendant and friend, Katt, who had helped the Crown Prince plan his intercepted escape from the cruelties of the Prussian court.[44] Fanny Burney translated the skills of an innovative eighteenth-century novelist into those of a poignant memoirist of Windsor court life under George III, whose deteriorating sanity brought the wide-eyed attendant to the Queen through several harrowing adventures.[45]

The most valuable and voluminous memoir literature of this era, however, would be produced by those who, while not principals, were still deeply engaged in the political systems they observed. The memoirs of Saint-Simon stand as a masterpiece of the genre, revealing with consummate literary power and psychological insight, more than any other testimony, the operation of the French court and its leading personalities through the first half of the eighteenth century. If the 29 volumes of the Boislisle edition present some dry desert between the fountains, as Macaulay put it, the fountains are there in abundance for the reader and the later historian.[46] An opponent of the rising absolutism he witnessed, and filled with hatred for the *arriviste* servants of this system, notably Mazarin, Colbert and later Dubois, Saint-Simon stood as a *frondeur* in the cause of recovering the political status of the *noblesse d'épée*. For him the great king was Louis XIII, to whom the Saint-Simon family owed its advancement, rather than Louis XIV whose talents the memoirist diminishes as he berates the corrupt courtiers, mistresses and royal bastards who held sway around the Sun King. Exercising his greatest influence during the Orléanist regency for the young Louis XV, and undertaking an important mission to Spain, Saint-Simon would be unremembered for his minor political role were it not for the scope and power of the memoirs which were composed after his departure from Versailles upon the death of the regent in 1723. From this point, Saint-Simon would occupy most of the rest of a long life composing his master-work, helped by the loan of Dangeau's detailed *Journal* of daily transactions at court from 1684 to 1720, mining the copious journals he had himself made as events unfolded and gathering information from reliable witnesses wherever possible. When the task was completed in 1751, the author anticipated that a generation or two must pass before it would be possible to publish the memoirs. A few extracts were released before the Revolution, but the import of the work would not be realized until the publication of full editions of the memoirs in the mid-nineteenth century. And by the time of the publication of the massive critical edition, beginning in 1879 and completed by 1928, if historians were fully aware of the political agenda and personal biases which both enlivened and marred his record, all agreed that this monumental apologia for the French aristocracy represented an unparalleled example of the genre of political memoir.[47]

English courts from the later Stuarts to the Hanoverians exhibited little of the glitter and grandeur of Versailles. Yet the constitutional dramas witnessed throughout this period compared in political import and fascination to the more revolutionary course of change under way in France. Moreover, eighteenth-century London produced a literary culture as highly developed and politically engaged as any European capital. As on the Continent, the British court memoir of this period served as the most characteristic genre of political and historical literature.[48] With political power concentrated geographically in London and personally in the circles around the monarch and his court, the court memoir was well able to exploit and reflect the highly personalized focus of the prevailing political system. Amongst a growing corps of British memoirists, several were outstanding – Lord Hervey, Lord Waldegrave and Horace Walpole – with Hervey rivalling Saint-Simon in the enduring appeal of his style and perception.

Hervey, like Saint-Simon, seemed perfectly placed and inclined to memorialize the political life around him. The second son of the wealthy Earl of Bristol, Hervey entered Parliament in 1725, aligning himself with Sir Robert Walpole, the Prime Minister. His proximity to power, however, would depend more on his court appointment as Vice Chamberlain to the royal family in 1730, and his subsequent enjoyment of the favour of Queen Caroline. With his privileged view on political transactions during the reign of George II, Hervey kept a detailed journal of what he saw and heard. The memoirs are prefaced with a commitment to candour that holds some shock even for the seasoned sensibilities of the modern reader: 'I am determined to report everything just as it is, or as it appears to me; and those who have a curiosity to see courts and courtiers dissected must bear with the dirt they find in laying open such minds with as little nicety and as much patience as in a dissection of their bodies; if they want to see that operation they must submit to the stench.' Hervey proceeded to dissect both the processes and the personalities of Georgian politics with a very sharp scalpel. His personal and political enemies, notably Pulteney, Bolingbroke and Frederick, Prince of Wales, are reduced verbally to cadavers. When it came to publishing Hervey in the mid-nineteenth century, the editor, John Croker, had no small task in removing 'every expression positively offensive to a delicate mind'.[49] By contrast, the full-length portrayal of the Queen – her management of the court, the King's mistresses and his political conscience – presents a characterization as sympathetic and convincing as it is revealing of political processes at the court of George II. Equally, the memoirs portray clearly the political subtlety of Walpole as Prime Minister, and the factors of loyalty, interest and *amour propre* which animated Georgian politics.

The memoirs of James, Second Earl Waldegrave, have neither the flare nor the malevolence of those of Lord Hervey; they share, however, a similarly proximate view on court transactions as Waldegrave succeeded to his father's position as a Lord of the King's Bedchamber in 1743. This appointment gave Waldegrave direct and continuous access to the monarch; his favour by George II was sealed in 1751 by an appointment as Lord Warden of the Stanneries, administrator of the Duchy of Cornwall estates. Of greater political import was Waldegrave's appointment in 1752 as governor in charge of the education of the Prince of Wales, the future George III. It was in this sensitive position, with George II seeking to impose a suitable household on the Prince, his grandson, and with the Prince and his mother, Augusta, Dowager Princess of Wales, determined to resist the King's incursions, that Waldegrave found himself supplanted at Leicester House by Lord Bute, and soon therefore forced to resign his governorship. Waldegrave would briefly play a central role in the political manoeuvring that followed the end of the Newcastle administration in 1756, coming near, as the memoirs reveal, to heading an administration himself. The King would reward him with a handsome sinecure after his loss of the governorship, and then invested him with the Garter for his efforts in the failed negotiations of 1756. But Waldegrave was deeply embittered by his treatment at Leicester House; he would take his revenge in the memoirs he began writing in 1757.[50] These not only attributed the constitutional precepts of George III on the monarchical prerogative to the perverse influence of his mother and Bute, but also lent discreet but deadly credence to the gossip of a sexual liaison between the Dowager Princess and Bute, whose qualities Waldegrave savaged.[51]

Horace Walpole, whose niece was married to Waldegrave, showed less discretion than his close friend in damning the reputations of Bute and the Dowager Princess, claiming that he was 'as much convinced of an amorous connection between B. and the P.D. as if I had seen them together', and elaborating this venomous charge in his *Memoirs*.[52] Walpole, son of Sir Robert, pursued literary interests with more passion than he pursued his political activities. His seat in Parliament, however, gave scope to his relentless curiosity, and placed him in a central position for recording the complex shiftings of faction and parties through the latter half of the eighteenth century. Indeed, Walpole's voluminous memoirs of the reigns of George II and George III mark an important shift in locus away from concentration on the court to Parliament and the highly politicized club-life of London. Although Walpole's writings are often biased, vindictive, unbalanced and inaccurate, they are unfailingly interesting, and contain a vast store of information on the leading personalities and transactions of Parliament which is unavailable elsewhere.[53]

The leading eighteenth-century memoirists recorded the widely varying political experiences of the governments which they served or observed. Despite the variations of content, many common elements of form and approach can be seen in their writings. They all, by now, wrote with a self-consciousness of the problematic, if fascinating, nature of memoir as a genre of historical literature. They were thoroughly familiar with the principal memoir literature of the past, Saint-Simon emphasizing the decisive effect the reading of memoirs exerted from an early point on his own career. The latter prefaced his work with a defence of his purpose and methods: 'Ecrire l'histoire de son pays et de son temps, c'est repasser dans son esprit avec beaucoup de réflexion tout ce qu'on a vu . . . , qui s'est passé sur le théâtre du monde.' Saint-Simon insisted, however, that memoirs and contemporary history like his own – which he called 'l'histoire particulière' as distinct from 'l'histoire générale' which dealt with a diversity of nations and institutions over several centuries – not be published until well after all the persons portrayed were dead. Only thus would the author be free to write without fear or influence from the living, and truth could be presented 'dans toute sa pureté'. No doubt Saint-Simon strove for truth as a witness and recorder, but the memoirs are intentionally much more rich in reflection than bare description, and the prism of the author's values colour and shape vividly the portrayal of character and episode.

Both Hervey and Walpole also asserted their commitment to truth and the reliability of their sources for information; unlike Saint-Simon, however, they made clear disclaimers against writing as historians. Hervey, in a shrewdly disarming introduction, avowed that his focus was to be on the 'more private transactions' and the 'little incidents less likely to be inserted in all other records of this reign'. He furthermore eschewed any claim to have played a major part in the dramas he witnessed:

I leave those ecclesiastical heroes of their own romances, Retz and Burnet, to aim at that useless imaginary glory of being thought to influence every considerable event they relate; and I freely declare that my part in this drama was only that of the Choruses in the ancient tragedies, who, by constantly being on the stage, saw everything that was done, and made their own comments upon the scene, without mixing in the action or making any considerable figure in the performance.[54]

Walpole claimed similar modesty: 'I am no historian. I write casual memoirs; I draw characters; I preserve anecdotes, which my superiors the historians of Britain may enchase into their weighty annals, or pass over at their pleasure.'[55]

The mounting distinctions being made by the middle of the century between memoirs and history proper, as well as the enduring attraction that memoirs held for eighteenth-century British readers, can be seen in the justifications given by Thomas Birch, Secretary of the Royal Society, for his selection of narrative sources from the Elizabethan era which had been unavailable to historians such as Camden. The *Memoirs of the Reign of Queen Elizabeth* were presented, in a widely used metaphor of the period, as exposing 'the true springs' of political conduct, and 'the real characters and sentiments of the great persons who adorned the scene of action at that time'. While the anecdotal details that often provided the main fare of memoirs might be 'too minute for a regular history', they were nevertheless 'more universally entertaining, and more descriptive both of manners and times, than those of a more public and solemn nature'.[56]

It was of course not accidental that the professed modesty of the mid-eighteenth-century memoirists in face of history coincided with major developments in the conceptualization, methodology, and practice of historiography itself. By this time the main prerequisites for a modern 'scientific' historiography were becoming available with the methodologies and new knowledge developed in such ancillary disciplines as diplomacy, numismatics, palaeography and philology, while a vast corpus of rich historical documentation was being compiled and analysed by antiquaries, bibliographers and librarians. Equally important were the new ideas deriving from Enlightenment thought which are to be seen operating to brilliant effect in Voltaire's historical works, notably his *Essai sur l'histoire générale et sur les moeurs et l'esprit des nations*.[57] Here the rationalism and secularism of the Enlightenment, the rejection of providential categories of historical explanation, a concern to base assertion on manifest evidence, and an expository style which dovetailed social analysis with narration in departing from the constraints of chronological form, together illustrated the scale of the break with traditional historiography. In Britain, Hume's *History of England* demonstrated that scholarly historiography could attract a wide and financially rewarding readership.[58] The new dependence on research and sources made accessible by the antiquaries can be seen to even greater effect in Gibbon's master-work, *History of the Decline and Fall of the Roman Empire*, which combined rationalist analysis with superb narrative style, and an interpretive framework designed to affirm the course of human progress.

The political culture of monarchy and court which provided such rich material for the eighteenth-century memoirist would be shaken and changed irretrievably by the revolutions that encompassed

America and Europe in the last quarter of the century. Revolution, ideology, terror, war, nationalism, imperialism – all would fuel the dynamics of both history and historiography. The new century, after the defeat of Napoleon and the political restorations, would see an unprecedented development of historiography. With the Göttingen school in the vanguard, the concepts and methods of the modern discipline of history would be clarified, codified and practised with increasing professionalism. If the court memoir had been the characteristic historical genre of the eighteenth century, national histories and scholarly monographs would predominate in the century of Ranke, Macaulay, Michelet, Parkman and Adams, while innovations in publishing and expanding literacy ushered in the era of mass readerships.

With the rise of scientific historiography, and the subsequent professionalization of history as a modern discipline, the former hegemony of the memoirist in writing contemporary history now came to an end. Indeed, despite the new surge of memoir literature flowing from the seminal revolutionary events in France and the drama-charged era of Napoleon, the genre of political memoir would decline in quality and stature in the first half of the nineteenth century. It is appropriate, therefore, to conclude this analysis with an assessment of the forms and functions of political memoir as they had developed by the late eighteenth century, while suggesting also some of the lines along which the genre would proceed in future.

There is a symmetry in the cycle of British Augustan memoirists rediscovering the distinctions which classical Augustans had themselves made between memoir and historiography. The protestations of modesty by such virtuosi as Hervey and Walpole should not be taken more seriously than they were intended. The leading memoirists of the monarchical regimes were conscious by the mid-eighteenth century of writing within a distinct genre, however variable and indeterminate its form might be. This consciousness clearly distinguishes these authors from such seventeenth-century memoirists as Clarendon and Burnet who alternated between autobiography and historiography, adopting the latter while asserting a special historical competence due to their political participation. The care that the best of the eighteenth-century memoirists took in the writing of their work was no less than that taken by Clarendon, the result being that, certainly in the case of Saint-Simon and Hervey, their memoirs would have a powerful influence on the subsequent development of their nation's literature as well as on historical perception.

The introductory section of this study argued that political memoir could best be comprehended as a polygenre – a literary amalgam of diffuse elements of recording, autobiography, biography, political analysis and contemporary historiography. It is of course true that of the many who have recorded their observations of events very few have exhibited the requisite industry and artistry to transmute the elements of memoir, whether separately or in fusion, into a literary testament of enduring value. Our survey has, for the most part, addressed only memoirs with some claim to belong in this latter category. It is when at least one of the elements of memoir is developed with intensity and skill that the potential for valuable memoir occurs. In rare cases this may result from merely the passive, if careful recording of observations which provide important descriptive information, not otherwise available, concerning historically important phenomena. The court journals of Dangeau provided Saint-Simon with invaluable chronology and sequential information, even though the latter scorned Dangeau's lack of artistry. There are, of course, vast stores of memoirs-as-simple-records – countless fragmentary diaries, letters, journals and other personal narrative sources – which, if seldom worthy of publication, nevertheless nourish the curious historian. But where recording is translated into narrative with a sense of the interrelationship of events, where personal political engagements and relationships are dramatized, where character is artfully portrayed in juxtaposition with circumstance and where political analysis exposes the 'hidden springs' moving government, the resulting amalgam has every capacity to fascinate and inform the reader. And in the extremely rare conjunction of dramatic circumstance, exercise of leadership, sophisticated political perspective, literary talent and the essential animus to write, as well as leisure and access to crucial documentation, the memoirist can function with mastery as contemporary historian – as in the case of Saint-Simon and Clarendon.

But even the greatest of these memoirists are not read today *as historians*; rather, they are read as narrative sources for information on the events, manners and especially the personalities which they portray, not least their own. They are enjoyed also as literature, capable of enlightening and entertaining the reader, even when, as with Hervey and Saint-Simon, they are sometimes biased as sources. Indeed, as the nineteenth-century historians went to work on the same history covered by our memoirists, submitting them to the critical canons of aspiring scientific historiography, Ranke and his rigorous disciples would exhibit a distinct preference for objective documentation over memoir. The latter would be subordinated to the status of narrative source, to be tested for the accuracy of the data which it could be made to yield, or assigned to the realm of literature.[59]

Nevertheless, as professional historiography was embracing scientific methodology, and as memoirists were disclaiming their competence as historians, the political memoir was being liberated to function in new forms and capacities. The memoirs of previous ages had circulated within the fairly narrow confines of the social and political élites of their times. Even as readerships began to expand significantly in the eighteenth century, the memoirists could seldom expect to see their works published within their lifetime. The rise of a newly literate mass readership during the nineteenth century, and the innovations in the technology and distribution of print which were in place by the latter part of the century, would open new opportunities to the political memoirist, especially in the wake of the bloody Civil War in America and the dramas of European imperialism. Then the world of the nineteenth century would be ended for ever, as the First World War levelled the terrain for the clashing mass cultures of the twentieth century. The new century of revolutions and world wars would prove extremely conducive and receptive to the offerings of the memoirists. But this is to introduce further chapters in the history of political memoir.

NOTES

1. That Mr Reagan was publishing his memoirs with Simon and Schuster, however, did cause some shocked surprise at Harper and Row, who thought they had tied the President down in a three million US dollar contract for an official biography to be written by Edmond Morris. *New York Times*, 1 February 1989, section III, p. 23.
2. Although President Kennedy was assassinated in office, his administration has been served well by memoirists, notably Theodore Sorensen, Arthur Schlesinger, and Pierre Salinger. For both Kennedy and Franklin Roosevelt books have been published reconstructing their words and thoughts in memoir form. *I, JFK* (New York, 1989); Bernard Asabell, *The F.D.R. Memoirs* (New York, 1973). Edward Heath's promised memoirs have not as yet appeared at the time of writing this essay.
3. Address by Lord Armstrong of Ilminster (formerly Secretary to the Prime Minister and the Cabinet), University of British Columbia, 14 March 1989. Literary agents predicted a possible US$8 million advance for Mrs Thatcher's memoirs. *Time*, 10 December 1990, p. 36.
4. Jomo Kenyatta, *Facing Mount Kenya* (London, 1938); Kenneth Kaunda, *Zambia Shall Be Free: An Autobiography* (London, 1962); Bishop Abel Tendekai Muzorewa, Norman Thomas (ed.), *Rise Up and Walk: An Autobiography* (London, 1978); Benazir Bhutto, *Daughter of the East* (New York, 1989).
5. *Publishers Weekly*, 10 February 1989, p. 34; *New York Times*, 1 February 1989. The five-million dollar estimated advance appears to have been the most accurate. *Time*, 10 December 1990, p. 36.
6. Details on the help Mr Reagan had in writing the memoirs can be found in *Publishers Weekly*,

10 February 1989, p. 34. With Michael Korda, Editor-in-Chief of Simon and Schuster, taking personal charge of the editing of Reagan's memoirs, there are comparisons to Mark Twain's role in the production and marketing of Ulysses Grant's memoirs. Michael Korda is himself a best-selling novelist. The Reagan memoirs were serialized first in *Time*, 5 and 12 November 1990, and published later in the same month by Simon and Schuster.

7. C.T. Onions (ed.), *The Oxford Dictionary of English Etymology* (Oxford, 1966), p. 568; R. Barnhart (ed.), *The Barnhart Dictionary of Etymology* (New York, 1988), p. 650.

8. *The Oxford English Dictionary* (Oxford, second edition, 1989), pp. 593–4.

9. Georg Misch, *History of Autobiography in Antiquity* (Westport, CT, 1974), Vol.I, pp. 185 and 187.

10. Ibid., p. 186. See also pp. 6, 7 and 15.

11. Roy Pascal, *Design and Truth in Autobiography* (Cambridge, MA, 1960), pp. 4–5.

12. Misch, I, p. 20.

13. Ibid., pp. 41–3.

14. Ibid., pp. 203–5.

15. Ibid., pp. 259–63.

16. Procopius' sixth-century *History of the Wars* recounts the military campaigns of the emperor Justinian and the Byzantine commander Belisarius, whom Procopius served as a leading adviser. His *Historia Arcana (Secret History)* includes a graphic indictment of the deeds of Justinian and Belisarius. Psellus' eleventh-century *Chronographia* contains a highly personalized account of the happenings of the Byzantine courts where he served as chief adviser to several emperors. John VI's largely autobiographical account was written after his deposition in 1354 and exile to a monastery. Byzantine historiography is reviewed in Matthew A. Fitzsimons *et al.* (eds.), *The Development of Historiography* (Port Washington, NY, 1967), Ch. 6.

17. M.R.B. Shaw (ed. and trans.), *Joinville and Villehardouin: Chronicles of the Crusades* (London, 1963).

18. Of these, the twelfth–thirteenth-century *Sverris Saga* is notable for its qualities both as history and as personal narrative. The introduction to the *Sverris Saga* tells how it was dictated in part by the Norwegian king to his secretary and librarian, Karl Jonsson, who also used information obtained from Sverri's contemporaries in compiling the saga. I am grateful to Jan Furst for sharing his knowledge of saga literature. See also Peter Hallberg, *The Icelandic Saga* (Lincoln, NE, 1962).

19. Eugen Hillenbrand (ed.), *Vita Caroli Quarti/Die Autobiographie Karls IV* (Stuttgart, 1979).

20. Rinaldo Fulin *et al.* (eds.), *I Diarii di Marino Sanuto* (58 vols.) (Venice, 1879–1903). Sanuto's diary/memoir is analysed in Robert Finlay, *Politics in Renaissance Venice* (New Brunswick, NJ, 1980).

21. Mark Phillips has used this memoir to extract a wealth of fresh information on the social and political history of Renaissance Florence: *The Memoir of Marco Parenti: A Life in Medici Florence* (Princeton, 1987).

22. For the bibliography of Piccolomini's manuscript, its publication in a highly expurgated version under his secretary's name in the later sixteenth century, and the discovery of the original work in the late nineteenth century, see F.A. Gragg and L.C. Gabel (eds. and trans.), *Memoirs of a Renaissance Pope: The Commentaries of Pius II* (New York, 1962), pp. 21–3.

23. Fourteenth- and fifteenth-century French memoirs are analysed in Denys Hay, *Annalists and Historians* (London, 1977), pp. 75–8.

24. Commynes' memoirs have been printed in eight languages and have appeared in over 120 editions since their first printing in Paris in 1524. S. Kinser (ed.), *The Memoirs of Philippe de Commynes*, Isabelle Cazeaux (trans.), (2 vols.) (Columbia, 1969, 1973), p. 81.

25. Annette S. Beveridge (trans.), *Babur-Nama (Memoirs of Babur)* (London, 1922; New Delhi, 1979).

26. *The Memoirs of Robert Cary, Earl of Monmouth, Written by Himself, and Fragmenta Regalia being A History of Queen Elizabeth's Favourites by Sir Robert Naunton* (Edinburgh, and London, 1808).

27. The memoirs of Sully, Richelieu, de Retz and Louis XIV are surveyed by George Peabody Gooch's essay, 'Political Autobiography', in *Studies in Diplomacy and Statecraft* (London, 1942), pp. 228–37.

28. 'The Author to the Reader', prefaced to *The History of the Most Renowned and Victorious Princess Elizabeth* (London, 1675), translated by Richard Norton from Camden's Latin *Annales Rerum Anglicarum et Hibernicarum regnante Elizabetha* (London, 1615).
29. James Spedding *et al.* (eds.), 'On the Fortunate Memory of Elizabeth Queen of England', *The Works of Francis Bacon* (London, 1857–74), Vol. VI, p. 305; cited in F.J. Levy, *Tudor Historical Thought* (San Marino, CA, 1967), p. 254.
30. For recent critical treatment of Ludlow's memoirs see A.B. Worden (ed.), *A Voice from the Watch Tower* (London, 1978).
31. Details on the making of Clarendon's *History* and *Life* can be found in George E. Miller, *Edward Hyde, Earl of Clarendon* (Boston, 1983), and Martine W. Brownley, *Clarendon and the Rhetoric of Historical Form* (Philadelphia, 1985). The standard editions are: Dunn Macray (ed.), *The History of the Rebellion and Civil Wars in England* (6 vols.) (Oxford, 1888), *The Life of Edward Earl of Clarendon . . . in which is included, A Continuation of his History of the Grand Rebellion* (2 vols.) (Oxford, 1857).
32. Miller, p. 143.
33. Lord Clarendon, *A Complete Collection of the Tracts* (London, 1747).
34. George Scott, 'The Epistle to the Reader', *The Memoirs of Sir James Melvil of Halhill* (London, 1683), taken from the third edition, 1752. Scott was a descendant of Melvil.
35. Bulstrode Whitelock, *Memorials of the English Affairs from the beginning of the Reign of Charles the First to the Happy Restoration of King Charles the Second* (London, 1853), p. iv. Whitelock was a parliamentary leader, holding office under the Commonwealth and Protectorate, but a moderate who was pardoned after the Restoration.
36. A series of essays by the late British historian George Peabody Gooch surveying outstanding political autobiographies and memoirs of the modern era illuminates many of the varieties and functions of memoirs written in the eighteenth century. Most of Gooch's essays were written first for the *Contemporary Review* and later published collectively as *Courts and Cabinets* (London, 1944). These are in addition to his 'Political Autobiography', in *Studies in Statecraft*.
37. Gilbert Burnet, O. Airy (ed.), *History of My Own Time* (2 vols.) (London, 1724, 1734).
38. The surviving sections of Burnet's autobiographical *Secret History* are published in H.C. Foxcroft (ed.), *A Supplement to Burnet's History of My Own Time; derived from his original memoirs, in his autobiography . . .* (Oxford, 1902).
39. Frederick's historical writings are assessed in G.P. Gooch, *Frederick the Great: the Ruler, the Writer, the Man* (New York, 1947).
40. Cited in Gooch, 'Political Autobiography', p. 240.
41. J.D.E. Preuss (ed.), *Oeuvres Historiques de Frédéric II, Roi de Prusse* (30 vols.) (Berlin, 1864ff.).
42. Catherine's fragmentary memoir would not be published until the mid-nineteenth century. Dominique Maroger (ed.), G.P. Gooch (intro.), Moura Budberg (trans.), *The Memoirs of Catherine the Great* (London, 1955).
43. F. Riaux (ed.), *Mémoires de Mme de Motteville sur Anne d'Autriche et sa cour* (Paris, 1855).
44. *Mémoires de Frédérique Sope Wilhelmine, margrave de Bayreuth, soeur de Frédéric Le Grand, depuis l'année 1706 jusqu' à 1742* (Paris, 1967).
45. Frances (Burney) Arblay, Charlotte Barrett, her niece (ed.), *Diary and letters of Madam d'Arblay* (7 vols.) (London, 1842–46).
46. A. de Boislisle (ed.), *Mémoires de Saint-Simon* (29 vols.) (Paris, 1879–1928).
47. For information on the making and impact of Saint-Simon's memoirs see Gooch, *Courts and Cabinets*, Chs. 7 and 8; and D.W. Brogan's introduction to Lucy Norton (ed. and trans.), *Historical Memoirs of the Duc De Saint-Simon: A Shortened Version* (3 vols.) (London, 1967, 1974).
48. This theme is developed in J.D.C. Clark's superb new critical edition of *The Memoirs and Speeches of James, 2nd Earl of Waldegrave, 1742–1763* (Cambridge, 1988), p. 6.
49. John, Lord Hervey, Romney Sedgwick (ed.), *Some Materials Towards Memoirs of the Reign of King George II* (3 vols.) (London, 1931), p. xi. See also Gooch, *Courts and Cabinets*, Chs. 11 and 12.
50. Waldegrave's *Memoirs* would first be published by John Murray in 1821, edited by Lord Holland from an inferior copy. The edition by Clark, taken from an earlier copy, and which includes ancillary reflections, satirical writings and speeches by Waldegrave, is much more

revealing.
51. For Waldegrave's seminal role in sowing the seeds of the scandal concerning Bute and the Dowager Princess, and the origins of the Whig interpretation of George III's constitutional retrogressions, see Clark, pp. 72–134.
52. Horace Walpole, *Walpoliana* (2 vols.) (London, 1799), Vol. I: p. 64. Walpole's *Memoirs of the Reign of King George the Second* were edited by Henry Richard Vassall Fox, 3rd Baron Holland, and first published in 1847. John Brooke has edited a modern critical version: Horace Walpole, *Memoirs of King George II* (3 vols.) (New Haven, 1985).
53. Walpole's *Memoirs of the Reign of King George the Third* were first published in 1845 in an edition by Sir Denis Le Marchant. A re-edited version by G.F. Barker is the standard (4 vols.) (London, 1894).
54. Hervey, pp. 2–3.
55. *Memoirs of George II*, Vol. I: p. xxxi.
56. Thomas Birch (ed.), *Memoirs of the Reign of Queen Elizabeth . . .* (2 vols.) (London, 1754).
57. In seven volumes (Paris, 1756). The eighteenth-century transitions to modern historiography are analysed in Hay, Ch. 8.
58. *History of England* (London, 1763); Hay, pp. 174–5.
59. Langlois and Seignobos' classic summation of nineteenth-century scientific canons of historiography exhibits little affinity with memoirs or 'psychological traces', which 'are often complicated and hard to unravel'. *Introduction to the Study of History*, G.C. Berry (trans.) (London, 1966, reprinted from the 1898 edition), pp. 65–6.

2
Bismarck's *Gedanken und Erinnerungen*

OTTO PFLANZE

Bismarck's memoirs are quite highly regarded by historians and even literary critics. After a survey of political autobiographies beginning with Babur, founder of the Mughal empire in the sixteenth century, and ending with Hitler's *Mein Kampf*, George Peabody Gooch concluded that Bismarck's *Reflections and Recollections* 'stand at the top of the list . . ., not merely because he is the greatest man who ever wrote a full-length narrative of his life, and not merely because the events he records are of world-wide significance, but because [the work's] value as a manual of statecraft is unsurpassed'.[1] A.J.P. Taylor was briefer: '*Gedanken und Erinnerungen* ranks with the most remarkable political memoirs ever written, not least for its artistic inaccuracy of detail'.[2] Even Ludwig Bamberger, one of Bismarck's liberal opponents, described it as a 'rich historical, political, and psychological monument to the strength of the human spirit and character', a contribution to world literature that would have been even more effective had it been objectively written. Caesar, Frederick the Great and Napoleon did not leave behind such a 'unique and brilliantly written account of their persons and their deeds'.[3] 'Are there any good German books?' someone asked Nietzsche. 'I blushed', he remembered, 'but then with the bravery peculiar to me in extreme situations, I answered: "Yes, Bismarck's".'[4] After re-reading the memoirs I am not sure what prompted these hyperbolic judgements. A partial explanation lies perhaps in the circumstances in which the work was written.

Historicism has taught us that every document is coloured in some degree by the circumstances of its origin. Bismarck's work was composed in the two years that followed his departure from office, while the sting of that event was still fresh and he was in open opposition to the policies of his successors. The issues that led to his dismissal have been much debated by historians. Basically, it seems to me, the issue was personal. From his early years Bismarck was driven by a dynamic, narcissistic compulsion to dominate and direct, for which his only outlet was politics, a compulsion that never left him until his death in 1898. In Kaiser Wilhelm II he confronted a young sovereign driven by a similar compulsion, who thought of himself as a latter-day Frederick the Great endowed with divine right.

Wilhelm was susceptible to flattery and suggestion by men eager to promote their own careers by clinging to his coat-tails, and yet Bismarck was unquestionably vulnerable to their insinuations. To many at court and in the government it seemed evident in March 1890 that the Chancellor, nearly 75 years old and long in poor health, was losing his grip on both domestic and foreign affairs. His extended absences from Berlin, while at his estate at Friedrichsruh, separated him from monarch and ministers and reduced his contact with the daily flow of government business. And yet Bismarck held on to the bitter end, forcing Wilhelm II to demand his resignation; even then, he took an excessive amount of time to write it out, scribbling at his desk even as his appointed successor, Leo von Caprivi, took charge of the chancellery outside his office door. What detained Bismarck that day was the belief that he must present in the letter of resignation his view of the events that had led up to his dismissal. Here began his struggle to capture public opinion, a struggle that soon led to the composition of his famous memoirs.

The apparent issues that led to the rupture of relations between Kaiser and Chancellor were several: Wilhelm's desire for additional social reforms with which to reconcile labour and weaken the socialist movement versus Bismarck's desire for a new, more repressive anti-socialist statute; Bismarck's belief that Germany faced an internal crisis that might require a *Staatsstreich*, which would end universal male suffrage, versus Wilhelm's wish not to begin his reign by an act of violence that might alienate the working man; Wilhelm's insistence that he had the right as sovereign to receive and instruct ministers and officials versus Bismarck's insistence that under a rule established in 1852 only the Prussian Minister-President and German Chancellor (he held both offices) could communicate directly with the Kaiser on civil and foreign affairs; and, finally, Bismarck's belief that the reinsurance treaty of 1887 with Russia should be renewed versus Wilhelm's conviction, inspired by Holstein and other advisers, that its terms contradicted those of the Austro-German alliance of 1879.

In the letter of resignation Bismarck chose to base his case primarily on constitutionalism. To invalidate the cabinet order of 1852, he wrote, meant a return to absolutism in Prussia. Without it neither ministerial responsibility nor a unified governmental policy was possible, both of which were essential attributes of a constitutional state. Until now his authority had rested on his many years in office and the trust placed in him by Kaisers Wilhelm I and Friedrich III. No longer possessing that trust, he had found it necessary to remind the ministers of the order of 1852. To retire from his Prussian posts and remain as imperial Chancellor was impossible. Even if it were practicable to separate domestic from foreign policy – which he doubted – he could not accept responsibility for the direction Wilhelm II now wished to pursue in foreign affairs. He had the impression, he concluded, that Wilhelm no longer had use for his experience and talents as a statesman. That being the case, he could retire from office without fearing that the public would judge that decision premature.[5]

On the afternoon of 18 March 1890, Bismarck finally finished and signed his 'request for release from office' with the familiar long vertical strokes of his pen. Forty-eight hours later came the Kaiser's acceptance. 'My dear prince! It is with deepest emotion that I see from your request of March 18 that you have decided to resign from the positions you have occupied for so many years with incomparable success.' He had hoped, the message continued, not to have to face the idea of parting from the prince 'in our life times'. 'With troubled heart' he had reconciled himself to the idea, but only in the knowledge that Bismarck's 'wish' was irreversible and with 'firm confidence' that 'your counsel and prowess, your faithfulness and dedication' would remain available 'to me and the fatherland'. In equally flowery language he paid tribute to the prince's achievements for Prussia, Germany and the Hohenzollern dynasty, as well as his 'wise and active policy' on behalf of peace, a policy that would be Wilhelm's 'guide for the future'. In conclusion, he conferred on Bismarck promotion to Colonel-General of the cavalry (rank of Field Marshal-General), the title 'Duke of Lauenburg', and the Kaiser's 'life-sized portrait'. On 29 March 1890, thousands crowded the streets of Berlin to applaud Bismarck and bombard him with flowers when he left for Friedrichsruh.[6] And yet the public's adulation of Bismarck did not necessarily translate into hostility toward the monarch who had dismissed him. By suppressing the prince's letter of resignation and publishing his own reply, Wilhelm won the first battle in the contest for public opinion. For the time being his version of the resignation, not Bismarck's, was generally accepted.

Bismarck retired to his estate at Friedrichsruh near Hamburg seething with anger toward those who he believed had intrigued against him and resolutely determined to oppose those policies of the new government of which he disapproved. He had, he declared, earned the right to criticize.[7] One possible forum was the Reichstag, of whose oppositional parties he had so often complained and whose electoral base he had so recently wanted to revise by a reactionary *coup d'état*. Even so he was not inconsistent. He had always maintained that Parliament's most valuable function was to criticize unwise policies of the government (a term inapplicable to himself).[8] Two days after his return to Friedrichsruh, the prince spoke privately of standing for the Reichstag, and on 22 May he publicly hinted at his availability for a by-election. In desperation his son, Herbert, pleaded with his father not to expose himself to 'his enemies and the general knavishness' of Berlin politics. In April 1891 he stood as a national liberal candidate in a by-election in Hanover and won only with the help of the Guelph party, composed of Hanoverian particularists with whom he had often feuded in earlier years. The possibility that he might speak in the Reichstag on crucial issues sent shivers down the spines of his enemies in the Berlin government.[9] But he never did. Instead, he yielded to the entreaties of his wife Johanna, his son Herbert and his physician Ernst Schweninger, not to honour that 'accursed' body with his presence. He feared to appear there 'like Banquo's ghost' or a 'person with the plague'.[10] If only grudgingly, he recognized that as a deputy he could never influence the chamber in the way he had as Chancellor.

In the newspaper press Bismarck found a more suitable forum for defending his personal interests and advancing his views on public policy. At this he was hardly a novice. Bismarck's political career coincided with the development of the newspaper into a mass medium, and he was one of the first statesmen to comprehend the value of exploiting it for political purposes. Within weeks of his dismissal he began to grant interviews, particularly to foreign journalists beginning with the *New York Herald*.[11] To his open annoyance, those newspapers that had been accessible to his influence as Chancellor, particularly the *Norddeutsche Allgemeine Zeitung*, now deserted him under official pressure. But he soon found a substitute in the *Hamburger Nachrichten*, which now became his principal mouthpiece. Its political editor, Hermann Hofmann, was a regular visitor at Friedrichsruh, carrying away with him notes, drafts and background information that soon appeared in articles widely read and reprinted throughout Germany and Europe. [12] Hofmann was a 'hired gun', but not so Maximilian Harden. Founder and editor of *Zukunft*, Harden was a brilliant, if convoluted, writer, an independent man of fearless rectitude, and a thorn in the flesh of the Kaiser and his government. For nearly two years (1892–94), he frequently visited Friedrichsruh, finding in Bismarck a valuable ally but not a master. [13] In southern Germany Bismarck found another willing collaborator in Hugo Jacobi, chief editor of the *Münchener Allgemeine Zeitung*, owned by the famous publishing house of J.G. Cotta. Eventually Jacobi became the editor of *Berliner Neueste Nachrichten*, financed by wealthy industrialists and titled aristocrats sympathetic to Jacobi's pro-Bismarck course. [14]

Hofmann, Harden and Jacobi were the most important channels through which Bismarck brought his views and interests to the attention of the public. On a less regular basis he employed many other journalists, pamphleteers, historians and literati for that purpose. To be invited to Friedrichsruh for an interview was a flattering opportunity for struggling newspapermen, whose desire to exploit the connection was no less avid than that of the host. One of these was Moritz Busch, Bismarck's old *Leibjournalist*, who came away with copious verbatim notes (and on one occasion with unauthorized copies of documents he had been given merely to read). Others earned the right to such visits by favourable articles, brochures and even books about the ex-Chancellor, the receipt of which at Friedrichsruh sometimes triggered an invitation and interview. In the Bismarck household these writers and journalists were known as the 'diaspora press', to be exploited at every opportunity to exalt the ex-Chancellor's image, discredit his foes and critics and advance his own views on past and present affairs. Father and son strove to keep these sometimes unsavoury scribblers under control by punishing their indiscretions with public denials and their deviations by threats of excommunication. Even when they faithfully executed the ex-Chancellor's wishes, they were sometimes disavowed when, by some miscalculation at Friedrichsruh, the public reaction to their writings was unexpectedly adverse. [15]

By the time of their composition the memoirs had become a potential weapon in the propaganda struggle with the Kaiser and his advisers. Although he toyed with the idea of such a work during the 1870s and 1880s, the first positive step was taken in late 1888, when he charged Moritz Busch with the preliminary task of sorting and ordering the necessary documents at Friedrichsruh and Varzin.[16] And yet little progress was made before March 1890, when the problem of sources became acute. Obviously the ex-Chancellor could no longer depend on free access to the archives. On 16 March Busch found him in his office surrounded by boxes of papers and a half-empty filing cabinet, concerned that the contents might be sequestered before he could make off with them. Herbert continued to function as State Secretary in the Foreign Office until his resignation was accepted on 26 March, and, according to one source, he ordered stacks of document files delivered to his quarters until Caprivi forbade it.[17] What father and son managed to take with them in the many chests (most containing household goods, including 13,000 bottles of wine) that were shipped from the Wilhelmstrasse to Friedrichsruh is unclear. But it did not suffice to document even the important episodes that the prince wished to relate. In any case Bismarck preferred to rely primarily on his memory, which was very selective.

The rumour that Bismarck intended to write memoirs spread rapidly. At least 43 publishing houses (including some in the United States) wrote to Friedrichsruh to inquire whether they might be of service, and there were also five offers of translation. But in July 1890 Bismarck had already signed a contract with the firm J.G. Cotta at Stuttgart, the most famous German publisher. Founded in the seventeenth century, Cotta had published the works of Schiller, Herder, Goethe, Fichte, Hebbel, Tieck and many other eminent authors.

Following the death of Karl von Cotta in 1888, the firm had been purchased by the brothers Adolf and Paul Kröner. Quite apart from the distinction of the publishing house they acquired, the Kröners had access to Bismarck through Hugo Jacobi, whose *Münchener Allgemeine Zeitung* was controlled by Cotta, and Max Duttenhofer, a Württemberg industrialist, whose brother, Carl, was a guest at Friedrichsruh in late May 1890. Carl carried with him a letter from Adolf Kröner and introduced it by speaking of the memoirs as a potentially 'lucrative business proposition'. Bismarck undoubtedly spoke the truth when he replied that, if he decided to write the memoirs, it would not be for money, which he would 'leave to others'. In any case the matter was premature: his papers were in great disorder, and he would have to overcome the 'inertia' that now afflicted him.[18] Two months later he signed a contract with Adolf Kröner that provided for six volumes with a royalty of 100,000 marks each – a flat sum with no additional royalties on sales, translations or future editions. The royalty was meagre, but so were the prospects, for the contract relieved the prince of all liability in the event that the work was never written.[19]

Ultimately Bismarck's choice of a collaborator was not Moritz Busch, the journalist, but Lothar Bucher, his long-time secretary and aide who had retired from the Foreign Office in 1886. Bucher soon had reason to doubt that the memoirs would ever be finished. At 73 years of age, this former radical was plagued by gout and bent and worn by years of dedicated public service. He was also a highly intelligent, learned and independent soul, whose conception of the memoirs differed markedly from that of his master. His idea was to produce a historical work, objective and balanced, based not only on Bismarck's memory but also upon such documents as were available. Bismarck, on the other hand, viewed his memoirs as one more opportunity to shape the image of himself and his deeds that he wished to imprint on the public mind. It was just another weapon in his continuing struggle against critics, detractors and Caprivi's 'new course'. Bucher's occasional attempts to keep Bismarck on the track of historical veracity went unheeded. 'It is not only that his memory is inadequate and his interest in the finished parts small', Bucher complained, 'but that he also begins to distort intentionally, even when the facts and events are clear. In no instance does he want to have been involved in anything that was unsuccessful'.[20]

Also distressing to the patient but ailing secretary was the slowness with which the work proceeded during the first weeks. Ernst Schweninger described the scene: 'Bucher, silent, out of sorts, peevish, sitting at a table with a blank sheet of paper, sharp of ear and pencil; Bismarck reclining on a chaise longue on doctor's orders and absorbed in a newspaper. Deep quiet – one could have heard a mouse. The prince said not a word, Bucher even less – and the page remained blank.' In late November 1890 Bucher had less reason to complain; the dictations assumed a steady pace, interrupted only by Bucher's vacations and Bismarck's annual cure at Bad Kissingen. They followed no chronological pattern, but wandered backwards and forwards in time, and from topic to topic and back again, sometimes prompted by the prince's reactions to current events. Afterwards Bucher had the task of separating and reassembling the text into chapters, divining the author's intent, pointing out lacunae, excising repetitions, inserting dates and documents, correcting and implementing.[21] For this he was an ideal, if grumbling, collaborator. By May 1892 the drafts of two volumes of *Erinnerung und Gedanke* (subsequently renamed

Gedanken und Erinnerungen) were ready. But the prince was already concerned about the candour with which he had described his relationships with and opinions about living personalities. 'I have seen three kings naked.' To tell the world how they looked unclothed would violate principle, and yet silence was also impossible. If the work were published posthumously, people would say, 'There you have it; now it comes from the grave; what a dreadful old man!'[22]

That May Bucher, suffering from a painful bladder ailment, went on leave in search of a cure; in October he died alone in a hotel room on Lake Geneva. His end was much mourned at Friedrichsruh, for without him there could be no thought of additional volumes. To Adolf Kröner's vexation, Bismarck made little progress thereafter in preparing the existing manuscript for publication. The ex-Chancellor's illness at Bad Kissingen in August–September 1893 added to the publisher's anxiety and the urgency of his appeals. Kröner did succeed in gaining the prince's permission to set the type, but only for the first volume. In early October the galley proofs of that volume arrived at Friedrichsruh. But again Bismarck made many changes – corrections of style, orthography and typography, striking out some lines and amending others. In 1894 his surface 'reconciliation' with Wilhelm II intervened to slow the process.[23]

Several Bismarcks contested with one another during these years. Bismarck the realist was eager to expose the incompetence of his successors; Bismarck the narcissist lusted to reveal how shabbily he had been treated; Bismarck the monarchist was reluctant to damage the dynasty's public image. Conceived as a weapon in the dispute with Wilhelm II, the memoirs had begun to look less like a sword and more like a boomerang. Bismarck made no clear decision on when to publish either volume. In Bucher's time he apparently wanted the second volume to appear 'posthumously'. Subsequently he spoke of delaying publication of volume one until his death; volume two, until the death of Wilhelm II. And so the corrected galley proofs of volume one and the manuscript of volume two still lay at Friedrichsruh when he died on 30 July 1898.

Three days after Bismarck died, Adolf Kröner alerted Friedrichsruh to expect the page proofs for volume one. When they arrived, Herbert saw that the pages did not contain the corrections Bismarck had made in the galley proofs, which had never been returned to Cotta. Before proceeding further, he decided to consult with Chemnitz Gymnasium Professor Horst Kohl, editor of *Bismarck-Regesten, Bismarck-Jahrbuch, Die Politischen Reden des Fürsten Bismarck*, and other works. Bismarck himself had often complained of gaps in the narrative he and Bucher had produced. With Herbert's co-operation, Kohl fleshed out volume one, writing an introduction, inserting letters from the Friedrichsruh archive and adding a large number of footnotes. But he also made stylistic and factual 'corrections', some needed, many not. As a result of Kohl's additions, volume one reached a size that made advisable its division into two volumes. The memoirs became a three-volume work.[24]

Kohl thought of himself as Bismarck's chosen literary executor and as the supreme authority on the ex-Chancellor's thoughts and purposes. Indeed the prince had shown great confidence in Kohl, permitting him to take to distant Chemnitz documents from the Friedrichsruh archive for copying and publication. The editors of the definitive edition of the memoirs published in 1932 detected instances in which this self-confident Bismarck loyalist had altered the text unnecessarily, even misleadingly, sometimes for the presumptuous purpose of shielding its author. And yet he did not change the basic character and contents of the work. Kohl was a swift and indefatigable editor who completed his task in a few weeks. Volumes one and two were published simultaneously with remarkable speed at Stuttgart on 30 November 1898. Volume three, to the manuscript of which Kohl was not given access, was not published until 1921.[25] The hiatus of nearly a quarter of a century in its publication, as well as its theme and method of composition, require that this volume be considered apart from its two predecessors – in the last part of this essay.

Delays in the writing and publication of the memoirs frustrated the initial purpose of their composition – that of supplying the Bismarck camp with a significant weapon in the public struggle against the foreign and domestic policies of Caprivi's 'new course'. By the time volumes one and two appeared Caprivi had been out of office for five years, Wilhelm II had lost his enthusiasm for social reform, the reinsurance treaty with Russia was gone beyond recall (Russia being already allied with France), Caprivi's attempt to reduce agrarian protectionism had been frustrated by the determined opposition and political influence of the landlord lobby and the first steps had been taken toward the construction of a high seas fleet and the inauguration of *Weltpolitik*. What *Gedanken und Erinnerungen* could still accomplish, however, was no less important to Bismarck and his son Herbert: namely, the moulding of Bismarck's image in the public mind and in history itself.

This purpose is already evident in the opening lines of the memoirs:

I left school at Easter 1832, a normal product of our state system of education: a pantheist, and, if not a republican, at least with the conviction that a republic was the most reasonable form of government. Why, I reflected, should millions of men continue to obey one person, when one could hear grown up people express so much bitter or contemptuous criticism of rulers? Moreover, I had brought away with me 'German-national' impressions from Plamann's preparatory school, conducted on Jahn's drill-system, in which I lived from my sixth to my twelfth year. These impressions remained in the stage of theoretical reflections, and were not strong enough to extirpate my innate Prussian monarchical sentiments. My historical sympathies remained on the side of authority. To my childish ideas of justice Harmodius and Aristogiton, as well as Brutus, were criminals, and Tell a rebel and murderer. Every German prince who resisted the Emperor before the Thirty Years War aroused my ire; but from the Great Elector onwards I was partisan enough to take an anti-imperial view, and naturally I found the Seven Years War was justified. Yet German-national feeling remained so strong in me that, at the beginning of my university life, I at once entered into relations with the *Burschenschaft*, a group of students whose aim was the promotion of national sentiment.

But their unwillingness to duel and their poor manners repelled him, and likewise the extravagance of their political views, which he attributed to deficiencies in their knowledge of history and practical affairs. 'Nevertheless, I retained my own private national sentiments and my belief that in the near future events would lead to German unity; in fact, I made a bet with my American friend Coffin that this aim would be attained in twenty years.' And yet he found the Hambach festival of 1832 and the Frankfurt uprising of 1833 'revolting'. 'Mob interference with political authority conflicted with my Prussian schooling.' But France's possession of Strassburg exasperated him when he looked at the map, and a visit to Heidelberg, Speyer and the Palatinate made him feel vengeful and militant.[26]

In dictating this passage Bismarck first used the word 'atheist' to describe his early religious beliefs, but later changed it to 'pantheist'. For a reborn Christian it looked better to have once believed in an immanent God than in none at all. His comment about the 'normal' product of state education was not a casual irony but a conclusion he reached in the late 1880s that Germany was producing too many educated persons, whose critical training inclined them toward nihilism and radicalism – one of the few convictions he continued to share with Wilhelm II. But the most remarkable aspect of this opening paragraph is the depiction of his fluctuating early views on Prussian autocracy and German nationalism.

There is no longer any reason to doubt that Bismarck's primary loyalty at least until the early 1860s was to the Prussian state or, as he often expressed it in these years, to the 'Prussian nation'. His experiences in the revolution of 1848–49 merely reinforced this emotional and political orientation. German nationalism was associated with radical liberalism, and national unity under liberal auspices was a threat to the social and political existence of Prussia. And yet Bismarck's Prussian nationalism did not lead him into a defensive, quiescent conservatism. On the contrary, he grew up with the conviction that Prussia must expand at the cost of the German small states, particularly those that lay between the separated halves of the Prussian state created by the treaty of Vienna. That treaty had established Austrian primacy in Germany and made it the principal protector of small state sovereignty. During the 1850s Bismarck reached the view that Prussia must remove the Habsburg obstacle to its expansion in Germany. In the years 1858–62, he came to appreciate that this could only be done in alliance with German nationalism. The victory could be won by conventional means – the striking power of the Prussian army, the discipline of its soldiers, and the brilliance of its generals. But its consolidation required a moral legitimation that only German nationalism could provide.

Once he chose this course, it was necessary for Bismarck to reshape his public image. Popularly regarded in the years 1862–66 as a black reactionary, he had now to redefine himself as a lifelong German nationalist without at the same time denying his Prussian heritage. His adoption of the idiom of German nationalism during the period 1860–66 can be traced in both personal and state documents of that period. The memoirs became yet another canvas for this self-portrait. So attractively and convincingly did he paint it that for two generations most biographers and hagiographers accepted his depiction as accurate. In Bismarck's person, in the socio-political establishment of united Germany, and in the constitutional order of the German Reich, Prussia and Germany became fused as one. This was a new configuration in German political life, one of profound consequence for the future.[27]

In the composition of the memoirs Bismarck's reflections generally took precedence over his recollections. The early chapters, for example, tell us almost nothing about his home life as a child. His father and mother are introduced into the record only in connection with his assertion that he was raised without prejudice either for the Junker aristocracy (his father's heritage) or against the bourgeoisie (his mother's heritage). As a statesman, he had ever been guided by the interests of state, never by favouritism toward the aristocracy. (In the same breath he tells us that the decline of agriculture – obviously, relative to industry – presented a grave danger to the state!) The record of his university years is limited to the above reference to the *Burschenschaft*. We are told nothing of his educational experience at the universities of Göttingen and Berlin, of his carousing and duelling (25 *Mensuren* (duels) in three semesters) at the former and cramming (for the state jurisprudence exam) at the latter.[28]

We are also left with the impression that his premature departure from state service at Aachen was owed entirely to boredom and disillusionment with the service itself. There is no mention of the distractions that eased his boredom: the French coquette with whom he had a brief liaison; Laura Russell, the English noblewoman, whom he came close to marrying; Isabella Lorraine-Smith, daughter of an English clergyman, the pursuit of whom caused him to desert his post at Aachen and pile up debts that threatened bankruptcy. What we do get is a long disquisition on the evils of bureaucracy and his assurance that he had never been a believer in the unlimited authority of monarchs. Public criticism in Parliament and the press was indispensable to prevent 'women, courtiers, sycophants, and visionaries' from influencing government policy.[29]

At the outset, then, it is clear that Bismarck's memoirs are to be a purely political autobiography, in which the personal side of the author's life has no place. We are told nothing about his attachment to two married women (Marie von Thadden and Katharina Orlova), which is not strange. But neither are we told anything about his religious conversion and his marriage to Johanna von Puttkamer. The only references to Johanna, his devoted wife for nearly half a century, are peripheral. For example: he mentioned her serious illness at Reinfeld in September 1854 only because it displeased the king that he hurried off to her at a critical moment in the Crimean affair.[30]

The women who dominated his thoughts in the memoirs were not those he loved but those he hated, particularly women whom he accused of meddling in affairs of state: Queen Elisabeth, wife of King Friedrich Wilhelm IV; Queen (later Kaiserin) Augusta, wife of King (later Kaiser) Wilhelm I; and two Victorias – Queen Victoria of England and Crown Princess Victoria of Prussia-Germany, daughter of Queen Victoria and wife of Crown Prince Friedrich Wilhelm (later Kaiser Friedrich III). Of these Queen and Kaiserin Augusta predominates in the reminiscences. This feud began in March 1848 when she, as Princess of Prussia, incurred his wrath by imperiously rejecting his attempt to exploit the name of her absent husband (who had fled to England) in launching a counter-revolution. Throughout the memoirs he returns repeatedly to what he regarded as her pernicious influence, her vulnerability to French and Catholic interests, and her continuing attempts to influence her husband at critical moments: advising against Bismarck's appointment in 1862, opposing his policies during the 'conflict time' of 1862–66, denouncing his advocacy of the bombardment of Paris in late 1870, and opposing his campaign against the Catholic church during the 1870s. Other villainesses appear from time to time: the wife of the Prussian envoy, Count Usedom, Bismarck's successor as Prussian minister at Frankfurt, and the wife of the Prussian Minister of Public Worship (*Kultusminister*) Heinrich von Mühler.[31] But Bismarck was not completely negative concerning political wives. Consider, for example, his description of the spouse of the Russian diplomat Peter von Meyendorff: 'a woman of masculine shrewdness, distinguished, honourable, and amiable'.[32]

Bismarck's problem was one of misanthropy more than misogyny. Few of the colleagues he experienced over the years met with his favour. In a chapter on 'the conflict ministry' he described in unflattering terms the cabinet ministers he inherited in 1862. Most he judged to be unfit for their positions; one, an impossible windbag. Only two met with his – qualified – approval: the Minister of War, Albrecht von Roon, who eased his appointment in 1862, and the Minister of the Interior, Friedrich zu Eulenburg, whom he judged capable but indolent. But their successors hardly pleased him more. The only minister for whom he had unqualified praise was Adolf von Scholz, Finance Minister in the 1880s, distinguished chiefly by his ability to appease the Chancellor.[33] 'I have only a limited capacity to admire other people', he once confessed, 'and my eye has the shortcoming that it perceives weaknesses much better than strengths.'[34]

Bismarck's memoirs have a disjointed character that stems from the method of their composition and compilation. The log of Bucher's daily dictations shows little consistency of theme or chronology.[35] The author talked about whatever happened to come to his mind. In the flow of dictation one thought often led to another, creating digressions that taxed and sometimes defeated Bucher's editorial skills – scissors and paste were not enough. The consequence is that some important subjects are dealt with sparsely, others not at all, while minor topics took up the space. Occasionally Bucher raised questions or provided documentation that led to the closure of gaps in the narrative. And yet Bucher himself was well aware that the remaining lacunae were huge. Had he lived a little longer and been disposed to put up with the exasperations of the job, a dubious assumption, the memoirs might have been fuller.

What strikes the reader first is the uneven allocation of space for Bismarck's years in power. In the original manuscript, as edited by Bucher and published in 1932, 12 chapters (147 printed pages) were devoted to nine years (1862–71), ten chapters (124 printed pages) to 17 years (1871–88) and ten chapters (107 printed pages) to two years (1888–90). Throughout the entire period Bismarck was responsible for both the foreign and the domestic policy of Prussia and the German Reich. And yet most of the space in his memoirs is devoted to foreign affairs. International politics were the scene of Bismarck's spectacular attainments before 1871 and of his most respected achievements thereafter. For that reason this aspect of his career has been given the greatest attention by biographers and historians, as well as by himself. But historians have, of late, begun to find that it was in internal affairs that he made his most profound impact on German and European history.[36] Germany's defeats in two world wars wiped out his diplomatic achievements. Neither Prussia nor the German Reich exists today, and Germany's frontiers are greatly reduced. But his internal exploitation of his external achievements left an enduring mark on German social and political history, creating structures and attitudes that influenced German social and political culture long after he fell from power.

Where internal affairs are concerned, the lacunae are many and serious. Although an entire chapter is devoted to his attack on political Catholicism (the *Kulturkampf*), the content reads more like a commentary than a history, and the commentary is devoted to a defence of his own record. We are told that the action was defensive, necessitated by Catholic opposition to German unity and to the consolidation of the German Reich after its achievement. What seems to have disturbed him most was the conviction that the Catholic clergy were responsible for the disproportionate growth of the Polish population relative to the German-speaking population in Prussia's eastern provinces. That the 'May laws' passed during the *Kulturkampf* did not achieve their purpose of reducing the influence of Catholic ultramontanism (the doctrine advocating supreme papal authority) and the political appeal of the [Catholic] Centre Party he attributed to the clumsiness of their design. He denied all responsibility for the legislative details and put the blame on *Kultusminister* Adalbert Falk. And yet the record shows that the struggle itself was Bismarck's invention and that he was an aggressive defender of the May laws as long as he thought their purpose was achievable. Once Falk was gone, he said, he had dispensed with the objectionable features, keeping only the 'indispensable part'. The most indispensable part was in Prussian Poland, where the *Kulturkampf* continued after 1880 in a determined, self-defeating effort to Germanize the Polish population. Of this the memoirs contain not a word.[37]

One would expect at least a chapter on the anti-socialist laws instituted by Bismarck in 1878 and renewed in the 1880s. But the references to social democracy, its rise and presumed menace and his effort to destroy it are very few and always incidental to other matters. The social insurance laws of the 1880s were an essential part of the 'stick and carrot' strategy of that campaign. Bismarck's government created the first state-supported social insurance system of modern times. But this monument to social progress, the only enduring institutional consequence of his career, is not mentioned at all in the entire work. Bismarck was disappointed. He had hoped to rid Germany of the Social Democratic Party by attacking its leadership and organizational structure through the anti-socialist laws and simultaneously to win the allegiance of the working class through a state system of social insurance. But the social democratic movement survived the repression, and German workers voted socialist in increasing numbers, despite the benefits accorded them in the form of accident, old age and medical insurance.

Nor do the memoirs offer any description or commentary on the tax 'reforms' that were the principal objective of Bismarck's domestic policy after 1875. Historians have in recent years elevated the protective tariff act of 1879 to a level of importance equivalent to the founding of the German Reich in 1871; it constituted, some argue, a 'refounding of the German Reich' by cementing an alliance between the big industrial and agrarian interests that became the chief economic-social bulwark of the regime.[38] But Bismarck scarcely mentioned the tariff act in the memoirs. Nor did he devote more than a passing remark to his continuing efforts in the 1880s to provide the Reich with a base of financial support independent of the federal states and beyond parliamentary control, to provide relief for landlords by abolishing surcharges on real estate taxes, and to provide relief for the poor by removing the lowest brackets of the Prussian 'class tax'. The passing remark was a reiteration of his prejudice against direct taxes in general and his preference for indirect levies, whose regressive effect he had so often disputed.[39]

The first ten years of Bismarck's chancellorship (1866–75) were made notable by his general collaboration with liberals, particularly the National Liberal Party, in the building and consolidation of the German Reich. And yet the subject of the achievements of those years is approached in the memoirs in a most oblique way. It is discussed in a chapter entitled 'Break with the Conservatives'. In 1866 the ultra-conservatives expected Bismarck to exploit Prussia's victory over Austria internally by trouncing the liberal opposition and revoking some of the liberal features of the Prussian constitution. Instead, he appeased the Prussian opposition with an Indemnity Act and took a revolutionary course in German affairs by securing adoption of a constitution (first for northern Germany and later for the German Reich) that provided for a national legislature based on universal suffrage. Prussia's ultra-conservatives were offended by Bismarck's 'white revolution' and fearful of its ultimate consequences for Prussia's socio-political order. Among the conservatives were aristocrats whom Bismarck had known since childhood and who now regarded him as a renegade Junker and a traitor to his social caste, its interests and traditions.

But Bismarck regarded them with equal venom as disloyal to his government and to himself. By 1872 the grumbling of the conservatives had mounted to the point of open rebellion. The most ferocious attacks that Bismarck suffered in public life came not from liberals, Catholics or socialists, but from ultra-conservatives and their allies among the journalists. Bismarck counter-attacked in the press, in Parliament and in the law courts. His memoirs offered yet another opportunity to denounce his conservative opponents, who, he claimed, were impelled by jealousy (for his elevation to the title *Fürst*), personal ambition and general malevolence. Their attacks, he said, were responsible for a serious deterioration in his health during the mid-1870s.[40]

In the succeeding chapter, entitled 'Intrigues', Bismarck lashed out at other opponents of these years, particularly at those whom he believed had conspired to replace him. Highest on the list of intriguers was Count Harry von Arnim, the German ambassador to France after 1871, of whom he provided this thumb-nail sketch: 'he posed as an ambitious and unscrupulous man, played the piano fascinatingly, and in consequence of his beauty and versatility was a dangerous character for ladies to whom he paid court'. Bismarck concluded that Arnim's proclivity for quoting Machiavelli was more than a pose. The diplomat seemed to be pursuing an independent foreign policy toward France,

conspiring to bring about a Bourbon restoration, using official information to speculate on the French bourse and undermining Bismarck's
position with the Kaiser Wilhelm. In 1874 Arnim was recalled from
Paris, then jailed, tried and convicted for misappropriating official
documents. Released on bail because of ill health, he fled the country
after his first conviction and never returned. From Switzerland he
petitioned the Kaiser, pleading less for clemency than for 'protection'
against Bismarck's hatred. But he damaged his case by publishing in
the German press an anonymous pamphlet glorifying himself and
vilifying the Chancellor. Ultimately he was also convicted of treason
and *lèse-majesté*. Among the ultra-conservatives Arnim's prosecution
was regarded as persecution, a vicious attack by Bismarck upon a
personal rival and yet another betrayal of his own caste. In his memoirs
Bismarck retold this story, denied that his motive had ever been
personal and even criticized the severity of the prison sentences
imposed by the courts. But this was no help to the exiled Arnim, who
died abroad in 1881.[41]

Naturally Kaiserin Augusta was also among the 'intriguers'.
Bismarck accused her of collusion with both Arnim and the French
Ambassador, Viscount de Gontaut-Biron. Augusta had an unfortunate
liking for Catholics and Frenchmen, he said, which stemmed from her
early experience as a princess of Weimar, where both were regarded as
exotic and hence superior. (He was convinced that her reader, Auguste
Gérard, was a French spy.) In the memoirs he accused Gontaut of
conspiring at St Petersburg in 1875 with the Russian Chancellor,
Prince Alexander Gorchakov, to portray Bismarck as a warmonger in
Europe's chancelleries and newspapers.[42]

The humiliation of the 'war in sight' crisis of 1875, a rare diplomatic
defeat, still burned in Bismarck's consciousness. He portrayed
Gorchakov, the Russian statesman, as a man of insatiable vanity who
envied the position the German Chancellor, once his protégé and now
the arbiter of Europe, had gained in the public mind. Furthermore, by
posing as the protector of France from renewed German aggression in
1875, Gorchakov had sought to further the formation of a Franco-
Russian alliance, the potential combination that gave Bismarck
nightmares. According to his own account, Bismarck had complained
to Gorchakov about the latter's misrepresentation of German policy,
but the Russian Chancellor had denied it. Tsar Alexander II, to whom
Bismarck turned next, merely puffed on his pipe, laughed, and urged
him not to take Gorchakov's *vanité sénile* too seriously. But the sting of
this reverse did not diminish. In the memoirs Bismarck lamented again

that the Tsar's disapproval had not sufficed 'to rid the world of the myth of our intending to attack France in 1875'.[43] By a political miscalculation, brought on by nervous exhaustion, Bismarck had exposed himself in 1875 to a minor diplomatic coup by his Russian rival, one he could neither forget nor fully avenge.

Among other 'intriguers' Bismarck also listed the leaders of the National Liberty Party, his principal parliamentary allies after 1866. When he tried in 1877 to persuade Rudolf von Bennigsen to enter the Prussian cabinet as Minister of the Interior, he found Bennigsen's terms excessive. The deputy from Hanover insisted on bringing with him two other leading liberals, Max von Forckenbeck and Baron Franz von Stauffenberg. Bismarck wanted Bennigsen as a colleague to assure the loyalty of the national liberals in the Reichstag; Bennigsen wanted Forckenbeck and Stauffenberg as ministerial colleagues to avoid isolation in a predominantly conservative cabinet. Kaiser Wilhelm was 80 years old; the succession of Crown Prince Friedrich Wilhelm could not be far off. Perhaps the dawn of liberal power was finally on the horizon. In the memoirs Bismarck protested that he did not try to 'drive the national liberals to the wall . . . That is one of those lying inventions with which people try to injure their political opponents . . . On the contrary, that is what these gentlemen tried to do to me.' To Bismarck Bennigsen's demand was proof that his rivals in the Cabinet, Parliament and palace were conspiring for his fall. 'The negotiations between some of my colleagues, some national liberals and some influential persons at court for the division of my political legacy had reached the point of agreement, or, at any rate, were not far from it.' Their purpose, he said, was to create a cabinet *à la* Gladstone, representing liberalism and Catholicism.[44]

Bismarck believed that this plot extended through Augusta and Alexander von Schleinitz, former Foreign Minister and now House Minister to the Kaiser, 'into the very palace of the old emperor'. Its 'active ally' at court was General von Stosch, head of the imperial admiralty – with whom Bismarck waged a longer and more bitter feud than the memoirs relate. Bismarck suspected Count Botho zu Eulenburg, the new Minister of the Interior, of being the conspiracy's candidate for the position of Chancellor. Eulenburg, Bismarck admitted, was clever, distinguished, and of a nobler nature than Harry von Arnim. 'But in his case also it was my experience to find that gifted colleagues and eventual successors, whom I was anxious to train up, did not retain a permanent feeling of goodwill towards me.'[45] Instead of assisting him in governing the country, his ministerial colleagues and their subordinate officials persisted in obstructing him. 'I ultimately had the impression of being face to face with a system of gradual pressure which aimed at ousting me from the political leadership.'[46]

When he dictated these suspicions (presented as facts) for his memoirs, Bismarck thought that he had become the victim in 1890 of the kind of plotting that he described here. And yet he did not simply read later events into earlier ones. Throughout his years in power he was continually on the alert for signs that others were seeking to supplant him. He found it difficult, perhaps even impossible, to accept that opposition of whatever kind in domestic affairs could have any explanation other than bad will and personal malice. He expected foreign powers to pursue their interests in international politics, but found it difficult to accept the same from the governments of federal states, political parties, and ministers of state within Prussia-Germany. These domestic quarrels and conflicts, he maintained, tore at his nerves and debilitated his physical and mental health. Nor did he change his mind about this self-diagnosis when a new physician, Ernst Schweninger, showed him in 1883 that the actual cause of his disorder was to be found in his personal life style, essentially his eating and drinking habits.[47]

It is now apparent that Bismarck's volumes cannot qualify as a 'full-length narrative' of his life. But can they qualify as a 'manual of statecraft'? Their claim to this status, if valid, must rest on the chapters dealing with foreign affairs.

In the early chapters the most frequent subject is that of missed opportunities in foreign affairs. Looking back, he found nothing much to praise in either the foreign or the domestic policy of his predecessors since Frederick the Great. For a century Prussia's monarchs and ministers had been content to leave their country a second-rank power in Europe. Deficient in 'independence and energy', they had neglected repeated opportunities to pursue a German 'national policy'. (On the policies followed by Stein and Hardenberg in the years 1806–23 he was strangely silent.)[48] In recounting his experiences during the years 1848–50 he deplored the weakness and indecisiveness of King Friedrich Wilhelm IV in both internal and foreign affairs. The king had lost his nerve at the outset of the revolution and had delayed for months, unnecessarily so, the launching of the counter-revolution. Revolutionary disorders in France and Austria, furthermore, had offered Prussia a chance to expand in Germany that was not seized. He concluded:

The fundamental error of Prussian policy during those days was that people fancied results could be attained through publicist, parliamentary, or diplomatic hypocrisies that can only be had by war or readiness for it, by fighting or by a readiness to fight; instead, they expected to be rewarded for virtuous moderation and oratorical demonstrations of our 'German sentiment'. Later these became known as 'moral conquests'. It was the hope that others would do for us what we dared not do for ourselves.[49]

Another lost opportunity came during the Crimean War. Austria's need of Prussian and German support at that time offered Berlin a chance to renew its demand for parity with Austria in the affairs of the revived German Confederation. As Prussian envoy to the Confederation's Diet at Frankfurt, Bismarck proposed that, if Austria called upon the German Confederation to join it in support of the assault by England, France and Piedmont on Russia, Prussia should respond by concentrating its forces in Silesia, where they could cross with equal ease either the Russian or Austrian frontiers. Here was the true fulcrum of European power. With 200,000 men Berlin would command 'the entire European situation', able to dictate a peace that would win for Prussia a 'worthy position in Germany'. The king's reply was memorable: 'A man of Napoleon's sort can commit such acts of violence, but not I.'[50]

Needless to say, Bismarck had the same criticism of Prussian policy under Wilhelm I in the Italian war and its aftermath in the years 1859–62. The invasion of Lombardy by France and Piedmont created in Vienna a critical need for Prussian support. Instead of exploiting Austria's weakness at this juncture, Wilhelm and his Foreign Minister Schleinitz nearly came to its defence, which would have transformed the war from an Austro-French into a Prusso-French contest.

The situation was not regarded from the point of view of a forward Prussian policy, but rather in the light of the customary endeavours to win the applause of the German princes, the Austrian emperor, and the German press, and of the undignified striving after an ideal prize of virtue for devotion to Germany. There was no clear conception of the nature of the goal, the direction in which it was to be sought, or the means of attaining it.

In Bismarck's opinion Prussia should have mobilized and sent Austria an ultimatum: 'Either accept our conditions in the German question or expect our attack.'[51]

After the Crimean War Bismarck engaged in an epistolary debate with an old patron, Leopold von Gerlach, in which the two men

argued out their respective views on foreign policy, Gerlach primarily
from the standpoint of an ideological conservative, Bismarck primarily
from that of a political realist. Gerlach maintained that the solidarity of
Europe's conservative powers should be the first objective of Prussian
foreign policy, which dictated alliances with Russia and Austria;
Bismarck, that self-interest rather than principle was the actual basis of
all foreign policy, which meant that Prussia must be willing to co-
operate with revolutionary France as well as conservative Russia
against Austria. France was an unavoidable piece on the chessboard of
European politics. 'Not even the king has the right to subordinate the
interests of the country to his own feelings of love or hate towards
foreigners.'[52] That Bismarck chose to print these long letters to Gerlach
in his memoirs shows how important they were in his political thinking.
They were fundamental to his conception of the European political
system, a conception that he wished to imprint on the German political
consciousness. They were perhaps the most essential part of the legacy
he wanted to leave behind for the political education of his people.

The most brilliant diplomatic campaign of Bismarck's political
career, and the one of which he was most proud, was that which
eventually led to the acquisition of Schleswig-Holstein by Prussia. The
crisis that produced the conflict with Denmark in 1863–64 was not of
his making. And yet he exploited it masterfully to accomplish a
territorial acquisition for Prussia that no one originally wanted but
himself – not Austria, whom he induced to join Prussia in the assault on
Denmark, nor German public opinion, which favoured a national
crusade against Denmark to secure sovereignty over the duchies for the
Duke of Augustenburg, nor the Prussian Landtag, whose liberal
majority favoured the Duke's cause, nor King Wilhelm I of Prussia, the
ultimate beneficiary. He tricked the Austrians again and again, forcing
them into one untenable position after another, until finally the future
of the captured duchies became the issue upon which Germany fought
a civil war in 1866.[53] And yet Bismarck's account of these events is
curiously disjointed and even distorted in the memoirs. The reason for
his restraint is to be found in the Austro-German alliance of 1879.
Austria had become an ally, and in the memoirs Bismarck chose to
stress that their co-operation in the Danish affair had been an early sign
that Austria remained Prussia's and Germany's natural comrade in
European politics. Their friction over Austria's failed attempt at reform
of the German Confederation in 1863 and the war of 1866 had been but
passing interruptions in their long history of mutual support.[54]

In Bismarck's account of the wars of 1866 and 1870–71, the

dominant theme is his struggles with Wilhelm I and his generals. Some of these frictions arose from Bismarck's occasional interferences in military decisions on the deployment and disposition of troops. But the fundamental issue was one of priority: would political or military expediencies guide the course of the war? The decisive victory over the Austrian army at Königsberg in 1866 left open the road to Vienna, and the generals wanted to march. King Wilhelm, who had undertaken the war with great reluctance, now wanted to lead his victorious troops into the Austrian capital in triumph and to crush the foe by annexing Austrian territory. But Bismarck had to be concerned that Napoleon III, who had counted on an Austrian victory, might now intervene to rescue Austria. In the general euphoria he did not lose sight of his political objective: the expansion of Prussia by incorporating the small and medium-sized states that lay between the separated halves of the Prussian state and the creation of a North German Confederation under Prussian hegemony (the first step toward German unification). The war of 1870–71 produced similar disagreements. After the victory at Sedan, the internment of Napoleon and the revolution in Paris, Bismarck was eager to find as soon as possible a French government (preferably Bonapartist or republican) willing to end the war before other European powers, particularly England and Austria, could intervene to impose their interests. Having tasted victory, the generals wanted to crush all French resistance without regard for diplomatic complications that might result from the extension of the war.[55] Bismarck's pages on these issues constitute a significant chapter in the history of this age-old problem, a practical and instructive illustration of what Carl von Clausewitz meant when he coined the famous dictum that war is properly never an end in itself but a continuation of foreign policy 'by other means'.

By an incautious statement to the Prussian Landtag's budget committee in 1862, Bismarck earned for himself a place in history as 'a man of blood and iron'. But this sobriquet is undeserved. He was never an advocate of war either for its own sake or for 'preventive' purposes. The risks were too great and the results too imponderable, quite apart from humanitarian considerations, to which he was not insensitive. The wars of 1864, 1866 and 1870 were classic examples of Clausewitz's dictum. They were fought for limited objectives on isolated battlefields; they altered but did not destroy the European balance of power. Bismarck was, in fact, one of the great practitioners of balance of power diplomacy. Something can be learned from his memoirs not only about his own foreign policy but also about the character and

conduct of international politics in a European political system composed of five major powers. And yet the reader must be wary here.
Bismarck's discussion of the necessities and strategies of foreign policy
is sometimes coloured by his current distress over the Caprivi government's course in external affairs; his narration of individual events, by
the desire to cleanse the record and an occasional inclination to over-
dramatize.

Scattered throughout the memoirs are Bismarck's analyses of
Germany's geopolitical position in Europe and the policies that
position dictated. Briefly, its central location with exposed borders on
three fronts – to the east, south-east and south – compelled Germany
to align itself with at least one, preferably two, major powers. Until
1866 *rapprochement* with Russia and France was essential for the
isolation of Austria in preparation for Prussia's enlargement and for its
hegemonic control over northern Germany. Once that goal had been
attained through Austria's defeat, France was no longer a potential
ally. No regime in Paris could tolerate, without major territorial
compensation, the consolidation of a united Germany on its northern
frontier, certainly not a Napoleonic empire, committed as it was to the
revival of past military glory. And yet Berlin, having taken the first step
toward national unity, had no choice but to take the next by winning
the south. Without eventual fulfilment of German aspirations for
'little-German' unification, the gains of 1866–67 could not be
consolidated.

In the chapter on the 'North German Confederation' Bismarck
related that after 1866 he was never in doubt that France was now not
only an unavoidable but also a necessary enemy. And yet he did not
relate all of the reasons for the necessity. By 1870 it was apparent that
the south German states would not voluntarily join the north in
creating a united Germany under the north German constitution. The
only issue capable of mobilizing the German nation and completing
that union was war with France. And yet Bismarck denied in the
following chapter ('The Ems Dispatch'), as so often in the past, that he
did anything to provoke such a war. He did not, he averred, promote
the candidacy of Prince Leopold of Hohenzollern-Sigmaringen to the
Spanish throne; the prince's election was entirely a matter between the
Spanish government and the house of Hohenzollern; and the French
were completely unjustified in regarding it as a German provocation. A
king of Spain, whoever he might be, could only promote Spanish, not
German interests.

Bismarck went so far as to claim that his first thoughts about the election, aside from some pride in the growing significance of the Hohenzollern name, were not political but economic – the dynastic link would promote trade between Spain and Germany! War resulted not from the candidacy itself but from the aggressive, belligerent reaction to it by the French Cabinet, Parliament, and newspapers in early July 1870. France's impudence in this matter was intolerable to the German people and to himself. He returned to Berlin from Varzin on 12 July determined to go to war rather than accept dishonour – only to discover that the King had continued to treat with the French Ambassador, Vincent de Benedetti, at Bad Ems.[56]

On 13 July Bismarck dined with Generals Roon and Moltke, all three depressed by the news of King Wilhelm's apparent complacency in the face of French insolence and by the arrival of a telegram reporting that Prince Leopold had withdrawn his candidacy in order to avoid war with France. Bismarck decided, he declared, to resign his office rather than accept responsibility for such a humiliation. But then came the famed dispatch from Bad Ems, in which Wilhelm reported that he had rejected a French demand that he guarantee to deny consent if in the future any Hohenzollern should renew the candidacy. The last sentence of the dispatch left to Bismarck's discretion the question whether the demand and its rejection should be communicated to other governments and the press. After obtaining from Moltke an assurance that Prussia's forces were ready and that nothing was to be gained and much lost by delay, Bismarck, by his own account, sat down and edited the dispatch, deleting words and joining sentence fragments in such a way that the message, although not falsified, seemed 'more decisive'. Now it appeared that Wilhelm, presented with a presumptuous demand, had closed the door to Benedetti and all further negotiation. The two generals rejoiced, for the result was less like an invitation to parley and more like a call to arms.[57]

This account, so satisfying to German and offensive to French sensibilities, was largely Bismarck's invention. The truth is that he had been deeply involved in the 'Hohenzollern candidature' for months, and there is good reason to believe that he seized on it as a means with which to provoke either a Franco-German war or, at least, an internal crisis in France that would offer the opportunity to complete German unification without French interference. Lothar Bucher knew the truth about this sequence of events for he was one of the emissaries whom Bismarck dispatched to Spain during his long promotion of the candidature.[58] But his protests to Bismarck went unheeded. Here Bismarck preferred myth to reality. And the 'Ems dispatch'? The files of the German Foreign Office contain neither an edited copy of the original dispatch nor a revised version in Bismarck's handwriting. The version that Bismarck released to the press was evidently dictated. The dramatic dinner scene could not have taken place as he described it.[59]

In 1892 Bismarck had good reason to deny and even falsify his early involvement in the Hohenzollern candidature, but there was no apparent reason for embroidering the dinner story of 13 July 1870. In fact, the editing story left the impression, untrue but never fully quashed, that he had falsified the king's message. The probable explanation lies elsewhere. Bismarck despised verbosity, repetition and other literary infelicities. Hundreds, perhaps thousands, of documents in the archives show the long bold strokes of his pencil, where he struck out words and whole passages in the text, writing his emendations in the blank half-page margins provided by the copyist. He was known to edit and annotate articles in the daily newspapers as he read them, pencil in hand, only to discard the papers when he was done. Evidently he liked to propagate the idea, furthermore, that he had altered the course of history with a few strokes of his foot-long lead pencil, while sitting at dinner with two generals who subsequently led Germany to a glorious victory over its traditional foe. So he invented the story, told it often,[60] and stuck to it in his memoirs even after Chancellor Caprivi had reported to the Reichstag that the relevant document in the archive was a dictation, not an edited telegram. How many other events of this kind he embroidered – particularly the dramatic conflicts he had experienced with Wilhelm I, to which they were the only witnesses – we shall probably never know.

Nothing in the memoirs rivals the simplicity of Bismarck's instruction to the Russian envoy Saburov in early 1880: 'All politics reduces itself to this formula: to try to be one of three, as long as the world is governed by the unstable equilibrium of five great powers.'[61] In the memoirs he explained the dilemma in less mathematical fashion. The 'nightmare' that disturbed his sleep was a possible renewal of Kaunitz's coalition (Austria-Russia-France) that had nearly defeated Frederick the Great. Germany had fought victorious wars against two great powers. Its task was to persuade one of the defeated to renounce its ambition to unite with the other in a war of revenge. France's history and the 'Gallic character' showed that it was unsuitable, leaving Austria as the viable candidate. Britain, which had abandoned Frederick the Great, had to be discounted because its constitution did not allow lasting alliances. Austria and Russia remained as Germany's only potential allies. 'In point of material force I held a union with Russia to have the advantage.' And the Russian alliance was also safer because of Russia's monarchical institutions and traditional dynastic friendship with Germany. By contrast the Habsburg Empire appeared less stable because of public unrest among the subject nationalities, including the Hungarians, and the continuing influence of Catholic clerics, whose plans for a Catholic alliance might one day be favoured by a *rapprochement* between Rome and Paris.

That he opted, nevertheless, for alliance with Austria in 1879 was, he asserted, the result of a threatening letter sent by Tsar Alexander in that year demanding proof of Germany's support, should Russia become embroiled with Austria in Balkan affairs. Lest Germany be caught with no ally at all, he negotiated with Austria the Dual Alliance of 1879. Reassured by this compact, he had striven subsequently to restore the Russian connection by re-establishing the Three Emperors' League (Russia-Austria-Germany). This tripartite combination, he stressed, was necessary to prevent Russia from coming to terms with France. It would enable Germany to avoid a two-front war. In victory neither Russia nor Germany could gain rewards worth the cost. The logical aim of Russian foreign policy was control over the Bosphorus, 'the key to Russia's house', an objective that Germany and Austria should not obstruct. Russia in Constantinople would be less dangerous to Austria and Germany, although more so to Great Britain.[62]

Anyhow, in the future not only military equipment but also a correct political eye will be required to guide the German ship of state through the currents of coalitions to which we are exposed in consequence of our geographical position and our previous history . . . Our reputation and our security will develop all the more permanently, the more, in all conflicts which do not immediately touch us, we hold ourselves in reserve and do not show ourselves sensitive to every attempt to stir up and utilize our *vanity*.

Germany, he continued, had nothing to gain by further aggression.

On the contrary, we ought, by honourable and peaceful use of our influence, to do all we can to weaken the bad feeling which has been aroused by our growth to the position of a truly Great Power, and so convince the world that a German hegemony in Europe is more useful and less partisan and also less harmful to the freedom of others than that of France, Russia, or England.[63]

This lesson in history and geopolitics was aimed at his successors in Berlin, a lesson that – unfortunately for Germany, Europe and the world – was never learned.

Naturally the open feud between Wilhelm II, Bismarck and the Caprivi government heightened the public's suspense over the contents of his memoirs. This was particularly true of those who might be injured by the ex-Chancellor's revelations and accusations. In 1895 rumours in the press that the work was finished caused Caprivi's successor as chancellor, Prince Hohenlohe, to attempt with threats and offers (500,000 marks) to gain control of and 'correct' the work through a blind consortium. But Adolf Kröner could not be tempted or bullied into parting with the rights to a work from which the Cotta firm stood to make millions.[64] Indeed the first two volumes of *Gedanken und Erinnerungen*, when finally released at the end of November 1898, became one of the more successful ventures in the history of the German book trade. The first printing of 100,000 copies was quickly exhausted despite its high price (20 marks for the cloth, 30 marks for the leather edition), and so likewise was the second printing of 200,000 copies.[65] The translated work was quickly published in other countries. In 1905 Cotta published a 'folk edition' edited by Horst Kohl and in 1913 a 'new edition'.[66] I have not been able to ascertain how many copies of these editions were printed.

The work sold well, even though it remained for nearly 25 years a torso without a head. The third volume, which related the story of the dismissal, was expected to appear shortly after the first two. Indeed, what became the first draft, relating the events of January to March, had been composed by Herbert Bismarck in April 1890. He worked from personal notes recorded daily at the time, and the result was not intended for publication but as a memory refresher. Bismarck used it as the basis for his own narrative, correcting and amending it page by page, and recasting it into literary form. In 1898 Herbert regarded it as unready for publication, and during the following months he tinkered with the wording, introducing small changes of an inconsequential sort. By the spring of 1899 a final draft suitable for the printer had been prepared in three copies. But there was patently another reason for delay – ambivalence. Of the three 'naked kings' Bismarck had seen, the depiction of Wilhelm II was least appetizing. As monarchists neither Bismarck nor Herbert was eager to present a German emperor to the world without his clothes. Much as they wanted to punish Wilhelm II, father and son dreaded the damage it would do to the institution of monarchy itself. The voyeurs would have to wait.[67]

After considerable friction, including a renegotiation of royalties (1,000,000 marks per volume, plus 25 per cent of sales, and 50 per cent of translation fees), Herbert finally signed a new contract with Cotta in

August 1900, but only with the proviso that the volume not be published until after his own death and in no case before 1910. The final manuscript was to be delivered to Cotta in a sealed packet for publication without change within one year thereafter. One complete copy was deposited abroad for safety; other copies elsewhere in Germany. By late 1904, Herbert was in bad health and, sensing his approaching end, concluded that publication of the volume during Wilhelm's lifetime was politically inadvisable. And so he sent to Adolf Kröner a statement to that effect, which resulted after Herbert's death in a new contract (13 March 1905) between his widow (Princess Marguerite) and Cotta incorporating that stipulation.[68]

Since Wilhelm II died in 1941 (aged 82), readers would have had a long wait. But the First World War intervened and in its wake came the end of the monarchy. Within days of the armistice, the flight of Wilhelm II to Holland and the declaration of the republic, Robert Kröner, who had succeeded his deceased father as head of the Cotta Verlag, called for the fulfilment of the contract. Herbert's will was no longer binding, he declared. The public had a right to know Bismarck's final message to the German people. To reinforce his case Robert evidently leaked some passages of the text to the press, arousing renewed speculation and demands for publication. In Berlin a young lawyer named Erich Eyck (later a Bismarck biographer) called for publication of the manuscript, as did Thomas Mann. At Friedrichsruh Princess Marguerite, and her son, Prince Otto, demurred because of the ex-Kaiser. 'Never hit a man when he is down', the princess declared. But Cotta threatened to take them to court, and the Bismarck lawyer advised – perhaps unwisely – that the prospects of fending off the attack were poor. The princess yielded but made a last-minute plea that an enigmatic reference to Wilhelm II's 'strong sexual development' should be excised from the text. It was not honoured.[69]

By November 1919 the work had been set in type and the printing nearly completed when Wilhelm's Berlin lawyers succeeded in getting a court order staying publication. The manuscript contained letters by the ex-Kaiser, they charged, that could not be published without his consent. The delaying tactics of the lawyers dragged the case out until 1921, when it was decided in favour of Wilhelm II! Naturally this legal combat received wide attention in the German press. By 1921 many stories had appeared concerning the volume, including verbatim quotations. Cotta had been either unable or unwilling to keep the thousands of copies printed in 1919 under lock and key. Swedish and English editions were imminent. Furthermore, the lawsuit gave the deposed Hohenzollern and his sons a bad image in Germany, one that threatened their hope of an eventual restoration. Wilhelm appeared bent upon denying the German people access to the last words of the George Washington of German history, including secrets that reflected on his own performance as Kaiser. Hence the last Hohenzollern Kaiser, now safely ensconced in Holland, decided on generosity. He renounced his legal rights, accepting from Cotta the sum of 200,000 marks, which he consigned to charity, 50,000 marks to cover his legal costs and reimbursement of one-half of the as yet unspecified court costs.[70]

The first printing of volume three, 200,000 copies, was quickly sold. An additional 175,000 copies were printed – the number limited to this figure because no more paper could be found. Like the two previous volumes, it was immediately translated and enjoyed a wide sale in foreign countries. The Cotta papers at Marbach show correspondence with publishing houses in Sweden, France, Italy, Spain, England, America (Harper and Brothers), Holland and Rumania. Its appearance, furthermore, revived public interest in the entire work, which was republished several times in single and multiple volume editions during the next ten years. Subsequent German editions appeared in 1932, 1942, 1951, 1952, 1959 and 1982. How many copies have been printed and sold over the years can no longer be determined, but it is safe to say that the total figure is well over a million. Doubtless the Cotta Verlag kept records, but only fragments have survived.[71]

The final volume bore the dedication: 'To my sons and grandsons for the better understanding of the past and as a lesson for the future.'[72] It is difficult to see how Bismarck expected his sons and grandsons to profit from the lessons this volume has to offer. Its principal theme is that Bismarck, though old and worn out, had remained in office driven by a sense of duty and honour and convinced that he alone, because of his long years in office and the knowledge and experience he had accumulated, could prevent a young and unschooled monarch from serious mistakes. But he had fallen victim to a conspiracy by a group of jealous, power-hungry men, headed by one of his own subordinates, the treacherous Karl von Boetticher, who aspired to supplant him as Chancellor and Minister-President. Eventually they gained the favour of the Kaiser, who dismissed Bismarck and had him rudely evicted from his quarters in the chancellery at 24 hours' notice for reasons that, Bismarck wrote, were never made clear to him.

This theme had its corollary. In the volume's first chapter Bismarck provided evidence (an exchange of letters in 1886) showing that Wilhelm's father, then Crown Prince Friedrich Wilhelm, thought of his heir as unripe and inexperienced, inclined toward vanity and presumption, with an outsized estimate of his own talents: 'it is *dangerous* as yet to bring him into touch with foreign affairs'. As the memoirs progress, it becomes clear that Bismarck came to share this judgement.[73] Wilhelm took seriously the ancient claim of the Hohenzollern to rule by divine right and wished to institute a kind of 'popular absolutism' in which the Kaiser would rule directly in the style of Frederick the Great, the ancestor with whom Wilhelm identified himself. 'Frederick the Great', someone had told him, 'would never have become Great if on his accession to power he had found and retained a minister of Bismarck's importance and authority.'[74] But Wilhelm also wished to become a modern, popular ruler, capable of attracting and holding the respect of all classes. The divine-right monarchy was to be based not only on God's will but on the devotion of the masses. To defeat both liberal reformism and social democratic subversion, the schools must teach loyalty to nation and dynasty and the state must intervene in the economic process to halt capitalistic exploitation of working men, and to promote their welfare.

Bismarck's message to his heirs (and, we may presume, to the nation) seems to have been that Wilhelm II was incapable of exercising in either domestic or foreign affairs the autocratic power that he claimed for himself and that the vision that inspired him was false, even catastrophic in its probable consequences. Throughout the memoirs, and particularly in volume three, Bismarck stressed that after Frederick the Great direct rule by the monarch became impossible because of the increasing size and complexities of modern government. For that reason constitutional monarchies had been instituted, providing for cabinets of responsible ministers headed by a prime minister and subject to the corrective criticism of press and Parliament. Cabinet government served the purpose of providing trained and experienced ministers, assisted by career officials, to administer the day-to-day tasks of government but also to shield the monarchy from the consequences of failure. Unsuccessful ministers could be dismissed, to be replaced from a pool of qualified successors. But an unsuccessful monarch might have to abdicate, an act that could endanger the institution of monarchy itself.

This seems to have been the essence of what Bismarck wanted to communicate, and who can gainsay its value? But the message was diluted and distorted by the character of its presentation. Throughout the memoirs we are treated to the spectacle of a man of formidable talents, perhaps of genius, driven by a narcissistic compulsion to dominate and govern, who did little to prepare for the inevitable day when others must take the helm. The supreme irony of his career is that he rescued the monarchy from the crisis of 1862 and preserved and even enhanced the authority that in 1890 was used to unseat him. No one was more responsible than he for the fact that the system of constitutional monarchy as practised in Germany did not function according to his prescription after his fall. If the pool of qualified successors was poor in quality, he had done little to fill it. His inability to tolerate independent personalities filled the highest positions in the Prussian and imperial services with the mediocrities of which his memoirs so caustically complain. His lamentations over the failure of Parliament to perform after 1890 the role he assigned it under the constitution was in part the consequence of his own manipulations of the party structure and his attempts to suppress the spirit of opposition during more than 27 years as Prussia's and Germany's leading minister.

Certainly Bismarck could not have prevented an incompetent from inheriting the throne he had done so much to protect. Whether earlier publication of his memoirs would have stimulated public awareness of Wilhelm II's shortcomings and whether that awareness would have had any practical consequence we will never know. But what of the grandson who inherited his title, name, estate, archives and the manuscript lying in the safe at Friedrichsruh? Herbert's only son, Prince Otto von Bismarck (1897–1975), was 22 years old when his mother, Princess Marguerite, concluded the final contract with the Cotta Verlag. Doubtless he had read and studied the manuscript that his grandfather dedicated to him. Did he learn from it a 'better understanding of the past and lesson for the future'? In 1933 he was an enthusiastic supporter of Adolf Hitler.

NOTES

The author is grateful to the Princeton University Press for permission to incorporate into this essay a number of passages from Otto Pflanze, *Bismarck and the Development of Germany* (3 vols.) (Princeton, 1990): I, *The Period of Unification, 1815–1871* (second edition, 1990); II, *The Period of Consolidation, 1871–1880*; III, *The Period of Fortification, 1881–1898*.

1. G.P. Gooch, 'Political Autobiography', *Studies in Diplomacy and Statecraft* (London, 1942), pp. 261–3. Ten years later Gooch had not changed his mind. 'Is it', he asked, 'an exaggeration to describe the Iron Chancellor's political testament as the most authoritative treatise on the art of government since the "Prince" of Machiavelli?' G.P. Gooch, 'Bismarck's Legacy', *Foreign Affairs*, Vol. 30 (1952), p. 517.
2. A.J.P. Taylor, *The Struggle for Mastery in Europe, 1848–1918* (Oxford, 1954), p. 585.

3. Ludwig Bamberger, 'Bismarck Posthumus', *Die Nation*, Vol. 16 (Berlin, 1898–99), p. 145.
4. Quoted in Harry Graf Kessler, *Gesichter und Zeiten: Erinnerungen* (second edition, Berlin, 1962), p. 250.
5. Heinrich Schulthess (ed.), *Europäischer Geschichtskalender* (Nördlingen and Munich, 1890), pp. 44–5; Wilhelm Mommsen, *Bismarcks Sturz und die Parteien* (Berlin, 1924), pp. 140 ff.; Georg von Eppstein (ed.), *Fürst Bismarcks Entlassung* (Berlin, 1920), *Bismarcks Entlassung*, pp. 189–94 and 199–202.
6. Ernst Gagliardi, *Bismarcks Entlassung* (Tubingen, 1927), Vol. I, pp. 153 and 170–1.
7. Herman von Petersdorff *et al.* (eds.), *Bismarck: Die gesammelten Werke* (Berlin, 1923–33), Vol. IX, pp. 167 and 347; Vol. XIII, pp. 412, 428 and 532; Heinrich O. Meisner, *Denkwürdigkeiten des General-Feldmarschalls Alfred Grafen von Waldersee* (Stuttgart, 1923), Vol. II, pp. 202 and 224–6; Arthur von Brauer, *Im Dienste Bismarcks* (Berlin, 1936), p. 358.
8. On coming to power in 1862, he said, his task had been to strengthen the crown; now the time had come to reinforce the role of Parliament (*Die Volksvertretung*). Bismarck, *Werke*, Vol. IX, pp. 32, 118–19 and 347–8; Vol. XIII, p. 431.
9. Manfred Hank, *Kanzler ohne Amt, Fürst Bismarck nach seiner Entlassung 1890–1898* (Munich, 1977), pp. 258–69; Wolfgang Stribrny, *Bismarck und die deutsche Politik nach seiner Entlassung, 1890–1898* (Paderborn, 1977), pp. 73–100.
10. Bismarck, *Werke*, Vol. IX, pp. 118–19, 178–9 and 347; Vol. XIII, pp. 428–30; Wolfgang Windelband (ed.), *Johanna von Bismarck: Briefe an ihren Sohn Wilhelm und ihre Schwägerin Malwine von Arnim-Kröchlendorff geb. von Bismarck* (Berlin, 1924), pp. 87–8; Sidney Whitman, *Personal Reminiscences of Prince Bismarck* (New York, 1903), pp. 27–8.
11. Heinrich von Poschinger (ed.), *Fürst Bismarck. Neue Tischgespräche und Interviews* (2 vols.), (Stuttgart, 1895–99), Vol. I, pp. 272–6.
12. We have two collections of the newspaper articles Bismarck is said to have written or inspired during these years: Hermann Hofmann (ed.), *Fürst Bismarck. 1890–1898* (2 vols.), (Stuttgart, 1913); Johannes Penzler (ed.), *Fürst Bismarck nach seiner Entlassung* (7 vols.), (Leipzig, 1897–98). After a critical comparison of these works Hank concluded that Penzler's volumes are the more reliable. Hank, *Kanzler ohne Amt*, pp. 176–80.
13. Hank, *Kanzler ohne Amt*, pp. 122–47. On Harden and his relationship with Bismarck, see Harry F. Young, *Maximilian Harden. Censor Germaniae* (Hague, 1959), pp. 36 ff.
14. Walther Peter Fuchs (ed.), *Grossherzog Friedrich I. von Baden und die Reichspolitik 1871–1907* (3 vols.) (Stuttgart, 1980), Vol. III, pp. 366–8; Fritz Stern, *Gold and Iron. Bismarck, Bleichröder, and the Building of the German Empire* (New York, 1976), p. 277.
15. Hank, *Kanzler ohne Amt*, pp. 89 ff.
16. Moritz Busch, *Tagebuchblätter* (Leipzig, 1899), Vol. II, p. 487 fn., Vol. III, pp. 94, 253–67 and 314–15. When the Kaiser was expected to stop off on 29 October 1888, Busch was sent to Hamburg for the day. 'Otherwise', Bismarck explained, 'he will ask who that is and what he is doing here. I will have to tell him, which will make him curious. Then he will confiscate the whole business, and that would not suit me well at all.' Ibid., Vol. III, p. 261.
17. Busch, *Tagebuchblätter*, Vol. III, pp. 275–81; Norman Rich and M.H. Fisher (eds.), *The Holstein Papers: The Memoirs, Diaries and Correspondence of Friedrich von Holstein, 1837–1909* (4 vols.) (Cambridge, 1955–63), Vol. I, p. 149.
18. Adolf Kröner to Bismarck, 30 April 1890. Carl Duttenhofer to Max Duttenhofer, 25 May 1890. Kläre Buchmann (ed.), *Cotta Almanach; 280 Jahre Verlag* (Stuttgart, n.d.), pp. 36–40.
19. Gerhard Ritter, 'Zur Entstehungsgeschichte des Werkes', Bismarck, *Werke*, Vol. XV, pp. iv–xxviii; Hank, *Kanzler ohne Amt*, pp. 231–5.
20. Hank, *Kanzler ohne Amt*, pp. 235–7; Busch, *Tagebuchblätter*, Vol. III, pp. 303–7, 310–11, 321–4 and 330–2.
21. Ritter, 'Entstehungsgeschichte des Werkes', Bismarck, *Werke*, Vol. XV, pp. x–xi.
22. Bismarck, *Werke*, Vol. IX, p. 111; Vol. XV, pp. vii–viii; Busch, *Tagebuchblätter*, Vol. III, pp. 314–15.
23. Hank, *Kanzler ohne Amt*, pp. 231–7.
24. Bismarck, *Werke*, Vol. XV, pp. xxiii–xxiv, 449 and 455.
25. The definitive edition of all three volumes was published as the final volume of Bismarck's collected works. Gerhard Ritter and Rudolf Stadelmann (eds.), *Erinnerung und Gedanke, kritische Neuausgabe auf Grund des gesamten schriftlichen Nachlasses*, in Bismarck, *Werke*,

Vol. XV (Berlin, 1932). The editors chose what they believed to have been the original title for the work, one proposed by Bucher and approved by Bismarck, but arbitrarily changed by Kohl to *Gedanken und Erinnerungen*. *Werke*, Vol. XV, p. xxiv. Manfred Hank, however, found that Adolf Kröner used the plural form of the title in a letter to Bismarck on 28 January 1893, as though it were understood to be the definitive title. Bucher derived the title from the memoirs of a member of the British Parliament: John Nicholls, *Recollections and Reflections* (London, 1820). Hank, *Kanzler ohne Amt*, pp. 237–8. The passages quoted in this essay (some of which are amended) are from *Bismarck, The Man and the Statesman. Being the Reflections and Reminiscences of Otto Prince von Bismarck. Written and Dictated by Himself after his Retirement from Office*, translated under the supervision of A.J. Butler (2 vols.) (London, 1898), and *New Chapters of Bismarck's Autobiography*, translated by Bernard Miall (London, 1920).

26. Bismarck, *Werke*, Vol. XV, pp. 5–6.
27. See Pflanze, *Bismarck and the Development of Germany* (second edition, 1990), Vol. I, pp. 66–70, 126–30, 306–11 and 504–6; Vol. II, pp. 93–126.
28. Bismarck, *Werke*, Vol. XV, pp. 14–16.
29. Ibid., pp. 6–14.
30. Ibid., p. 104.
31. Ibid., pp. 20, 29–30, 87–91, 135–7, 162 ff., 207, 307, 315 ff., 334, 361–2 and 432–5.
32. Ibid., p. 148.
33. Ibid., pp. 204–7.
34. Bismarck to Leopold von Gerlach, 2 May 1857. Bismarck, *Werke*, Vol. XIV, p. 464.
35. Bismarck, *Werke*, Vol. XV, Anhang XI, Synoptische Tabelle 2, pp. 656–79.
36. See especially Hans-Ulrich Wehler (ed.), *Der Primat der Innenpolitik* (Berlin, 1965, third edition, 1976), translated as Eckart Kehr, *Economic Interest, Militarism, and Foreign Policy: Essays on German History* (Berkeley, 1977); and Hans-Ulrich Wehler, *Das deutsche Kaiserreich 1871–1918* (Göttingen, 1973), translated as *The German Empire, 1871–1918* (Dover, 1985).
37. Bismarck, *Werke*, Vol. XV, pp. 330–42.
38. Helmut Böhme, *Deutschlands Weg zur Grossmacht. Studien zum Verhältnis von Wirtschaft und Staat während der Reichsgründungszeit 1848–1881* (Cologne-Berlin, 1966).
39. Bismarck, *Werke*, Vol. XV, p. 385.
40. Ibid., pp. 343–55.
41. Ibid., pp. 356–60.
42. Ibid., pp. 360–2.
43. Ibid., pp. 362–6.
44. Ibid., pp. 366–73.
45. Ibid., p. 373.
46. Ibid., p. 378.
47. Ibid., pp. 378–9; Otto Pflanze, 'Toward a Psychoanalytical Interpretation of Bismarck', *American Historical Review*, Vol. 77 (1972), pp. 419–44.
48. Bismarck, *Werke*, Vol. XV, pp. 183–96.
49. Ibid., pp. 31–57.
50. Ibid., pp. 71–3.
51. Ibid., pp. 191–2.
52. Ibid., pp. 110–26.
53. See Pflanze, *Bismarck and the Development of Germany* (second edition), Vol. I, pp. 253–67; Lawrence Steefel, *The Schleswig-Holstein Question* (Cambridge, 1932).
54. Bismarck, *Werke*, Vol. XV, pp. 229 ff. and 250–68.
55. Ibid., pp. 269–81 and 312–29.
56. Ibid., pp. 282–304.
57. Ibid., pp. 305–11.
58. Josef Becker, 'Zum Problem der Bismarckschen Politik in der spanischen Thronfrage', *Historische Zeitschrift*, Vol. 212 (1971), pp. 529–607, 'Der Krieg mit Frankreich als Problem der kleindeutschen Einigungspolitik Bismarcks, 1866–1871', in Michael Stürmer (ed.), *Das Kaiserliche Deutschland, 1870–1918* (Düsseldorf, 1970), pp. 75–8 and 'Bismarck, Prim, die Sigmaringer Hohenzollern und die Spanische Thronfrage', in *Francia*, Vol. 9 (1981),

pp. 436–71; Raymond Poidevin and Jacques Bariéty, *Les rélations franco-allemandes: 1815–1975* (Paris, 1977), pp. 79–83; Lawrence Steefel, 'Bismarck and Bucher: The "Letter of Instructions" of June 1870', in A.O. Sarkissian (ed.), *Studies in Diplomatic History and Historiography in Honour of G.P. Gooch, C.H.* (London, 1961), pp. 217–24, and *Bismarck, the Hohenzollern Candidacy, and the Origins of the Franco-German War of 1870* (Cambridge, 1962), p. 85.

59. William L. Langer, 'Bismarck as a Dramatist', in Sarkissian, *Studies in Diplomatic History and Historiography*, pp. 199–216. For the original and revised texts of the dispatch see Ernst Walder, *Die Emser Depesche, Quellen zur neueren Geschichte herausgegeben vom Historischen Seminar der Universität Bern* (Bern, 1959), Vols. 27–29, pp. 62–8. Since the edited original has never been found, Josef Becker presumed that it never existed and that Caprivi was correct when in the 1890s he described the revised text to the Reichstag as being dictated. See J. Becker, 'Zum Problem', pp. 530–1.

60. Robert Pahncke, *Die Parallel-Erzählungen Bismarcks zu seinen Gedanken und Erinnerungen* (Halle, 1914), pp. 154–72.

61. J.Y. Simpson, *The Saburov Memoirs or Bismarck and Russia* (New York, 1929), p. 111.

62. Bismarck, *Werke*, Vol. XV, pp. 388 ff., 398 ff. and 417 ff.

63. Ibid., pp. 420–2.

64. Alexander von Müller (ed.), *Fürst Chlodwig zu Hohenlohe-Schillingsfürst: Denkwürdigkeiten der Reichskanzlerzeit* (Stuttgart, 1931), pp. 74, 83–5 and 113–14.

65. Under the contract of 1890, Cotta paid 200,000 marks for two volumes. Kohl received 5,000 marks, and Herbert, brother Wilhelm, and sister Marie shared the remainder equally. Hank, *Kanzler ohne Amt*, p. 243. How much Cotta made from the venture can no longer be ascertained because of the fragmentary character of its archive at Marbach. According to Horst Kohl, the American publisher (Harper) paid 200,000 marks for the right to publish the English translation. Hank, *Kanzler ohne Amt*, p. 245, fn. 4.

66. Bismarck, *Werke*, Vol. XV, p. xxvi, fn. 89.

67. Ibid., pp. v–vi.

68. Ibid., pp. xxvi–xxvii. Kröner agreed to pay 100,000 marks for volume three, and Princess Marguerite surrendered the royalty on sales and the translation fees. Hank, *Kanzler ohne Amt*, pp. 247–8 and 685.

69. Bismarck, *Werke*, Vol. XV, pp. xxvi–xxviii. From letters in the Bismarck family archive, Manfred Hank has fleshed out and corrected significantly the sparse account of these events in *G/W*. See his *Kanzler ohne Amt*, pp. 249–57.

70. Rechtsanwalt Siebert to Robert Kröner, 25 August 1921. Cotta Ms., Bismarck II, *Deutsches Literaturarchiv*, Marbach.

71. The archives of the original Cotta Verlag are available at the *Deutsches Literaturarchiv* at Marbach on the Lahn. The files relating to *Gedanken und Erinnerungen* are meagre – a few ledgers, legal briefs and correspondence concerning the judicial proceedings of 1919–21, and huge bundles of newspaper clippings. For the letters to and from the publisher we are dependent on the files of the Bismarck family archive stored in a room over the combined stable-garage of the manor house at Friedrichsruh.

72. Bismarck, *Werke*, Vol. XV, p. 451. Horst Kohl published this dedication, intended only for volume three, in his 1904 'people's edition' of volumes one and two. He was never permitted to see the manuscript of volume three but had been told of its dedication, which he appropriated without authorization for the earlier volumes as well. Subsequent multiple-volume editions copied the error.

73. Bismarck, *Werke*, Vol. XV, pp. 455–6.

74. Ibid., p. 504 fn.

3
Partial Recall:
Political Memoirs and Biography
from the Third French Republic

ROBERT YOUNG

'Neither the State, nor Justice, nor Religion, nor Education, nor any serious business could *function* if the truth were wholly visible. Judges, priests, teachers, all must be robed.'[1] So Paul Valéry counselled his readers – French readers who, according to Nathan Leites, had been primed for generations, centuries even, to understand and respect the importance of not telling everything.[2] But I propose to state my intent at the outset.

I have chosen to work essentially with *political* memoirs, those left by people who were formally engaged in French national politics. This excludes, for the most part, the memoirs of soldiers, diplomats, civil servants and media people, some of whom have left excellent – if understandably tendentious – accounts of their careers and of the events they witnessed. But I have narrowed my focus for a reason. As a putative biographer of Louis Barthou, I am interested in whatever relation there may or may not be between biography and memoir, particularly as Barthou left no such account. It is true that he might have done so, had he not died by assassination in 1934. It is also true that he might not have, for he considered most political memoirs to be 'fardés, truqués et trompeurs'.[3] In short, I am finishing a biography of a politician who held national political office for over 40 years, but who left no political memoir or private papers. I will explain later how I came to be in this apparent predicament, but for the moment will only acknowledge that, as I am clearly unlikely to argue the indispensability of memoir as a source for biographies of politicians, it seems rather more judicious for me to argue in reverse. Grudgingly, I must also acknowledge in advance that the tendentious quality attributed to non-historians may not be confined to them.

The case to be advanced for the dispensability of political memoir has three component arguments. The first, and most familiar, is focused on the limitations and imperfections of the genre which, when marshalled together, may speak to the advantages of not having such a source to impede one's interpretation and arguments. The second derives from one's particular objective as a historian, to whom, after all, the political memoir is just another source. Any source, consulted for a specific and limited purpose, may be perfectly useful and reliable – despite our sense that, overall, on issues that relate to the memorialist directly, there is too much distortion and special pleading. If, however, the memorialist himself is our primary target, then the reliability of the memoir as source is of larger concern. But so too may be the *political* character itself if, for instance, the memoir is more narrowly conceived and restricted to politics than one would prefer. Finally, the dispensability of political memoirs depends heavily on the availability of other kinds of sources, and on our abilities to exploit them.

I do not wish to dwell upon the known common faults of memoirs of almost any sort. Whether or not one is as severe as Montesquieu who summed up these self-portraits – 'c'est faire une assez sotte chose' – we might agree with his appreciation that they usually reveal 'un goût de se contempler' and a 'désir d'être absout'.[4] By the latter he meant, of course, that self-justification was usually central to the memorialist's motivation, an objective sought by either exaggerating or minimizing one's role in some particular affair. It is this reasoned, calculated element to which we all try to be alive, that element which features prominently in so many French assessments of memoir as a genre of writing. However, there is another possibility, more disturbing, and just as credible.

It may well be that the *décideurs*, those who voted in cabinet, never did know, or, better, never did fully understand, why they had done so. Having voted, on the basis of a surface understanding, between two presented alternatives, they had little or no sense of the preliminary negotiations and trade-offs. No very complete awareness of how competing departments of the bureaucracy – military, industrial or financial – had engaged in silent warfare among themselves, while business, union, consumer and religious lobbyists had worked away in the press, in the corridors of parliament, in the committee rooms, in the Prime Minister's own *cabinet*, possibly even at his own dining table. Without putting too much force on the bludgeon, one might ask those familiar with the BBC television series *Yes, Minister* whose memoirs they would find more profitable to read: those of the minister or those of his permanent under-secretary.

Further charges may be made against political memoirs. The memoir, if we accept Montesquieu's attitude toward things auto-biographical, may be a place where people who do not know the truth do their best to lie about it. To which charge may be added other blemishes. First, if strictly political, the memoir produces a slightly disembodied effect, as if parents, siblings, spouses and children, education and recreation, travel and personal health have no bearing on the career political. Second, if too narrowly political, the memorial-ist leaves uncertain how much he knows, or cares, of the world beyond the conventionally defined, domestic political élite. Accordingly, the memoir can testify to the world of party, parliament and probably the friendly press, but seldom to popular movements and culture, to international business and finance (both private and state oriented) or to international politics, whether collectively organized or other-wise. Ultimately, the memoir is often a combination, the product of a diary, edited and annotated after the fact, and a historical recollection, which is shaped more by conditioned reflexes than by reflection. Sometimes, it is difficult for the historian to distinguish one from the other, as may be seen, for example, in the bewilderment of Professor Duroselle, reviewing the diplomat Hervé Alphand's *L'étonnement d'être. Journal, 1939–1973.* If this is all diary and not recollection, Duroselle asks, how can Alphand place the wrong ambassador in Rome in August 1939 and mistake the date of France's entry into the Second World War?[5]

We historians of the Anglo-Saxon world, knowing the limitations of this kind of source, do our best to use the assets of memoirs while compensating for their liabilities by cross-checking key points against other kinds of documentation. One does precisely the same thing, of course, with French memoirs; however, in their case I have begun to wonder if there are not some rather special kinds of considerations.

Certainly there are some striking features. For instance, the pro-minent political figures of the Third Republic who have commanded at least one sound, source-referenced biography number 13: Thiers, Gambetta, Ferry, Boulanger, Waldeck-Rousseau, Combes, Briand, Caillaux, Clemenceau, Herriot, Laval, Blum and Pétain. But of these 13, only Combes, Clemenceau, Caillaux and Herriot left memoirs as such, and that of Combes was largely confined to his premiership, that of Clemenceau to the war years, while that of Caillaux skimmed over

the last 20 years of his career.[6] Of the 12 Presidents of the Republic
between MacMahon and Lebrun, only the latter left us with what
could seriously be called memoirs – and that, with limited worth
because they are not very informative. Of the 34 premiers from 1871 to
1914, only three in my estimation left substantial memoirs – Combes,
Caillaux and Freycinet.[7] And of the 20 premiers between 1914 and
1940, only seven left significant memoir testimony – Herriot, Paul-
Boncour, Flandin, Reynaud and, arguably, Clemenceau, Laval and
Blum.[8] In a society where the associations between politics, journalism
and literature have been very pronounced, that is to say where
politicians commonly engage in active writing careers, the incidence of
political memoirs seems surprisingly low.[9] I use the word 'seems'
because there is more to be said about the French *mémoire*.[10]

For one, its connotation in French is a good deal more ambiguous
than it is in English. The first definition in *The Concise Oxford
Dictionary* is a 'record of events, history written from personal knowledge or special sources of information'. That in *Dictionnaire de la
Langue Française: Petit Robert* is 'écrit destiné à exposer, à soutenir
la prétention d'un plaideur'. There are, we are told, *mémoire ampliatif*
and *mémoire en défense* – concepts and language both taken directly
from the legal world of prosecutors and defendants. There follow a
second, a third and a fourth definition before we reach *mémoire* in our
English sense, a written record of events as prepared by a direct
witness. And when we do so arrive, at the end of the etymology, we find
for the sake of illustration a line from Gide: 'Les Mémoires ne sont
jamais qu'à demi sincères.'[11]

In other words, there is something more complex here than simply
mistaking *mémoire* in the defendant's sense with *mémoire* in that of
the putative historian. Gide, I would guess, was not thinking of the
Palais de Justice, but rather of the Château de Versailles and the court
of Louis XIV, and brilliant if crabbed courtiers like Saint-Simon. His
memoirs, at least, were among the most famous in French literary
history. Though history, in our sense, they were not. Summed up, and
for all their genius, they were 'une oeuvre de passion, d'orgeuil et
de colère', written by one who made absolutely no pretence of
impartiality.[12] Neither did Chateaubriand, the most famous French
memorialist of the past two centuries. Even before writing his
Mémoires d'Outre-Tombe he had ground his axe on Bonaparte, with a
zeal that even a staunch republican like Barthou found woefully
lacking in *mesure*. Speaking of the pamphlet *De Buonaparte et des
Bourbons*, Barthou wrote: 'Son génie s'encanaillait. Il est un partisan,

qui oublie trop d'être français.'[13] The memoirs themselves were more subdued in this respect, but also explicit enough to admit that their author was constructing a monument to himself. 'Je n'entretiendrai pas la postérité du détail de mes faiblesses, je ne dirai que ce qui est convenable à ma dignité d'homme, et, j'ose le dire, à l'élévation de mon coeur.'[14] I do not know whether Valéry, a century later, necessarily had in mind Saint-Simon or Chateaubriand – names with whom the autobiographical account had become synonymous – but I do know he explained the genre with some contempt: 'quand on ne sait plus que faire pour étonner et survivre, on se prostitue, on livre ses pudeurs, on les offre aux regards.'[15]

We have then the appearance of a curious fusion of Robert's first and fifth definitions, plaintiff in the court of a magistrate, plaintiff in the court of a king, both offering testimony, both making a case, both looking, in Montesquieu's words, for absolution. Not history, as we would expect it, not 'truth' as we aspire to it, but what de Retz, another renowned memorialist, called 'faits vus à travers un tempérament'.[16] It could just be candour, it could also be cynicism, of the sort inscribed in French culture ever since we were left with the maxims of one of de Retz's contemporaries, the Duc de La Rochefoucauld. It was he, for example, who observed among the political élite of his own day: 'The proof that men know their own weak points better than is commonly supposed is that they never make a mistake when you hear them discussing their own behaviour.'[17] And in the wake of them all, de Retz, Saint-Simon, La Rochefoucauld and Chateaubriand, all shamelessly partisan, we find the assessment of an anonymous reviewer of Bertrand Barère's memoirs in 1843 : 'A man who has never looked on Niagara has but faint idea of a cataract; and he who has not read Barère's *Mémoires* may be said not to know what it is to lie.'[18]

'Honesty and Lies' is the title of one chapter in Leites' *The Rules of the Game in Paris*; and one cannot take lightly that current in the French intellectual or cultural tradition which flows on the side of the fox, on the side of the clever, the imaginative, the romancer, the liar. 'I mistrust this unruly honesty of yours', says one of Guitry's characters. Colette has one of hers rejoice in the 'relaxations . . . of lying', while Jules Renard goes so far as to talk of the 'sensual gratification of telling lies'. As for his wife, he tells her to be frank with him, knowing 'she can tell from the look in my eyes just how far she can go'. Gide took lying just as seriously, insisting that it was 'something absolutely sacred', while Montherlant diagnosed the inability to lie as a 'genuine sickness'. It was the latter who found the sort of phrase the French would call *délicieuse*, certainly for its form and apparently for its content: 'you should have kept all that to yourself so that I could go on pretending I hadn't understood.'[19]

I certainly do not pretend to know, but I wonder, if the apparently low incidence of memoirs among so many prominent politicians of the Third Republic has something to do with both the etymology and the cultural associations of the word *mémoire*. One can hardly present oneself in the most favourable light if everyone assumes one's memoir is in the finest tradition of French *mémoires*, that is to say that one will dissimulate with grace and indict with passion. And again, if Leites is to be believed, there is absolutely no point in trying to disperse so much scepticism with an opening, categorical denial. That is what Pierre Flandin tried while sitting in an Algiers prison in 1944. Prison, he wrote, made one more contemplative and reflective – which may well have been true, and impartial – which may well not. But if Leites is correct, Flandin lost credibility when he laid claim to the truth, *la vérité*, because assurances of truth were seen as preludes to lies, because propagandists in peace as well as in war had taught a recognition of what Proust called 'the inverted signs by means of which we express our feelings with their contraries'.[20]

In sum, at their very best memoirs were an art form, essays in persuasion; if not that, then nothing, at least nothing worthy. Try to tell the truth, and be disbelieved; say you are going to tell the truth, and be distrusted. It was not much of a choice, as Paul Cambon appreciated in April 1921. In a private letter he wrote:

N'attendez pas mes mémoires, vous ne les lirez jamais . . . Je trouve d'une inconvenance inqualifiable cette démangeaison d'écrire de gens qui ont été mêlés à la politique et qui font des romans avec des indiscrétions souvent imaginaires et toujours dangereuses . . . Les souvenirs politiques n'ont du reste d'intérêt que lorsqu'ils révèlent ce qu'il faut taire, autrement ce ne sont que papotages et propos mondains.[21]

These are prophetic words when one surveys some of the review literature which has greeted the *mémoires* of so many French politicians, memoirs even more than usually destined for controversy given the embarrassments of defeat, collaboration and liberation. Appraising Laval's quasi-memoirs from Fresne, Crane Brinton said, rightly enough, that they were 'no more than a collection of notes . . . scribbled for his future defense against the charge of treason'. Albert Guérard said, more roughly, that they were nothing more than an

attempt 'to save his skin'.[22] Discredited for other reasons was André Le
Trocquer, whose memoirs Henri Michel described as superficial,
incomplete and inaccurate, while two reviewers of Georges Scapini's
literary efforts summed them up as nothing more than 'un plaidoyer'.[23]
And so it continued, Guérard complaining about the imprecision of
President Lebrun's light memoir, Georges Bidault being criticized for
an artefact filled with 'abuse and egomania . . . invective and regrets'
and Georges Bonnet pilloried for his 'pretentious and windy farrago of
half-truths and evasions'.[24]

Even those upon whom fortune had smiled eventually, men like
Jean Monnet, Paul Reynaud and Charles de Gaulle, found their
records more highly regarded than their memoirs. Monnet's published
recollections were described with considerable sympathy by André
Kaspi as a 'livre de militant' and by Douglas Johnson as a 'carefully
slanted autobiography'. Reynaud, several reviewers seemed to agree,
was just trying too hard. By his telling, those around him were 'idiots,
crooks and poltroons', a contrived and exaggerated depiction which
curiously diminished his own stature. As Harvey Goldberg put it,
Reynaud managed to turn a respectable record into something that
seemed more dubious than it was, distracting readers with the 'drum-
beats of self-justification'.[25] De Gaulle's war memoirs were greeted
with a mixture of admiration for all that he had done and outraged
astonishment over all that he claimed. Arthur Funk said it was a pre-
meditated attempt 'to perpetuate the heroic myth', John Cairns that it
was inspired in tone, even style, by the *Mémoires d'Outre-Tombe*. For
what has been said of Chateaubriand's memoirs could be said with no
less truth of those left by de Gaulle. The ultimate source of power is
'the animating ego of its creator'.[26]

Apart from having demonstrated yet again what a formidably
exacting profession history is, I trust too that I have said enough to
reinforce the caution with which historians approach political memoirs.
True enough among Anglo-Saxon writers, it seems to me doubly so
when it comes to the Frenchman who sets out to write and the Frenchman who bothers to read the political *mémoire*. I am stressing the word
'political' again, because I wish to shift my emphasis momentarily to
the adjective and, accordingly, to the second argument I advanced for
the *dispensability* of political memoirs.

It is one thing to turn to Laval for some glimpse of Franco-Italian
relations in 1935, or to Flandin for his account of the Rhineland crisis
in 1936. In each case there is limited use and limited liability. But if one
were contemplating a biography of either, both use and liability would

increase. Too often, Georges Bonnet's testimony would interfere with greater accuracy – and some would say the same of Bidault. But equally restricting, it seems to me, is the kind of political memoir that is rigorously, indeed unrealistically political. Even for the political biographer, such a memoir is restricting when it does not offer glimpses of what lay behind the office, and particularly if it sacrifices introspection to the lesser task of sorting out events. But if the goal should be to place politics within the context of a life, instead of the other way round, then I think the political memoir may be even more deficient.

It would not be appropriate in this essay to say more than the briefest word about a philosophy of history. As a still putative biographer, I am interested in reconstructing the life of another, by which I mean interpreting that personality within the context of his times and in the broadest fashion possible, including politics, but not excluding what I can put together of this man's private life, his tastes in music, literature and art, his passions, his emotions and so on. To which someone may be tempted to ask: why bother with Barthou's bibliophilia when it is his politics that are more significant? To which my reply is two-fold. First, his politics remain obscure without a knowledge of his non-political life. Second, his life would be incomplete without the politics; and it is that goal – the life diversified, complex, contradictory – which interests *me*.

This may explain why I have found the inability to rely on Barthou's political memoirs quite congenial. In fact, as a reader I much prefer the set of charming letters he penned in 1932 from Switzerland and published the following year as *Promenades autour de ma vie.*[27] He says next to nothing of politics – after more than 40 years as a deputy and a senator – but recalls experiences from his youth, his first encounter with the writings of Hugo, musical highlights in the music of Beethoven, Wagner, Debussy and Fauré, moments in the presence of the actress, Mme Bartet, the poet, Coppée, the dramatist, Rostand, and the novelist, Loti. In a sense, for him these were the real rewards of politics, power used to gain access to those he considered men and women of genius, and ultimately to secure – by politics and literature – the only title he wanted engraved on his tomb at Père Lachaise: *membre de l'Académie Française.*

None the less, these memoirs could not have begun to support the weight of the 'social' biography I became convinced was possible without the availability of other sources; and these form my third and final argument for the dispensabiity of political memoirs.

Readers will be thoroughly familiar with the range of what I mean by 'other sources', not the least of which are the interpretations advanced by our scholarly predecessors. But as primary documentation important to the political biographer, I would list the private papers of the subject's political colleagues, the official records appropriate to his ministerial career, press reports, parliamentary speeches, minutes of parliamentary committees, published or unpublished collections of diplomatic documents – assuming foreign policy had some importance to his career. These would be supplemented, when possible, by oral interviews with the subject's contemporaries and, with requisite caution, by use of their published *mémoires*. The same sources would also be invoked by the biographer interested in breaking the shackles of politics, simply by keeping an eye out for non-political things of interest. Furthermore, one would add to the inventory of primary sources: legal documents pertaining to his birth, marriage and death, his ostensibly non-political speeches, his newspaper, magazine and book contributions on subjects apparently as unrelated to his own life as to current politics.

In this latter respect, Louis Barthou left the equivalent of a large, multi-volume published archive, from which can be extracted ample and diverse testimony. Some of this is evidently conscious and I should say deliberately self-revelatory. Some of it is much less so, indirect, arguably inadvertent and left to a reader's powers of inference. Unconscious though the latter may have been on his part, I, however, must return to my purpose here – which is not Barthou – and to the demands of the argument I wish to present. In the interests of the latter, I offer four brief illustrations of the uses I believe can be made of such source materials, and in ways that I think offer substantial compensation for the absence of a memoir. The first three I will direct towards the political, the fourth towards the character of my subject, although given what I have stated above about my conception of this biography, it should not come as a surprise if there is some convergence.

The first illustration is of the conscious, if somewhat subtle sort. In 1923, when he was 61 years of age, Barthou published a small volume entitled *Le Politique*.[28] It was a kind of introduction to parliamentary politics for the average reader, complete with a walking tour of the Palais Bourbon, an explanation of the committee system, the procedures by which cabinets are formed and the like. It is not a memoir in the conventional sense; and yet when one penetrates the perplexing codenames he adopted for his political contemporaries, and for himself, there are useful and entertaining glimpses of Namnetus (Briand) and Mosanus (Poincaré), and a short but revealing passage where the latter and Gallus Maximus (President Millerand) concur on the necessity of the Ruhr occupation. More personally revealing is his open recognition that Léronensius (himself) suffered from his reputation of being too clever, a reputation which he suggests was the work of those more clever still. Similarly revealing is his last chapter, 'La Retraite'. In total it comprises four lines, beginning with, 'Il n'y a pas de retraite pour le *Politique*', and ending with 'Le *Politique* espère toujours'.[29] Thin though it may be, *Le Politique* is therefore a considerable asset for anyone interested in Barthou's conception of politics.

A second illustration of the conscious observation may be drawn from his extensive career in journalism. There is, for instance, a large corpus of his writings on political issues throughout the 1880s in the form of his reports and editorials in the Pau-based paper, *L'Indépendant des Basses Pyrénéees*. Later there is his regular fortnightly column in *Journal de l'Université des Annales* for most of 1920, 1930 and 1931, as well as his more sporadic but continuing contributions to the print media throughout the entire course of his career. As a result, we know his position on reform of the divorce laws, on unions of public employees, on separation of church and state, on Boulangism, socialism, anarchism and clericalism. We know too his views on Lloyd George and Chicherin, Mussolini and Hitler, as well as on colleagues like Méline, Floquet, Ferry, Poincaré, Briand and Clemenceau. Accordingly, if we do not have memoirs as such, we certainly have *souvenirs*, fragmented, scattered, but in abundance.

My third illustration, while still addressed to politics, is of that variety which I have called unconscious – Barthou exposing himself to inference. Some might call it a type of content analysis. Whatever the nomenclature, the fact is that Barthou wrote voluminously on subjects that were ostensibly non-political, including history – from which I have chosen this my third and a fourth illustration.

Louis Barthou was a student of history as well as a politician, and probably – like most people – in that order. It is clear to me that, thanks to his father's influence, he knew the democratic Republic was good and the Church malign before he knew much about either. He knew as well that France was even greater than the Republic, knew it as an eight-year-old in 1870 when he saw his father share his tears with a Bonapartist. And he knew too, from *foyer*, temperament and school discipline that order was a virtue rivalled only by that of moderation.

When, therefore, he entered politics in 1889 he was a moderate in patriotism, republicanism and anti-clericalism. When he turned his hand to history his heroes – for he was a hero-worshipper – were already part of his intellectual *formation*. At the same time, however, these histories represent a conscious and resounding affirmation of Barthou's deepest political convictions – of the sort so deep they are often not articulated in normal parliamentary exchange or in the heat of electoral campaigns.

He had three great historical heroes, and devoted a full volume to each of them: Mirabeau, Danton and Lamartine.[30] It was no accident, I think, that what he saw as the overriding characteristic of their political lives – apart from their love of France – was precisely what he saw in his own: the moderate intent on forging unity by reconciling the exposed flanks of opposing extremisms. Mirabeau's, he wrote, was the 'politique de juste milieu', a man trying to reconcile 'l'autorité royale et la liberté nationale'. Danton, too, he described as 'obsédé par un désir de rapprochement et d'union', but it was a desire that led him, like Mirabeau, under 'le canon de tous les partis'. To Barthou, himself so pilloried by the nationalist right and the internationalist left, Lamartine was another kindred spirit. Wise men, sensible men, distrusted dogma and the inflexibility of dogmatists, and were themselves distrusted for it. Lamartine came under the suspicions of the republicans he had joined, as well as the legitimists he had left, because he was a proponent of gradual rather than wholesale reform. Clearly he struck a vibrant chord in Barthou with his remark: 'Ne vous y trompez pas, Messieurs, c'est parce que je suis progressif de cette façon, que je me crois aussi conservateur.'

More could be said on this subject of historical writing used as a mirror of contemporary politics, but to do so usefully would mean saying much more about those politics as well as about the history. However, to support what I have said about how these histories reflect Barthou's own political convictions, and at the same time to advance the argument as promised above, let me identify some of the *personal* connections which are to be found between Barthou and the three men whose effigies he had inscribed on the handle of his ceremonial sword at the Académie Française.

Eloquent speaker, erudite, a man who never submitted to the disciplined constraints of any formal political party, Louis Barthou was pleased to discover the same qualities among all three of his political heroes. Taken individually, they were equally attractive. Like Mirabeau, Barthou had an exceptional memory, loved music and detested the whispering concert-goer; and like him, too, he was to endure the accusations of being an intriguer, a womanizer and an employer of ghost-writers, as well as the grief of losing his only son. Lamartine lost a daughter, but recovered from the tragedy as best he could, an early riser and bibliophile, like his historian Barthou, and like him similarly endowed with impressive powers of recall. As for Danton, Barthou respected his sometimes brutal candour, forgave his romantic dalliances and praised a quality which he admired wherever he found it – the ability to endure unjust criticism in silence.[31] Personal qualities and attributes such as these, signalled by the praise or censure written into these works of history, provide greater substance to a biographer's understanding, a substance not always found, and certainly not always as evident, in many political memoirs. Taken together with the moderate's political creed of conciliation and adaptation, these personal qualities strike me as throwing essential light on the man behind the politician. And in this case, those qualities, like the creed, are signalled to us by a source which makes heroes of others rather than, like the memoir, of oneself.

Having stated above what I proposed to do, I have reached that point where I think I may have achieved my purpose. If the achievement seems modest, so too was the goal. Memoirs, autobiographies, recollections, whatever we call them, are tainted sources. But it takes no perspicacity to say so, because they have that in common with so many of the sources the historian must work with. What is more, we only add to the problem with our own limited powers of recall. Like the memorialist we do not remember everything, do not understand everything that happens around us and, to be candid, do not believe in the desirability of recording everything we do recall and think we do understand. The world is full of editors and readers and colleagues who consider partial recall a benefaction.

I have presented the problem of the memoir, and its attendant limitations, from the point of view of a biographer. Although there is nothing disingenuous about my critique of memoirs, or about my positive appraisal of other sources where one might find direct and indirect commentary from one's subject, I confess to wishing Monsieur Barthou had turned his hand to a memoir of the political genre. Placed within the context of all the other sources one is obliged to use, such a document might have led to more confusion and perplexity, might have demonstrated how little he understood, how limited his influence, how constrained his horizons, how inflated his ego. But those weaknesses, grand or petty, are critical to a biographer. Let not all the talk of the memoir's defects obscure the fact that this is a document which reveals character, for better or worse. If it is only data we are after, it may be disappointing, even dangerous. If it is character, people, then the very infirmities of the memoir are what make it whole.

NOTES

1. Paul Valéry, *Degas, danse, dessin* (Paris, n.d.), p. 76.
2. This essay is much indebted to Leites' engaging and provocative *The Rules of the Game in Paris* (Chicago, 1969).
3. Louis Barthou, 'Le Général Lyautey jugé par ses lettres', *Revue Hebdomadaire*, Vol. ix, No. 3 (1920), p. 268. This biography was published as *Power and Pleasure: Louis Barthou and the Third French Republic* (Montreal, 1991).
4. Jacques Rueff, *De l'Aube au Crépuscule. Autobiographie de l'Auteur* (Paris, 1977), p. 9.
5. Reviewed in *Relations Internationales*, No. 13 (1978), p. 120. For comments on the discrepancies between Poincaré's unpublished diary and his 10-volume *Au Service de la France*, see Gerd Krumeich, *Armaments and Politics in France on the Eve of the First World War* (Leamington Spa, 1984), pp. 282–4, notes 62, 95 and 113.
6. See Emile Combes, *Mon Ministère, 1902–1905* (Paris, 1956); Joseph Caillaux, *Mes Mémoires* (3 vols.) (Paris, 1942–47); Edouard Herriot, *Jadis* (2 vols.) (Paris, 1948–52); Georges Clemenceau, *Grandeurs et misères de la victoire* (Paris, 1930). Pierre Laval's *Laval Parle ... Notes et mémoires* (Paris, 1948), written on the eve of his execution, is not a contemplative memoir in any sense. In Blum's case, although we have significant memoir traces in *A l'échelle humaine* (Lausanne, 1945) and *L'histoire jugera* (Montreal, 1943) there is no coherent volume or volumes of memoirs.
7. Charles de Freycinet, *Souvenirs, 1848–1878* (2 vols.) (Paris, 1912). For the sake of these admittedly subjective estimates, I have counted each premier's name only once, despite the fact that they may have headed two or more administrations.
8. Joseph Paul-Boncour, *Entre deux guerres* (3 vols.) (Paris, 1946); Pierre Etienne Flandin, *Politique Française, 1919–1940* (Paris, 1947); Paul Reynaud, *Mémoires* (Paris, 1960–63); *Au coeur de la mêlée, 1930–1945* (Paris, 1951).
9. In his chapter on the writing careers of French cabinet ministers between 1871 and 1914, Jean Estèbe indicates that these men were much more likely to write about history, politics, literature, economics, science, technology and law – in that order – than to compile volumes of *souvenirs*. See *Les Ministres de la République, 1871–1914* (Paris, 1982), pp. 186–7.
10. The following statistics, based on my selective judgement and assembled in haste, are likely to imply a precision in which I do not believe. In fact this crude survey offers nothing more than an impression. That said, of French, Italian, German and British Prime Ministers between 1914 and 1940, this survey suggests the following incidence of memoir writing. French: 7/20 or 35 per cent (Herriot, Boncour, Flandin, Reynaud, Clemenceau, Laval and Blum); Italian: 4/8 or 50 per cent (Giolitti, Salandra, Orlando and Mussolini); German: 8/17 or 47 per cent (Bethmann-Hollweg, Michaelis, Ebert, Scheidemann, Marx, Luther, Brüning and Papen); Britain: 3/7 or 43 per cent (Asquith, Lloyd George and Churchill).
11. *Dictionnaire de la Langue Française: Petit Robert* (Paris, 1982), p. 1179.
12. Ch. des Granges and J. Boudot, *Histoire de la Littérature Française des Origines à nos Jours* (Paris, 1962), p. 477.
13. Barthou, 'Ce que Napoléon aurait fait sur la Marne', *Conférencia* (5 September 1931), p. 261.
14. Pierre-Georges Castex and Paul Surer, *Manuel des Etudes Littéraires Françaises* (Paris, 1954), Vol. II, p. 638. See also Jonathan Keates, 'Chateaubriand', in Justine Wintle (ed.), *Makers of Nineteenth Century Culture, 1800–1914* (London, 1982), pp. 112–13.
15. Rueff, *De l'Aube*, p. 9.
16. Granges and Boudot, *Histoire*, p. 475.
17. La Rochefoucauld, *Maxims*, Leonard Tancock (trans.) (Harmondsworth, 1981), No. 494, p. 99.

18. John Bartlett, *Bartlett's Familiar Quotations* (Toronto, 1968), p. 596b.

19. See Leites, *Rules of the Game*, pp. 301–11.

20. Flandin, *Politique Française*, p. 8. Then see Leites' discussion of the language of opposites in his chapter 'Stark Language and Veiled Meaning', in which the Proust quotation is found on p. 324.

21. Paul Cambon to Mlle Baudot, 13 April 1921, in Paul Cambon, *Correspondance* (Paris, 1946), Vol. III, p. 393. My thanks to Dr Michael J. Carley for bringing this letter to my attention.

22. Crane Brinton, *Saturday Review of Literature* (2 October 1948), p. 10; Albert Guérard, *The Nation* (16 October 1948), p. 442.

23. *La parole est à André Le Trocquer* (Paris, 1962); and Georges Scapini, *Mission sans gloire* (Paris, 1960). The former was reviewed by Henri Michel, *Revue d'Histoire de la Deuxième Guerre Mondiale* (April 1964), pp. 108–9; the latter by François Boudot and Jean-Marie d'Hoop, in ibid. (October 1962), pp. 81–5.

24. Lebrun's *Témoignage* (Paris, 1945) was reviewed by Guérard in *Books Abroad* (Summer 1966), p. 291. *Resistance: The Political Autobiography of Georges Bidault*, Marianne Sinclair (trans.) (New York, 1967) was reviewed by Michael R. Gordon, *American Political Science Review* (September 1968), pp. 1003–4. Bonnet's *Défense de la paix* (2 vols.) (Geneva, 1946–48) was so described in A.P. Adamthwaite's doctoral dissertation on Bonnet's foreign policy (Leeds, 1966), p. 10.

25. Harvey Goldberg on Reynaud's *Au coeur de la mêlée* (translated as *In the Thick of the Fight*), in *Nation* (31 March 1956), pp. 261–2; also Paul Johnson on the same book in *New Statesman and Nation* (24 September 1955), p. 368; and finally a review in *Time* (23 January 1956), p. 96. Jean Monnet's *Mémoires* (Paris, 1976) were reviewed by Kaspi in *Relations Internationales*, No. 8 (1976), pp. 389–97, and Douglas Johnson, in *Times Literary Supplement* (10 December 1976), pp. 1530–1.

26. See Funk on de Gaulle's *The Call to Honour* (New York, 1955), in *Journal of Modern History* (March 1956), pp. 299–303; John C. Cairns, 'Charles de Gaulle', in Peter Dennis and Adrian Preston (eds.), *Soldiers as Statesmen* (London, 1976), pp. 135 and 148; and Jonathan Keates' piece on Chateaubriand in *Makers of Nineteenth Century Culture*, p. 112.

27. *Promenades autour de ma vie* (Paris, 1933).

28. *Le Politique* (Paris, 1923).

29. Ibid., p. 125.

30. *Mirabeau* (Paris, 1913); *Lamartine. Orateur* (Paris, 1916); *Danton* (Paris, 1932).

31. Despite this host of shared personal qualities, despite too his predilection for making personal comments in the course of his text, on no occasion in these three volumes did Barthou ever make an association between his heroes and himself. Though their virtues were his, one would have to read elsewhere to discover that fact.

4
Indian Nationalist Voices: Autobiography and the Process of Return

MILTON ISRAEL

I consider autobiography very unreliable as a source of objective truth. It is practically certain that nobody can ever write the truth and nothing but the truth about his or her intimate experience. I really don't understand why intelligent people risk to compose autobiographies. That itself is a matter of psychoanalytical study.

M.N. Roy

The diary and memoir tradition was particularly strong among Indian rulers and their court writers who recorded daily events and the affairs of family and state, often including reflective passages on their significance. While the style and context of these chronicles (*Tawarikh*) are essentially Muslim in origin, it is important to emphasize the over-lapping mix of indigenous Hindu, Muslim and eventually European traditions of historical record keeping and recovery. The desire to document accurately particular events, land boundaries and donations to temples, with specific reference to dates and times, is reflected in inscriptions dating back to the sixth century. Similarly, a seventeenth-century biographical sketch of an extraordinary young monarch, Harsha Vardhana, written by Bana, one of his courtiers, is a major source for our understanding of his 41-year reign.[1]

Our knowledge of the Mughal imperial courts and of the lives of the emperors in the sixteenth, seventeenth and eighteenth centuries is largely dependent on the contemporary *Tawarikh*, memoirs, auto-biographical and biographical writing. Babur, Humayun and Akbar[2] either dictated their daily record and retrospective memoir or allocated the responsibility to some court official. Jehangir[3] wrote much of his own memoirs, the *Tuzuk-i-Jahangiri*. The material concerning the first 12 years of his reign was made into a volume by the Emperor and a number of copies were distributed in his court.[4] Like memoirists of other times and other cultures, the Mughal princes could be selective about what events were to be included in their record and how their roles were to be described. Babur suppressed the narrative of a military defeat, and Jehangir tended to gloss over details concerning his rebellion against his father.[5] But there was also Jehangir's finely crafted portrait of Akbar and his extraordinary frankness about acts and decisions others might have excluded. When he determined that his father's senior minister and adviser, Abu-l-fazl would be likely to enhance the differences between the Emperor and his heir, Jehangir moved quickly and provided posterity with a detailed description of his actions.

It became necessary to prevent him from coming to Court. As Bir Singh Deo's country was exactly on his route and he was then a rebel, I sent him a message that if he would stop that sedition-monger and kill him he would receive every kindness from me. By God's grace, when Shaikh Abu-l-fazl was passing through Bir Singh Deo's country, the Raja blocked his road, and after a little contest scattered his men and killed him. He sent his head to me in Allahabad.[6]

Bimsen Saksena's memoir, *Tarik-i-Dilkasha* (Pleasant Story), is the most valuable contemporary account of Aurangzeb's reign (1658–1707). He held high office in the Mughal government and had the opportunity to see both the Mughal Emperor and the great Maratha leader, Shivaji. His book provides critical personal assessments:

I have found the men of the world very greedy, so much so that an Emperor like Alamgir who is not in want of anything, has been seized with such a longing and passion for taking forts that he personally runs about panting for some heaps of stone [i.e. hill forts]. What shall I say about the men of weak intellect, who are the majority of the people? I have never found any man free from greed and desire by looking at whom one may gain composure of mind.[7]

It includes, as well, sensitive and informative descriptive passages:

How can I give the description of the palace of this ruler? It is a huge wooden building and is so big and massive that if a man starts seeing it in the morning he will not be able to go through it till evening. It is no wonder that if a man goes alone there he gets lost. But the palaces of the old owners, which are known as *Dad Mahal* are not so attractive. But the building whose foundation was laid down by Qutb Mulk Abul Hasan on the bank of the river, is quite attractive. There are four palaces, facing each other, and in the centre is erected a big tank. This tank is so big that boating is done in it for the sake of pleasure and that he used to enjoy boating in the water of that tank from evening till midnight. He used to get the entire area properly illuminated and having all the provisions at hand, he used to gain full pleasure from those luxuries.[8]

Among non-princely memoirists, Ananda Pillai, an eighteenth-century Hindu merchant, left a detailed diary of 25 years of business transactions, political intrigue and personal reflections. He served as chief agent for the French colony, Pondicherry, acting as an intermediary between French traders and people in the countryside. His lack of nationalist identity in relations with the French is reflected in a description of Dupleix, the colony's governor.

Owing to these qualities, he has acquired such a reputation as to make all people say that he is the master, and that others are useless individuals. Because God has favoured him with unswerving resolution, and because he is governing Pondicherry on an occasion when she is threatened with danger, her inhabitants are confident and fearless, and are even able to defy the people of towns opposed to them... This is due solely to the skill and administrative ability of the governor. If he did not occupy this position, and if the danger had occurred in the times of his predecessors, the inhabitants of this city would be a hundred times more disturbed and terrified than the followers of the invader: such is the general opinion regarding M. Dupleix. Besides this, if his courage, character, bearing, greatness of mind, and skill in the battlefield, were put to the test, he could be compared only with the Emperor Aurangzib, and Louis XIV; and not with any other monarch. But how am I to paint all his high and praiseworthy characteristics? I have described him only so far as my simple mind allows me. People of better capacity could do this more completely than I.[9]

Despite an easy acceptance of French rule, there was no diminution of his commitment to his fatalistic Hindu traditions.

This great man has been arrested and put with his property on board ship. Such is the fate of the man who seeks his own will without the fear of God; but he who acts with circumspection, and refrains from molesting the upright, escapes falling into sin. But a man's thoughts depend upon the times and seasons. Who then can be blamed? Such is the world. He who is destined to happiness will be wise; and he who is destined to misery will be foolish. Do not the Vedas say so? What was to be has come to pass.[10]

Another eighteenth-century memoirist, Abu Taleb, travelled to Europe, returning after three years with a critical assessment of English society.

The first and greatest defect I observed in the English is their want of faith in religion, and their great inclination to philosophy [atheism]: The effects of these principles, or rather want of principle, is very conspicuous in the lower orders of people, who are totally devoid of honesty. They are, indeed, cautious how they transgress against the laws, from fear of punishment; but whenever an opportunity offers of purloining anything without the risk of detection, they never pass it by . . .
　　The second defect most conspicuous in the English character is pride, or insolence. Puffed up with their power and good fortune for the last fifty years, they are not apprehensive of adversity, and take no pains to avert it.
　　Their third defect is a passion for acquiring money and their attachment to worldly affairs.[11]

There has, in fact, existed in India from the classical period a whole genre of biographical writing, *Charitra* or *vamshavali* (genealogical details), written in Sanskrit or local languages. These were generally stories of the lives of heroic leaders and the battles they fought. The Sikh aspect of this tradition concerned the lives of the Gurus produced in *gurumukhi* script. In the medieval period they were increasingly influenced by the political chronicles of the Mughal courts, but they were clearly meant to be available to a broader audience. *Powada* (Marathi) or *Kummi* (Tamil) are historical ballads, often biographical in nature, describing events with specific dates and the actions of leading protagonists. Throughout Maharashtra and Rajputana these songs were particularly associated with warrior classes and sung not only during the life of the particular hero but long after his death.[12]
　　The British encouraged the translation and search for these records and, with the spread of printing and publishing during their time in power, facilitated access. Their influence was particularly pervasive in two other areas. They produced a substantial Anglo-Indian auto-biographical literature which made an impact on style and focus. In addition to the new set of imperial princes – viceroys, governors, commissioners and district officers, who perceived their roles to be significant, were recognized as powerful and often left an auto-biographical record – they brought over to India a substantial number of their countrymen and women in a range of ordinary occupations, who thought their experiences were worth documenting as well. The result was a continuing flow of diaries, travelogues, memoirs, collections

of letters and personal accounts which have enlivened our knowledge of Anglo-Indian colonial society and perspective. Merely being in India for an extended period seemed to suggest that one's experiences were sufficiently unusual to record and share with others. The possession of power which appeared to come automatically with membership of the imperial race suggested as well that what they did was important and writing it up was an obligation.[13]

In the context of the developing nationalist struggle against their rule in the nineteenth century, the British also stimulated these nation builders to search out their own heroes, especially those whose achievements and life stories would be useful to the cause. An example of this phenomenon is the seventeenth-century Maratha king, Shivaji,[14] whose historical reputation within Maharashtra had been assured in numerous eighteenth-century biographies in Marathi; but who re-emerged in 1895 as an Indian national hero under the patronage of B.G. Tilak, a major nationalist leader. Similarly, Raja Ram Mohan Roy, an early nineteenth-century social and religious reformer in Bengal, became, over time, the 'father of modern India'.[15] Most significantly, in the context of their overarching educational policy, the British made an extraordinary impact on the perspective of modern Indian political memoirists, many of whom came to view India's past and its recovery through alien eyes.

The image of India in the West has always been informed by an element of wonder. India was 'fabulous' and 'opulent'. It was also 'curious', 'frightening', even 'repulsive' in the range of stereotypes conjured up over time by travellers, scholars and administrators – both on the spot and in their armchairs. Whatever else India might be, it was clearly presumed to be different from the West, and Indians, a different kind of people. India became, in fact, the premier example of 'the other' culture – exotic where it held to its own traditions and merely hybrid where it adapted to modern influences from the outside. This presumption of fundamental difference was further entrenched during the period of British imperial rule as the contrast between western power and Indian weakness was generalized to include all aspects of culture and civilization. In his 1835 'Minute on Education', T.B. Macaulay left no doubt about the need for reform and the critical role to be played by the English language in the massive cultural transfer that was intended.

The question now before us is simply whether, when it is in our power to teach this language, we shall teach languages in which by universal confession there are no books on any subject which deserve to be compared to our own; whether, when we can teach European science, we shall teach systems which by universal confession whenever they differ from those of Europe differ for the worse; and whether, when we can patronise sound philosophy and true history, we shall countenance at the public expense medical doctrines which would disgrace an English farrier, astronomy which would move laughter in girls at an English boarding-school, history abounding with kings thirty feet high and reigns 30,000 years long, and geography made up of seas of treacle and seas of butter . . .[16]

It is this presumed element of irrationality and other-worldliness in the Indian perception of time past that is pertinent to the central theme of this essay. Among the array of attributes and flaws subsumed in the western image of India was the problem of a society without a useful past because no effort had ever been made to describe it accurately. Indians were, apparently, a people without history. The Hindu perceived time in cycles of experience and cycles of lives – each circuit obliterating a portion of the one that came before and, therefore, eliminating the possibility and idea of historical context playing a role in contemporary society. Similarly, the need or desire to leave an accurate record as a legacy to future generations appeared to be foreign to the traditions of the subcontinent.

If Indian history were to be recovered and made available to its people, it was assumed by many of those who perceived the loss as a significant problem that British scholars would have to do it. Those who accepted the challenge rarely underestimated the significance of their work. While working on his *History of Orissa*, Sir William Hunter noted a singular achievement in the entry in his diary for 17 December 1870: 'Today I pieced together my evidence about the Yavans, and reconstituted that lost race of warriors and kings – resuscitated in fact, a buried dynasty.'[17]

While the introduction of the canon of the professional historian was an important aspect of the general cultural impact of Britain in India, it is clear that some of the pieces of the historical puzzles being unravelled in the nineteenth century had been deliberately left behind. Remembering the past, being concerned about one's place in it and leaving a record was not alien to Indian tradition. In the preface to his translation of the Mughal Emperor Humayun's memoirs,[18] Major Charles Stewart considered it necessary to emphasize the similarities rather than the differences between eastern and western historical writing and perspective: 'I take this opportunity of declaring that I have scarcely ever met with an idea in any European poet, or a passage in any historian, that I have not found a parallel to it in Oriental writers.'[19] Western perspective played a far more complex role, however, in the political environment of late-nineteenth-century Indian nationalism.

'To support the official world and its garrison', Meredith Townsend has noted, there was 'except Indian opinion, absolutely nothing'.[20] The founders of the Indian National Congress and a generation of its leaders seemed to recognize no necessity to eliminate that regime in order to achieve their immediate goals. In fact they appeared to complement each other. In his 1897 Presidential address to the Congress, C. Sankaran Nair described the relationship.

Just look for a moment at the training we are receiving. From our earliest school-days the great English writers have been our classics, Englishmen have been our professors in Colleges. English history is taught us in our schools. The books we read are English books, which describe in detail all forms of English life, give us all the English types of character. Week after week, English newspapers, journals and magazines pour into India for Indian readers. We, in fact, now live the life of the English. Even the English we write shows not only their turns of thought but also their forms of feeling and thinking. It is impossible under this training not to be penetrated with English ideas, not to acquire English conceptions of duty, of rights, of brotherhood. The study and practice of the law now pursued with such avidity by our people, by familiarizing them with reverence for authority and with sentiments of resistance to what is not sanctioned by law, have also materially contributed to the growth of mental independence.[21]

In subsequent years there was continuing debate about the nature and degree of 'mental independence' that had in fact resulted from this massive anglicizing experience and whether it would be possible to build the Indian nation on the basis of Indian terms. More significantly, there appeared to be no confidence that 'Indian terms', as opposed to 'British terms', of reference could be or should be isolated and utilized as the sole basis for defining independence goals. In an exchange of letters with Jawaharlal Nehru in 1936, J.S. Barnes, a retiring Reuters official, lamented the dominance of British perspective in India: 'Why can't Indians be Indians, learn things independently of England and judge things for themselves? Until they can do that, I see little hope of their doing anything worth doing in the way of constructive work. It is an absolute tragedy.'[22]

In response to Barnes' suggestion that 300 young Indians ought to be sent to France, Italy and Austria – 'universal centres of European culture' – Nehru agreed that 'we had got too much into the habit of looking at the world through British spectacles'. He regretted that it was not possible to implement such a plan but noted that it might not produce the desired results. The contemporary world seemed to be 'in a curious way', and Nehru was not certain 'how long European culture itself will last'. It was clear to Nehru that his outlook was 'largely coloured' by the British background of education. 'I suppose I cannot help it', he noted, 'although I try to see things straight. When the world itself is so crooked it is not easy to have a straight view of anything.'[23]

Many of the participants in the Indian nationalist movement – both those in major leadership roles and those whose contributions were less notable – shared with British memoirists the conviction that they were involved in extraordinary events that needed to be recorded. Although only a small representative group will be considered in this essay, their autobiographical writings, in a range of languages and substantial in scale, provide an intimate human perspective often lost in the generalizations which tend to dominate a vast canvas. Placed in the context of a substantial analytical literature concerning these events, these memoirs provide a major source for the history of the period. Politicians, businessmen, newspapermen, communal leaders and princes have contributed to the memoir and autobiographical literature of the nationalist period and virtually all of this material can be described as political. These writers have used their pens to enhance their own roles and attack their enemies. Some have sought to provide an accurate record. Others were committed to proselytizing on behalf of their own ethnocentric goals among a particular community. Much of the memoir literature produced during the struggle was deliberately propagandist in content and was sometimes suppressed by British authorities.

Throughout the period of nationalist struggle, there was a range of lesser confrontations among indigenous groups and individuals which informed and constrained the larger battle with the British Raj. The hegemonic nature of British authority in India allowed for dominance without absolute control. To maintain their administration and give effect to their policies, they were required to depend on the collaboration of traditional feudal élites as well as the westernized educated classes who recognized some degree of common purpose. Similarly, those who rose to the leadership of the Indian National Congress could not assume that the shared goal of ending British control would allow them a free hand in conducting the campaign. The potential for division and violence had resulted in a commitment to accommodation and a rejection by most mainstream leaders of any form of revolution. It also placed a heavy burden of responsibility on the pen as principal weapon.

The design of the nation-building goals and the means to achieve them required an extraordinary preparation by those who sought a leadership role. It was necessary to find some order in their world, to achieve a comfortable understanding of their own developing identities and then to share their conclusions and attract a following. A description of that period of change and adjustment is a common prologue shared by many of these nationalist memoirs. For some, however, the issue is not resolved, the centre is not found;[24] and the control of the terms of reference for a freedom struggle that is both national and personal remains unresolved.

Partha Chatterjee has described the 'universal framework of thought' which evolved in the post-enlightenment period of European intellectual history and presumed to define the tenets of modernity for everyone. Its self-proclaimed universality explicitly denied its cultural source and was, therefore, another form of perpetuating colonial domination.[25] Here is the ultimate impact of the British imperial experience on the political memoir literature of Indian nationalism. The nature of the relationship between national culture and so-called universal modernity, both before and after independence, is a major theme which Indian political memoirists seem compelled to address. The resolution of any fundamental conflict appears to be essential in the complex process of returning home.

The western-educated leaders of the Indian nationalist movement describe their contact with European culture in the context of rejection, embrace or a range of intermediary adaptive devices. But there is always involvement and a sense of the impact the contact has made on their development and role as nationalist leaders. Surendranath Banerjea, a founder of the Indian National Congress and a dominant moderate leader in the late nineteenth century and early twentieth century, speaks for those who welcomed these new ideas and integrated them into their Indian lives. He charged a group of Calcutta students with a daunting task: 'You must live in a high and holy atmosphere fragrant with the breath of the gods. Burke, Mazzini, Jesus Christ, Buddha, Mohammed, Chaitanya, Ram Mohun Roy, Keshub Chunder Sen must be your constant companions.'[26]

Mazzini had made a particularly profound impression on his mind, although Banerjea notes in his memoirs that it was necessary to adapt his revolutionary views to the Indian situation.

The purity of his patriotism, the loftiness of his ideals, and his all-embracing love for humanity, expressed with the true eloquence of the heart, moved me as I had never before been moved. I discarded his revolutionary teachings as unsuited to the circumstances of India and as fatal to its normal development, along the lines of peaceful and orderly progress; but I inculcated, with all the emphasis that I could command, the enduring lessons of his noble life, lived for the sake of others, his lofty patriotism, his self-abnegation, and his heroic devotion to the interests of humanity. It was Mazzini, the incarnation of the highest moral forces in the political arena – Mazzini, the apostle of Italian unity, the friend of the human race, that I presented to the youth of Bengal. Mazzini had taught Italian unity. We wanted Indian unity.[27]

Lala Lajpat Rai, an early-twentieth-century nationalist leader from the Punjab, and no friend of Banerjea's moderate views, noted in his autobiography the extraordinary impact that a Banerjea speech on Mazzini had made on him. Rai published a life of Mazzini in Urdu in 1896, and also translated into Urdu Mazzini's *Duties of Man*. 'I made Mazzini my Guru, including the revolutionary message,' he declared, 'and so he continues to be to this day.'[28]

These memoirists describe, as well, a range of negative responses to the western message. Some, like Abu Taleb, emphasize the superiority of Indian spirituality in contrast to western materialism. Banerjea, while accepting the western message, insisted it was not entirely original. In an Oxford University speech reproduced in his memoirs, he makes the case for an easy and natural relationship between Indian and British political culture:

You have only to walk across the way, and place yourselves in the Bodleian Library, to witness the ancient records of Indian industry, Indian culture, and Indian ethics . . . self-governing institutions formed an essential feature of the civilization of the Aryan race, and we come from the Aryan stock.[29]

Paradoxically both the embracers and the opposers tended to envision their own stereotypical India – purely spiritual or fundamentally democratic.

These political memoirs often describe the process of changing viewpoint in the context of explicit self-analysis. Both M.K. Gandhi's *My Experiments with Truth* and Jawaharlal Nehru's *Toward Freedom* deal with the rejection and embrace of western culture as a prelude to a process of return to a personally satisfying relationship with the traditions of their homeland. In the years after the First World War, the need and desire to mobilize a mass following required the development of a new kind of relationship. Nehru notes that he and his class took the peasant for granted. After venturing into village-level political work in the early 1920s, he could still only envision a vague impression. 'My mental picture of India contains this naked, hungry mass.'[30] But he recognized the need to make contact; for him this symbolized contact with India. The British had not created that chasm between the classes, but they had clearly enhanced it. Among the multitude of paradoxes tossed up by the colonial experience, the western education which had informed the viewpoint of these new leaders with progressive social and political ideas concerning this vast underclass further alienated many of them from a traditional culture not easily shoved aside.

In the early years of the Second World War, C. Rajagopalachari reflected on India's place in the struggle and the likely impact of a British victory or defeat. 'It is not a question of Great Britain failing or Germany failing,' he insisted. 'I do not expect a millennium for India upon Great Britain's success. It is a case of this rotten civilization proving itself a failure. We who got mixed up in it must suffer either way.'[31] While there was a range of views among India's nationalist leaders about the degree of benefit or suffering which had resulted from Britain's imperial control, there was no question about their having become 'mixed up' in a situation beyond their control, which demanded a personal response that absorbed much of their lives and was the central theme in their memories of the past. Each story is different, however, reflecting an individual encounter with British power and western culture. For some, their parents were already 'at home'[32] in Anglo-India and this early rapport tended to inform their views and define their identities throughout their lives. Surendranath Banerjea noted in his memoirs that his grandfather was 'a Brahmin of the old school, rigid in his orthodoxy'. But he had given Banerjea's father 'the best kind of English education available at the time'.[33] As a result, the conflicting focus of eastern orthodoxy and western culture met in his home as 'in every educated home in Bengal'. But, Banerjea insists, the 'atmosphere of controversy' was not burdensome and there was no debate regarding the English education he would receive and his Anglo-Indian career goals.[34] In retrospect, near the end of a life devoted to the continuing nationalist struggle, he reiterated an undiminished commitment to this British legacy: 'An Englishman once publicly declared that I was more English than most Englishmen. I freely confess that I have a genuine admiration for those great institutions which have helped to build up English life and the fabric of British constitutional freedom.'[35]

Jawaharlal Nehru received a similar inheritance from his father. He describes the increasingly westernized lifestyle of his childhood, and his father in those days as 'a nationalist in a vague sense of the word', but one who 'admired Englishmen and their ways'.[36] His subsequent education at Harrow and Trinity College, Cambridge, was meant to prepare him as well for success in British India. Although his eventual commitment to full-time politics and opposition to the British Raj carried him far beyond Banerjea's moderate appeals for change, he had no desire to eliminate the impact of his initial and positive encounter with Britain. But the task of working out an acceptable accommodation of the mix of influences in his life, with his nation-building mission, remained a lifetime's burden.

Others were required to begin their rebel careers within their families. Abdul Kalam Azad[37] described his father as 'a man who believed in the old ways of life' and had 'no faith in western education'. He shared with most Indian Muslims of his time a conviction that modern education would 'destroy religious faith', and Azad received his early education 'in the old traditional manner'.[38] But his exposure to the writings of reformers, especially those of Sir Syed Ahmad Khan,[39] began the process of change and rejection.

This was a period of great mental crisis for me. I was born into a family which was deeply imbued with religious traditions. All the conventions of traditional life were accepted without question and the family did not like the least deviation from orthodox ways. I could not reconcile myself with the prevailing customs and beliefs and my heart was full of a new sense of revolt. The ideas I had acquired from my family and early training could no longer satisfy me. I felt that I must find the truth for myself. Almost instinctively I began to move out of my family orbit and seek my own path.[40]

He adopted the name 'Azad' meaning 'free' as a reflection of his new independence from inherited beliefs, and committed himself to revolutionary politics. His political career would remain, however, a Muslim one, dominated by a personal search for an accommodation between Muslims and Hindus in a national context primarily informed by British political norms, values and institutions.

In their autobiographical writing, these nation builders describe their efforts to gain control of the terms of reference for a freedom struggle that is both national and personal. While the British presence provides the major stimulus for adaptation and change, the range of possible responses was not limited to some form of acceptance or rejection of an anglicized identity. Lajpat Rai learned during his college years 'to respect the ancient Aryan culture which became my guiding star for good'.[41] The politicized environment into which he graduated required choices to be made. Rai joined the revivalist *Arya Samaj* and committed himself to the development of the 'idea of Hindu nationality'.[42]

Reflecting the range of possible influences rising from this great cultural and political encounter, M.R. Jayakar[43] refused to make choices.

In Jayakar the counter thrusts of nationalism and provincialism, secularism and communalism, socialism and capitalism, Hindu Raj and British Raj are allowed to do battle but are never rationalized to the extent that would allow accommodation with those who controlled the movement at the centre and constantly made the trades that were essential to remain in power. He refused to be absorbed into an easy liberalism which in his view endangered his orthodox Hindu traditions, denied the importance of his Maratha heritage, pandered irresponsibility to the ill-prepared masses and impugned the significance of British institutions and political ideas which he considered India's only great benefit from the period of British control.[44]

As a result he remained on the margin of everyone else's orthodoxy – both new and old, continually denied the recognition and central leadership role which he coveted. In the preface to the first volume of his memoirs he sets the tone by quoting the poet Bhavabhuti's response to the critical rejection of one of his plays: 'There may be living somewhere at present, or may be born in future years someone, whose sentiments are in accord with mine – for time is boundless and the earth spacious enough.'[45]

A final example of remembering this initial cultural dialogue is M.N. Roy's description of his first six years as a revolutionary. For him, there was never any possibility of any accommodation with the British regime. After an initial association with *Yugantar*, a Bengali revolutionary organization, he left India in 1914. His initial plan was to procure arms for the struggle at home; but his encounter with Marxist ideas in New York changed both his immediate plans and his goal for the future. ·

Roy describes a socialist meeting in New York which Lajpat Rai addressed concerning the Indian nationalist struggle. When Rai was asked what the difference was for an Indian peasant – to be exploited by Indian capitalists or foreign imperialists, he responded angrily: 'It does make a great deal of difference whether one is kicked by his

brother or by a foreign robber.'[46] The audience, however, was unconvinced, and Roy was made uncomfortable: 'Suddenly a light flashed
through my mind; it was a new light.'[47] Thus began his mental voyage to
commitment to a greater revolution.

I was still a nationalist: cultural nationalism is a prejudice that dies very hard.[48]

The road from revolutionary anti-imperialist nationalism to communism was
short.[49]

The new ideal of freedom was not to be attained within national or
geographical boundaries.[50]

These freedom fighters reached out to a range of intellectual
patrons. Roy discovered Marx and Lenin. Lajpat Rai and Banerjea
perceived themselves as Mazzini's heirs. Abul Kalam Azad had been
initiated into the struggle by Mustafa Kamal Pasha and the Young
Turks. M.K. Gandhi reflected on his debt to Tolstoy and Ruskin. Each
in turn carried their legacy back to India and incorporated it in some
way into a developing understanding with their sense of her essence
and their plans for her future.

The memoir literature of Indian nationalism reflects the extraordinary role of a handful of individuals in the leadership and design
of its programmes. They shared a conviction that their participation
was important, even essential, and their views needed to be spread
widely in order to attract a large constituency. Nehru, Gandhi, Azad,
Jayakar, Rai – all insisted on controlling the words and views of a
newspaper in order to respond to the words and views of other men's
newspapers.

There were for some the vast crowds of peasants who attended their
meetings and treated them with extraordinary deference. Nehru
describes the crowds that came to his house in Allahabad just to see
him. The experience was 'embarrassing', 'annoying' and 'irritating'.

Yet there they were, these people looking up with shining eyes full of
affection, with generations of poverty and suffering behind them, and still
pouring out their gratitude and love and asking for little in return, except
fellow feeling and sympathy. It was impossible not to feel humbled and awed
by this abundance of affection and devotion.[51]

Gandhi's response was typically less romantic than Nehru's. He felt
burdened by his 'Mahatmaship': 'I was the victim of their craze for
darshan.'[52]

The excitement of the 'rebel' life is also reflected in the memories of these leaders. Going to gaol became an opportunity to rest and write, although a sentence that lasted too long or frequent imprisonment was often difficult to bear. While defending his moderate political views to a new generation of more radical colleagues, Banerjea reminded his critics that he claimed the honour 'of being the first Indian of my generation who suffered imprisonment in the discharge of a public duty'. Noting that younger leaders 'now make imprisonment a qualification for public service', he insisted that he possessed it 'even from their standpoint' and that he was 'qualified long before any one of them'.[53]

Lajpat Rai provides a list of the books he read during his six months of deportation in Mandalay Fort,[54] while Gandhi laments in the introduction to his memoirs that the work had been delayed by his release from Yeravda Prison: 'I should indeed have finished the autobiography had I gone through my full term of imprisonment.'[55] Less significant participants who managed to 'court arrest' could experience vicarious *darshan* by being locked up in the same cell or cell block that had once held one of the nationalist luminaries.[56]

Jawaharlal Nehru has noted the close proximity of personal experience and historical events: 'It has not been difficult for me to envisage history as a living process with which I could identify myself to some extent.'[57] For him and many of India's nationalist leaders, the long struggle against the British – its progress or decline – was personified in their own actions, goals and responses to major issues. For Surendranath Banerjea, representing the first generation of moderate nationalism, the introduction of non-cooperation under the leadership of M.K. Gandhi was both a personal tragedy and a national defeat. He describes in his memoirs the tradition of tolerance 'ingrained in the Hindu nature' and the regrettable results of the victory of extremist policies. For Banerjea, he and his generation of moderate political leaders had achieved an ideal accommodation of Hindu and western values. Now both seemed to be in jeopardy in India: 'The present spirit of opposition and intolerance observable among some of our people was unknown; and reverence for the head and elders of the family was the resounding note of the Hindu household.'[58] Those like himself, who had once been lionized as India's national leaders, were now ignored or reviled as collaborators of the alien regime. His memoirs were required, therefore, to carry the added burden of reminding the new generation of leaders of earlier achievements.

The need for Reminiscences such as these has become all the more pressing in view of recent developments in our public life, when unfortunately there is a marked, and perhaps a growing, tendency among a certain section of our people to forget the services of our early nation builders.[59]

Lajpat Rai also wrote defensively. But he sought support for extremist views in an earlier period when Banerjea's moderates were in the ascendancy. Rai had considered publishing his memoirs for some time, but was concerned that such reflections would fall into the hands of 'enemies of my nation'. These 'enemies' were his own countrymen, not the British; and he recognized that such continuing division would lengthen the struggle for independence: 'Our internal enemies are so numerous, and cleavages so fundamental that it appears very unlikely that these cleavages would vanish speedily or that the internal enemies would be vanquished very soon.'[60]

He wrote, after 32 years of public life, to describe the nature of the relationship between the Indian people and their British rulers in his time, and the resulting constraint on the progress of the freedom movement. While he assumed that 99 per cent of the English-educated intelligentsia were in sympathy with extremist views, only 5 per cent appeared to be prepared to make the necessary sacrifices. Among the traditional élites, the situation was no more promising. The 'old fashioned Pandits and Maulvis' were in his view 25 per cent traitors, 50 per cent indifferent and 25 per cent available to the nationalists. The commercial community was 99 per cent apathetic, as were the agriculturalists. Among the landed classes, he assumed the familiar situation: 50 per cent traitors, 25 per cent apathetic and 25 per cent anti-British.[61] It was a dismal picture of accomplishment near the end of his nationalist career, but, he noted, 'each generation engaged in it should know where those who went before erred'.[62]

While Banerjea and Rai were summing up their life's work, Nehru and Gandhi wrote in mid-career.[63] But all of these works reflect a commitment to personal viewpoint, and a troubled and complex relationship with colonial experience. All of them are propagandist, meant to be used to proselytize and mobilize. M.N. Roy had no intention of writing an autobiography and did not live to complete it. But he used the opportunity to 'set the record straight' and demystify a reputation and point of view which had kept him on the margin of mainstream nationalist policy and decision-making: 'A full story of my experience during those years may be told some day, not as the auto-biography of an individual, but as a part of the history of the time.'[64]

Others on the margin because of the nature of their roles wrote about their relations with great men and events, and the resulting distinction it gave to their own lives. This was particularly true among newspapermen: 'Since leaders sought the press and we ourselves had become leaders, our offices in turn soon became the rendezvous of political workers and the non-official headquarters of Congress activity.'[65]

Abul Kalam Azad did not actually write his autobiography. Drafts of chapters were prepared for him after detailed discussions, and amended according to his instructions. Azad included relatively little about his personal life, concentrating on the central mission of his public career: Hindu–Muslim relations. In this context the book is in large measure the lament of one who was confident he had achieved a resolution to the communal problem and had averted the partition of India – only to be undermined by the two paramount leaders – Gandhi and Nehru.

Azad argues that Gandhi's approaches to Jinnah added to Jinnah's importance and enhanced Muslim support for him. But the *coup de grace* was delivered by Nehru who rejected practical and sensible advice in order to protect an elusive ideal: 'Jawaharlal has a weakness for theoretical considerations.'[66]

This is particularly evident in Azad's argument for a federal constitution in India, insisting that a unitary government was unsuitable in a country with such a range of differences. Particularly in Muslim majority provinces, Azad suggested, all matters except defence, communications, and foreign affairs were to be administered by the province. 'This would eliminate from the minds of the Muslims all fears of domination by the Hindus.'[67] Gandhi agreed but Nehru hedged. Nehru was concerned about the need for central planning and unconvinced about the level of popular support among Muslims for Jinnah's leadership.

Azad was convinced that his approach would have achieved success and reluctantly implies that it was Nehru who lost Pakistan and the possibility of Hindu–Muslim amity in India, by rejecting a practical unity, with shared power, in favour of a theoretical unity that never existed.

He has worked and suffered for Indian freedom, and since the attainment of independence, he has become the symbol of our national unity and progress. I have nevertheless to say with regret that he is at times apt to be carried away by his feelings. Not only so, but sometimes he is so impressed by theoretical considerations that he is apt to underestimate the realities of a situation.[68]

Azad's book seeks to set the record straight and establish the significance of his role in the history of a freedom struggle always presumed to be led by others. There was reluctance, however, to publish anything that would be significantly damaging to Nehru, the head of the government in 1959 in which Azad was a minister. Thirty pages of text dealing with incidents and reflections of a personal character were not included in the original published edition. A sealed copy of the whole book was given to the National Archives and National Library, to remain unavailable to scholars and the general public for 30 years. These 30 pages were published in 1989 and met with a brief but noisy public confrontation when an attempt was made to keep them sealed. As anticipated, Azad had suppressed personal criticism of Nehru but there was no significant change in the thrust of his argument. In the centenary year of Nehru's birth, however, these long-awaited memoirs provided added fuel to the revisionist attack on Nehru's reputation as founding father.

In the same year that Azad's memoirs were published, with the discreet suppression of the 30 offending pages, Dr N.B. Khare published his autobiography. He was a former congressman, who had been forced out of office as chief minister of the Central Provinces after a confrontation with Congress leaders.[69] He too blamed Gandhi and Nehru for the partition and he cited Azad's memoir in support. But his argument is cast in the unrestrained language of politicized Hindu revival. It is a bitter book, the lament of an unreconciled loser who became deeply involved in local politics and the communalist Hindu Mahasabha after being routed from a high position in the Congress. Although very personal, it too is representative of a range of outsiders who lost internal struggles or were never able to participate as decisions were made by others on their behalf.

Thus Pakistan was brought into existence as a result of thoughtlessness, lack of wisdom, greed for power, indecent haste and dark conspiracy . . . There is no example in the whole history of the world, of a powerful political organization acting treacherously towards the country. The Congress bent its knees before the Muslim League, played into the hands of British Imperialism and committed this act of treachery. History will never forget this.[70]

It seems appropriate to use a very broad and inclusive definition of political memoir for the group these writers represent. In addition to the standard autobiography, they published collections of letters and press editorials. They also wrote highly personalized histories of India in their time and in the past. These historical surveys take the form of long pauses in an autobiographical narrative, or are published as standard histories with no apparent autobiographical mission.[71] In all of these works the theme of cultural challenge and response informs the discussion of other major issues such as relations between the élite and the mass of the population and communalism. Finally, all of these books reflect some degree of distance of the élite from the central problems requiring solution.

With regard to the question of a new pattern of social structure which would unite or unify, Indian historian Romila Thapar has noted that those wanting change were 'not in communication with those who formed the largest section of the social structure'. As a result, ideas 'remained confined to a small section of society . . . tended to mill around within that section resulting in compromise and reformism and a weakening of the original urge for change'.[72]

Because M.K. Gandhi and Jawaharlal Nehru attained positions of extraordinary power and influence in the movement, their memoirs and reflections, and the manner in which they attempted to resolve the personal and public problems produced by the colonial environment, are of special significance. Their leadership and perspective became major issues themselves in the response of their followers and among those who rejected their methods and goals.

In the introduction to his autobiography, M.K. Gandhi notes the concern of a friend who considered such writing to be 'a practice peculiar to the West'. In response, Gandhi assured his readers that his book was not a real autobiography but only the story of his 'experiments with truth'. Since he viewed his life as consisting of 'nothing but those experiments', the description took the shape of autobiography.[73] The result was a political memoir which might be described as the ultimate personification of the Indian nationalist struggle.

Writing in the mid 1920s after having obtained a dominant position in the movement, he insisted that his primary concern was the search for self-realization, the truth that would allow him to attain the ultimate goal of *Moksha* (salvation). What he had done, and described in his book, were personal experiments performed in the open so that others might benefit.[74] But he recognized that there were limits to what could be shared. Some things were 'known only to oneself and one's maker', and simply not communicable.[75]

Although Gandhi insisted that he retained an open mind and there was no infallibility about his conclusions, he made clear that any significant changes were a deviation from his 'Truth': 'For me they appear to be absolutely correct, and seem for the time being to be final.'[76] If this were not the case, Gandhi asserts, he would be unable to base any action on them: 'So long as my acts satisfy my reason and my heart, I must firmly adhere to my original conclusions.'[77] He did not make it easy for those who followed, or tried to follow him. Although he conceded that he acted on the basis of 'relative truth as I have conceived it', until absolute truth was realized, he insisted, there could be no deviation from a path that was 'straight and narrow and sharp as the razor's edge'.[78] He deliberately cast himself in the distant role of Guru and prophet: 'I believe in the Hindu theory of Guru and his importance in spiritual realization.'[79] After reading Carlyle's *Heroes and Hero Worship*, he notes: 'I read the chapter on the Hero as a prophet and learnt of the Prophet's greatness and bravery and austere living.'[80] It was with this calculated persona that Gandhi returned to India in 1914.

Gandhi's narrative of his development from a shy and introverted student to a confident leader of a mass political movement was for him a story that needed to be shared – especially with India's new leaders. He had willingly accepted the penalty of becoming an outcast when he sailed for England to read law. Like many others, he sought to enter into the mainstream of British Indian society and his goal was reflected in an initial series of experiments with clothing, dancing, elocution, violin-playing, meat eating – adapting himself to the western 'truth' that appeared to be his and India's future.

Having completed his legal studies, he returned to India and then moved to South Africa where the second phase of experiments reflect a different goal – the process of return to an Indian persona in the context of the struggle for his personal civil rights, and then those of the whole resident Indian community. In this context the means to serve India's interests and eventually to achieve her liberation from British control were worked out in a series of experimental encounters with South African authorities. The result was *satyagraha* (truth/force), a means to achieve self-purification in the first instance and then participate in the purification of the whole nation. Its essence was *Ahimsa* – resistance to a system, not its authors.

For Gandhi the return to an Indian identity required the rejection of virtually the whole alien system. It was clearly too much to ask from most of his new colleagues and he recognized and accepted the constraints which tended to isolate him from those who called him 'Mahatma' and 'dictator'.

A reformer cannot afford to have close intimacy with those he seeks to reform.
I am of the opinion that all exclusive intimacies are to be avoided. And he who
would be friends with God must remain alone to make the whole world his
friend.[81]

In Natal he had received loyal and enthusiastic support in the civil
rights struggle. But his call for sanitary reform and contributions to
famine relief attracted only polite indifference: 'I saw that I could not
so easily count on the help of the community in getting it to do its own
duty, as I could in claiming for its rights.'[82] The experience taught
Gandhi the need of the reformer for 'infinite patience': 'It is the
reformer who is anxious for the reform, and not the society, from which
he should expect nothing better than opposition, abhorrence and even
mortal persecution. Why may not society regard as retrogression what
the reformer holds as dear as life itself.'[83]

The introduction of his system of civil disobedience into Indian
politics produced a profound change in the nationalist struggle. At
Champaran in 1917, Gandhi described his intercession on behalf of
Bihari indigo farmers in typical personal terms: 'It is no exaggeration
but the literal truth, to say that in this meeting with the peasants I was
face to face with God, Ahimsa and Truth.'[84] But this was quickly
followed by the apparently inevitable fall from grace of his would-be
followers. In addition to the confrontation with landlords and government, he had initiated sanitation projects, a cow protection programme
and established a number of schools. After he left, however, all these
initiatives collapsed: 'My co-workers and I had built many castles in
the air, but they all vanished for the time being.'[85]

Throughout his life in nationalist politics, Gandhi insisted that there
was an alternative choice. Gandhi's memoirs, and the whole of his vast
literary legacy, reflect the confidence of a man who had found his
'truth' in his traditional culture. He describes the journey which
demonstrated conclusively for him the possibility of return, of being at
home again.

In April 1944, in the twenty-first month of his imprisonment in
Ahmadnagar Fort, Jawaharlal Nehru waited for Europe's struggle to
end so that India could get on with its own. As he had done in the past,
Nehru turned to his books and his pen, to the history of the world and
India's place in it, to the part he had played and would be likely to play
in the future.

When Nehru began writing *The Discovery of India*, he was 55 years
old and had been involved in nationalist politics for 32 years. Yet the

old questions concerning the relationship of East and West, and in particular the impact the colonial experience had made on his life and perspective, still remained unresolved.

India was in my blood and there was much in her that instinctively thrilled me. And yet I approached her almost as an alien critic, full of dislike for the present as well as for many of the relics of the past that I saw. To some extent I came to her via the West, and looked at her as a friendly westerner might have done. I was eager and anxious to change her outlook and appearance and give her the garb of modernity. And yet doubts arose within me. Did I know India – I who presumed to scrap much of her past heritage? There was a great deal that had to be scrapped, that must be scrapped; but surely India could not have been what she undoubtedly was, and could not have continued a cultured existence for thousands of years, if she had not possessed something very vital and enduring, something that was worthwhile. What was this something?[86]

After five months and 1,000 hand-written pages he recognized that India was too vast a canvas to be comprehended, however long one wanders in her past or observes contemporary affairs. He had to settle for a romantic image of a nation-in-making: 'The unity of India was no longer merely an intellectual concept for me; it was an emotional experience which overpowered me.'[87] He looked for signs that indicated that 'the old enchantment' was breaking down; that India generally was capable of modernization and change. But he continued to return to his central theme of separation between two worlds, and his capacity to reach out and lead both to some rational and practical synthesis: 'She is a myth and an idea, a dream and a vision, and yet very real and present and pervasive.'[88] He discovered the 'old witchery' everywhere, implicitly living up to the British stereotypes, to the West's East, and to Nehru's fears: 'Today she swings between a blind adherence to her old customs and a slavish imitation of foreign ways.'[89]

Both Nehru and Gandhi had recognized the limitations of nationalism as a sufficient ideological context for the resolution of India's problems. Gandhism moved beyond nationalism to reach the masses on their own terms. Nehru's commitment to socialism was meant to achieve the same goal, but on alien terms which required a continuing process of negotiation. While Gandhi rejected the British/western system, Nehru embraced it. He insisted there was no choice, while Gandhi described the problem as a moral issue, only requiring moral courage to achieve resolution. For Nehru, a modern socialist/

industrial state would solve the practical and compelling problem of economic deprivation and provide a better life for the vast impoverished peasantry. For Gandhi, that solution only produced and entrenched new problems, and denied any possibility of a moral order. It was the Raj without the British.

Gandhi's 'experiments' reflected a willingness to abandon western institutions and ideas, including the concept of civil government itself. Nehru needed government, the state, the institutionalized nation in order to achieve his goals. He could not conceive of civil life without them. For Gandhi, in the role of prophet or guru, the possibility always remained to struggle on alone if others could not share his goal and the commitment to his means. Nehru could not accept that. He could not be alone.

Gandhi confronted the dark side of Hindu culture with a radical programme for reform. He was totally unromantic about his tradition and was willing to confront and offend. With regard to the vast mass of pilgrims who gathered in Allahabad for the Hindu festival *Kumbh Mela*, he noted more evidence of their absent-mindedness, hypocrisy and slovenliness, than of their piety.[90]

For Nehru, viewing the same gathering, religious reform was not the issue. He envisioned the possibility of diverting that religious energy to political action.[91] There were few true Gandhians among the nationalist leadership. His policies were widely recognized as impractical. But Nehru's vision seemed to many no more acceptable and no more likely to be achieved.

Nehru's description of the 'Indian problem' always reflected ambivalence in perspective and purpose. He criticized Indian marriages as 'wasteful', 'vulgar' and 'extravagant', but felt compelled to note the benefits as well: a little colour in the drab life of the peasant; the in-gathering of family for the middle classes. He denounced religion in India: 'Blind belief and reaction, dogma and bigotry, superstition and exploitation, and the preservation of vested interests.'[92] But there had to be something else, an Indian essence which 'supplied a deep inner craving of human beings'.[93]

Nehru searched in his writing for a source of easy companionship with Indians and India – something that would allow him to be comfortable in the two worlds he occupied. Regarding the Englishman's stereotypes, he insisted that: 'He never makes an attempt to understand that somewhat obvious and very unmysterious person, the Easterner.'[94] But there is always the reiteration of the fundamental mystery that was a barrier for him as well.

I realized more than ever how cut off we were from our people and how we lived and worked and agitated in a little world apart from them.

But the barriers were too solid to disappear, and I peeped over them with wondering eyes at this phenomenon which I failed to understand . . . But all these shouting crowds, the dull and wearying public functions . . . touched me on the surface only . . . My real conflict lay within me.[95]

His 'Englishness' remained the source of a fundamental displacement and isolated him from the countrymen he tried to embrace: 'Indeed I often wonder if I represent anyone at all, and I am inclined to think that I do not . . . I have become a queer mixture of the East and the West, out of place everywhere, at home nowhere.'[96] The sense of isolation extended to his anglicized colleagues as well. He noted that he got on better with the Englishman than other nationalist leaders: 'Probably I have more in common with him than the liberals or others who co-operate with him politically in India.'[97]

In 1926, he travelled to Europe with his wife and remained there, largely in Switzerland, for a year and nine months. His experience dramatically affected his perspective and goals. The Indian struggle became for him an element in a world struggle and the process of accommodation with traditional India that had occupied his mind was now made more complex with this broadening of the stage for action.

On our mountain top, surrounded by the winter snow, I felt completely cut off from India as well as the European world. India and Indian happenings seemed especially far away. I was a distant onlooker, reading, watching, following events, gazing at the new Europe, its politics, economics and the far freer relationships, and trying to understand them.[98]

He became an active participant in the League Against Imperialism, a committed socialist and a supporter of the Russian communist experiment. He also became an even more distant colleague for those who had remained at home: 'My outlook was wider and nationalism by itself seemed to me definitely a narrow and insufficient creed.'[99]

In 1934, Nehru outlined a radical socialist agenda for the nationalist movement in his Congress Presidential address.

For a short while I seemed to carry the Congress in the direction I wanted to go. But I realized soon that the conflict was deep-rooted, it was not so easy to charm away the suspicions of each other and the bitterness that had grown in our ranks.[100]

In India the old problems and conflicts continued, and I had to face the old difficulty of how to fit in with my colleagues.[101]

Like Gandhi, Nehru described his memoir as a means to trace 'my own mental development' rather than a survey of recent Indian history. But there was conscious intermixing: 'I lived through the past I was writing about.'[102]

Gandhi sought a reformed and purified East that left most of his followers behind. Nehru sought a purified West and achieved a similar response. There was the encounter with the British and with India. There was also the extraordinary encounter with each other. Nehru's memoirs describe a Gandhi who is the personification of India, an India that Nehru sought to change – even eliminate.

A country pays a heavy price when it mortgages its mind to one man. When it does it in succession to two men whose ideas on politico-economic matters differ so radically at vital points, it is self-evident that the country is beginning to lose its capacity for independent thinking and will accept any carrot or reconcile itself to any stick.[103]

Nehru met Gandhi for the first time in 1916. Gandhi's South African reputation had preceded him but the ambivalent response that would continually inform their relationship was there at the start: 'He seemed very distant and different and unpolitical.'[104] Over the next 32 years, Nehru reiterated the litany of his shortcomings – but always subsumed in an overarching appreciation of his strengths. Gandhi was reactionary: 'So, while some looked to the future, others looked back to the past.'[105] He was intolerant of opposition to his non-violent, non-cooperation programme: 'Individuals might make of it a religion or incontrovertible creed. But no political organization, so long as it remained political, could do so.'[106] Yet he had courage and style and he produced results. He attracted a following in the 1920s among intellectuals, in part because of the absence of choice. But there was more: 'Consciously and deliberately meek and humble, yet he was full of power and authority, and he knew it.'[107] His views remained 'almost incomprehensible to an average modern,' lamented Nehru. 'What a problem and a puzzle he has been.'[108]

For Nehru, non-cooperation was simply not enough, and Gandhi's constructive programmes did not fill the political gap: 'We ignored the necessity of thought behind the action. We forgot that without a conscious ideology and objective the energy and enthusiasm of the masses must end largely in smoke.'[109] There was, however, a critical constraint to the socialist solution he advocated. In 1929, he served as President of both the Indian National Congress and the Trade Union Congress. In his memoirs he recalled his attempt to bring the two closer together, and his failure: 'It was, perhaps, a vain hope, for nationalism can only go far in a socialistic or proletarian direction by ceasing to be nationalism.'[110]

Nehru recognized the need to constrain the socialist argument in his autobiography, aware of the range of opponents who would read it and confirm their rejection of his leadership.

Again, I would repeat that I am not at present considering the question of how to effect the change, of how to get rid of the obstacles in the way, by compulsion or conversion, violence or non-violence . . . But the necessity for the change must be recognised and clearly stated. If leaders and thinkers do not clearly envisage this and state it, how can they expect ever to convert anybody to their way of thinking, or develop the necessary ideology in the people?[111]

But the effort was largely in vain. In 1936, Nehru proposed the establishment of an Indian Civil Liberties Union. The rejection he received from M.R. Jayakar was representative of the conservative core of Indian nationalism. In Jayakar's view Nehru did not possess the broadmindedness required in a promoter of such an organization, as reflected in 'the intolerance of views displayed by you in your Autobiography toward all who do not agree with your political views'.[112]

Gandhi was capable of supporting a 'decaying system' that produced 'misery' and 'waste', arguing that the status quo could be affected by a change of heart.

The socialism and communism of the West is based on certain conceptions which are fundamentally different from ours. One such conception is their belief in the essential selfishness of human nature . . . Our socialism and communism should therefore be based on non-violence and on the harmonious co-operation of labour and capital, landlord and tenant.[113]

As always, Nehru rejected and embraced Gandhi, as he rejected and embraced India: 'He came to represent India to an amazing degree and to express the very spirit of that ancient and tortured land. Almost he was India, and his very failings were Indian failings.'[114]

In 1935, Gandhi called off the Civil Disobedience Movement when he appeared to be losing control. Nehru was angry and frustrated. He accommodated because he had no choice, but his inability to influence and control his own situation, if not India's, was an increasingly heavy burden.

Suddenly I felt very lonely in that cell of Alipore Jail. Life seemed to be a dreary affair, a very wilderness of desolation. Of the very hard lessons that I had learned, the hardest and the most painful now faced me: that it is not possible in any vital matter to rely on anyone. One must journey through life alone – to rely on others is to invite heartbreak.[115]

The leaders of Indian nationalism were not able to assume the existence of a stable civil structure requiring only the removal of the British to satisfy a shared freedom mission. They were required to play the role of nation builders as well. The resulting internal competition of ideology, viewpoint and goal became the central focus of the struggle, informed but not controlled by the overarching system of institutions, norms and values which the British had introduced. The memoirs of those who participated reflect the fundamental nature of the confrontation. It was at its base a confrontation between civilizations, but played out most dramatically in the lives of a handful of individuals who made the choices on behalf of the rest.

NOTES

1. Stanley Wolpert, *A New History of India* (New York, 1982). With regard to ancient historiography see also A.K. Warder, *Indian Historiography* (Bombay, 1972); V.S. Patnaik, *Ancient Historians of India* (Bombay, 1966); C.H. Philips, *Historians of India and Pakistan* (London, 1960).
2. The first three Mughal emperors of India, 1526–1605.
3. The fourth Mughal emperor, 1605–28.
4. Alexander Rogers (trans.) and Henry Beveridge (ed.), *The Tuzuk-i-Jahangiri* (Delhi, 1968), pp. vi–vii.
5. Ibid., p. viii.
6. Ibid.
7. V.G. Khobrekar (ed.), Sir Jadunath Sarkar Birth Centenary Commemoration Volume, English translation of *Tarikh-i-Dilkasha* (Memoirs of Bhimsen relating to Aurangzeb's Deccan campaigns) (Bombay, 1972), p. 223.
8. Ibid., p. 151.
9. Stephen Hay (ed.), *Sources of Indian Tradition, Vol. II: Modern India and Pakistan* (New York, 1988), p. 6.
10. Ibid., p. 9.
11. Ibid, pp. 13–14.
12. I am indebted to my colleague, N.K. Wagle, for information and insight regarding these materials.
13. This literature is vast in scope and provides the basis for an understanding of Anglo-India as a colonial sub-culture.
14. Shivaji Bhonsle (1627–80). He gathered together a range of Maratha kingdoms into a confederacy, providing a base for Hindu nationalist opposition to Mughal rule. It is in this context that his name and reputation were 'nationalized' in the late nineteenth century as part of the struggle against British rule.
15. See David Kopf, 'Ram Mohun Roy and the Bengal Renaissance: An Historiographical Essay', in V.C. Joshi, *Ram Mohun Roy and the Process of Modernization in India* (Delhi,

1975), pp. 21–45.
16. T.B. Macaulay, 'Minute on Education', 1835, reproduced in Edward Thompson and G.T. Garratt, *Rise and Fulfilment of British Rule in India* (Allahabad, 1958), p. 661.
17. F.H.B. Skrine, *Life of Sir William Wilson Hunter* (London, 1901), p. 193.
18. Humayun was the second Mughal emperor (?–1556).
19. Major Charles Stewart (trans.), *The Tezkereh Al Vakiator or Private Memoirs of the Mughal Emperor Humayun* (New Delhi, 1970), p. vi.
20. Meredith Townsend, *Asia and Europe* (London, 1920).
21. *Congress Presidential Addresses*, second edition (Madras, 1917), p. 363.
22. J.S. Barnes to Jawaharlal Nehru, 9 December 1936, Jawaharlal Nehru Papers, B-30.
23. Jawaharlal Nehru to J.S. Barnes, 22 April 1937, Jawaharlal Nehru Papers, B-30.
24. V.S. Naipaul's phrase.
25. Partha Chatterjee, *Nationalist Thought and the Colonial World* (Tokyo, 1986), Ch. 1, pp. 1–35.
26. S.N. Banerjea, *A Nation in Making* (Bombay, 1925), pp. 130–1.
27. Ibid., p. 40.
28. Lala Lajpat Rai, *The Story of My Life*, in V.C. Joshi (ed.), *Lajpat Rai Autobiographical Writings* (Delhi, 1965), p. 81.
29. S.N. Banerjea, *A Nation in Making*, pp. 107–8.
30. Jawaharlal Nehru, *Toward Freedom* (New York, 1941).
31. C. Rajagopalachari to G.A. Natesan, 18 July 1940, Natesan Papers.
32. Peter Berger's term in *Homeless Mind* (New York, 1973).
33. S.N. Banerjea, *A Nation in the Making*, p. 1.
34. Ibid., p. 2.
35. Ibid., p. 19.
36. Jawaharlal Nehru, *Toward Freedom*, p. 36.
37. Azad was the major Muslim leader in the Indian National Congress.
38. Maulana Abul Kalam Azad, *India Wins Freedom, An Autobiographical Narrative* (Bombay, 1959), p. 2.
39. Sir Syed Ahmad Khan initiated a reform and modernization movement in the Muslim community in the nineteenth century.
40. Maulana Abul Kalam Azad, *India Wins Freedom*, p. 3.
41. Lala Lajpat Rai, *The Story of My Life*, pp. 28–9.
42. Ibid.
43. M.R. Jayakar was a twentieth-century Bombay nationalist leader closely associated with the responsive cooperation position in opposition to non-cooperation.
44. Milton Israel, 'M.R. Jayakar and the Bombay Nationalist Press', in N.K. Wagle (ed.), *Images of Maharashtra* (London, 1980), p. 9.
45. M.R. Jayakar, *The Story of My Life* (Bombay), Vol. I, p. 4.
46. *M.N. Roy's Memoirs*, sponsored by the Indian Renaissance Institute (Bombay, 1964), p. 28.
47. Ibid.
48. Ibid., p. 59.
49. Ibid., p. 60.
50. Ibid., p. 217.
51. Jawaharlal Nehru, *Toward Freedom*, p. 151.
52. Mohandas K. Gandhi, *An Autobiography: The Story of My Experiments with Truth* (Ahmedabad, 1927), p. 286. *Darshan* refers to the benefit received from being in the presence of a great or especially pious man.
53. S.N. Banerjea, *A Nation in the Making*, p. 69.
54. Lala Lajpat Rai, *The Story of My Life*, pp. 169–71. Included in the list were: Justin McCarthy, *History of our Time*; Herbert Paul, *History of Modern England*; Herbert Spencer, *Autobiography*; Lecky's *History of the Rise and Influence of Rationalism in Europe*; Hallam's *History of the Middle Ages*; Motley's *Rise of the Dutch Republic*; and Bryce's *The American Commonwealth*.
55. M.K. Gandhi, *An Autobiography*, p. xiii.
56. This was particularly the case among newspapermen who tended to write about their

experience in their papers or in memoir accounts. Going to gaol became a standard form of credentials for nationalists.

57. Jawaharlal Nehru, *The Discovery of India* (Calcutta, 1946), p. 8.
58. S.N. Banerjea, *A Nation in the Making*, p. 2.
59. Ibid., preface.
60. Lala Lajpat Rai, *The Story of My Life*, p. 4.
61. Ibid., p. 8.
62. Ibid., p. 10.
63. Gandhi was 58 in 1927, when his autobiography was published. Nehru was 46 in 1935.
64. M.N. Roy, *M.N. Roy's Memoirs*, p. 4.
65. J.N. Sahni, *The Truth About the Indian Press* (New Delhi, 1974), p. 88.
66. Abul Kalam Azad, *India Wins Freedom*, p. 129.
67. Ibid., p. 140.
68. Ibid., p. 160.
69. Dr N.B. Khare, *My Political Memoirs or Autobiography* (Nagpur, 1971). The so-called 'Khare Affair' in 1937 raised a number of important constitutional issues for the new Congress governments in the provinces.
70. Ibid., p. 117.
71. Jawaharlal Nehru's *Discovery of India* is the most notable example.
72. Romila Thapar, 'Summary of Discussion', in Bisheshwar Prasad (ed.), *Ideas in History* (London, 1968), pp. 328–9.
73. M.K. Gandhi, *An Autobiography*, p. xiv.
74. Ibid.
75. Ibid.
76. Ibid.
77. Ibid.
78. Ibid., p. xv.
79. Ibid., p. 64.
80. Ibid., p. 49.
81. Ibid., p. 14.
82. Ibid., p. 158.
83. Ibid.
84. Ibid., p. 304.
85. Ibid., p. 314.
86. Jawaharlal Nehru, *The Discovery of India*, p. 51.
87. Ibid., p. 27.
88. Ibid., p. 598.
89. Ibid., p. 599.
90. M.K. Gandhi, *An Autobiography*, p. 285.
91. Jawaharlal Nehru, *Toward Freedom*, pp. 150–1.
92. Ibid., p. 240.
93. Ibid., p. 241.
94. Ibid., p. 70.
95. Ibid., p. 154.
96. Ibid., p. 353.
97. Ibid., p. 93.
98. Ibid., p. 121.
99. Ibid., pp. 128–9.
100. Ibid., p. 358.
101. Ibid., p. 364.
102. Ibid., pp. 8–9.
103. Frank Moraes, *Witness to an Era* (London, 1973), p. 11.
104. Jawaharlal Nehru, *Toward Freedom*, p. 75.
105. Ibid.
106. Ibid., p. 82.
107. Ibid., p. 110.
108. Ibid., p. 190.

109. Ibid., p. 75.
110. Ibid., p. 148.
111. Ibid., p. 323.
112. M.R. Jayakar to Jawaharlal Nehru, 13 July 1936, Jayakar Papers, 151.
113. Jawaharlal Nehru, *Toward Freedom*, p. 325.
114. Ibid., p. 313.
115. Ibid., p. 325.

5

Japanese *Nikki* as Political Memoirs

JOSHUA MOSTOW

The term 'political memoir' is commonly used to denote works that partake of both 'history' and 'autobiography'. Political memoirs are a kind of autobiography, and to understand what kind of autobiography we might contrast them with, for instance, 'spiritual autobiography' (note that we speak less commonly of 'spiritual memoirs' or 'political autobiography'): we expect a spiritual autobiography to concentrate on the author's internal, religious development, and pay attention to the external environment where this development took place only to the extent that it had an influence on or helps explain that spiritual growth. Political memoirs, on the other hand, are about the author, not as a spirit or religious, but as a politician, and we expect to be told of the author's spiritual life, for instance, only to the extent that it was politically relevant. Further, we expect the author to have been a fairly big player in, or an unusually close witness to, the major political events of the day. In fact, our image of the genesis of a political memoir probably corresponds quite closely to that given by Georges Gusdorf: '[m]any great men, and even some not so great – heads of governments or generals, ministers of state, explorers, businessmen – have devoted the leisure time of their old age to editing "Memoirs" . . .'.[1] And while the genre of autobiography has St Augustine, political memoirs seem to be an undeniably post-Renaissance activity. Nor should we ignore the word 'men' in Gusdorf's description, for political memoirs seem to be even more a men's club than politics itself. Indeed, Gusdorf would have us restrict the authorship of autobiographies not only to post-Renaissance men, but to western men:

autobiography is not to be found outside of our cultural area; one would say that it expresses a concern peculiar to Western man, a concern that has been of good use in his systematic conquest of the universe and that he has communicated to men of other cultures; but those men will thereby have been annexed by a sort of intellectual colonizing to a mentality that was not their own. (Gusdorf, p. 29)

There is a body of texts, however, that can be considered 'political memoirs' in a sense somewhat different from that outlined above. These texts are considered 'memoirs', but they are usually characterized as 'literary memoirs', which are understood to be, almost by definition, apolitical. In what follows, I will argue that these memoirs *are* political, not only in the sense that all writing is political, but also in that these works were specifically commissioned by major political figures, for specifically political reasons. A brief excursion into the world of visual art may help clarify the situation.

The *Chûden gyokaizu*, a copy of an original attributed to Fujiwara no Nobuzane (1176?–1266), depicts a moon-viewing party and concert hosted in 1218 by Emperor Juntoku, shown in the painting playing the biwa,

the higher-ranking ministers [are] on the veranda nearby; and the other poets trail around to the side of the building, their distance from the centre in inverse proportion to their rank. In the last section we come upon . . . squeezed in at the very end, Nobuzane himself, in the earliest self-portrait in Japanese painting. This copy has been handed down in the Kujô family, descendants of Kujô Michi'ie, Minister of the Right in 1218 and the man shown seated closest to the Emperor in the painting: it is likely that the Kujô family commissioned the original as a gift for the emperor and kept the copy for themselves.[2]

This 'occasion portrait', as Graybill calls it, includes a self-portrait of the artist, and yet was commissioned by someone else, both to win favour with the emperor and to illustrate, literally, the Kujô family's closeness to the imperial authority. The literary works under consideration function in almost the same way: while they include much auto-biographical information about the authors (all middle-ranking female courtiers), they were in fact commissioned to serve the political purposes of high-ranking ministers of state.

Such is the corpus of texts from classical Japan called *ôchô joryû nikki*, or 'court women's diaries', written from the late tenth century through to the end of the late fourteenth century. But to understand how such remarkable works, written by women, in Asia, in pre-modern times, came about, and how they functioned, both literarily and politically, we must first briefly review the origins of history writing, biography, and diary-keeping in ancient China, whence Japan originally borrowed its writing system and literary genres.

The texts I will identify as political memoirs belong to a much larger genre, called *nikki*, a word that in modern Japanese translates as 'diary', and whose graphemes can be rendered literally as 'day record'. The word itself is Chinese in origin (modern pronunciation *jih chi*) and appears to have been first used by Wang Ch'ung (AD 27–97?), a rationalist Confucian philosopher, in his *Lun hêng* (completed AD 82 or 83), translated as 'Balanced Discussions' or 'Critical Essays'. Wang used the term in reference to the *Spring and Autumn Annals* (*Ch'un ch'iu*), which are the oldest historical records in China, recording court events and astronomical phenomena in the state of Lu from 722 to 481 BC, arranged by season, month, and sometimes giving the exact day as well.[3]

Such record-keeping was eventually regularized into a number of discrete genres, such as the 'Diary of Activity and Repose' (*ch'i chü chu*) covering, or rather uncovering, the diurnal and nocturnal activities of the emperor (Loon, p. 41). These, in turn, were incorporated into yet other diaries. As Lien-Sheng Yang explains:

The successive Diaries of Activity and Repose, supplemented with such works as the *Shih-cheng chi* or Records of Current Government prepared by the chief ministers or their subordinates, served as a major source for compilation of the *Jih-li* or Daily Records; these in turn became the primary source of the *Shih-lu* or Veritable Records of the emperor. Both the Daily Records and the Veritable Records were in the chronicle style; biographies of important persons, however, were supplied in the entries which recorded their deaths.[4]

The early annals were supplemented by oral exegeses, called 'traditions' (*chuan*). The content of these included hearsay and folk-tales and they were, therefore, more popular than the documented material of the annals themselves, and tended to concern specific historical actors. The first work of comprehensive and synthetic history was the *Shih chi* or 'Records of the Historian', written by Ssu-ma Ch'ien (145–90? BC). His history begins from the earliest times and continues up to the author's own lifetime at the beginning of the first century BC. It comprises 130 chapters, divided into five groups: (1) imperial annals, (2) aristocratic annals, (3) genealogical tables, (4) treatises on various aspects of government and (5) 'biographies' (*chuan*), where the 'traditions' about famous individuals are systematically brought together.[5] It is among these biographies that we find the first autobiography, called a *tzu-hsü* (self-account), in which Ssu-ma Ch'ien recounts 'the genealogy of his family, giving a brief summary of his father's life and his own'.[6] Yet the formality of the occasion, a dynastic history, precluded any revelations.[7] Indeed, as Pei-yi Wu writes: 'Chinese historiography posed probably the most formidable obstacle to what is nowadays valued in an autobiography – a personal voice, a private point of view, or any self-revelation.' Nor do we get any inside information on the Han court or Ssu-ma Ch'ien's version of important events, such as are preserved, rather, in an extant letter to a friend.[8]

In fact, Chinese literature so divided the generic pie that anything like 'political memoirs' were presented in several different genres: analysis and comments on politics were contained in memorials to the throne; personal history was contained in official self-accounts; and the emotional reactions to all these events were contained in poetry, a genre second only to history in literary importance, and read as both autobiographical and political. Of China's earliest collection of poetry, the *Book of Odes* (*Shih ching*), for instance, Ssu-ma Ch'ien writes: 'most of the three hundred poems of the *Book of Odes* were written when sages poured forth their anger and dissatisfaction' (Watson, p. 55). It was not until the end of the Sung dynasty that we see the emergence of what might be considered true political memoirs – what Wu calls 'annalistic autobiography' (*tzu-hsü nien-p'u*) – beginning with that of the prime minister and general in command during the final days of the dynasty, Wen T'ien-hsiang (1236–83) (Wu, pp. 32–9).

During the seventh century, the Japanese adopted not only the Chinese form of government and its language and script, but also their literary genres, specifically history. By 720 they had composed the *Nihon shoki* (Written Records of Japan) in Chinese, tracing the earliest history of their country and justifying the rule of the Yamato clan descended from the Sun Goddess Amaterasu, as imperial family. As regards form, the Japanese followed the chronicle model of *The Spring and Autumn Annals*, rather than the standard dynastic history format established by Ssu-ma Ch'ien. This, of course, gave less prominence to the biographies of individuals and no autobiographical writing appears at all.[9]

The adoption of Chinese bureaucracy led to the adoption of its tools as well, the daily records of court, composed in what is called *kiroku kanbun*, or 'record Chinese': the emperor's activities were recorded by chamberlains (*kurôdo*) in the *tenjô nikki*, or 'Emperor's Diary'; the proceedings of the Great Council of State (*dajôkan*) were recorded in the *geki nikki,* while those of the Ministry of Central Affairs (*nakatsukasashô*) were recorded in the *naiki nikki.* All other ministries and organs, such as the Inner Palace Guards, kept such daily records. The first reference to *nikki* of this sort dates from 821. In addition, many individual government officials kept their own daily records, one of their main purposes being 'the minute recording of correct ceremonial' procedure.[10] As one such diarist wrote, on a rainy day in the eighth month of 1133:

Quiet day at home. Fine rain and misty. Alone, I spread out the table of contents . . . and wrote in the missing public functions. This is both to disperse uncertainties at the present time and to provide against their being forgotten and abandoned in the future.[11]

Recording *nikki* were also written in Japanese by women, but these specifically referred to the polished records of poetry contests (*uta-awase*), an important venue for court activity.[12] The earliest surviving record is by Lady Ise and dated 913. Ise herself was a lady-in-waiting to Emperor Uda (r. 887–97), the monarch responsible for reintroducing Japanese verse into court after it had been all but entirely supplanted by Chinese verse in the early 800s. Poetry in the Chinese model was, of course, not an amusement but both a way to criticize one's ruler, tactfully and implicitly, and a means of self-cultivation. As Confucius is reported to have said (*Analects* XVII:9): 'An apt quotation from the Odes may serve to stimulate the imagination, to show one's breeding, to smooth over difficulties in a group and to give expression to complaints.'[13] Thus, already by the early 900s we see two kinds of *nikki* in Japan: those concerning the daily activities of court, written by men in Chinese; and those centred on *belles-lettres,* written by women in Japanese. By the tenth century the *nikki* genre came to encompass types of more personal memoirs as well (Cranston, p. 91).

Commissioned records of poetry matches, such as that by Lady Ise, led to commissioned records of other exchanges of poems, specifically those in epistles (of which poems were an essential part). In 961 Fujiwara no Takamitsu appears to have taken his family, who were *de facto* rulers of the country, somewhat by surprise when he suddenly renounced the world and became a hermit at the age of 23. A lady-in-waiting close to the family appears to have been commissioned by Regent (*kanpaku*) Koretada (also called Koremasa, 924–72) to 'publish' an account of the event and the family's reaction to it,[14] mainly through editing the letters (and poems) exchanged between Takamitsu in retreat on Mt Hiei and the various members of his family back in the capital. At this distance it is difficult to know what the motivation for this commission was. One possibility is that it was 'spin-control' – the work presents so many sad and touching poems that it is easy to overlook the fact that nowhere does it attempt to explain *why* Takamitsu left the world so abruptly.[15] The other possibility is that Takamitsu's action was simply being used as grist for the Fujiwara culture-mill, and provided an opportunity to depict the clan at its most sensitive and heart-rending.

The next extant work is known today by the title of *The Pillow Book of Sei Shônagon (Makura no sôshi)*, and is usually viewed as a miscellany (*zuihitsu*), rather than as a journal. Yet the generic term for 'miscellany' did not exist in Sei's day[16] and, as will be seen below, there is good evidence to believe that her work was at least partly commissioned by chief of the Fujiwara clan and head of state, Michitaka (953–95).

But first, some political background: Emperor Ichijô ascended the throne in 986 at the age of six, with Kane'ie (his maternal grandfather) serving as regent. In 990, Kane'ie's son, Michitaka (see chart below), presented his daughter Sadako (or Teishi, about 16 years old at the time) to court, and she became the ten-year-old Ichijô's consort (*nyôgo*). It is supposed that Sei Shônagon entered Sadako's service somewhere around this time.

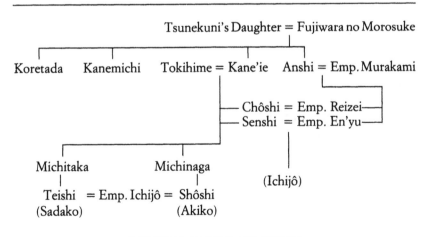

FUJIWARA FAMILY RELATIONS

In the seventh month of 990 Kane'ie died; Michitaka took over as regent, and his daughter, Sadako, was elevated to the position of empress (*chûgû*). For the next five years Michitaka was at the height of his fortunes, capped in 995 by the presentation of another daughter as the consort of the crown prince. However, in the ninth month of that year Michitaka fell ill, dying a month later. There ensued a power struggle between Michitaka's children, Taka'ie and Korechika, and his brother Michinaga. Michinaga engineered his nephews' banishment in 996 and in 999 presented his daughter Akiko (Teishi) to Emperor Ichijô, in direct competition with Sadako. There was an uneasy competition between the two empresses for almost two years, and then in the twelfth month of 1000, Sadako died while giving birth to her third child.

It was in this kind of political milieu that in 994 Michitaka commissioned a dedication of the full canon of the *sutras* at Shakuzen Temple. Sei's description of this 'media event' is the longest entry in her journal and we must suspect that she was given a quantity of paper by Korechika a few months later at least partly to prepare a clean copy of her account. The account is mostly a panegyric of Michitaka and Sadako, as Sei writes:

Watching the Chancellor [Michitaka] as he sat down in front of the Empress [Sadako] and started talking to her, I wished that I could somehow arrange to let outsiders have a glimpse of the scene, so that they might observe how perfectly she made her replies.[17]

'Outsiders' here, of course, does not refer to some bourgeois readership, but to almost everyone at court except the very few courtiers (mostly women) allowed to see the empress in her casual moments. Sei's memoirs, then, and those of the women who followed her lead, provide intimate glimpses of the major political figures, male and female, at court. While we do not get accounts of secret discussions at the centre of political activities, her record has proved a valuable source for obtaining a sense of the personalities of the period, as well as being a treasure trove for cultural history. Moreover, the intent of Sei's writing was clearly political: in the first instance, to present her empress and masters in a positive light and to manifest the cultural flourishing their administration supported; in the second instance, to provide a retrospective commemoration of the Empress Sadako's court and salon, a motivation for such memoirs that became increasingly dominant in later centuries.

In any event, some time after the eighth month of the same year as the ceremony, Emperor Ichijô had paper supplied for the copying of Ssu-ma Ch'ien's *Records of the Historian*. A quantity of paper seems to have been left over, and Korechika and Sadako gave it to Sei – it is tempting to believe that it was given so that she might serve as a contemporary (Japanese and feminine) counterpart to the classic (Chinese and male) recorder.

Regardless of whether Sei's memoirs were specifically commissioned or not, we do know that some form of her work was produced shortly after she had retired from court upon Sadako's death. Indeed, a strong argument can be made for women's *nikki* deriving, at least in part, from the earlier tradition of *banka*, or elegiac lament. As Gary Ebersole has convincingly demonstrated in his recent book, *Ritual Poetry and the Politics of Death in Early Japan*, these laments were an integral part of a ritual complex designed to accommodate and control the power struggles that occurred after the death of a sovereign or potential successor to the throne.[18] It is, then, no accident that a significant number of extant women's *nikki* are centred on the death of an imperial loved one: Ise includes her *banka* on Empress Onshi (Haruko, 872–907) in her *nikki*; the *Takamitsu nikki* records Emperor Daigo's grandson Takamitsu's 'death to the world' when he took religious vows; Izumi Shikibu's *nikki* is essentially a *memento mori* for Prince Atsumichi (981–1007); Fujiwara no Takako's *nikki* (discussed below) opens on and revolves around the death of Emperor Horikawa (r. 1086–1107); and Lady Nijô's *Confessions* come to an end with the death of Emperor Go-Fukakusa (r. 1246–59). Many of these 'memoirs', then, are in fact 'memorials' for political masters.

In 1008 it was Akiko's turn to give birth and Michinaga, her father and regent (*sesshô*) since 995, apparently assuming it would be a boy, seems to have, at the very least, 'encouraged' Murasaki Shikibu, the famous author of *The Tale of Genji* and companion to Akiko, to make a record of the event.[19] She had, after all, been called on one occasion 'Our Lady of the Chronicles' (Bowring, p. 137).

As the official histories were written in Chinese, a language it was considered unbecoming for women to know too well, female readers were in principle excluded from participating in the entire genre of history, a logical result when the purpose of history was thought to be to aid those in government – positions from which women had been excluded since the last ruling empress, in 770. However, the official histories were so dry that it may be doubted how many men read them either.

Accordingly, the eleventh century saw the rise of Japanese vernacular history, starting with *A Tale of Flowering Fortunes* (*Eiga monogatari*), a narrative account of life at court from 887 to 1028, written in the narrative form of a literary romance (*monogatari*). The first 30 chapters of this work have been attributed to Akazome Emon (fl. 976–1041), a younger contemporary of Murasaki Shikibu who, like her, was a renowned poet, and served Michinaga's wife, Rinshi. Akazome was in addition the wife of Ōe no Masahira (952–1012), whose family had been involved in the writing of the last of the six national histories (*rikkokushi*) and the aborted seventh, the *Shinkokushi*. The author of the *Eiga* must have had access to the kind of archives the Ōe family would have kept, and included in these archives must have been the records and memoirs of palace women.[20] In fact, Murasaki Shikibu's account of the birth of the future Emperor Go-Ichijō (r. 1016–36) is incorporated almost verbatim into the *Eiga monogatari*.

The period covered by Akazome in the *Eiga* was treated again, this time by a man, in *The Great Mirror* (*Ōkagami*). This work in turn led to a number of sequel 'mirrors' (the *Ima kagami*, *Mizu kagami*, *Masu kagami*, and so on), representing a tradition of continuous and co-operative masculine vernacular history that spanned some six centuries.[21] The women too, however, continued the tradition of Murasaki Shikibu and Akazome Emon; as the latter wrote at the end of her chapters: 'There will be other events following the ones I have described. Someone who witnesses or hears about them must be sure to write them down' (McCullough and McCullough, Vol. II, p. 774). And in fact, ten chapters were added to the *Eiga* by two later women, bringing the work up to 1092.[22]

The remaining works in this tradition stay in the *nikki* format, rather than the larger and more synthetic format of the *monogatari*. They are, consequently, more narrow in scope and more personal in content. The first of these is the *Sanuki no Suke nikki* (Diary of the Assistant Handmaid of Sanuki Province), a record by Fujiwara no Nagako of the last days of Emperor Horikawa (r. 1086–1107), and her first year in the service of his five-year-old successor, Emperor Toba (r. 1107–23). Like Murasaki Shikibu's *nikki*, the *Sanuki no Suke nikki* was used as source material for the *Ima kagami* (c. 1180), but it seems more likely that Nagako saw herself continuing the *Eiga monogatari*, starting her journal where the latter had left off, in the middle of Horikawa's reign (Brewster, p. 14).

While Nagako's work seems to have been a self-motivated continuation of the 'unofficial history' (*gaishi*) started with the *Eiga*, the thirteenth century saw a return to the essentially commemorative works sponsored by powerful patrons. Yumiko Hulvey suggests, for instance, that the *Ben no Naishi nikki*, covering the 13-year reign of Go-Fukakusa (r. 1176–1270), may well have been commissioned by his father, Emperor Go-Saga (r. 1242–46).[23] Likewise, the *Nakatsukasa Naishi nikki* describes the author's 13 years of service to Emperor Fushimi (r. 1288–98), beginning while he was still Crown Prince, and continuing through to the second year of his reign. All these works, then, were written by the female personal attendants of the monarch and seem designed to record, preserve and celebrate the cultural splendour of their respective emperors. Such artistic splendour was, of course, considered a direct result of a beneficent reign. The final extant work of this tradition is the *Account of Takemuki Palace* (*Takemuki ga ki*) by Hino Nako, which spans the turbulent Nanboku-chô period (1333–92), the only officially recognized time in its history that Japan had two competing courts and monarchs.[24]

Politically, if not culturally, Japan saw tremendous change in 1185 when Minamoto no Yoritomo (1147–99) established administrative control of the country in Kamakura, 300 miles east of the emperor's court in Kyoto, beginning Japan's 700-year history under military rule. The move from an aristocratic society to a feudal one had a negative impact on the political and economic status of women. Though the division of property among male and female heirs was initially permitted, marriage gradually became virilocal, with the woman moving into the man's house, rather than uxorilocal, where the woman remained in her own house after marriage, as it had been in the earlier Heian period (794–1185).[25] Virilocal marriage put Japanese women under constant patriarchal control, significantly restricting their freedom of movement.

Yet the distance between Kamakura and Kyoto necessitated more travel than at any previous time. This combination of circumstances led to the rise of the travel diary, whose chief authors were men.

At the same time, the greatly weakened authority of the court seems to have also weakened the barriers between previously gender-based literary genres, and we see men starting to write *nikki* in Japanese (for the first time since a few isolated attempts in the early 900s), such as that by Minamoto no Ienaga (1173–1234), a chamberlain under Emperor Go-Toba (r. 1183–98).[26]

Male court poets (a group that now included major politicians, rather than, as in the previous period, solely professional authors), rather than women, now wrote records of imperial or shogunal journeys and progresses to various shrines and temples. Such *nikki* of course reinforced the original political motivation for such trips. The *Account of the Journey of the ex-Emperor Takakura to Itsukushima* (*Takakura-in Itsukushima gokôki*, 1180) by Koga Michichika (1149–1202), for instance, portrays a humble and suffering Takakura making his long way to the ancestral shrine of the Taira clan in Itsukushima, apparently in an attempt to placate the military ruler Taira no Kiyomori (1118–81), who at that time had Takakura's father, the ex-Emperor Go-Shirakawa (r. 1156–58), under house arrest.[27]

By the Muromachi period (1333–1573), women were no longer writing memoirs, and the spatially oriented travel diary had completely supplanted the diurnally centred *nikki*. The most famous of the travel diaries, however, were written by 'aesthete-recluses'[28] whose politics were the rejection of politics. And even those kept by politicians, such as Nijô Yoshimoto (1320–88), who at various times held the posts of chancellor, prime minister, and regent, were written in the persona of poet rather than statesman.

There were still records of progresses: *The Visit to Itsukushima of the Lord of the Deer Park* (*Rokuon'in-dono Itsukushima Môde no Ki*, 1389) by Imagawa Ryôshun (1326–1414?); and *Journey to Fuji* (*Fuji kikô*, 1432) by Asukai Masayo (1390–1441), recording what we might be tempted to call the 'routine manoeuvres' put on by the Shogun Ashikaga Yoshinori (1394–1441). As Keene states (p. 204): 'Yoshinori's purpose in making the journey was not purely aesthetic. He intended to affirm his authority with respect to Ashikaga Mochiuji (1398–1439), the chief shogunate officer (*kubô*) in Kamakura, who was suspected of harbouring seditious ambitions.' Again we see how these accounts served the same functions as those apparent in the *Chûden gyokaizu*: courtiers accompanying the shogun not only recorded poems written on the famous sites encountered, but also included verses of fulsome praise for their ruler:

> Everyone who bathes
> In the glorious sunlight
> Will surely recognize
> You, my lord, as the god of
> The land of the rising sun. (Keene, p. 205)

Keene argues that with such diaries the courtiers thus 'intended to ingratiate themselves with a hateful despot', which he calls 'a lamentable perversion of tradition' (p. 206). But such an assessment can hardly be accepted.

In fact, with the pacification of the country under Tokugawa rule (1600–1868), the ability to travel was seen as proof and affirmation of peace and beneficent rule, and the panegyric element becomes dominant. *A Journey to Mount Nikkô* (*Nikkô-zan kikô*), written in 1617 by Karasumaru Mitsuhiro (1579–1638), for instance, records the transfer of the deified Tokugawa Ieyasu's remains to the sumptuous mausoleum of Nikkô. Yet the same approach was used for lesser mortals. Ogyû Sorai (1666–1728) wrote *Travels of Gentlemen Emissaries* (*Fûryû shisha ki*) in 1706 after being sent by Yanagisawa Yoshiyasu (1658–1714) to check the geographical particulars in an inscription Yanagisawa was writing about a place he had never visited. The trip, of course, was unnecessary, as Yanagisawa, sight unseen, had none the less been accurate in all particulars; as Sorai wrote (Keene, p. 344):

> The gentlemanly emissaries, delighting in quiet pleasures,
> Have aimlessly wandered over a space of a thousand *ri*.
> This journey has taught them the greatness of their lord's favour;
> Sated with famous mountains, they return without profit.

Memoirs, then, were written chiefly in this period to commemorate journeys. Such journeys, however, could be occasioned by momentous political events. Thus we have a number of diaries from Japan's invasion of Korea in 1592[29] and, more significantly, records of officials' journeys to ports where western ships were arriving to open Japan forcibly. Yet even on these occasions, the commissioner was more likely to record a poem made at a famous scenic spot along the way than any details of the actual negotiations, as seen, for instance, in the 'Nagasaki Diary' of Kawaji Toshiakira (1801–68) (Keene, pp. 386–91).

Eventually Japan did open to the West, and underwent a major transformation in the guise of the Meiji Restoration. As Carmen Blacker has noted: 'For these astonishing changes we can hold responsible both the impersonal forces of history and the very personal power of certain individual men.'[30] This importance of individuals, both in history and in a historiography that strove to have each geopolitical unit of the country represented by a famous figure in the Restoration, contributed to the revalorization of diaries, memoirs and autobiographies. We can see the re-emerging importance of diaries in that of Kido Takayoshi (1833–77). As Sidney D. Brown describes it:

Kido seems to have begun his diary simply as a memorandum for his own information. Early entries are laconic. The name of the guest is given, and possibly the subject discussed, but little more . . .

As time went on the diary served as a form of psychotherapy for Kido. He vented his frustrations on its pages so often that a man who was by most accounts a genial extrovert and inveterate socializer in real life projected the image of a mordant, chronic complainer in his daily entries. He did become a terribly unhappy man when his proposals began to be rejected in Meiji councils; and his diary became a record of the dark mutterings of a discontented statesman.[31]

Travel diaries, too, took on a new function when the destinations were no longer in Japan but in Europe, and the prophets of modernization, at the time synonymous with westernization, used their accounts of their travels in the west to promote western enlightenment, as seen, for example, in the voluminous writings of Fukuzawa Yukichi.[32]

The Sino-Japanese War of 1894–95 brought about the firm establishment of both a modern newspaper press and the genre of political memoirs in Japan. Unlike the emergence in Japan of the novel and other western literary genres, however, the emergence of modern political memoirs in Japan does not seem to have been an attempt by Japanese to imitate a western genre; instead, as had been the case in the seventh century when the Japanese had adopted *nikki* along with the governmental system of the Chinese, so the *function* of political memoirs came as an integral part of western democratic government. For it is not the keeping of political memoirs that is important, it is the publishing of them. By the end of the nineteenth century we find Japanese politicians leaking information to the press, or publishing unsigned editorials. It was with the same motivations that modern political memoirs appeared, in an attempt to inform and influence public opinion. It was in this context, then, that works such as the *Kenkenroku*,[33] or *The Secret Memoirs of Count Hayashi Tadasu*[34] appeared.

None the less, the old motivations did not completely disappear and, as in the fourteenth century, we find faithful servants recording the thoughts and deeds of their masters for posterity. The best example of this are the Harada–Saionji memoirs. As Harada explained them:

This record was begun from 1929. The basic reason for undertaking it, at the time of the London Treaty, was that in the atmosphere of distortion and falsehood then prevailing, little of the true situation was understood. In particular, His Majesty's [Hirohito's] attitude and the nature of the counsel given him by the *genrô* [Saionji], by those about the throne, and by the Cabinet Ministers were subject to much falsification and misinterpretation

... since from my own position I was cognizant of the true facts, I deemed it essential to record them in written form ... An edited version will be published at some suitable occasion – I should imagine not until some ten or fifteen years after Prince Saionji's death.³⁵

As it turned out, the memoirs did not have to wait so long – they were seized as evidence and translated into English by the International Prosecution Section of the International Military Tribunal for the Far East in 1946, along with the diaries of other government leaders such as Kido Kôichi.³⁶ In fact, to some extent, the Tokyo War Crimes Trial became a battle of the diaries, with Kido attempting to devalue Harada's and using those of Honjô Shigeru to 'ascribe all the responsibility to the military'.³⁷ Political memoirs had become, now quite literally, a matter of life and death.

NOTES

1. 'Conditions and Limits of Autobiography', in James Olney (ed.), *Autobiography: Essays Theoretical and Critical* (Princeton, 1980), p. 28.
2. Maribeth Graybill, 'From Courtly Pastime to Family Business: Portrait Painting by Fujiwara Nobuzane and His Descendants', paper delivered at 1990 College Art Association of America, draft, pp. 6–7.
3. P. van der Loon, 'The Ancient Chinese Chronicles and the Growth of Historical Ideals', in W.G. Beasley and E.G. Pulleyblank (eds.), *Historians of China and Japan* (Oxford, 1961), p. 25.
4. Lien-Sheng Yang, 'The Organization of Chinese Official Historiography: Principles and Methods of the Standard Histories from the T'ang through the Ming Dynasty', in Beasley and Pulleyblank, p. 45.
5. A.F.P. Hulsewé, 'Notes on the Historiography of the Han Period', in Beasley and Pulleyblank, pp. 35–6.
6. Burton Watson, *Ssu-ma Ch'ien: Grand Historian of China* (New York, 1958), p. 40.
7. Pei-yi Wu, *The Confucian's Progress: Autobiographical Writings in Traditional China* (Princeton, 1990), p. 43.
8. Translation in Watson, pp. 57–69.
9. G.W. Robinson, 'Early Japanese Chronicles: The Six National Histories', in Beasley and Pulleyblank, pp. 213–18.
10. Edwin A. Cranston (trans.), *The Izumi Shikibu Diary: A Romance of the Heian Court* (Cambridge, MA, 1969), p. 90.
11. *Chûyûki* (covering the years 1087 to 1138), by Fujiwara no Munetada, from Donald Keene, *Travellers of a Hundred Ages* (New York, 1989), p. 76.
12. Interestingly, the original meaning of the Chinese character for 'historian', *shih*, appears to have represented 'a hand holding a vessel used to contain tallies at archery contests, and that the official designated by this character in Shang times was originally charged with the duty of keeping track of hits at these contests' (Watson, p. 70).
13. D.C. Lau (trans.), *The Analects* (Harmondsworth, 1979), p. 45.
14. Nitta Takako, personal interview with Lynne Miyake, 29 June 1982; Lynne K. Miyake, *Tonomine Shosho Monogatari: A Translation and Critical Study* (unpublished Ph.D. dissertation, University of California, Berkeley, 1985), p. 59.
15. Later texts, whose production was still controlled by the Fujiwara, would mistakenly suggest that it was due to the death of his sister, Empress Anshi, but she was, in fact, alive and quite

active in court politics at this time (Miyake, p. 153).

16. Jin'ichi Konishi, *A History of Japanese Literature* (Princeton, 1986), Vol. II, p. 257.
17. Ivan Morris (trans.), *The Pillow Book of Sei Shônagon* (abridged edition) (Harmondsworth, 1971), p. 221.
18. Gary Ebersole, *Ritual Poetry and the Politics of Death in Early Japan* (Princeton, 1989).
19. Harada Atsuko, 'Murasaki Shikibu nikki no shihatsu: Michinaga-ke eiga no kiroku', *Kokubungaku kô* (June 1971); cited by Richard Bowring, *Murasaki Shikibu: Her Diary and Poetic Memoirs* (Princeton, 1982).
20. William H. McCullough and Helen Craig McCullough (trans.), *A Tale of Flowering Fortunes: Annals of Japanese Aristocratic Life in the Heian Period* (Stanford, 1980), Vol. 1., pp. 43–5.
21. Joseph K. Yamagawa (trans.), *The Ôkagami: A Japanese Historical Tale* (Tokyo, 1966), p. 388.
22. Jennifer Brewster (trans.), *The Emperor Horikawa Diary by Fujiwara no Nagako: Sanuki no Suke Nikki* (Honolulu, 1977), p. 14.
23. Shirley Yumiko Hulvey, 'The Nocturnal Muse: Ben no Naishi Nikki', *Monumenta Nipponica* Vol. 44, No. 4 (1989), p. 392.
24. On the *Takemuki ga ki*, see Keene, pp. 163–72.
25. Wakita Haruko, 'Marriage and Property in Premodern Japan From the Perspective of Women's History', Suzanne Gay (trans.), *Journal of Japanese Studies*, Vol. 10, No. 1 (1984), pp. 87–8.
26. Ishida Yoshisada and Satsukawa Shûji (eds.), *Minamoto Ienaga Nikki zenchûshaku* (Tokyo, 1968); see Keene, pp. 103–6.
27. Herbert Plutschow and Hideichi Fukuda (trans.), *Four Japanese Travel Diaries of the Middle Ages* (Cornell University East Asia Papers), No. 25 (1981), pp. 25–43.
28. Mezaki Tokue, 'Aesthete-Recluses During the Transition from Ancient to Medieval Japan', in Earl Miner (ed.), *Principles of Classical Japanese Literature* (Princeton, 1985).
29. See Keene, pp. 254–9.
30. Preface, *The Autobiography of Yukichi Fukuzawa* (Eiichi Kiyooka, rev. trans.) (New York, 1966), p. v.
31. Translator's Introduction, *The Diary of Kido Takayoshi*, Vol. I: 1868–1871 (Sidney D. Brown and Akiko Hirota, trans.) (Tokyo, 1983), pp. xxiii-xxiv.
32. *Fukazawa's Seikôki* (Fukazawa's Record of Sailing West) is discussed by Keene in his *Zoku Hyakudai no kakyaku* (Kanaseki Hisao, trans.) (Tokyo, 1988), pp. 56–68.
33. Gordon M. Berger (trans.), *Kenkenroku: A Diplomatic Record of the Sino-Japanese War, 1894–95* (Princeton, 1982).
34. A.M. Pooley (ed.) *The Secret Memoirs of Count Hayashi Tadasu* (London, 1915). Pooley calls Hayashi 'the first Japanese statesman to realize and utilize the power' of the press (p. 10), and notes that Hayashi was responsible for the premature publication of the abortive Cassini Convention. On the evolution and role of the press in early modern Japanese politics, see Albert A. Altman, 'Shinbunshi: The Early Meiji Adaptation of the Western-Style News-paper', in W.G. Beasley (ed.), *Modern Japan: Aspects of History, Literature and Society* (London, 1975), pp. 52–66.
35. *Fragile Victory: Prince Saionji and the 1930 London Treaty Issue from the Memoirs of Baron Harada Kumao* (Thomas Francis Mayer-Oakes, trans.) (Detroit, 1968), pp. 46–7.
36. *The Diary of Marquis Kido, 1931–45: Selected Translations into English* (Frederick, MD, 1984).
37. Hane Mikiso (trans.), *Emperor Hirohito and His Chief Aide-de-Camp: The Honjô Diary, 1933–36* (Tokyo, 1982), p. 19.

6

'Let Us Now Praise Famous Men': Political Memoirs and Biography in Canada

ROBERT BOTHWELL

'Let us now praise famous men,' the saying goes, 'and our fathers that begat us', a saying out of Ecclesiasticus beloved in sermon literature, and in the anticipation of the soon-to-be-dead. The effect is, however, seldom what was anticipated. Famous men would prefer to see the out-lines of their biography set down in the sermon or eulogy that follows their passing; and to help the preacher or eulogist they frequently leave behind some rough notes, in the form of an autobiography, for which the eulogist is duly grateful. It is thus through eulogy that self-praise is transformed into praise *tout court*: the first, but not the last, ratification of the deceased's standing as a fragment of the collective memory.

It is natural, indeed aesthetically inevitable, that political auto-biography and its first cousin, political biography, have become some-what suspect. It is perhaps less inevitable that they should also have become intellectually suspect, even disreputable, in the eyes of some historian-critics, for whom the *méthode biographique* is a survivor of an earlier, more primitive, era in historiography.

Prime Minister Mackenzie King, that perceptive observer of life, put the problem thus, when reflecting on the death of his great rival, R.B. (Lord) Bennett in June 1947: 'how strange a parallel in at least one particular our lives were, namely, life devoted almost exclusively to public affairs and very much alone with the result that much of what is richest and best in life, home and happiness, were missed altogether.'[1] King was unwittingly defining what many social historians consider to be the great defect of political biography, namely, the omission of 'what is richest and best' in favour of the poverty of the biographical approach. The energy spent on biography, they might suggest, is better directed to the great waves and curves of *histoire événementielle*. They might go further and argue that political biography exemplifies the argument that 'the evil that men do lives after them', while the good, their daily, humdrum lives, is often interred with their bones.

To judge by the public appeal of such books, remarkably few bookbuyers agree with them, a point to which I shall return. It is also true, as a glance at current Canadian bibliographies shows (the one I use is the quarterly bibliography of Canadiana in the *Canadian Historical Review*), that no area of Canadian historical publishing, be it labour,[2] women's studies, economic history, sport, crime, is without its biographical component – sometimes a very heavy biographical component. Since many of the lives being recounted are truly public lives, they do not lack a political component.

The most striking parallel with political biography is in the fields of sport and crime, where the audience's attention is overwhelmingly focused on individuals – where, indeed, the nature of the *événements* described compels attention to excellence in sports, or to forensic brilliance or turpitude in crime.[3] Of course, I realize that with the improvement of modern technology it could be argued that in sports at least we are witnessing the deployment of carefully crafted chemical aggregations, a true inwardness that might give pause to those who are prone to emphasize the 'scientific' study of history as opposed to mere personality. To that end, I would predict the appearance of a new molecular subdiscipline of history; its thought centre could, perhaps, be located in Transylvania.

It is apparent that there is an inexhaustible desire on the part of publishers to publish, and, to a lesser extent, on the part of consumers to buy, autobiographies and biographies. In Canada they have a great deal of choice, although interestingly, at the top of the heap – the memoirs of governors-general and prime ministers – there is less than might be expected. Of nineteenth-century prime ministers, only Sir Charles Tupper left a memoir, and in the twentieth century up to 1957, only Sir Robert Borden. Mackenzie King intended to write his own life, and set up a small research enterprise to start this work, but at 74 years of age his energy was limited, and he died before he could accomplish anything.[4] Since Mr King intended to incinerate his own diary as he progressed with his book, historians must regard his demise as a peculiar form of providential intervention.

That leaves the prime ministers since 1957. Pearson and Diefenbaker each produced three volumes; their books were highly sought after although, to judge from the number of copies that remained unsold, not quite as much as their publishers anticipated. Pierre Trudeau, it is said, has examined his voluminous papers, stored in Ottawa; but he does not appear to have commenced work systematically to set down his own understanding of himself and his times. With the example of Mackenzie King before him, and his seventieth birthday now behind him, he should perhaps do so. As to Turner, opinions differ, although a kind of political Festschrift was planned to coincide with his retirement from the Liberal leadership and politics. Joe Clark has not yet had the leisure to start work on his memoirs. And as for Brian Mulroney, it is too early yet to comment.

The prime ministers of the twentieth century did not go unchronicled in their own time. English and French-language Liberal journalists narrated the good deeds of Sir Wilfrid Laurier. One of Laurier's biographers later became so annoyed that he changed parties and became a Tory – and was subsequently knighted. Another, L.O. David, was rewarded with a seat in the Senate – creative use for that august body.

By the time Sir Wilfrid's next biographer, Oscar Douglas Skelton, set to work, the Liberals were out of power: only Skelton's *The Day of Sir Wilfrid Laurier* appeared during its subject's lifetime; his majestic *Life and Letters of Sir Wilfrid Laurier* was published in 1921, two years after Sir Wilfrid's death. Skelton was the first academic political biographer in Canada, and Laurier was not his only biographical subject. Skelton also set a precedent, not frequently imitated, of speedy completion; and he also set a professional standard for political biography in Canada. As R.C. Brown has observed, it was not Skelton's admiring portrait of Laurier that was the innovation; 'rather it was . . . the skilfully documented analysis of the political and economic obstacles confronting his hero throughout Laurier's career'.[5]

Skelton's biography called forth the most famous book review in Canadian history, the Winnipeg editor J.W. Dafoe's *Laurier: A Study in Canadian Politics*, published in book form in 1922. Dafoe, as much as Skelton, was an eloquent witness to his times; he pursued the times as well as the lives further in an important study of his patron and Sir Clifford Sifton, Laurier's minister of the interior in 1929. Both Laurier and Sifton are the subject of more recent biographies: in Laurier's case a popular account by Joseph Schull (1965) that added little to what Skelton and Dafoe had set down, and a later, graceful biography by Richard Clippingdale. Sifton received exhaustive treatment in David Hall's two-volume biography. Though Hall was obliged to treat the

complex issues of Sifton's day thoroughly, he demonstrated that
biography had advanced since Skelton's day with a perceptive and
convincing sketch of Sifton's locality and mentality.[6]

Laurier's successor, the introspective Sir Robert Borden, lived long
enough to witness Laurier's biographers at work, but he did not have
to be told how important it was to ensure one's place in history. Borden
first essayed the reinterpretation of his own times in his *Canadian
Constitutional Studies*, originally the Marfleet lectures at the University
of Toronto, and *Canada in the Commonwealth*, similarly delivered as
lectures at Oxford in 1927.[7] Borden had formerly been a part-time
professor; he applied his knowledge of academic work by procuring
the research and editorial assistance of a combination of professors,
archivists and an external affairs official.[8]

Borden's version of the recent past, stressing Canadian prowess and
British obduracy if not obtuseness, did not go unquestioned at the
time, or later. Borden fiercely defended his positions in correspondence
with the recently founded *Canadian Historical Review*; nor did he limit
his watchful eye to history.[9] In 1930 he found it necessary to instruct
the youthful R. MacGregor Dawson in the true meaning of civil service
reform, evidently to the satisfaction of both parties.[10] Later still, Borden
satisfied his epistolary taste by inventing and writing to an imaginary
newspaper, the *Limbo Recorder and Guardian*; the correspondence,
carefully filed, turned up in his papers and was eventually edited and
published by his nephew, Henry Borden, in 1971.[11]

But for years Borden's main project was his own memoirs. After
leaving office Borden hired the Ottawa lawyer W.F. O'Connor, the
draftsman of the War Measures Act, to sort and arrange his papers; the
'O'Connor series' became the foundation of all Borden scholarship. In
October 1928 Borden started dictating his recollections, and remained
at this task for seven years. In the end Borden's energy flagged before
completion, and the memoirs therefore expired in 1920, the year he left
the prime ministership and active politics. That was appropriate, for
what Borden was overwhelmingly concerned to accomplish was a
justification of his public career. The memoirs hardly revealed 'the
whole man', but Borden indirectly revealed his vanity and his tendency
to self-justification.

The memoirs were edited and published, after Sir Robert's death, by
his nephew Henry.[12] Henry evidently did not consider them to be
definitive, for he later helped – through the University of Toronto,
where he was chairman of the board – to sponsor another two-volume
life of his uncle, by the historian R. Craig Brown. It was another

testament to the close connection between autobiography and biography – though the Borden biography at no time suffered from editorial interference or control from the Borden family.

Arthur Meighen, Borden's successor, was not concerned about producing his autobiography, though he did produce a volume of speeches, and co-operated with his eventual biographer, Roger Graham. It was Meighen's classmate, William Lyon Mackenzie King, who would prove to be pre-eminent in the field of Canadian biography.

Officially, King never published an autobiographical word on his own behalf. He always had it in mind to write his memoirs, and his diaries were clearly composed with such a project in mind. The autobiography would act as a kind of filter, after which the great King diary, stretching over 57 years, would be discarded as just so many memoir notes. But we were never to know what King would have written on his own behalf, because as mentioned earlier he died before his enterprise was properly under way. That does not mean that we are deprived, for Mackenzie King had kept an anxious eye on his reputation throughout his political life. He knew that in the eyes of many Canadians, even many who had never met him, his reputation was not unspotted. He had, for example, stayed home during the First World War, and was consequently and unfairly depicted as a slacker.

Almost as soon as he became Liberal leader in August 1919, King was writing to a reporter on the *Toronto Star*, John Lewis, that he should write something about his 'constructive service' to industry during the war. Lewis was not averse; indeed he was promoted from the service of the *Star* in January 1920 to be editor of political literature for the National Liberal Federation.[13] Lewis continued in that post for five years; as a culmination to his service he produced a biography of King in time for the 1925 election. His reward, as for L.O. David before him, was to be made a senator. Happily David was present to witness the event, a testament to how enduring political reward in Canada can be.

It was natural that King should expect Lewis's service to continue, and he turned to the senator for a revision in time for the 1935 federal election. Time and inertia had caught up with Lewis, and he declined the honour on the grounds of ill health. Instead, King turned to Norman McLeod Rogers, a professor of political science at Queen's University. The intention was that Rogers would do the actual drafting, and that in due course Lewis would append his signature to the revised version of Mackenzie King's life story. Rogers worked diligently, prompted and corrected, and eventually supplemented, by his subject. King was particularly anxious to set down his views on social policy as a response to R.B. Bennett's 'new deal' speeches. No consideration was too small for King. In recognition of this fact, his publisher admitted that 'your thoroughness has amazed me; after over forty years of experience I am not easily amazed by the eccentricities of genius'.[14]

There was only one hitch: Senator Lewis refused to have anything to do with the rebirth of his book. 'I was quite amazed at Lewis' attitude', King wrote. 'He seemed quite insane and claimed he was dead and did not care to be resurrected.' One might have thought that Lewis, rather than Rogers, was the ghost; the result was the promotion of the real author to full credit, with a brief acknowledgement of his precursor on the title page.[15]

Such was Canadians' partisan fervour during the 1935 election that 10,000 copies of this rather dreary book were printed and, apparently, disposed of. While the Rogers book was a minor factor in the election – which King won – it is interesting and useful as a key to the inspiration of the Liberal chief, not to mention his abounding vanity and self-absorption. Rogers soon collaborated with King in a larger sphere; elected to Parliament in 1935, he became Minister of Labour.

This was not the end of the tale of Mackenzie King's biographies. Two more were published during his lifetime. One, by the German savant Emil Ludwig, so tickled King's fancy that he gave it the same devoted attention he had bestowed on Rogers' product. Ludwig, who described himself as a portraitist, was granted a 'sitting' with King in November 1943. 'I pray', King wrote in his diary, 'that his thought and hand may be guided in what he writes.' Ludwig, according to the Prime Minister, had 'a genius for portraiture and letters'. According to J.W. Pickersgill, King's principal secretary, 'The result could not be called [Ludwig's] greatest book'.[16]

King's encouragement to Ludwig bore strange fruit. There was, in the wings, another portraitist, European-born, and a refugee. But while Ludwig swam in the mainstream of contemporary European culture, Robert Rumilly's sphere was narrower. A right-wing French refugee, he decided to make his fortune in Canada when he judged things had got too warm for him at home. Rumilly did not allow his convictions to interfere with earning a living; soon, he was publishing flattering portraits of Canadian (especially French-Canadian) political figures. Since the Liberals were the dominant party, Rumilly cut his cloth to suit, and it was no surprise when, in the middle of the Second World War, he approached one of King's ministers for an interview with the Liberal leader. King put him off, and time passed until news reached Rumilly that Ludwig, *universellement connu*, had procured an interview immediately.[17]

It is hard not to sympathize with the spurned biographer. Rumilly was already far advanced in his work, a standard chronicle of King's career, and all he did was to add a final chapter – a chapter that was somewhat different in tone from what had gone before. The final words predicted the Prime Minister's political demise and the obliteration of his party: their fate was 'sealed'. The manuscript was delivered to the publisher and 15,061 copies duly printed – an interesting comment on King's standing in French Canada.

Word of the altered state of Rumilly's feelings reached the Liberal party. It acted quickly. Approaching Rumilly and his publisher, the Liberals bought, through an intermediary, all extant copies of the book, *before* they got to any bookshop, for C$14,500. The book's very existence was kept a secret, while Rumilly moved on to make his living and reputation as a spokesman for the anti-Liberal Union Nationale party in Quebec.[18]

Some years later the Liberals toyed with the idea of republishing Rumilly's work, with a new conclusion – the author having sold *all* rights – so as to embarrass the Union Nationale, but by then Mackenzie King had retired from politics and there seemed little point in resuscitating bygones.[19]

The post-war reputation of King was placed in the hands of the Librarian of Parliament, Arthur Hardy, who penned what is probably the least notable of the biographies of Mackenzie King. Hardy's work failed to satisfy at least one of King's numerous critics. Late in 1950, just after King's death, a former civil servant named Frank Grierson[20] published a 'histology and vision' of King's life. In the final chapter, King is welcomed into heaven by Saint Peter over the protests of 'His Satanic Majesty', who – in the opinion of the author – had a far better claim on King's immortal soul.[21]

King had no intention of leaving his worldly reputation to chance. His diary would act as the foundation for a biographical monument; his will established literary executors with the power to donate all his papers and books 'as I have not directed to be destroyed or otherwise disposed of'.[22] We are not in much doubt as to King's intentions, but the definitive pronouncement was, happily for history, buried in the diary for 1949; it was not read by any of the literary executors until it was too late. One of King's friends did make a considerable fuss over the continued existence of the diary, but her objections were overridden. The diaries were essential, in the executors' judgement, for a balanced biography. They were therefore preserved and, eventually, opened.[23] They remain an invaluable monument to the life of a late Victorian Canadian, an autobiography in fact, if not in intention.

King's rival, R.B. Bennett, Conservative Prime Minister from 1930 to 1935, did not leave memoirs. There was a campaign biography, like King's for the 1935 general election; presumably its sales were rather less than for the Rogers volume. Bennett's one-time crony, Lord Beaverbrook, did write a life, entitled *Friends: Sixty Years of Intimate Personal Relations with Richard Bedford Bennett*, and published it in 1959. A.J.P. Taylor, Beaverbrook's own biographer, described the book as neither good nor a biography; the assessment seems just. It is, however, a memoir, though not a penetrating one.[24]

Louis St Laurent, King's Liberal successor in 1948, left no memoir, though his sister, a teaching nun at a Saskatchewan college, wrote a laudatory memorial of him in her Ph.D. thesis. St Laurent was embarrassed by the effort, and did his best to conceal its existence; its revelation by the press would only humiliate his sister, whom he loved.[25]

The autobiographical enterprises of John G. Diefenbaker and Lester B. Pearson are described in Chapter 13. In both cases researchers, professionally trained, were employed; and in both cases the enterprise took a number of years and a certain amount of official or unofficial support.

The acclaim and publicity that attended the publication of Pearson's and Diefenbaker's memoirs probably inclined others to follow their path. Some, indeed, had already embarked on it. Judy LaMarsh and Walter Gordon, two of Pearson's ministers, left behind memoirs to demonstrate their own strengths and their former leader's failings.[26] Donald Fleming, Diefenbaker's Minister of Finance, was rumoured to have tried for years to obtain a publisher for his recollections. They eventually emerged in 1985, over 1,300 pages long, and heavy with Fleming's accumulated sense of grievance against his former leader.[27] As far as is known, these three memoirs were written with little professional help.

The same cannot be said for the memoirs of some of Pierre Trudeau's ministers. One, Don Jamieson, left behind a diary which has now been published. Jean Chrétien enjoyed assistance from Ron Graham in writing his memoirs – and very successful they were, with queues in front of bookshops for autographs from the author. Jack Horner was assisted by Diefenbaker's and Pearson's chief researcher,

John Munro. Eugene Whelan followed the same well-trodden path. In the case of Chrétien and some others, such as Don Johnston, it was clear that the memoirs were less an epitaph – though certainly a eulogy – than a campaign document for struggles dreamt of, but, as yet, unfought. The assistance received was less historical in nature than editorial – rather like speech writing, in fact. It is only too bad that the rigours and time lags of publication remove the immediacy that accompanies speech writing, as in the case of the long-suffering speech writer, toiling for an ungrateful minister, who handed his chief a speech at the last minute, and then sat back to wait for page four, which contained the immortal words, 'That's it, you bastard. I quit!'

NOTES

1. King diary entry for 27 June 1947, in J.W. Pickersgill and D.F. Forster, *The Mackenzie King Record* (Toronto, 1970), Vol. 4, pp. 56–7.
2. A glance at the 'social and labour history' category of the June 1988 issue of *Canadian Historical Review* discloses 19 books or articles (but mainly books) that are biographical in nature.
3. The same June 1988 issue of *Canadian Historical Review* lists such gems as *Greenspan: The Case for the Defence*, by Greenspan; *Paddy Nolan: He left them laughing when he said Goodbye*; *Never Let Go: The Tragedy of Kristy MacFarlane*; 'George Goulding: A Case Study in Sporting Excellence'; *Study: The Incredible Obsession of Brian Molony* (not a satire on the Prime Minister), and so forth.
4. C.P. Stacey, *A Very Double Life: The Private World of Mackenzie King* (Toronto, 1976), pp. 214–15.
5. R.C. Brown, 'Biography in Canadian History', *Historical Papers*, Vol. 69, No. 2 (1980), pp. 241–5.
6. John W. Dafoe, *Laurier, A Study in Canadian Politics* (Toronto, 1922); Joseph Schull, *Laurier, The First Canadian* (Toronto, 1965); Richard Clippingdale, *Laurier, His Life and World* (Toronto, 1979); David J. Hall, *Clifford Sifton* (2 vols.) (Vancouver, 1981, 1985).
7. *Canadian Constitutional Studies* (Toronto, 1922), and *Canada in the Commonwealth* (Oxford, 1929).
8. R.C. Brown, *Robert Laird Borden: A Biography* (Toronto, 1980), Vol. 2.
9. Ibid., pp. 203–4.
10. Dawson altered his conclusions and emerged on good terms with Sir Robert.
11. Henry Borden (ed.), *Letters to Limbo* (Toronto, 1971).
12. *Robert Laird Borden: His Memoir* (2 vols.) (Toronto, 1938).
13. Mark Moher, 'The "Biography" in Politics: Mackenzie King in 1935', *Canadian Historical Review*, Vol. LV (June 1975), p. 240.
14. George Morang to King, 18 March 1935, in ibid., p. 245.
15. Ibid., pp. 244–5.
16. Quoted in J.W. Pickersgill, *The Mackenzie King Record* (Toronto, 1960), Vol. 1, p. 588.
17. Georges-Emile LaPalme, *Le bruit des choses reveillées* (Montreal, 1970), Vol. 1, p. 327.
18. Ibid., pp. 326–8.
19. Ibid.
20. Grierson described himself as an Ottawa resident of 30 years' standing who had first entered 'the east Block' where the Prime Minister's office was located around 1920. Frank Grierson, *William Lyon Mackenzie King: Histology and Vision* (Ottawa, n.d. [1950 or 1951]), p. 89.
21. Ibid., pp. 109–10.

22. King's will was published in a 'Mackenzie King Memorial Edition' of *The Canadian Liberal*, Vol. 3, No. 5 (September 1950), pp. 53ff.
23. One of the executors, J.W. Pickersgill, came across King's real intention very late: he made a note opposite the diary entry, initialled it, and dated the note. On King's intentions, see Stacey, *A Very Double Life*, pp. 12–13.
24. A.J.P. Taylor, *Beaverbrook: A Biography* (London, 1972), p. 639.
25. National Archives of Canada, St Laurent Papers. To this the historian is tempted to add that it would certainly have illuminated the degree-granting standards of her Alma Mater.
26. Judy LaMarsh, *Memoirs of a Bird in a Gilded Cage* (Toronto, 1969); Walter Gordon, *A Political Memoir* (Toronto, 1977).
27. Donald Fleming, *So Very Near* (2 vols.) (Toronto, 1985).

7
Rulers of the Waves: British Naval Memoirs

BARRY GOUGH

Marshal Foch said he never wrote his memoirs because he had nothing to hide. British naval officers wrote many memoirs and they had much to hide, or to keep quiet about.[1] The recollections or memoirs of a number of officers and men of Britain's Senior Service contributed piecemeal over four centuries until 1919 reinforce the presupposition that naval memoirs are not marginal but mainstream to English historical literature. Naval memoirs are not official history; they are individual expressions from highly individualistic persons: they are testimonies of lives lived in distant locations and in difficult circumstances, in peace and in war, in times of government favours, and in periods of savage retrenchment. They are attempts to imprint personal experience on the corporate memory not only of the Service but of the nation and even humanity. They are examples of how man seeks posterity by the written word. Almost invariably these memoirs are written after achievement, great or small. They are after the fact. That many of them were not published at the time, but were brought forward by record societies or devoted relatives or close friends gives added value to the desire of the individual or survivors to make a statement about the progress of humankind. Far from being a line of enquiry into the anecdotal or the record of individual heroics, the study of a nation's naval memoirs may yield a result that is greater than the sum of its parts.

The earliest English naval memoirs or recollections were known only to the writers and perhaps to their family and friends. Only later through the publications of the Navy Records Society, founded in 1893 by distinguished historians and naval officers, have these pioneering records been known to the wider world. Perhaps the first naval memoir came from the pen of Phineas Pett (1570–1647), a shipwright and commissioner of the Navy. The best text of it survived owing to the energies of the diarist and naval administrator Samuel Pepys, who copied it. Written over long intervals of time, it was compiled for motives that are difficult to detect. It was probably commenced to explain Pett's defence regarding a royal inquiry into a disputed ship contract in 1609, and afterwards the memoir was continued partly for the author's recreation and partly for the edification of his children.[2] Other officers kept journals and letterbooks, and all officers were obliged to file their report of proceedings and their remarks on navigation at the end of a ship's commission. But very few for this early period seem to have concerned themselves with writing an auto-biography or a memoir. The Navy Records Society has published Bartholomew James's *Journal*, 1752–1828, Sir William Dillon's *Narrative*, 1790–1839 and James Trevenen's *Memoir*, 1759–90, but they hardly constitute a corpus of literature, disparate as they are individually in focus and intent.

The first published English naval memoir seems to be that of the great administrator Samuel Pepys. Entitled 'Memoirs Relating to the State of the Royal Navy of England, for Ten Years, Determin'd December 1688' (printed in London in 1690), this was a *pièce justificative*, composed after Pepys had been obliged to resign the secretaryship of the Admiralty following the 1688 Revolution. The only book by the celebrated diarist published during his lifetime, *Pepys' Memoirs* as the work is called, specifically concerns Pepys' last years of naval administration. It is a fragment of history, part of what Pepys intended to complete on the naval history of England during the Dutch wars. The immediate occasion for *Pepys' Memoirs* was controversial rather than historical: they were published to defend the Special Commission of 1686 on naval affairs and its members, including Pepys, against 'a strong combination' . . . 'raised for the discrediting of the same'. The work succeeded in diminishing the parliamentary opposition. It also served to redeem Pepys in the critical eyes of many who saw his era of administration as one of mis-management.[3] It signifies the political intent in naval administrative memoirs, a theme recurrent in the work of Sir John Briggs, of which more below. But in one area Pepys' memoir stands alone: in financial value. In 1989 a London antiquarian bookseller offered a prime copy of the first edition for $US3,500 – a price its author would claim worth every penny.

The Royal Navy was (and is) a corporate entity, and the first major naval memoirs came as a form of corporate memoir, the first of which was John Campbell's *Lives of the Admirals and other Eminent Seamen* (1742–44), which went through many subsequent editions. The collective biography of the eighteenth century rested on contributions filed by the individual entrants. Three prime examples of this subgenre can be mentioned. The first is John Charnock's six-volume *Biographia Navalis; or Impartial Memoirs of the Lives and Characters of Officers of the Navy of Great Britain*, published in 1794. This recounted the great naval lives from 1660 to the date of publication. Charnock, a Barbados-born, Winchester and Merton College-educated naval volunteer, re-entered civilian life after inheriting a considerable fortune which he 'quickly lost in a life of dissipation'. Thereafter he had to rely on his pen for a living. 'The rewards of his writings, however', records Peter Kemp, 'were unable to keep pace with his debts and he was committed to the King's Bench prison where he died' in 1807.[4] One wonders what role drink plays in the writing of memoirs; fortunately for naval memoirs poor Charnock completed his task before the gaol gate closed shut on him. Charnock's goals were highly honourable. He wrote in his preface that historical memoirs of his era were of heroes, and in these works calumny and panegyric were often used. He classified the memoir as 'this monster in literature'. To this he hastily added, 'The more exalted the rank, and meritorious the service of any particular personage, the greater extent does he furnish for those lists in which the tournament is to be held for the establishment or destruction of his [the subject's] posthumous reputation.' He continues, in a cautionary note:

It probably would be, in some respects, a wise and wholesome act of literary legislation were it [the memoir] expressly forbid, under pain of being everlastingly consigned to moths and book-worms and promulgation of opinion as to individual merits or delinquency till time had mellowed the asperity of prejudice, as well as cooled the warmth of partiality and friendship; for it is a certain and serious truth, that among the worst means of attaining a true knowledge of a man's character, are the accounts written of him during his life, or soon after his decease.

Biography, by contrast, claimed Charnock, explored 'those inmost recesses of private life'. As for his scope, he took all naval commanders since the Restoration. He included in this collective work anecdotes of the public service in time of war, and added that they could not be expected of officers 'in time of profound peace', which is obvious. This was a distinguished and renowned contribution to letters, and the British Museum and the College of Arms aided him in the enterprise, and so, too, did the officers and their relatives. It was a magnificent achievement.

Charnock's work was followed by Lieutenant John Marshall's *Royal Naval Biography*, first published in 1823 and a work which went through numerous editions. It carried the subtitle, *Memoirs of the Services of all the Flag Officers . . . whose Names Appeared on the Admiralty List of Sea Officers*, and it included historical and explanatory notes, details of naval actions and events for the period of 1763 to the date of publication. A movable feast, this was a work of undoubted dedication by an enterprising officer on half-pay, who after 1815 devoted his time to compiling this work which was finally completed in 1835. It occupies 12 volumes. Marshall was not naive in his approach, and quoted Dr Samuel Johnson on his title page:

Failures, however frequent, may admit of extenuation and apology. To have attempted much is always laudable, even when the enterprise is above the strength that undertakes it. To deliberate whenever I doubted, to enquire whenever I was ignorant, would have protracted the understanding without end, and perhaps without improvement. I saw that one enquiry only gave occasion to another, that book referred to book, that to search was not always to find, and to find was not always to be informed; and that thus to pursue perfection, was, like the first inhabitants of Arcadia, to chase the sun, which, when they had reached the hill where he seemed to rest, was still beheld at the same distance from them.

A delightful image, reminiscent of Sisyphus. Marshall devoted his life to recording particulars of the lives of his contemporaries in the profession, and it seems that herein lies the key. He had gone to sea at the age of nine and knew many of these men. Their gallant exploits were saved from obscurity by Marshall's endeavours. He frankly wrote that the promotion of their merit was important in encouraging a faith in the Navy and thus the nation. Glory was tied to national security. Their lives were meritorious examples for youth. He sets out to avoid the panegyric and the censure. He begins with the Duke of Clarence, the Lord High Admiral of the British Fleet, then proceeds to John Jervis, Earl of St Vincent, the highest-ranking Admiral next to the Duke and a great sea fighter, and then works his way downward to the more junior persons. This work is a bit of a Who's Who, and contains addresses (but not clubs) and lists family as well as political connections. Since this work encompasses the great age of fighting sail it is a veritable treasure trove for scholars working on the French and Napoleonic Wars and the naval war of 1812.

We now come to a slightly less generous, more self-serving work, by James Ralfe, *The Naval Biography of Great Britain consisting of Historical Memoirs of those Officers of the British Navy who distinguished themselves during the Reign of His Majesty George III*, published in four volumes in 1828. This work was floated on subscription, by over 100 subscribers. Maps of battles were included and also longer memoirs. The scope of the work was to review the professional services of those great men – about 30 per volume – Rodney, Howe, Hood, Duncan, St Vincent and Nelson among others. The emphasis is on ability, not on political connections. These men are described as 'models of valour, fortitude and perseverance; in short, of every military excellence and virtue. Such men never die; their examples and actions are always before us, encouraging us by the one to imitate the other.' Like Charnock and Marshall, Ralfe decries the cynics:

though [these officers] have ever been the theme of universal panegyric, there never was a period in which were displayed greater skill, courage, and enterprise: at no period of our history were there ever so many instances of the superiority of British seamen; at no period of our history were there ever so many instances of general and individual bravery evinced; at no period of our history were there ever so many brilliant examples of devotion to their king and country displayed, as during the time embraced by this work. Throughout the whole of that long and eventful period they always maintained the characteristics of British valour, naval and scientific skill, justice and clemency in the hour of victory, and a disposition to lighten to the evils of war . . . What benefits have they not thereby ensured to posterity! Who is there that is not astonished at their achievements, and proportionably proud of their bravery and constancy?

Amen to all that, and Rule Britannia!

In truth, Charnock, Marshall and Ralfe were part of a very much larger genre of memoir-biography – biographical dictionaries. Among them you can find the general ones, the statesmen ones, the women-of-wit-and-beauty ones and the idiots and invalids ones – all of them before Sir Sidney Lee and *The Dictionary of National Biography*. But the tradition of the collective biographical memoir did not die out, and H. Algernon Lockyer put together a memoir of distinguished naval commanders (1842) and Sir John Barrow, a Secretary of the Admiralty, wrote many portraits of sailors based on testimonials written by their subjects. William O'Byrne's *Naval Biographical Dictionary*, 1849 (enlarged, but incomplete, 1861), contained up-to-date details of service, and reports by sailors of their exploits: it is the sole memoir of countless young lieutenants engaged in little-known gunboat actions on the *Chesapeake*, some pirate chases in the China seas, or a storm in the Bermuda triangle. The collective memoir continued well into the Victorian age. For example, in 1890 John Brighton published a slim work entitled *Personal Recollections of three British Admirals*, and the three worthies were Broke-Middleton, Dunsanay, and Nova Scotia's Provo Wallis. This did not prevent the personal recollections being compiled by individuals, of course, that of Provo Wallis being an example: John George Brighton's *Admiral of the Fleet Provo W.P. Wallis: A Memoir* (London, Hutchinson, 1892) was compiled from interviews with and memoirs by the great 'Bluenoser' (Nova Scotian). In this instance, John George Brighton had been motivated to investigate the history of the War of 1812 as he had heard or read very little about it in England. His Wallis *Memoir*, it hardly need be said, did not make much of a dent in English historical appreciation of that forgotten war at sea.

We now come to the memoir of England's greatest naval hero. On 21 October 1805, 'England's glory', the Right Honourable Horatio, Lord Viscount Nelson, Vice-Admiral of the White, Knight of the Order of the Bath, Duke of Bronte in Sicily, and so on, died at the memorable battle of Trafalgar. Immediately writers rushed to publish his 'memoirs'. The first, an anonymous *Authentic Memoirs of the Brave and Much-Lamented Admiral Lord Nelson, the Idol of his Country . . .*, was published before the end of the year.[5] Even before steam presses, lithographic reproduction and computer typesetting, the publication of instant memoirs was possible: by the end of the year no fewer than 12 'memoirs', 'biographical memoirs' and 'lives' of Nelson had appeared.[6] Much of the content of those works derived from official dispatches and gazettes, and very little of it had Nelson's own story. Until Robert Southey's *Life of Nelson* (1813), long the classic account, established the compelling story as a work of great literature, many of the early perspectives were hastily compiled and designed to sell to an eager public – one that still exists in Britain today, we might note. Moreover, not until Southey's 1854 version did there appear the 'Memoirs of Nelson's Services. Written by Himself'.[7] David Hannay applied further touches to Southey, in an edition of 1897, which includes a codicil to Nelson's will. J.M. Dent's edition of the same work in 1906 was perhaps the first to boast an index. Illustrations – engravings and woodcuts – had appeared from the beginning. But each publisher added something new: a snippet from 'a nephew of Nelson' graced James Ridgeway's *Notes on the Character of Admiral Lord Nelson* (1861).[8] George Lathom Browne's *Nelson, the Public and Private Life . . . as Told by Himself, his Comrades and by Friends* (1891) included no fewer than 11 appendices, including details of the Wellington and Nelson interview.[9] The 'Memoirs of Nelson's Services' that Southey's 1854 edition printed was one of the few things that Nelson wrote about himself. After the Battle of the Nile, Nelson sent the editors of the leading naval periodical, *The Naval Chronicle*, at their request, a characteristic 'Sketch of his Life' as did Collingwood after Trafalgar. Nelson's brief, astringent record of his career contains none of the vanity that some have attributed to the great fighter and tactician; rather, it is a steady-handed, beautifully written and spare account of his progression through the Service. It speaks, as one would expect, of duty and honour.

As a Ph.D. student at the University of London I sought to find out how the material bases or foundations of British naval authority – coal, spars, provisions, supplies and the like – contributed to the rise of Esquimalt, Vancouver Island, as a naval base.[10] I was obliged to read a good deal of what is now called international history, and to study Anglo-Russian and especially Anglo-American relations. My first obligation, however, was to understand the Royal Navy. Where does one begin to read the history of the Royal Navy? I had reviewed Samuel Pepys' celebrated diary as an exercise in historiography, and I had read Mr Secretary Nicholas's correspondence about the Duke of Buckingham's ship-money levies; but these seventeenth-century readings were a pretty flimsy start. A kindly Rear-Admiral in the Royal Navy, P.W. Brock – himself British Columbia-born, and the son of the dean of the University of British Columbia – became my 'in-Service' mentor on these things. He put me on to reading Victorian memoirs written by admirals who had been on the Pacific Station, as that command was called. Among these were *Two Admirals*, written by Admiral John Moresby, the record of a 100 years' naval service by Sir Fairfax Moresby (after whom Moresby Island, in the Queen Charlotte Islands, off the coast of British Columbia is named) and his son John.[11] This book was first published by John Murray in 1909. It was dedicated to John Moresby's grandson, Fairfax Donald Mackeson, Naval Cadet, RN, with this added inscription: 'Fear God. Honour the King.' Also among these books was Mary Augusta Phipps Hornby Egerton's *Admiral of the Fleet, Sir Geoffrey Phipps Hornby, G.C.B.: A Biography*, one of the finest examples of an autobiographical memoir

of filial devotion that one could find, and on such a grand subject too.[12]
This central figure in the 'pig war' over the San Juan Islands (off the
coast of Washington, USA) was one of the pre-eminent sailors of the
late Victorian era. These books were records of individual lives in a
very large and fluctuating national armed service. From these or other
memoirs I never was able to find out how the Navy worked. I only
discovered *that* by reading Admiralty Board Minutes in the Public
Record Office, Kew. There in the minutes of the Lords Commissioners
of the Admiralty one could follow the processes of thought about how
Britannia's will was being exercised in its multitudinous obligations.
First came the in-letters: a report on an act of piracy on some distant
shore, a record of some slaver driven on to the reefs off some mosquito-
infested coast, or a statement by some aggrieved British trader against
local insurgents or pirates. Then would come the out-letters, the
official view written after considerable deliberation: send more gun-
boats, file some strongly worded diplomatic protest, and almost
invariably, back the man on the spot. It was in the last of these that I
uncovered the secret of how the Navy in the Victorian age worked:
almost invariably the young lieutenant or the senior captain on some
faraway station knew what to do in the circumstances; he had the
canny ability to know what their Lordships in Whitehall would or
would not approve. Because the Navy was the tool, so to speak, of the
Foreign Office, the officer commanding a sloop-of-war or a gun vessel
had to be able to anticipate how his actions would be received. Failure
to comply with instructions, or to exceed what was morally or
professionally acceptable in the circumstances, was sure to result in
censure, embarrassment, unemployment and exclusion. It has been
said of the British public schools that they could kick you out but
would never let you down; the same was true of the Navy, for it was not
in the interest of the Senior Service to have embittered, unemployed
officers making public complaints about the Service. The point is that
the naval memoir, which is itself based on day-to-day journals by the
man on the spot, supplements very richly the official report, filed by
that man at the time. When one couples the two – the memoir and the
report – the historian gains an enhanced understanding of the circumstances of the day, a heightened appreciation of the circumstances,
often trying, in which the *Pax Britannica* was being exercised.

    The British naval memoir reached its pre-eminence in the Victorian
age and continued to be a form of literature well into the mid-twentieth
century. One can say that its rise as a genre and its modification as a
literary form followed the rise of the Royal Navy as the arbiter of world

influence in the late eighteenth and throughout the early nineteenth and twentieth centuries; axiomatically one can postulate that its gradual disappearance from the bookshops reflects the less dominant role naval affairs have taken in British and international relations in recent years. The British naval memoir, too, reached its pre-eminence in the era of inexpensive printing. Steam-powered printing, which made *The Times* of London a national daily by the mid-1840s, delivered throughout England by courtesy of the precursors of British Rail, allowed for inexpensive mass production. In an era when naval and military heroes could obtain front-page newspaper coverage, their memoirs were equally popular. No means exists of determining sales and print runs, but from what can be gleaned from reviews one can only speculate that these naval memoirs were sought-after collectors' items for the Victorian and Edwardian gentleman's library, besides being obvious acquisitions for the growing number of institutes, learned societies, clubs and public and private libraries. The growth of public education and of literacy, the emergence of a public consciousness about naval affairs and national and imperial security on and over the seas, and the growth of the naval reserve and cadets are other reasons why naval memoirs became significant as publication achievements.

That having been said, it is important to differentiate between the work that could be read for vicarious interest – the travelogue, of which Philip Howard Colomb's *Slave Catching in the Indian Ocean* (1873) is a first-class example – and that relating to national and imperial defence, Admiral Percy Scott's being a sterling example.[13] Naval officers, if not on half-pay and perhaps thereby confined to the beach, were great travellers. Some became celebrated travel writers – Sir Basil Hall in South America and on the Kamchatka coast of Siberia is but one example. Others wrote on specific themes. For instance, certain naval officers were keen sportsmen, and their memoirs reflect this. Mention can be made of a premier example: Admiral Sir William Kennedy, KCB. The recipient of the Royal Humane Society's medal, he was author of the excellent memoir *Hurrah for the Life of a Sailor! Fifty Years in the Royal Navy*, first published in 1900.[14] The book was written to 'give some grown-up boys an idea of a sailor's life'. That life during hostilities and peacetime had included the Crimean War, the Opium Wars, and service on the Pacific, Newfoundland and East Indies stations. Kennedy wrote extensively of his adventures for *Boy's Own Paper* and even more so for that large public interested in hunting and fishing. He wrote four books on sport, travel and adventure in the

Pacific, South America, Newfoundland and the West Indies.[15] Taken together, Admiral Kennedy's literary contributions are considerable. His equal love of the Service and of stream and field are to be found on each and every page. No critic of the Service, no challenger of authority, Kennedy's memoirs are at once a delight and a realization that not always did one record one's experience with a political intent; in Kennedy's case he sought to tell others how he had had fun and to show others how they could do likewise. His last preface was written in his stream-side sporting chalet in Sweden; he then disappears from history, perhaps closer to the Naval Valhalla than others.[16]

In pre-radio, pre-television days, table conversation and recreational reading must have been more widely extended than nowadays. Subjects for discussion must have focused on imperial or national derring-do. In the eighteenth century, for instance, we know that Admiral Edward Vernon was famous for his naval exploits against the Spanish in the Caribbean; later vilified by the lower deck for watering down the rum portion, 'Old Grog' was a hero to Parliament, press and public.[17] The same was true of, say, Richard Howe, who in addition to his skills in naval warfare, negotiated and otherwise put down mutinies in the Navy, or of Earl St Vincent, the famous fighting admiral and distinguished naval administrator. The attention given Lord Nelson was universal and remains celebrated to this day. In the late nineteenth century – the heyday of the naval memoir – the vicarious was being balanced with the political. Philip Colomb or John Moresby could write their 'cruise reports', to coin a term, but the likes of a Humphrey J. Smith could go one step farther in his 1933 recollections and state that the Edwardian Navy as a World Police Force ('with a capital W', as he put it for emphasis) was hardly ready for battle, that the senior officers knew nothing of active naval warfare and even less of strategy and tactics, and that the Service was due for the shake-up which Sir John (Jacky) Fisher brought to it in the first decade of the twentieth century.[18] Admiral Sir Percy Scott's devastatingly critical *50 Years in the Royal Navy*, published in 1919 after the First World War and the inconclusive Battle of Jutland, took many shots at those who stood in the way of the Navy's reform and regeneration. Scott was a gunnery expert, and his work is mainly a description of his efforts to improve gunnery in the British fleet. He details the conservatism and opposition to change in the Navy, the resulting problems, and politicians' meddling in technical matters. His intent was to clarify matters of vital concern to the nation and to expose the weaknesses and the defects of administration. His book advocated the recruitment of an educated, practical and progressive seaman, not the development of a cumbersome, over-organized naval staff. It derogated the civilian intrusion into the Navy, and explains Lord Jellicoe's role in reorganizing and modernizing the Navy. The commander of British naval forces at Jutland was in need of such support, for Jellicoe was then under much criticism by press, Admiralty Boards, and in-Service rivals for failure to defeat the Imperial German High Seas Fleet in the famous encounter in the North Sea in 1916. All these complaints were legitimate enough, but in a sense ahistorical, *ex post facto*. In preparing his invaluable *Naval Administrations, 1827 to 1892: The Experience of 65 Years* (London, 1897), Sir John Henry Briggs, a chief clerk of the Admiralty, wrote that he was driven to record his experiences because in his view there was a serious necessity for an adequate Navy, thoroughly prepared and ready for war to protect the best interests of England and the Empire. Happily, Briggs concluded, the rejuvenation of the Service was under way by 1897. Political will or lack of it, administrative talents or lack of them, threat of war or its absence – these to Briggs were the key to Britain's preparedness at sea. As he saw it from his desk, the most important factor was the statesmanship and leadership of the First Lord of the Admiralty, a member of Cabinet. The fortunes of the British fleet depended on political will.

Generally speaking, the Victorian naval memoir was not full of complaint about Lords of Admiralty and politicians. Rather, the choice of words was invariably guarded, and those admired in the Service were praised while those not admired were omitted from the discussion. This tells us something about navies: 'Fear God. Honour the King' was the Royal Navy's motto. While personalities were admired, even encouraged (or tolerated) within the Service, the larger obligation was to the Crown and the state. The individual officer answered to his superiors but he held a Royal commission. In such circumstances, he zealously kept his secrets.

The ties that bound were not only those of commission, duty, honour and the traditions of the Service; they were linked by those of class. These are very deep waters indeed for a historian, but by and large the officers in the Navy were persons of landed or mercantile wealth, with the occasional parson's son or customs officer's lad thrown in. Such persons joined the Navy as volunteers first class at the tender age of 12, and were put under the immediate care of the ship's captain. In a few years they became midshipmen, and would then qualify, after examination, for a commission. By the age of 20 or 21 they might have become lieutenant, RN, and promotion to commander and captain would follow in due course, depending on circumstances, patronage, capability and good fortune. The progressions would follow, with time and increasing rarity, to rear-admiral, vice-admiral, admiral, and admiral of the fleet. Michael Lewis in his *Social History of the Navy* has provided an excellent analysis of the social mix and promotion rates of these persons.[19] Together they formed one of the distinct and significant segments in British society.

Of course, the exceptions to the rule often obtain more attention than the norm. The memoir of Henry D. Capper, OBE, RN, is very unusual. It is a memoir of a sailor who went aft – *Aft – From the Hawsehole*, as his record is entitled.[20] This work was dedicated to his wife, 'Whose sweetness of disposition has made home delightful; and whose unflagging interest and support, always given me in every enterprise, have made possible any little success in my life'. But read between the lines: this work is not dedicated to a patron but to a spouse, and rightly so – for poor Mrs Henry D. Capper (Christian and maiden names not given) had to endure a lifetime of her husband's class-conscious quest for upward mobility. This memoir is a record of naval service, largely of an undistinguished sort. But it is essentially an explanation of how thin-skinned Henry, rebuffed by a cousin who carried a commission in the Queen's Navy, determined at all costs to be similarly commissioned. Here then is not the story of a Sir Joseph Porter, KCB, polishing up the handle on the big front door, but of a determined lad who did the near impossible: go from able seaman to lieutenant-commander, a wearisome personal progress of some 30 years.

Capper never had a patron, and he did not come from one of the great naval, military or even clerical families that gave England her sea warriors. He was born in Portsmouth in 1855, the son of a dockyard employee. He went to sea at a very early age, and sailed in the 1869 Flying Squadron, thus visiting many of the great imperial dockyards and arsenals. In 1873, aged 18, he went to Port Royal, Jamaica, and joined the sloop *Spartan*. There young Capper took up one of the enduring passions of his life: temperance. This was not a chosen road to Service advancement! But Henry induced many sailors and boys to join the newly founded Good Templars, and a ship's Lodge was formed. 'Stopping grog' meant appreciably diminished punishments and higher ship efficiency. The ship soon lost its reputation as 'the drinkenest ship in the Squadron'. It was on the North American and West Indies station that Capper was able to meet but not rub shoulders with the likes of Charles Beresford, MP, Captain John Fisher (later

Admiral Lord Fisher of Kilverstone), Admiral Sir William King-Hall, and Captain Richard King. Here too he was able to extend his good works – founding a Sailors' Home in Bermuda. Here also he began to write of his experiences in the form of a little booklet, *The Sailors' Rest, and How I Spent Three Days There.* These good deeds put him in touch with Miss Agnes Weston, rightly dubbed 'The Mother of the Navy', editor of the *Brigade News* (later *Ashore and Afloat*), and also with Miss Sarah Robinson of Portsmouth, also a promoter of temperance and British Sailors' Homes.

Henry Capper took the seaman-gunners course at HMS *Excellent*, Portsmouth, and qualified as a gunner. He served as a gunboat gunner on the west coast of Africa, and became a warrant officer. This was not enough however. Ambition stalked poor Capper, and he had no desire to serve years on the quarterdeck with no prospect of promotion aft. But he built up his sea time – on the China Seas, and as gunner in HMS *Canada* on the North American and West Indies station. There he renewed his acquaintance with Lieutenant Harry Boldero of HMS *Pylades*, who 'succumbed to the malign effects of the Newfoundland fogs' and whose mother, incidentally, wrote a review of his life under the title *A Young Heart of Oak* (London, 1891). This service took him to places of enchantment: to Admiral Benbow's grave in Kingston, Jamaica, to Quebec, where Capper rightly noted that Admiral Saunders had made possible James Wolfe's feat of arms, and to Charlottetown, Prince Edward Island, to celebrate the good Queen's Jubilee. At the latter place Capper had to be reminded by Captain Lewis Beaumont that there were officers and there were officers – and that warrant officers were inferior socially to their service juniors, midshipmen and clerks. Such 'undisguised social ostracism of myself and colleagues because we had risen from the hawsehole', recalled Capper, left another wound on his delicate psyche, but fuelled his desire to end such unjust and unfair discrimination.

Capper returned to England and had another spell in the gunnery school *Excellent*, and was installed in his career. He informs the reader of the history of men in his plight, remarking that the last warrant officer to be commissioned was Admiral Sir John Kingcome, sometime Commander-in-Chief at Esquimalt. The system of 'tarpaulins' dated from Cloudesley Shovel, a shoemaker's apprentice who became an admiral during Queen Anne's reign (1702–14). (A 'tarpaulin' was a captain who had risen by promotion through service in the Navy, as opposed to 'gentleman' captains who in Tudor and Stuart times were courtiers appointed directly.) Benbow, Lawson, May and James Cook were among the gallery of 'tarpaulins'. Capper quotes Campbell's *Lives of the Admirals*[21] that contribution to the public service had often resulted in the Crown's due reward, a system that had lapsed in the Victorian era. Even gallantry could not bring promotion in a class-ridden service. Denied promotion, Capper took up his pen, and lobbied the sailor-politicians such as Admiral Richard Charles Mayne, MP, Commander G.E. Price, MP, and Lord George Hamilton, the First Lord of the Admiralty. Subsequently, a Committee on Manning the Navy was set up, and reforms were finally effected by the Selborne scheme in the early twentieth century. We must not leave this sketch of Capper and the perilous climb up the 'tree of promotion' without observing that he was of the Navy but never really of the officer corps, at least not an insider. Earl Jellicoe of Scapa, writing in the preface to *Aft – From the Hawsehole*, gives us a very distant and cold appreciation of Capper. Doubtless a number of British leaders had been obliged to put up with Capper's needling. A frank female had once told Capper that she disliked his futile attempts to subvert the Navy and take it out of the hands of the nation's ruling families. Capper retired in 1910, and never really had a proper command at sea. And one cannot imagine him arriving in a phaeton at the 'In and Out Club' or speaking on any defence matter at the Royal United Service Institution. None the less, his memoir is a unique document which exposes the prejudices and the traditions of the Navy. A version of the 'Snakes and Ladders' game was sold by Hamleys in London 100 years ago for a shilling in which it took 83 squares for a young John Bull to climb from entry to admiral, a distinctly anomalous progression, as Capper's book explains.[22]

Many naval memoirs were never published in their time. Good memoirs of officers of the Royal Navy are rare; those of Canadians serving in the Royal Navy are rarer still. *At Sea and By Land: The Reminiscences of William Balfour Macdonald R.N.* which finally reached print in 1983, the autobiographical vignette of a Victoria-born Canadian of a prominent family, is a treasure.[23] As Macdonald confessed in tones of Scottish mirthfulness:

I know that autobiographies are usually written by those who have gained distinction in life, in other words, those people of sufficient importance to have their obituary notice carefully prepared and all ready to pop into the daily papers when the distinguished life has ended. I am afraid I am not in that category, but I am tempted to write down adventures and happenings that can never occur again to anyone, for in this modern world sailing ships and cannibals are out of date.

Macdonald, aged 12 and well connected, passed the necessary examination for entry into the Navy on board HMS *Swiftsure*, Admiral Stirling's flagship at Esquimalt. Then followed the rigorous training on board *Britannia*, the searing jibes as a 'scabby colonial', and the violent passage to manhood. The smallest 'snotty' (or midshipman) survived all this and more, and found himself sent to the Pacific and then to the Australian station and as lieutenant to undertake cruiser and gunboat actions in the islands of the head-hunters. 'During our many months of patrolling [in the New Hebrides and other island clusters], we had to punish many cases of cannibalism; the natives could never understand where their offence lay.' The gunboat actions provided the one relief from the monotony of Oceania, and Macdonald was relieved to have a change of command – back to Esquimalt and the chance to undertake a treasure-hunting expedition with Admiral Palliser to the Cocos Islands, a hushed-up affair of uncertain value to the Crown and the Navy. The China station was his next posting, and with China in disarray Macdonald did not want for excitement. In 1910 the Royal Canadian Navy was established and Macdonald (wary of 'side-shows') reluctantly assumed command of the cruiser HMCS *Niobe*, destined for training duties at Halifax. Macdonald's Canadian career had a singular misfortune: the *Niobe* went aground off Sable Island. Raised from this ignominy by the forcing flame of war, Macdonald served in a number of capacities in the First World War and in 1920, 'Exchanging the sword for the ploughshare, I became a market gardener in a still-suspicious and troubled world'. His last years in Hampshire until his death in 1937 were a quiet conclusion to this imperial odyssey. This naval memoir is a valued source for the student of the gunboat navy, and is no less important for its explanation of the Navy's transition from sail to steam.

Sir John Fisher, famous naval reformer of the Edwardian era, never completed his autobiography though he had plans for one, to be entitled 'Visions'. He compiled two sets of essays, or more correctly, impressions: *Memories* and *Records*, both published by Hodder & Stoughton.[24] These works showed no pattern except that he worked backwards. '"The last shall be first" is good for Autobiography', he wrote in one of his untiring biblical references. Fisher had been cautioned by a friend, Sir George Reid, 'Never write an Autobiography. You only know one view of yourself – others see you all around'. Fisher was never stuck for an answer. He replied, 'But I don't see any harm in such "Memories" as I now indite! In regard to Sir G. Reid's observation, there's one side no one else can see, and that's "the inside"!' In his preface to *Memories*, Fisher adds:

I believe that the vindication of a man's lifework is almost an impossible task for even the most intimate of friends or the most assiduous and talented of Biographers, simply because they cannot possibly appreciate how great deeds have been belittled and ravaged by small contemporary men. These yelping curs made the most noise, as empty barrels do! and it's only long afterwards that the truth emerges out of the mist of obloquy and becomes history. Remember it's only in this century that Nelson has come into his own.

To his publisher he wrote:

Lord Rosebery is emphatic that I should write the book. He says that people with peculiarities should always write books if they feel a call. My having a call entirely depends upon my having a fat and mindful female stenographer, under thirty, capable of driving a Rolls Royce, and apt in colloquial French, and of pleasing appearance and healthy enough to work eighteen hours a day when required. No limit to the salary I will give her. If you come across such a gem will you kindly send me a telegram.

Apparently Fisher was at work on 'Visions' at the time of his death.

The editor of Hodder & Stoughton doubtless had his hands full with the quixotic, egotistical and puzzling Fisher, and in a letter published on the occasion of Fisher's death, Sir Ernest Hodder-Williams noted that it was a matter of very high honour to have had Fisher as an author, and one who endeared himself to the publisher's staff. Fisher had telegraphed to Hodder-Williams on Trafalgar Day 1919 this message: 'To my amazement received six copies of book [*Memories*] and your greatly appreciated letter at daylight this great Nelsonic day. Deeply value your wonderful exertions, and may I ask for my gratitude and admiration being offered to all your splendid staff? Heaven bless you all.' Hodder-Williams recalled that at the Admiralty Fisher was accustomed to sending countless telegrams; in the space of the few weeks during which *Memories* was being prepared 1,000 words of instructions, exhortations, protestations and congratulations had reached the firm's editorial offices. 'Lord Fisher was most long suffering', admitted the publisher:

for we were compelled, of course, to ask his permission to edit some of the more turbulent passages in his writings. (It is true the word 'emasculated' with a whole series of exclamation marks, appeared frequently in his correspondence at this time.) I well remember his joyous laugh when I told him later of the precautions we had taken, and of the times the manuscript and the proofs had been read and re-read. Although it is contrary, I understand, to general belief, Lord Fisher was most anxious not to wound the personal feelings of any man living. There is fine proof of this in the manuscript of

Memories which is before me, where a long passage dealing, and dealing faithfully, with Lord Beresford [Fisher's inveterate rival] is crossed out with the splutter of the quill pen, and these words added as a note: 'Within a few hours of penning the above remarks I had news of his death. *De mortuis nil nisi bonum*. I have scratched out what I had been going to say.

'It is pathetic and noble, too', concluded Hodder-Williams, that Fisher told him that the royalties from *Memories* put his bank balance on the right side for the first time in years. This allowed him to take a holiday in the south of France with friends. He returned home to England to die, and to a Navy funeral, the most celebrated of its kind since Nelson's.

And what of *Memories* as a book? And what does it tell us about the Navy? Frankly, it is not much of a memoir and it tells all too little about the Navy. But it is vintage Fisher! Sharp, to the point, entertaining, biblical. The editor was smart enough to add his own preface, an apologia:

Readers of this book will quickly observe that Admiral of the Fleet Lord Fisher has small faith in the printed word; and those who have enjoyed the privilege of having 'his fist shaken in their faces' will readily admit that the printed word, though faithfully taken down from his dictation, must lack a large measure of the power – the 'aroma', as he calls it – which his personality lends to his spoken word.

The publisher adds that if Fisher had had his way there would have been no such book, but that he undertook the task for the nation and the Navy as a matter of duty. These *Memories* were a compromise between the no-book of Fisher's wish and the orderly, complete autobiography that the public wished to possess.

Great Britain's naval ascendancy was matched by an important growth of substantial literature. The stages of this growth are several in number and various in character. The earliest naval memoir, by Phineas Pett, was of uncertain, mixed intent. Pepys' *Memoirs* was politically motivated. In the eighteenth century collective biographies appeared of the great (and not so great) naval personages. The Napoleonic Wars brought another phase: Nelson produced, on request, his own brief memoir, which was a recounting of his services at sea. This work became the basis of the most celebrated memoir in British naval annals, to which was added all manner of details and appendices on Nelson's life. The next phase is that of the *Pax Britannica*. During the years 1815–1914 much of the memoir material was travel literature: what 'Captain X' did when he was on the West Indies station, what he did when in command of the Pacific station, and so on. These are valuable windows on the Victorian and Edwardian navies and useful views of the wider world. The fourth and final phase is the Navy at war, 1914–18, and its aftermath. This demonstrates the high art of memoir writing, and in this phase naval reform, war at sea, the deflection of strategy by politics, and the complexities of 'official history' are matters of significance and worthy of greater attention than I have given.[25] The British naval memoir must rank as one of the earliest and most developed forms of memoir, and as such the memoirs of the Senior Service are an integral branch of English literature, little known and under-appreciated. The imprint of British naval experiences on national and world memory was firm. As the poet Henry Newbolt put it:

> Admirals all, for England's sake,
> Honour be yours and fame!
> And honour, as long as the waves shall break
> To Nelson's peerless name!

As Robert Louis Stevenson wrote so correctly of British admirals:

Their sayings and doings stir the English blood like the sound of a trumpet, and if the Indian Empire, the trade of London, and all the outward and visible ensigns of our greatness should pass away we should still leave behind us a durable monument of what we were in the sayings and doings of the English Admirals.[26]

Even so, the inexorable passing of the years gradually erases from public memory the deeds and experiences of these men. The past looks farther away in the telescope while the pages of history seem more and more congested as the present catches up with the past. Except for the serious student of history the events of whole centuries are packed into a few pages. 'Events that were cataclysmic to those who witnessed them', wrote Admiral Sir William James in 1947 with telling understanding, 'shrink with the passage of years and even the names of those who moulded the destiny of nations fade into obscurity'.[27] In that splendid regard, the British naval memoir is a special slice of time, a fragment of human experience, a time capsule of character confronting circumstance. It is, too, the corporate memory of a gallant sea service whose world-wide influence was always out of proportion to its size and whose role in the shaping of modern history is remembered more conspicuously by its fighting skills and discipline than by the numerous individual autobiographical fragments that recount the dedication to duty that comprised the sinews of British naval might.

NOTES

1. Astute students of history, upon reading this essay, may note that there is no historiography of the subject. I have been previously chided for failure to provide a historiographical discussion for work that is *original*. In this instance the work is also *original*: diligent enquiries in various libraries especially in the Library of the National Maritime Museum, by myself and helpful librarians, failed to uncover anything on the topic. I wish to thank George Urbaniak, colleague and friend, for the anecdote on Foch. I can only wish that British admirals exhibited equal mirth. I acknowledge with thanks the assistance of my research assistants Margaret Palmer, Alana Wall, Peter Postrozny, Rick Rakosy and especially Daryl Pidduck. I also wish to thank the following who read my work in draft and provided suggestions: Alan Pearsall, John Hattendorf, Malcolm Murfett, Roger Knight, N.A.M. Rodger, Barry Hunt, James Boutilier, W.A.B. Douglas and James Goldrick.
2. W.G. Perrin. (ed.), *The Autobiography of Phineas Pett* (London Navy Records Society, Vol. LI, 1918), p. civ. Pepys' manuscript copy of this is in the British Library, London, Add. Ms. 9298. Another version, an early-eighteenth-century transcription, is to be found in the Harleian Collection (Harl. 6279), also in the British Library. The Perrin edition is a collation of the two with a clear preference for the Pepys copy.
3. J.R. Tanner (ed.), *Pepys' Memoirs of the Royal Navy* (Oxford, 1906; New York, 1971), introduction. Richard Ollard, *Pepys* (London, 1984), pp. 31 and 13.
4. Peter Kemp (ed.), *Oxford Companion to Ships and the Sea* (London, 1975), pp. 154–5.
5. *Catalogue of the Library of the National Maritime Museum, Volume 2, Part 1* (London, 1969), item 292.
6. Ibid., items 886–901.
7. Robert Southey, *Life of Nelson* (London, 1854), pp. 5–12.
8. *Catalogue of the Library of the National Maritime Museum*, item 965.
9. Ibid., item 968.
10. Published, in revised form, as Barry M. Gough, *The Royal Navy and the Northwest Coast of North America, 1810–1914: A Study of British Maritime Ascendancy* (Vancouver, 1971).
11. John Moresby, *Two Admirals: Sir Fairfax Moresby, John Moresby: A Record of a Hundred Years* (new and rev. ed.) (London, 1913).
12. Mrs Fred Egerton, *Admiral of the Fleet, Sir Geoffrey Phipps Hornby, G.C.B.: A Biography* (Edinburgh, 1896).
13. Percy Scott, *50 Years in the Royal Navy* (London, 1919).
14. London and Edinburgh, 1900; another printing, London, 1910.
15. Admiral Sir William Kennedy, *Sport in the Navy and Naval Yarns* (London, 1902); *Sport, Travel and Adventure in Newfoundland and the West Indies* (Edinburgh, 1885); *Sporting Adventures in the Pacific* (London, 1876); *Sporting Sketches in South America* (London, 1892).
16. He died on 9 October 1916; *Who Was Who, 1916–1928* (London, 1929), p. 579.
17. Gerald Jordan and Nicholas Rogers, 'Admirals as Heroes: Patriotism and Liberty in Hanoverian England', *Journal of British Studies*, Vol. 28 (July 1989), pp. 201–24. Kathleen Wilson, 'Empire, Trade and Popular Politics in Mid-Hanoverian England: The Case of Admiral Vernon', *Past and Present*, Vol. 121 (November 1988), pp. 74–109.
18. Humphrey J. Smith, *A Yellow Admiral Remembers* (London, 1934).
19. Michael Lewis, *The Navy in Transition, 1814–1864; A Social History* (London, 1965).
20. *Aft – From the Hawsehole: Sixty-two Years of Sailors Evolution* (London, 1927); quotations at pp. 81 and 95. An appreciative obituary is to be found in *The Times*, 30 May 1931.
21. Campbell, *Lives of the Admirals* (new edition, London, 1781), Vol. 3, pp. 367–73.
22. John Winton, 'From Sailor Boy to Admiral', *Seascape* (June 1988), pp. 19–21.

23. S.W. Jackman (ed.), *At Sea and By Land: The Reminiscences of William Balfour Macdonald, R.N.* (Victoria, BC, 1983). Quotations at pp. 19, 54 and 130.

24. The Wilfrid Laurier University Library contains a valuable copy of Fisher's *Memories* (London, 1919) which contains numerous clippings of an avid collector, including Sir Ernest Hodder-Williams' article in *The Church Weekly*, 15 July 1920, here quoted at length.

25. Among the pre-eminent 'modern' British naval memoirs are those of Sir Roger Keyes, *Adventures Ashore and Afloat* (London, 1939; London, 1973), A.E.M.C. Chatfield, *The Navy and Defence: The Autobiography of the Admiral of the Fleet Lord Chatfield* (2 vols.) (Toronto, 1942), Andrew B. Cunningham, *A Sailor's Odyssey: The Autobiography of the Admiral of the Fleet* (London, 1951).

26. Quoted in Admiral Sir W.M. James, *The Influence of Sea Power on the History of the British People* (Cambridge, The Lees Knowles Lectures on Military History for 1947, 1948), p. 44.

27. Ibid., p. 45.

8

The Relativity of War: British Military Memoirs from the Campaigns of Marlborough to the First World War

TIM TRAVERS

Over the past few years there has been a revival of interest in the conduct and experience of the First World War, which is often given special status as the 'Great War'. This revival of interest has included a renewed attempt to explain the significance of the literature of that war, most recently, for example, in Modris Eksteins' fine book *Rites of Spring: The Great War and the Birth of the Modern Age*, published in 1989. But the most influential work so far has been the book by Paul Fussell, *The Great War and Modern Memory* (1975), which argues that the First World War created a new kind of twentieth-century literature, and even a new attitude to life: 'I am saying that there seems to be one dominating form of modern understanding; that it is essentially ironic; and that it originates largely in the application of mind and memory to the events of the Great War.' Thus, according to Fussell, the British memoirs of the First World War were an attempt to express the contrast between the initial innocent expectations of the war and the grim reality of the absurd and uncontrollable world of the Western Front. In the process of trying to describe this, Fussell argues, the British memoirs of the war created a literature of irony which struggled to find new forms of myths, images and metaphors to express the full horror of the trenches. And Fussell believes that, in using such language to produce their memoirs, writers such as Siegfried Sassoon, Robert Graves and Edmund Blunden were in fact writing fiction.[1]

Fussell's analysis has become the standard explanation of British literature of the war, and his arguments have also reinforced the 'mud and blood' image of the Western Front, of revulsion against the horror of the trenches, and against the stupidity of generals and their staffs. But are there problems with Fussell's analysis? It seems that there are, especially in two areas. In the first place, Fussell has ignored the much greater range of British First World War military memoirs that actually exist. For every Siegfried Sassoon and Robert Graves there were a dozen writers such as Charles Douie, whose memoir *The Weary Road* (1929) presented a patriotic and enthusiastic portrait of the war, although he was equally as intense and inward looking as his more famous colleagues. And in the second place, Fussell, and many historians of the First World War, have tended to see the Western Front as the ultimate war experience, as Armageddon, and have ignored the historical context of past wars. For Fussell and other analysts of the literature of the First World War, the war was an event so unique as to create a whole new way of thinking, as reflected in British and other memoirs of this catastrophic war. Modris Eksteins, for example, argues that the Great War has totally changed the way we think and live. According to Eksteins, in order for 'our preoccupation with speed, newness, transience, and inwardness . . . to have taken hold, an entire scale of values and beliefs had to yield pride of place, and the Great War was . . . the single most significant event in that development'.[2] Yet it is possible to argue the reverse – that the war was really a vehicle for the expression of already existing social and intellectual trends – in other words, that the war did not create a whole new way of thinking through the memoirists, but rather that the writers of these memoirs simply reflected not so much the war, but already prevailing social and intellectual trends.

Fussell and Eksteins tend to see the First World War as exceptional in its horror and carnage, with its own 'mud and blood' image that sets it apart from all other wars in its stupidity and casualties. All of this is reinforced by the tendency to refer to the First World War as the 'Great War'. It is significant that both Fussell and Eksteins use the mythic phrase 'the Great War' in the titles of their books, as do many other authors, such as Denis Winter in his *Death's Men: Soldiers of the Great War* (1978), or James Munson (ed.), *Echoes of the Great War* (1985). This unique image of the First World War has been continuously updated in popular films such as *Oh What A Lovely War* and *Gallipoli*, and contributes to the concept of the First World War as having a particular and overarching significance beyond all other wars. There is obviously much to be said for these arguments regarding the war and its memoir literature as the turning point of the modern age, yet one cannot help feeling that a greater sense of context and historical appreciation of past wars and their literature might suggest a different analysis. This would be, first, that the First World War should not be seen in the mythic and unique way that Fussell and others have seen it. And second, I would venture to suggest that the memoirs and literature of wars actually reflect not so much the particular war in question but even more the social and intellectual currents of the time.[3]

We turn first to the question of the uniqueness of the First World War. The military historian Correlli Barnett has pointed out that the rates of casualties in proportion to troops involved were no greater than in some campaigns of the past. Hence while there were approximately 57,000 British casualties on the first day of the Battle of the Somme, out of a total Fourth Army strength of some 500,000, Napoleon lost 44,000 men out of 100,000 at Aspern-Essling in 1809 in two days, and another 30,000 out of 175,000 in one day at Wagram two months later. The battles of the Civil War in the US were actually more costly in terms of rates of casualties compared with numbers involved, with casualty rates often reaching over 80 per cent in the regiments involved at Antietam and Gettysburg, while we are only too familiar with the numbers of civilian casualties in the Second World War, including the results of the atomic bombs at Hiroshima and Nagasaki. A moment of reflection would also allow us to see that the First World War was no more horrible or terrible than other wars in the past. A British memoir of the Peninsular War by an officer of the 43rd regiment describes the British assault on the fortress of Cuidad Rodrigo, which rivals any horror from the trenches of the Western Front:

I saw one of the unfortunate soldiers in a blanket, with his face, head, and body, as black as a coal, and cased in a black substance like a shell; his features were no longer distinguishable . . . but still the unfortunate man was alive. [and later] . . . small groups of soldiers seeking shelter from the cart wheels, pieces of timber, fire-balls, and other missiles hurled down upon them [by the French]; the wounded crawling past the fire-balls, many of them scorched and perfectly black, and covered with mud, from having fallen into the lunette, where three hundred soldiers were suffocated and drowned . . .[4]

Indeed, far from being unique to the Western Front, some incidents of war seem to be gruesomely repetitive over the centuries. Take for example this passage from a British memoir of the siege of New Orleans in 1814, in which the author observed a wounded soldier who for two hours continued 'to raise his arm up and down with a convulsive motion, which excited the most powerful sensations amongst us; and as the enemy's balls every now and then killed or maimed some soldiers, we could not help casting our eyes towards the moving arm, which really was a dreadful magnet of attraction . . .'. Yet just over a century later, Siegfried Sassoon observed something very similar during the assault of the Manchester Regiment at Mametz on 1 July 1916, and recorded in his diary: 'There were about forty casualties on the left . . . Through my glasses I could see one man moving his left arm up and down as he lay on his side; his face was a crimson patch.'[5]

We turn next to the relationship of memoir to war, and of memoir to the dominant social and intellectual currents of the time. It will be useful here to compare British memoirs over a period of 200 years, starting with the memoirs of the Marlborough wars, then considering the British memoirs of the period of the Napoleonic wars of the early nineteenth century, and concluding with the British memoirs of the First World War.

The British military memoirs of the Marlborough wars are essentially narrative campaign accounts with the personality of the author submerged in the attention paid to strategy, tactics, the doings of generals, battles, times, places, names, numbers of casualties, marches and the outcome of campaigns. This is limited war, with limited reports of personal experience and limited viewpoints, for a limited readership (novels in this period apparently sold 1,000 to 3,000 copies), in a narrative campaign tradition, emphasizing mainly the heroic qualities of generals, and the glory of victory. Thus the title of the memoir by John Millner, a Sergeant in the Royal Regiment of Foot of Ireland, itself explains this narrative tradition: *A Compendious Journal of all the Marches, Famous Battles, Sieges, And other most note-worthy, heroical and ever memorable actions of the Triumphant Armies, of the ever-glorious Confederate High Allies, in their late and victorious war against the Powerful Armies of proud and lofty France, in and on the confines of Holland, Germany, Flanders, so far as our successful British Troops extended in Conjunction therein. Digested into Twelve Campaigns, begun AD 1701, and ended in 1712.* Another memoir by a member of the rank and file follows much the same format, although breaking out occasionally into condemnation of the notorious transport ships of the time: 'ye Pox above board; ye Plague between Decks: hell in ye fore-castle, and ye Devil att ye Helm . . .', and on another occasion berating the French enemy for their hellish 'inventions of throwing of bombs, boylying Pitch, Tar, Oyle and Brimstone wth Scalding Water . . .'. A slightly more forthcoming memoir was composed by Matthew Bishop, another private soldier, illustrating the fact that members of the rank and file tended to write slightly more lively narratives than officers, perhaps because of their different perspective. Bishop asserted that his narrative would set out to provide salutary lessons and examples, the chief of which appeared to be that no man was honourable who set out to do 'any thing for Gain, or Interest of any Kind'. Thus Bishop castigated his fellow soldier John Jones, who had found an interesting method of raising funds by searching the battlefield for spent cannon-balls and then selling them back to the same artillery that had fired them. More questionable was the general military practice, which Bishop detested, whereby his comrades plundered the dead, dying and wounded on the battlefield, whether these were Allied or enemy bodies. Bishop's goal was fame not gain. However, despite such flashes of homespun philosophy, plus some sympathy for the wounded (he could not sleep after the battle of Malplaquet (1709) because of the cries and groans of the wounded), and an interest in the relations between officers and men, Bishop essentially also followed the narrative campaign tradition.[6]

By and large, the narrative campaign tradition was continued in the memoirs of higher-ranking officers, such as that of Brigadier Richard Kane, who principally focused on the doings of Marlborough and the French general Tallard, and on details of battles, strategy and tactics. He was, however, sufficiently independent of mind to criticize Marlborough for changing plans at the battle of Ramillies (1706), and for wasting lives by trying to force the village of Blenheim instead of waiting outside and firing into it. If anything the memoirs of Captain Robert Parker were an even more straightforward rendition of the campaigns of Marlborough, with each chapter designating a particular campaign, as in John Millner's account, and stressing marches, battles, casualty numbers and the actions of generals. A typical passage from Parker concerns the behaviour of Marlborough on the morning of the battle of Blenheim: 'The Duke received the Holy Sacrament this morning at the hands of his chaplain . . . and upon mounting his horse, he said, "This day I conquer or die." A noble instance of the Christian and the hero! Our army consisted of 181 squadrons and 67 battalions.'[7]

Toward the middle of the eighteenth century, however, and visible in the edited versions of Marlborough campaign memoirs brought out in the nineteenth century, the moral and religious revivals of the mid- to late eighteenth century were having an impact. Thus, military memoirs were now interwoven with conversion experiences, and with moralizing. Hence Colonel James Gardiner, who fought in the Marlborough campaigns, and who was wounded at Ramillies while part of the Forlorn Hope assault, recorded his conversion from a life of folly, vice and Deism to a truer Christianity, and had much to say about swearing and the moral conduct of officers and soldiers. Similarly, Lieutenant-Colonel Blackader of the Cameronian Regiment wrote in his diary for April 1701: 'Gunpowder does not more suddenly flash up when a spark of fire falls upon it, than corruption, when Satan throws in his fiery darts. But I find to my unspeakable comfort, when I sin, I have an Advocate with the Father.' Not surprisingly, Blackader railed against the 'Cursing, swearing, [and] filthy language' of the British army, as well as its self-conceit and general sinfulness. During the indecisive campaign of 1703, Blackader recorded in his diary, on 17 May, that 'the English army are sinners exceedingly before the Lord, and I have no hopes of success . . .'. But the greatest overall difference with these later memoirs is that personal experiences, albeit religious, have emerged, so that, as Blackader noted, his diary was a spiritual register of his experiences.[8]

The military memoirs of the Marlborough campaigns really reflect the age in which they were written as much as the campaigns themselves. The calm rationalism and common sense of the Augustan age, the civilized golden mean, the inevitable and necessary order of things, the well-ordered structure of society, the attention paid to the heroic (Christian) individual, the sense of a benevolent divine order, are all reflected in the limited narrative campaign memoir which, until the mid-eighteenth century, removed personality and exotic detail in favour of a calm well-balanced sequence of events. These memoirs highlighted only the top of the hierarchy in the form of heroic military leaders, and otherwise related a cold, well-ordered sequence of events, places and numbers. It was one specific view of war, but from a very narrow perspective. Only the religious revival of the mid-eighteenth century pointed towards an interest in the individual personality of the memoirist and his experiences as valuable in themselves. Therefore, the British military memoirs of the early eighteenth century may be termed the 'heroic narrative campaign memoir', although another applicable term might be the 'remote memoir', referring to the detached, uninvolved quality of the writing.

However, with the Napoleonic War period (1790s–1815), there emerges the romanticized British military memoir, emphasizing the horrors of war with graphic and exaggerated descriptions; and romantic descriptions of life, love, travel and battle scenes in exotic locations. A military genre of literature is now established for the new reading public of the middle classes, for example, the military titles put out by the publishers Colburn and Bentley. A reviewer for this press describes one of their military memoirs: 'While reading *Sailors and Saints* the floor of our room has seemed to reel; we have fancied we have felt the saltspray of the sea on our face – so completely have we been absorbed in the graphical descriptions . . .'. Of another title, *Tales of Military Life*, the reviewer notes: 'their adventures are equally tinged with the marvellous, the pathetic and the humorous'.[9] Plainly, the publisher was intent on selling copies by appealing to the romantic imagination, or perhaps one should say by appealing to the melodramatic imagination, since the convention of the melodrama, with its desire to say and speak all, to resort to cliché, overemphasis and overstatement, and to exploit all the dramatics and excitement that reality permits, reflects rather well the intentions of most early-nineteenth-century military memoirists.[10] Another major difference from the eighteenth-century memoir was the emergence of the individual personality of the author. As the English scholar David Daiches has keenly pointed out: 'in the Romantic period the tendency was for the writer to draw on his own personality either as an illuminating case history or as a gesture of defiance or showmanship or "alienation", rather than to objectify it in terms of a cause or a system', as in the eighteenth century.[11]

The military memoirs of Captain John Cooke, describing his Napoleonic period experiences, and published in the early 1830s, are an example of Daiches' argument, revealing Cooke's personality in a brightly written and lively series of incidents, some horrible, some amusing. They tend to foreshadow the techniques of Graves and Sassoon in alternating pastoral or attractive interludes with the terrors of the battle front. Thus Cooke contrasts the story of the assistant surgeon losing his false teeth on the march, and the whole regiment looking for them, with the wounding of Lieutenant Considine shortly afterwards, hit in the thigh by a musket ball. When he was hoisted up by four soldiers Considine's 'screams are dreadful, and two of the soldiers fall dead, pierced by balls'. Considine and the other wounded are placed on carts, and Cooke notes 'the sick, wounded and dying with pallid countenances expressive of unheard-of agonies . . .'. Then again, in his memoir of France in 1814 and the 1815 New Orleans campaign, Cooke describes an enjoyable evening party in France, where a sham fort was constructed, to be stormed by various ladies, especially Mlle L., who advanced with 'petticoats above her knees . . .', and later on that night party games were played, including the pinning of a piece of paper on the trousers of an individual, which everyone then tried to set alight. But only a few pages later, Cooke philosophized about the arbitrary nature of death in the campaign, prefiguring the very similar experience of the First World War, where a constant aspect of the Western Front was the randomness of death and wounding, even when far from the front line. As the historian Denis Winter has remarked of the Western Front: 'In France, no man was safe.' But 100 years earlier, Cooke discusses a very similar attitude:

How often have I seen officers and soldiers struck down in the columns of reserve, without having ever seen the face of an enemy, or without having drawn their swords or pulled a trigger . . . How often have I seen men killed or maimed while fast asleep in the trenches at the siege of a fortress. Upon one occasion an officer had both his legs carried off by the bursting of a shell when he was in his hut, wrapped in the arms of sleep . . . But again I repeat that balls and bullets are so capricious that they often strike high or low, and near and far off, without ceremony or distinction.[12]

Indeed, there are a number of similarities between the memoirs of the early nineteenth century and those of the First World War, suggesting again that the latter should not be seen as so unusual. For example, one of the constant references both in the war memoirs of the Napoleonic period and those of the First World War was the death and wounding of fellow comrades, and shock at their sudden removal from life. This was often accompanied by a kind of survivor guilt, as explained by the psychiatrist Robert Jay Lifton: 'the survivor can never, inwardly, simply conclude that it was logical and right for him, and not others, to survive . . . [he feels] that his survival was made possible by others' deaths. If they had not died, he would have had to; and if he had not survived, some one else would have.' This feeling was much stronger in the memoirs of the First World War, but it is implied also in those of the Napoleonic period, even though the British army then was a professional force and inured to the expectation of death and often fatal wounding. Thus Sir Richard Henegan's memoirs of the Peninsular campaign, while often more of a travelogue, become personal when he discusses the death of friends, particularly that of young Robert Manners, who died after Waterloo. Henegan described how Manners had to have his leg amputated, but lamented that he might have been saved if only he had remained where the operation took place, but instead, being removed in a jolting cart, he haemorrhaged and died. Captain Cooke described the unhappy death of Lieutenant Uniacke, with one eye gone, and flesh torn off his arms and legs, and exclaimed sadly: 'He had taken chocolate, with our mess, an hour and a half before!' Young Lieutenant Moodie, writing his memoir of the Dutch campaign of 1814, spent much time describing the dead and wounded, whether in hospital or at the front. Thus in the hospital where Moodie was being treated, in the bed on his right, Ensign Martial died of a shoulder wound, and on his left, General Skerret died the next night, soon to be followed by Captain Campbell (in the bed opposite), who had suffered a severe grapeshot wound in his back, but even so talked incessantly in the hospital. On the field of battle, Moodie noted particularly that Second Lieutenant Bulteel had lost his head to a cannon-ball, and that Captain Mackenzie had his leg shattered by a shot. Implied in all this is some wonder that the authors of these memoirs had survived but their fellow officers and friends had not.[13]

Again, just as in the First World War, the memoirs of the other ranks seemed to show both a more calm acceptance of death, and a greater interest in the relations between officers and men. Thus John Green, a soldier in the 68th Durham Light Infantry, simply relates the death of Sergeant Dunn, who had both his legs shot off, without comment, and subsequently notes without surprise how a shot had broken bayonets and sent one blade through the neck of a nearby comrade. The man survived, but Green does not express a sense of relief at the man's escape. However when Green himself was wounded, he tells an interesting story that throws light on the relations between officers and men. After receiving his wound, Green appealed to Captain Gledstanes to save him: '"Sir, am I to be left in this condition, to be killed or taken by the enemy?" "No, my man", said this amiable officer, "I will assist you"', and he gave Green a stick for one leg, and held his right arm for support on the other side. Green was also promptly seen by two surgeons, although when Green cried out at the probing of his wound, the surgeon was stern: '"Silence", said the surgeon, "it is for your good".'[14]

There are other anticipations of the Western Front in the First World War in the memoirs of the early nineteenth century. For example, in writing of the assault on Badajoz, Captain Cooke describes the same kind of illumination of the trenches as occurred with the star shells of 1914–18: 'At ten a carcass [shell] was thrown from the town; this was a most beautiful fire-work, and illuminated the ground for many hundred yards; two or three fire balls followed, and, falling in different directions, showed a bright light, and remained burning.'[15] Other similarities of the two periods of war include the premonition of death of others, which is recalled by so many Western Front veterans. The death of Lieutenant-General Sir Thomas Picton at Waterloo is amply prefigured in his edited memoirs. Shortly before departing for the final struggle with Napoleon, Picton was walking with friends when he saw a freshly dug grave. Picton jumped into the grave and laid himself along the bottom, saying 'Why, I think this would do for me', and observed that the grave was an exact fit. In another incident, he said to a friend, 'When you hear of my death, you will hear of a bloody day . . .', and on a third occasion told a friend that these would be his last words with him.[16]

A final comparison concerns the horrors of war, of which enough has probably already been quoted to show that the First World War had no monopoly on that feature. It is, however, surprising how many passages of the early 1800s use the same metaphors as were used in those of 1914–18, for example machine-gun bullets acting as a scythe in cutting down lines of attacking men on the Western Front is not very different from an incident at the siege of New Orleans in 1815. Here Captain John Cooke noted that one attack by 3,000 men of the 7th and 43rd Regiments left only 1,000 survivors, 'and they fell like the very blades of grass beneath the scythe of the mower'. Like his First World War descendants, Cooke went on to criticize the staff work and the plans of the general which resulted in such a botched attack. However, in his account of the same action, Cooke employed the exaggerated melodramatic style of the early nineteenth century, which reveals a very different sensibility from the memoirs of the First World War. Thus he described the inferno encompassing the two British regiments 'enveloped by the clouds of smoke that hung over their heads . . . [and] the echo from the cannonade and musketry was so tremendous in the forests, that the vibration seemed as if the earth was cracking and tumbling to pieces . . .'. Then narrowing his focus, Cooke recalled the reactions of a soldier lying near him. This soldier 'had received a blow from a cannon-ball, which had obliterated all his features; and although blind, and suffering the most terrible anguish, he was employing himself in scratching a hole to put his money into'.[17]

The military memoirs of Captain John Cooke and his colleagues are a fair representation of the memoirs of the early nineteenth century, which reflected the romanticism of the prevailing intellectual currents of the time, and which may be termed the 'romantic' or 'melodramatic' memoir. Despite some interesting anticipations of the First World War, these memoirs have an exaggerated melodramatic quality, which is very different from the British memoirs of 1914–18. These twentieth-century memoirs were written mainly in the late 1920s and early 1930s, and to a large extent followed what may be called the psychological model. David Daiches has argued that the fiction of the 1920s developed as a result of three factors: the collapse of public standards of significance; new notions of time as subjective; and new psychological notions of the complexity of consciousness. The twentieth-century novel therefore developed themes which stressed the importance of private consciousness, and the relations between such private individuals and their small, intimate group of friends.[18] To a considerable extent, British First World War military memoirs are really about how often lonely individuals gradually become part of a small intimate group of friends and comrades under intense circumstances, this process leading to a good deal of soul-searching and psychological self-analysis. The irresistible mechanism of the war, and the follies of staff and generals, provide a common background or theatre for this process to take place. Most of the better-known memoirs seem to follow this track, namely those by Siegfried Sassoon, Robert Graves, Edmund Blunden, Cecil Lewis, Henry Williamson, Charles Carrington, and so on.

It will not be possible here to discuss the whole range of First World War British memoirs, but instead a close look at the evolution of Siegfried Sassoon's memoirs will illustrate the development of the First World War psychological memoir. Sassoon left detailed notes on his state of mind both during the war and as he wrote his memoirs, thus providing a useful case study. Many of the letters to and from Sassoon and other memoirists during the First World War stress the death and wounding of friends, hence Sassoon's fellow officer in the Royal Welch Fusiliers, Robert Graves, writes to a friend in 1918 that most of his contemporaries have 'gone west', with the few exceptions of the 'maimed, the blind and the insane'. Sassoon received similar letters from his fellow officers, like Joe Cotterill, who also thought in late 1917 that 'Truly we shall all be mad or dead presently'.[19] The death and wounding of friends clearly had a very profound effect on Sassoon, as did his dislike of militarism and the mechanism of war. He found the latter very difficult to deal with because he was both irresistibly part of the machine of war, being deeply committed to his regiment and to his brother officers, and being enthusiastic about participating in various regimental attacks on the Western Front, but at the same time he was strongly opposed to his own participation in the war. In a 1917 note to himself, Sassoon wrote: 'He had resolved to inscribe his hatred and contempt of war in pages of burning criticism and satire. And already he was beginning to forget his grievance against Militarism as he became part of the irresistible mechanism once more.' Other aspects of the war that bothered Sassoon were the humbugs, war profiteers and guzzlers back home – a common complaint by many memoirists – as well as the political tyrants who kept the war going.[20]

Sassoon was a frequent critic not only of the machine of war, but also of the generals and their staff officers, although, on occasion, particularly in his published memoirs, he defended them. But more common was his very personalized style of criticism of senior commanders. For example, Sassoon saw 60 generals observing an army demonstration in May 1916:

gross stupidity and materialism set a mark on every face: they strutted and straddled and guffawed; conceited and complacent; one felt their minds obsessed by meaningless decorations. They were more vain of all their glories than any woman of her gauds. That was in the merry month of May. At the end of June [i.e., the Battle of the Somme] they began their game of staking thousands of lives . . . .

This personalized dislike of the incompetent outward trappings of the higher commanders often concerned food. Hence at a hotel in France, Sassoon saw a red-faced and petulant Brigadier General at the next table guzzling food 'as though the successful prosecution of the war depended on the solidity of his mid-day repast. The Fusilier [Sassoon] . . . felt an almost irrepressible desire to pour a plate of soup down his neck. "To hell with all these incompetent bald heads!" he thought . . .'.[21]

There is no doubt, however, that the stress of the war itself had a more powerful effect on Sassoon than has been generally realized. In the published version of his memoirs (*Memoirs of an Infantry Officer*), Sassoon tended to omit sections that emphasized the strain of trench life, and he toned down the negative aspects of the British Expeditionary Force. For example, one section that Sassoon omitted in the published version concerned a brother officer, Durley, and his story of an attack:

Haunted by Durley's eyes, I wondered whether I ought to have allowed him to talk so much about that September show. And the horror of going out again myself loomed a little larger. For every morning when I awoke, my first conscious thought was this: 'you've got to go out again, you've got to go out again'. It was the same for all of us. We were under sentence of death, until our individual Fates had come to a haphazard decision about us.[22]

Partly under stress such as this, and partly because of the dislikes enumerated above, in 1917 Sassoon publicly declared his protest against the war. As is well known, Sassoon was saved from a court martial by Robert Graves, who arranged a medical board which sent Sassoon to Craiglockhart hospital for treatment for nerves and shell shock. What is less well known is the fact that although Sassoon always publicly denied that he was suffering from mental strain, or shell shock as it was called (and this has been accepted by biographers), nevertheless it would seem that Sassoon did indeed suffer a nervous breakdown of some sort.

Thus Sassoon notes in a manuscript source that his experience in early 1917 was 'bad enough to leave me a bit overstrained'. Then a brother officer in the Royal Welch Fusiliers, Geoffrey Harbord, wrote in mid-1917: 'You tell me you have been pretty shaken and if you give it [medical treatment] a miss now anyway till they are right again you may get them [the nerves] permanently wrong.' The most compelling evidence is in the letters of Sassoon's psychiatrist at Craiglockhart hospital, the celebrated W.H.R. Rivers, who wrote to Sassoon early in 1918. Rivers recommended the Palestine front for Sassoon, because 'We must remember that you are extremely sensitive – as shown by the . . . fainting incident and it is a question whether you would not have more chance of being useful there than in France'. Rivers concluded by writing that he was glad 'that your severe attack of "war-neuroses" had no lasting effects'. This is at variance with the published memoir, where Sassoon sees his stay at Craiglockhart as a sham, and where Rivers is portrayed as an authority figure who provided reality and integration for Sassoon, and who essentially offered Sassoon the choice of staying at Craiglockhart for the rest of the war, or of returning to the Western Front.[23]

Sassoon's attitudes and intense experience in the First World War were such that when he came to write the second volume of his memoirs in 1928 and 1929, published as *Memoirs of an Infantry Officer* in 1930, it is understandable that his book reflected the introspective and 'psychological' currents of the late 1920s and 1930s. In a notebook which he kept as he wrote his memoirs, Sassoon jotted down that 'The main value of the book must be in what is revealed *unconsciously*'. Sassoon wanted to write about not what he noticed, but what he was. Particularly after being wounded in April 1917, Sassoon noted that his narrative 'is a psychological record'. Then after reading the official history of the Royal Welch Fusiliers, Sassoon wrote that the history 'accentuates my notion that the important quality in my book must be my own "psychological story"', in other words, 'the secret drama inside a soldier's head'. At the same time, Sassoon was determined to be accurate, and in contrast to Fussell's claim that the memoir was 'in every way fictional', it is very clear that Sassoon made every effort to be factual concerning the Royal Welch Fusiliers and the war itself, and to avoid post-war omniscience, as he remarked several times in his working notebook. Sassoon wrote that he refused to fake anything, or the whole book would be a fake. He would not claim any 'typical experience' as his own. Even in regard to his own mental and emotional experiences, Sassoon tried hard to 'get back into my own skin' – the exact evidence of his eyes and mind as they then were.[24]

Sassoon's memoirs, then, seem to reflect the whole subjective and introspective trend of the period from the 1890s to the 1930s, which has been seen by historians as the period of the revolt against positivism. Despite the concentration on Sassoon's experience, in this matter Sassoon was representative of the great range of First World War writers. As T.E. Lawrence remarked: 'The worst thing about the war generation of introspects is that they can't keep off their blooming selves', Hence almost the whole range of British war memoirs of the 1920s and 1930s can be said to have been written from the point of view of internal experience, apart from some senior generals who wrote as representatives of their generation of the late nineteenth century, and one or two later memoirs by members of the other ranks. Thus the great majority of First World War British memoirs may be termed the 'psychological memoir'.[25]

It can be argued, therefore, that while the British memoirists of the First World War, just like their counterparts in the early eighteenth and nineteenth centuries, might catalogue the incidents and events of a particular war, in reality what they were actually recording were the already existing intellectual and social currents of their times. In this essay, these reflective memoirs have been labelled the early-eighteenth-century 'heroic narrative campaign' memoir or 'remote' memoir; the early-nineteenth-century 'melodramatic' or 'romantic' memoir; and the early-twentieth-century 'psychological' memoir. Thus, it is time to stop seeing the Western Front as a unique and ultimate war experience of mythic proportions which, through the memoirs of Sassoon, Graves, Blunden and others, produced a whole new world of meaning and understanding for European consciousness, as in the arguments of Paul Fussell and Modris Eksteins. The First World War was no more and no less terrible than other wars of our conflict-strewn past, and primarily reinforced the prevailing anti-positivism of the period.[26]

NOTES

1. Paul Fussell, *The Great War and Modern Memory* (Oxford, 1977), pp. 35, 310 ff.
2. Modris Eksteins, *Rites of Spring: the Great War and the Birth of the Modern Age* (Toronto, 1989), p. xiv.
3. This second argument is supported by George Mosse's recent and very useful book, *Fallen Soldiers: Reshaping the memory of the World Wars* (New York, 1990.)
4. Correlli Barnett, 'A Military Historian's View of the Literature of the Great War', *Essays by Divers Hands* (Oxford, 1969), p. 12. *Memoirs of the Late War: comprising the personal narrative of Captain Cooke, of the 43rd Regiment Light Infantry* . . . (London, 1831), Vol 1, pp. 128 and 149.
5. Captain John Henry Cooke, *A Narrative of Events in the South of France and of the attack on New Orleans, in 1814 and 1815* (London, 1835), pp. 240–1; Siegfried Sassoon, *Memoirs Of An Infantry Officer* (London, 1930), p. 76.
6. John Millner, *A Compendious Journal* . . . (London, 1733). Following in the narrative tradition, Millner took pains to record the enemy casualties at the battle of Blenheim (1704), which were 23,409, with 38,609 prisoners, and 12,484 Allied casualties, ibid., pp. 125 and 128. John Marshal Deane, *A Journal of the Campaign in Flanders* (of 1708) (London, 1846), pp. 6 and 26. *The Life and Adventures of William Bishop of Deddington in Oxfordshire* (1701–11) (London, 1744), pp. vi–viii, 224, 210, 216, 180–5, 205, 210, 215, 240 and 253–6.
7. Brigadier Richard Kane, *Campaigns of King William and the Duke of Marlborough; with remarks on the Stratagems by which every Battle was won or lost, from 1689, to 1712* (second edition, London, 1747), pp. 68 and 51. Captain Robert Parker, *Memoirs of the most Remarkable Military Transactions, From the Year 1683 to 1718* (Dublin, 1746; London, 1747), also available in a modern edition from which the above quote comes. David Chandler (ed.), *Robert Parker and Comte de Merode-Westerloo, The Marlborough Wars* (London, 1968), p. 37. There is apparently some question as to whether Parker may have plagiarized from Kane, or the other way around, or that both copied from a third source, ibid., pp. xvi–xviii.
8. P. Doddridge, DD, *Some Remarkable Passages in the Life of the Honourable Colonel James Gardiner, who was slain at the Battle of Preston-Pans, September 21, 1745* (second edition, London, 1748), pp. A3, 10, 30 and 116. Andrew Chrichton, *The Life and Diary of Lieutenant Colonel J. Blackader . . . who served with distinguished honour in the wars under King William and the Duke of Marlborough, and afterwards in the Rebellion of 1715 in Scotland* (Edinburgh, 1824), pp. 158, 218 ff., 175, 218, 212 and 142.
9. *Memoirs of the Late War: comprising the personal narrative of Captain Cooke, of the 43rd Regiment Light Infantry* . . . , Vol. 1, end pages.
10. Peter Brooks, *The Melodramatic Imagination: Balzac, Henry James, Melodrama, and the Mode of Excess* (New Haven, 1976), pp. 13 and 41.
11. David Daiches, *A Critical History of English Literature* (second edition, New York, 1970), p. 935.
12. Denis Winter, *Death's Men: Soldiers of the Great War* (Harmondsworth, 1979), p. 131. *Memoirs of the Late War: comprising the personal narrative of Captain Cooke, of the 43rd Regiment Light Infantry* . . . , Vol. 1, pp. 62, 78 and 84. Captain John Henry Cooke, *A Narrative of Events in the South of France and of the attack on New Orleans, in 1814 and 1815* pp. 34, 36, 39 and 52–3.
13. Robert Jay Lifton, *History and Human Survival* (New York and Toronto, 1971), p. 169, where Lifton is referring to the *hibakusha* of Japan, but the concept evidently has a general application. Sir Richard Henegan, *Seven Years' Campaigning in the Peninsula and the Netherlands; from 1808 to 1815* (London, 1846), Vol. 2, p. 333. *Memoirs of the Late War: comprising the personal narrative of Captain Cooke of the 43rd Regiment Light Infantry*, Vol. 1, p. 121. Lieutenant J.W. Dunbar Moodie, 21st Regiment of Fusiliers, *Narrative of the Campaign in Holland in 1814* (London, 1831), Vol. 2, pp. 310 and 305.
14. John Green, *The Vicissitudes of a Soldier's Life* (Louth, 1827, reprinted Wakefield, 1973), pp. 100 and 189–90.
15. *Memoirs of the Late War: comprising the personal narrative of Captain Cooke, of the 43rd Regiment Light Infantry* . . . , Vol. 1, p. 143.

16. H.B. Robinson, *Memoirs of Lieutenant General Sir Thomas Picton* (London, 1835), Vol. 2, pp. 338–9.
17. Captain John Henry Cooke, *A Narrative of Events in the South of France and of the attack on New Orleans, in 1814 and 1815*, pp. 236, 247–8, 204, 234, 240.
18. Daiches, *A Critical History of English Literature*, pp. 1154–5.
19. Robert Graves to Cyril Hartman, ? January 1918, and compare with Graves to Hartman, 15 June 1918, Special Miscellaneous Collection, M 4; Joe Cotterill to Sassoon, 16 October 1917, see also Cotterill to Sassoon, 17 September 1916, SS 1; and Geoffrey Harbord to Sassoon, 13 September 1917, SS 3; Sassoon Papers, PP/MCR/C26, Imperial War Museum (hereafter IWM). Sassoon's reaction to the wounding and loss of friends is in Sassoon, *Memoirs of an Infantry Officer*, pp. 107, 112, 251 and 284.
20. Sassoon, 'At the Base', *c.* 1917, SS 1, Sassoon Papers, IWM. Ibid., and Sassoon, *Memoirs of an Infantry Officer*, pp. 284 and 291.
21. Sassoon, 'On Returning to the War Zone', 1916; 'At the Base', *c.* 1917, SS 1, Sassoon Papers, IWM. Yet in his memoirs, Sassoon sometimes defends the high command, Sassoon, *Memoirs of an Infantry Officer*, pp. 83 and 185.
22. Sassoon, 27 February 1929, Manuscript of 'Memoirs of an Infantry Officer', SS 3, Sassoon Papers, IWM.
23. Sassoon, 'Tempo', Notebook (kept while *Memoirs of an Infantry Officer* was being written), SS 4; Geoffrey Harbord to Sig (Sassoon), 29 July 1917, SS 3; W.H.R. Rivers to Sig (Sassoon), 1 February 1918, SS 7; Sassoon Papers, IWM. Sassoon, *Memoirs of an Infantry Officer*, pp. 331 ff. For a biography that cannot decide about Sassoon's mental state, see Michael Thorpe, *Siegfried Sassoon* (Leiden, London, Oxford, 1966), pp. 101 ff.
24. Sassoon, Notebook, including 'A Foreword (for myself only)', SS 4, Sassoon Papers, IWM. Fussell, *The Great War and Modern Memory*, p. 104. Even Robert Graves, who wrote perhaps the most consciously crafted memoir of the war, spent some time defending the historical accuracy of his book, *Good Bye To All That* (London, 1929) in his *But It Still Goes On* (London, 1930), pp. 18, 20, 25 and 27–8.
25. T.E. Lawrence, cited in Robert Wohl, *The Generation of 1914* (Cambridge, MA, 1979), p. 120. Modris Eksteins has much to say on the introspective First World War memoir in his *Rites of Spring*, pp. 290–9. The inward-looking anti-positivist movement of the 1890–1930 period is very well described in H. Stuart Hughes, *Consciousness and Society: The Reorientation of European Social Thought, 1890–1930* (New York, 1958).
26. Another criticism of Fussell exists in J.M. Winter, *The Experience of World War I* (London, 1988), pp. 227–9. Winter argues that Fussell is wrong on three counts. First, that Fussell is too exclusively Anglo-Saxon in his focus. (This seems unfair since Fussell set out specifically to deal only with British memoirs.) Second, that Fussell ignores what is old in the literature, namely a literature of bereavement and a literature of separation. (Some of the concerns of the present essay are similar.) Third, that Fussell ignores the literature of those who did not serve in the war, such as T.S. Eliot and Pasternak, but whose works have had an equally powerful effect on the modern imagination. (This seems a cogent argument.) See also the review of Fussell's Second World War memoir book by Brian Morton in the *Times Higher Education Supplement*, 1 September 1989, p. 13.

9

The Diplomatic Life: Reflections on Selected British Diplomatic Memoirs Written Before and After the Great War

ZARA STEINER

Old diplomats do not die; they write their memoirs. Throughout the nineteenth century and still today, British diplomats have felt called upon to record the events of their lives in prose and verse. Every major library in Britain has on its shelves those fine red volumes published by Edward Arnold before and after the Great War and the many memoirs produced by John Murray extending to the contemporary period. It would be amusing to identify the first diplomatist to write for posterity. One would like to know, too, whether and what retired ambassadors like Sir James Rennell Rodd, GCB or Sir Horace Rumbold Bart, GCB, GCBG, were paid for their labours and how many copies their multi-volumed recollections sold. It may well be that in the Victorian and Edwardian periods, readership was restricted to that 'inner circle' to which diplomatists belonged both by birth and profession but that this audience expanded during the inter-war period and after when explanations were sought for two catastrophic wars.

There are obvious reasons why diplomatists, and I use the term to cover members of both the Foreign Office and the diplomatic service, should have been so prolific. In the first place, we are dealing with an élite trained to write. Almost all, in the pre-1914 period, were sent away to schools where the study of the classics was central to the curriculum. Schoolboys even in the inter-war period were still expected to construe Latin and Greek passages and to write elegiacs. All boys were, by necessity, letter-writers from an early age, though these first epistles were often short and not always sweet. If they went to university, and this became more normal after the Lansdowne reforms of 1904–5, there was again an emphasis on writing, whether one did Greats or Modern History or, as in the case of Charles Hardinge, the Mathematical Tripos.

Further changes in the Foreign Office bureaucratic regime in 1905–6 meant that relatively young men were expected to write minutes or memoranda on incoming dispatches and selected subjects of interest for the perusal of their superiors. If juniors still did a good deal of work which 'dulled the wits', they were encouraged to have 'a little say in high matters however wide of the mark at first'.[1] Seniors corrected prose in the department and in foreign posts; neither bureaucratic jargon nor Americanisms were tolerated. Dispatches were not written in the Cherokee English of today's electronic messages but in a manner acceptable to highly literate superiors. Though drafted by hand (the first lady typists were introduced into the Foreign Office in 1889 and the memoir material is full of young diplomats learning to type in their first posts), non-telegraphic communications and even departmental memoranda could go on for several pages. Vansittart's memoranda were often so long, prolix and literary that they were not read. Not only were diplomats abroad asked to contribute to the Annual Report, that onerous task instituted by Eyre Crowe to act as a memory bank for the Foreign Office, but ambassadors and ministers might, on their own initiative, prepare descriptions of the situation in their posts on arrival or departure, and members of their staffs sent home reports on special problems or on trips outside the capital.

There were as many complaints then as now that the Foreign Office did not read what they were sent. It was to avoid just such a result that Owen O'Malley, having been the repeated victim of Foreign Office indifference, began his report on a trip through Russia in 1942 with the following eye-catching opening:

The following account of a journey through Russia consequent upon the evacuation of the British Legation at Budapest is impressionistic and prejudiced. 'It is necessary', said Sir Stafford Cripps in Moscow, 'to study this country and people with an open mind and to see both sides of the question.' So indeed it is for him but because I have never lived there, have rarely spoken to Russians, am ignorant of their art, science and literature, have made no study of their interminable statistics, and in fact know practically nothing about Russia and the Russians, it does not follow that my superficial impressions are ill-founded.

I fully admit my prejudice, for I dislike every avoidable form of governmental interference with private thought and conduct. I wish to make and keep for myself and my children as much money as I properly can; I believe in the utility of a privileged and of an hereditary aristocracy. I enjoy the companionship of persons of condition and breeding; I respect tradition, and – I believe in God. Especially I abhor dirt; as nurse used to say, 'Cleanliness is next to Godliness.'

But just because I was prepared in advance to be disgusted by what I knew to be a dirty, ruthless, communistic, revolutionary and atheistic country, it doesn't follow that my experiences were without importance.[2]

Ambassadors in the nine embassies of the pre-First World War period had less cause for complaint. They reported officially to the Foreign Office on a regular basis, exchanged private letters with the Foreign Secretary, the permanent under-secretary, and, in shorter form, with the head of the department responsible for the affairs of their embassy. All were accomplished letter-writers. Even after the amalgamation of the Foreign Office and the diplomatic service in 1919, men might spend the greater part of their lives abroad. In the days before aeroplane travel was common, this could mean virtual exile. Apart from six months at the Foreign Office at the start of his career and a brief period of three months at the end of 1915, Nevile Henderson spent his entire 34 years in the service in foreign posts. Writing letters to family, friends and colleagues was often the only way to maintain contacts which, under ordinary circumstances, were ill-nourished by irregular home leaves of a maximum three or four months' duration. Many diplomats, according to these memoirs, kept diaries or, as in the case of Harold Rumbold, depended on their wives to fulfil this function. Such diaries and letters were the source material for future memoirs.

One is dealing with a group of men for whom writing was second nature. If the style of writing and the length of memoirs gradually changed from the leisurely and somewhat florid recollections of the mid- and late-Victorian periods to the brisker and shorter accounts of the mid-twentieth century, almost all are highly readable. Diplomacy was a profession which depended on written communication. Speech-making was less common than today (Spring-Rice was noted for his unusual excellence in this respect) and of secondary importance. But diplomats were expected to write clearly and well.

For the most part time was found for correspondence and diary-writing and even for writing and publishing books of verse and prose of all descriptions. Admittedly, permanent under-secretaries – Charles

Hardinge, Robert Vansittart, William Strang in their memoirs and Alexander Cadogan in his diary – repeatedly complained of the heavy burden of work and the long hours consumed by Foreign Office business. A few like Arthur Nicolson were overwhelmed by the paperwork but, in general, the permanent heads of the Foreign Office had to get through the files or else the whole office system would grind to a halt. Vansittart's schedule is instructive: 'I would reach my office at 10, leave at 7, play cards at the St James for an hour, then dinner and read boxes till 12 – if I had dined out, till 1 or 2.'' In moments of crisis, as in the months after the outbreak of war in 1914, the pace was so hectic that a three-shift system was introduced into the Foreign Office. But generally, especially for the men in the 'third room' (the room where the most junior clerks worked), the work was routine and far from taxing. Though the reforms of 1905–6 were to change the office atmosphere, non-bureaucratic types still found the clerical work wearisome and the fixed hours irksome.

Owen O'Malley, a Foreign Office man, speaks of the 'almost cloistral peace' reigning in the Western Department in 1911,

if we got home from work in time to change for dinner and if one of us was generally away in the country from Friday to Tuesday, this did not mean that we did not, on the average, do a good day's work for very little pay; to be precise, for £3 a day. The Marmadukes and Archibalds of fiction must have long been extinct; at least I never met them.[4]

Abroad, too, the head of chancery and some of his staff, particularly in a large embassy, had hectic moments on bag day (the bags went every night from Paris but only once a week or at even longer intervals from other embassies except during crises when intensified diplomatic activity was reflected in a stream of communications from London). Yet anyone sampling these memoirs will quickly realize that official life in some embassies and many legations was leisurely at best and excruciatingly dull at worst. A young man coming to St Petersburg or Peking might well expect to have the time to travel, to learn the language, and generally to get the feel of the country. The range and number of languages acquired in the course of the normal career abroad would astonish most modern diplomatists; the £100 addition to one's salary while in the country for knowledge of the language was only an added incentive.

In the smaller posts, such as at Copenhagen or The Hague, where there was still the old sense of living as part of the ambassador's family, one's hours were regulated by the schedule of the minister. At Copenhagen, for instance, Sir Reginald Tower lived at the Plaza Hotel, and the diplomatic staff met for breakfast at 8.30, then at the Jockey Club for lunch at one, and dinner at eight. The pace was set by the ambassador or minister or, more often, by the head of chancery. But even under efficient seniors, diplomats had hours of the day, days in the week, and weeks in the year when they could write, travel, hunt and paint. Rennell Rodd published numerous books of verse as did Robert Vansittart who, even as a junior member of the Paris embassy, had a play performed on the Paris stage to the British ambassador's (Lord Bertie's) deep indignation. Memoirs are filled with drawings and verse composed during service abroad, not all as satiric (or bad) as Hughe Knatchbull-Hugessen's examples in *Diplomat in Peace and War*. Inspired by a Foreign Office instruction on the use of metal paper-fasteners, Knatchbull-Hugessen wrote an eight-stanza verse which begins:

> Vainly we hoped the yards we spin,
> Though caught with clip or pierced with pin
> Could boast coherence greater still
> Through lucid phrase and drafting skill;
> (And H.M. Consuls not a few,
> Must certainly have thought so too),
> We may have hugged the vicious thought
> That pins concealed in some report
> Would help the minds of those who read
> To find the point of what we said,
> (And surely H.M. Consuls too
> Shared this intelligible view).[5]

Spring-Rice was 'poetically inspired' by a Foreign Office circular instructing Heads of Mission to warn staff against marrying foreigners:

> And, diplomats, remember this
> – there's wisdom in obeying –
> The undiluted British Miss
> is dull perhaps, but paying.[6]

Some capitals were inaccessible and had few home visitors. Diplomats relieved the monotony of life in Sofia by travelling to Belgrade, Bucharest, Philippopoli and Constantinople. Diplomats in Tehran, where the diplomatic circle was small, or in Cairo, Peking or Tokyo, used their weekends or periods of more extended leave to

travel far afield. Men coming home or going out to their posts explored
unknown territories; Owen O'Malley, coming back from China, went
through Indo-China and Cambodia, relying on the hospitality of British
consuls along the way. Posts such as The Hague were scarcely centres
of diplomatic activity; Sir Horace Rumbold spent eight years in this
pleasant back-water wondering if he would ever get an embassy before
retirement. In the South American posts, commercial negotiations,
often the only diplomatic activity, could take months; but more time
was spent in waiting than in negotiating. There was, moreover, in the
inter-war period, a commercial counsellor who could attend to the
detailed bargaining. The second-in-command was generally delighted
when heads of missions went on leave or were ill (memoirs are full of
diplomats and, worse still, their children and wives, becoming ill and
asking for home leave) so that they could take charge of the mission
and feel less of a fifth wheel, as sometimes happened in larger posts. It
is for such reasons, among others, that so many diplomatic memoirs
are filled with descriptions of the social life of the capital, balls and
dinner parties, hunts of such number and kind that one is ready to join
the anti-blood sports league. More humane sports are also recorded –
especially polo, tennis and mountain climbing – together with travels
of the most arduous and dangerous nature, to places Sir Henry Lunn
had not yet discovered.

Lord Hardinge recalled that since the staff at the Berlin embassy in
the mid-1880s was not overworked, he was able to spend a good deal of
time sketching on the lakes at Potsdam, and that under Sir Mortimer
Durand at Tehran, following the example set by the minister, little
work was done except in the chancery.[7] Knatchbull-Hugessen
describes daily existence at the summer legation in Persia:

Life at Gulhek was almost a dream of delight. In summer one could sleep out
on a balcony . . . A little work till about midday, a plunge into the very cold
waters of the bathing pool, a glass of sherry, luncheon, an obligatory siesta in
the burning heat of the summer afternoon, tea, tennis, dinner – what could be
a more delightful programme . . .[8]

Cranley, the future Earl of Onslow, writes: 'St Petersburg was,
however, very dull at the beginning of the [Russo-Japanese] war. There
was little doing and little to report. I devoted my time to shooting and
learning Russian.'[9]

In Paris, on the other hand, both before and after the Great War,
chancery work was always heavy. Experiences differed depending on

the times and the nature of the work. 'A few days after I arrived in Brussels . . . in 1926, I took up to my chief, Sir George Grahamme, a telegram of a more than usually humdrum nature, he gave me a sour look and remarked gloomily, "When I first came here it was the Ambassadors' Conference, Fiume, Vilna, Rapallo, the Ruhr . . . now it's pig castings."'[10] Much depended on the ambassador or minister and the diplomat himself. 'Tokio was the only post I ever had where the work was really light', Nevile Henderson writes, 'in spite of the fact that the entire purely diplomatic staff consisted of the ambassador, the counsellor and two secretaries.'[11] In the far eastern missions, in Cairo and in Constantinople, the work was done by often brilliant and always highly knowledgeable oriental secretaries or dragomans, and this considerably lightened the work for the others. In the course of a long career, most men served in a dozen or more posts abroad but there was always time to cultivate the habit of writing. Given the leisure of retirement, even if one took a City directorship or went to the country to farm, it was almost inevitable that diplomats should turn to writing their memoirs. Nevile Henderson, terminally ill after his return from Berlin in 1939, wrote three books before his death in 1942 – a defence of his time in Berlin, an autobiography and a book about his dog Hippy.[12]

What do memoirs tell the reader about the diplomatic life? Judging from a small sample of those written about the pre- and post-1914 period, it is clear that all these men are writing about a small and highly privileged élite. Early chapters in most memoirs start with descriptions of 'old and distinguished families', related to each other by blood or marriage. Most were brought up in country homes of varying sizes and degrees of luxury. They were raised by nannies and governesses before being sent away to prep. schools and public schools, with Eton leading the list, and then on to Oxford and Cambridge. Whether of the aristocracy, like the future Earl Osborne who learned his languages at home, or from gentry families who studied their French and German and Italian or Spanish abroad in *pensions*, future diplomatists usually spent time with Scoones, the great crammer who boasted that every member of both services had passed through his hands except Lord Bertie.

There are exceptions to this composite portrait even before the Great War and a real, though not lasting, change took place in 1919 when the Foreign Office, desperately in need of recruits, held special qualifying examinations for service men. This was how William Strang, who came of farming people, went to a state school and to the

University of London, came into the Foreign Office. 'It admitted a few misfits, and the wastage was rather heavy, but I think that it was as satisfactory as any other system would have been; so many of the men of that generation had been killed.'[13] The differences in the personalities, lives and memoirs of Robert Vansittart, permanent under-secretary between 1930 and 1938, and William Strang, who occupied the same office between 1949 and 1953, warns the reader against facile generalizations about men of roughly the same generation. 'Van' was, in the Russian ambassador's words, 'flesh of the flesh of the ruling class of Great Britain', yet this larger than life figure could not be conventionally typecast in any other sense. No previous (or later) permanent under-secretary projected such a political image of himself or acted less like a civil servant. Few, if any, have lived on such a grand scale. William Strang, on the other hand, despite his unconventional background, fitted well into that category of officials who were more at ease in the Foreign Office than in the embassies abroad and whose modesty and reserve characteristically concealed great intelligence. It was typical of that 'irreproachable, if somewhat unapproachable' (Lord Gladwyn's description) man that as permanent under-secretary, he lived in London, 10 minutes away from the Foreign Office so that he could walk to work; and that he should have written an administrative history of the Foreign Office, a subject which would never have engaged the far more prolific Van's attention.[14] Strang was an 'Office' man in the mould of Eyre Crowe; Vansittart, who admired Crowe, represented all that his former chief mistrusted. Vansittart's memoirs are highly literary, wonderfully descriptive of colleagues and politicians, British and foreign, and very long. Lord Strang's *Home and Abroad* is far less self-indulgent, about events rather than people, more discreet and shorter.[15]

Even within a narrower spectrum, there were noticeable differences between such contemporaries as Lord Cranley (later Earl of Onslow) or Eustace Percy (later Lord Percy of Newcastle), son of the 7th Duke of Northumberland, a Scot like Sir Nevile Henderson, whose grandfather prospered in England and was worth nearly half a million when he died, Owen O'Malley, whose roots were in Mayo and whose father was Chief Justice in various colonies and a Judge of the extra-territorial courts in Egypt and the Ottoman empire, or David Kelly who was born in Adelaide and whose father was a professor of classics. But the distinctions historians draw between those who came from aristocratic or gentry families, or the differences between those recruited before and after the Great War, tend to fade as one reads these memoirs which, almost without exception, underline the shared experiences of an upper-class élite with a strong *esprit de corps* that obscure such lines of demarcation.

There was plenty of room for eccentrics and misfits in the service. Arthur Hardinge, ambassador in Madrid during the Great War and cousin of the more conventional Charles Hardinge, who went to see the Queen with a black morning coat hastily put on as an afterthought over brown tweed trousers and waistcoat and who would 'dictate at random brilliant letters and memoranda on any subject and in almost any language without always taking notice whether anyone was there to take down or not', was only one of many such examples.[16] Sir Clare Ford, whose appointment as ambassador at Constantinople was, according to Charles Hardinge, 'deplorable in every way', brought his mistress with him, a fact soon known to all, including the Turks.[17] David Kelly writes in his autobiography:

There was one Minister who reported imaginary interviews with a Government which refused to receive him any more; another who, in a year wrote only one despatch – requesting more pay . . . and even a very successful Ambassador in Washington signed a despatch unread, drafted by a clever but irresponsible secretary, which created consternation by its vigorous rejection of the Secretary of State's instructions.[18]

Whether in the Foreign Office or in the diplomatic service, despite the exceptional presence of a few ex-consular officials such as the ambassador at Constantinople, Sir William White, and his socially unacceptable wife, most, in the words of a future permanent under-secretary and ambassador to France, 'speaking metaphorically, speak the same language; they have the same habits of thought, and more or less the same points of view, and if anybody with a different language came in, I think he would be treated by the whole diplomatic service more or less with suspicion'.[19]

The limits to toleration are rarely openly expressed in memoirs, especially those published after 1945. When men such as these were deciding on careers, the chief alternatives to the Foreign Office were the services or, in the case of Vansittart, a literary career, or, for Lord Gladwyn, an All Souls Fellowship. 'Nobody in my family had ever been "in business" or, as it was formerly expressed "connected with trade", and I [Owen O'Malley] accepted this restriction as valid for myself.'[20] Esme Howard's experiences with a West Indian rubber syndicate and his appointment as consul-general in Crete were

exceptional in every respect. It is in Sir Francis Oppenheimer's
Stranger Within: Autobiographical Pages and other consular memoirs
that one finds the record of diplomatic snobberies with respect to trade
and traders.[21] The consular service remained the 'Cinderella service'
until the Scott–Eden reforms of 1943, and British consuls were treated
as second-class citizens even after these changes were introduced. Sir
David Scott, of impeccable Buccleuch lineage and head of the consular
department in the 1930s, fought a hard and long battle to bring consuls
in from the cold, but he could not break down the age-old prejudices of
the service. Though diplomats reported on commercial and economic
matters and, in some posts, found the bulk of their work of an economic
nature, the Foreign Office was slow to recognize that it 'could no
longer afford to consider its responsibility limited to strictly political
matters and leave all commercial and financial questions blindly to the
departments technically concerned'.[22] David Kelly, second in command
of an American department which covered British relations with the
whole American continent, was one of a few who, like Frank Ashton
Gwatkin from the far eastern consular service and head of the newly
formed Economic section of the Western department in the mid-1930s,
recognized the central importance of economic diplomacy in the international politics of the day.

There were limits to toleration and some were excluded by general
consent from the diplomatic ranks. There were Catholics by birth and
conversion, both at the Foreign Office and in the diplomatic service
and even a Christian Scientist (the future Lord Gore-Booth), but Jews
and infidels were mainly beyond the pale. When the British ambassador in the United States in June 1920 suggested that the ideal senior
staff in Washington should consist of at least one Roman Catholic,
a Jew, a Scots Presbyterian, and an Anglican, Charles Hardinge commented, 'We could not find enough Jews and Scotch Presbyterians to
go round.'[23] Interestingly enough, given the not infrequent examples of
slighting references to Jews, Horace Rumbold, a far more cosmopolitan
figure than his son, was horrified by the anti-Semitic movement in
Austria where he was ambassador: 'there is no more pernicious
influence in Vienna than that of its bigoted, overbearing leader, the
Burgomaster Dr Lueger . . .'.[24] The private secretary did not look
kindly on the foreign born (though there were successful candidates
from the dominions even before 1914) and, if you had a foreign-
sounding name, it was wise to change it.

If these memoirs underline the social coherence of the services, they
also contain repeated references to the financial difficulties of the

diplomatic life. In the pre-1919 period, an attaché received no pay at all for two years on the sound financial grounds that if there were 'enough d—d fools in the world like you' to work for nothing the Treasury were not going to pay them.[25] When the young diplomat became a Third Secretary at the end of that period his salary was only £150. Counsellors were paid between £500 and £1,000 and though there were ways of augmenting these salaries, they were hardly princely. The taxed salaries of ambassadors and heads of mission covered not only their personal remuneration but also *frais de représentation*. The highest salary, £11,500, was reserved for the Paris embassy. Given the costs of maintaining that building and conducting a social life fitting the position of the British representative in Paris, ambassadors to France were (and continued to be) men of considerable means.

It was obvious then why candidates for the diplomatic service, though not for the Foreign Office, had to have a guaranteed personal income of £400 a year. Charles Hardinge's father declined to give such a guarantee; fortunately his godmother, Lady Lucan, died and left a small legacy to boost his allowance of £200 or £300 a year. Hardinge's financial difficulties were solved by his marriage; his father-in-law, Lord Alington, was wealthy enough to travel from Vienna to Constantinople in a special train, an act of extravagance which impressed even the Sultan.[26] Hardinge's wife was lady-in-waiting to the future Queen Alexandra, a key factor in the rise of this extremely ambitious diplomat.

Few could live abroad on £400 a year. Nevile Henderson found that, even with a parental allowance of £600, he could not have managed at St Petersburg, one of the most costly postings, without the £60 and lodgings he received as private secretary to Arthur Nicolson, as well as his steady earnings from bridge.[27] Vansittart, whose father's disastrous excursions into the world of business resulted in the loss of his allowance and his inheritance, was continually in financial difficulties. He turned his literary talents to good use but, for a man who loved the good life and liked to gamble, the lack of funds was a serious impediment to life in Paris. Two marriages to wealthy women (the first, an American divorcee who was the daughter of an American banker, died in 1928) restored his fortunes and allowed him to live in style at his beautiful William and Mary house, Denham Place. For those less wise in their choice of wives, the middle years, before they came into their inheritances, could be difficult ones.

Diplomacy was a wealthy man's profession. Even after the 1919 reforms, when it was no longer necessary to have a private income, the costs of life abroad dissuaded eminently suitable candidates from applying for the service. In the pre-First World War period, it would have been impossible for any but the comfortably placed to think about the diplomatic service. The Earl of Onslow warned his son that persons of extravagant habits were scarcely suitable for such a career. Even Cranley sought less expensive postings such as Tehran or Tokyo where life was refreshingly cheap.

Clerks, in distinction to diplomats, were paid from the start; junior clerks earned from £200 to £500, the assistant under-secretaries £1,000 to £1,500, and the permanent under-secretary £2,500 in 1914. A man like Eyre Crowe lived modestly even when permanent under-secretary. 'Can't the man [Lord Curzon] realize', Crowe used to say, 'that long after he has gone home in his Rolls-Royce, I have to catch a No. 11 bus for Elm Park Road and sup off sardines or cold sausages before dealing with the evening's telegrams?'[28] According to Vansittart, the scrupulously honest Eyre Crowe left £200. To show its respect to a man who commanded unusual loyalty, the Office raised a five-figure sum for his family.[29] It was easier to live comfortably on a restricted income in London than abroad. Again, Crowe was exceptional. Despite the financial differences between clerks and diplomats, the majority of the office, before 1919, were drawn from families 'in society' and if they had less money than some, they were accustomed to the lifestyle of the upper classes. Thomas Sanderson, Lord Salisbury's long-serving permanent under-secretary (1894–1906), who had left Eton when his father lost his money, thought himself fully entitled to be raised to the baronage.[30] Owen O'Malley notes that when he entered the Western department in 1911, four out of six men were the offspring of noble families.[31] Clerks were often the younger sons of the same families who served in Parliament, or in the army and navy, or even in the diplomatic service.

Financial pressures were somewhat eased when the Foreign Office and diplomatic service were amalgamated and a combined scale of emoluments established in 1919. The £400 a year requirement for the diplomatic service was abolished.[32] However, moves abroad still had to be financed out of private pockets and the upkeep of a legation, not to speak of an embassy, required a major outlay. In 1919, after eight years in the diplomatic service, Owen O'Malley's gross salary was £594 12s. 8d. By 1937, it had risen to £1,045 net, less than his wife's (Ann Bridge's) literary earnings of £1,300. O'Malley was forced to sell 'Brigend', the farm at Ockham ('I was the first member of the Foreign Office to live in the suburbs and go up and down to London every day') in order to afford the move and upkeep of the legation in Mexico.[33] It has to be remembered, as these autobiographies make clear, that whether in London or abroad, the diplomat lived comfortably during the 1920s and 1930s. Lord Gladwyn, speaking of his little house in Chelsea and a small income, notes that in 1929 he could afford a married couple, a lady's maid, and a motor car without overdrawing. When his son was born, a nanny was employed.[34] David Kelly, who had a house at 7 Hyde Park Square, speaks of a 'newly engaged butler who became absurdly familiar and had to be dismissed and the only person of the new staff to appear was a timid young girl who felt she should go back to her family in Bournemouth' in 1939.[35] It was one of the real perks of serving abroad that one had servants (the counsellor in Peking had 18) and, with certain notable exceptions, comfortable housing, and most of the appurtenances of the pre-1914 world.

Until 1938, private-house entertainment in the great houses of London was still possible, and the English preferred, and could still give, lunches and dinner for 20 or 30 people. Embassy life was still on the grand scale, though posts had grown in size and were losing their familial atmosphere. Berlin, for instance, according to Nevile Henderson, employed 10 people before 1914, but almost 100 in 1938. It may be that only old-fashioned diplomats like Sir Horace Rumbold would worry about the problem of entertaining the British community in Vienna on the occasion of the Queen's Diamond Jubilee, for this community was almost entirely made up of governesses and teachers, musical and other students, a few electrical engineers, some gasfitters and a trainer or two:

I and my staff and that of the Consulate-General were in full uniform, my wife and our dinner guests being also en grande toilette. In curious contrast with these surroundings there began to pour in at nine o'clock a stream of nice, somewhat shy ladies in the simplest of evening attire, not a few in plain morning gowns, with a sprinkling of men mostly in every-day clothes, until the room was filled by a crowd of people . . . few of whom either my wife or I knew even by sight but whom, as they arrived, we cordially welcomed in true White House fashion . . . by the time I had shaken hands with, and toasted, Baron Natty's veteran trainer, Mr. Butters, I felt that I had done the best I could under the circumstances.[36]

There were interchanges between the Foreign Office and the diplomatic service on an individual basis and their number increased in the pre-1914 period. 'Without these', Knatchbull-Hugessen writes, 'there would have been a serious lack of mutual comprehension, those who controlled foreign affairs from London knowing nothing of conditions abroad and those who served abroad lacking personal contact with their colleagues at home'.[37] Senior officials in the Foreign Office were rewarded with legations and embassies; Sir Francis Bertie was one. Both Charles Hardinge and Arthur Nicolson came back to the Foreign Office as permanent under-secretaries. Yet there was strong opposition, on both sides, to amalgamation and distinct differences between the 'grubs' and the 'butterflies' remained. Lord Gladwyn speaks of the difference between the operator, the tough sensible man of the world who performs well in the diplomatic arena, and the adviser who prefers to put his thought on paper:

A successful professional diplomat is surely a well informed, agreeable and socially-minded character with a profound knowledge of his fellow men and a certain natural cunning, who knows exactly when to slip a word in edgeways that will influence the mind of his own chief or that of the foreigner with whom he is negotiating.[38]

Lord Strang claims that Office types must be 'willing to face cheerfully the sometimes painful austerities of service at home in contrast to the more spacious lives of many of their colleagues abroad'.[39] Strang felt he was freer to read whatever he wished in London and could range as far afield from his official duties as he wanted. Eyre Crowe's *Lesebuch* suggests a similar breadth of interests that could be indulged in London; his only fear was that he might be appointed to an embassy.

We do know from these memoirs that even in the days before the term 'bureaucratic politics' had entered the political vocabulary, some men flourished in Whitehall while others only looked forward to their eventual release. Charles Hardinge clearly functioned as well in London as he did abroad, whereas Arthur Nicolson was clearly unhappy in the permanent under-secretary's chair. Owen O'Malley enjoyed his overseas appointments (all but Mexico), though he loved 'Brigend' and left his hens and pigs with a heavy heart. Philip Currie and Francis Bertie, who left the Foreign Office for top appointments in the diplomatic service before the Great War, had difficulties in shaking the bureaucratic habits of a lifetime in London. Amalgamation in 1919 gave the private secretary, who remained the key figure for appointments, greater flexibility in assignments and made financially possible transfers that could not have taken place before 1919. It did not, however, eradicate the differences in the nature of the work done and the preferences as well as the capabilities of the men concerned at home and overseas.

Diplomats were not only the sons of politicians but, on occasion, became politicians themselves. Yet despite their political allegiances (one had to resign if running for Parliament), they served under chiefs of the opposing parties without difficulty, and loyally served governments of whatever political complexion. Irish politics seem to have been the most divisive of the pre-1914 splits, and the political animosities of the Liberal period of rule far sharper than was usual in British politics. Arthur Nicolson was a strong Ulsterman and the chief clerk, Sir Hubert Montgomery, was a Covenanter (his father was a member of the Ulster provisional government); yet both served under Sir Edward Grey, a Liberal who did not share their views. Cranley, whose father was a member of the Conservative 'shadow cabinet', and who corresponded with and met many of the highest-ranking Conservative politicians, was private secretary to Sir Edward Grey. Admittedly, he was considered a renegade and was excluded from some Conservative houses in London. His connections did not make him suspect in Grey's eyes. Vansittart claims he only voted once, in 1931, for Duff Cooper, a diplomatic friend, who became a Conservative politician. Vansittart was private secretary to Stanley Baldwin, Ramsay MacDonald, and Arthur Henderson, and worked harder for Henderson than for any other foreign secretary, even Lord Curzon. In fact, despite the socially conservative views of many of these writers (Gladwyn underlines his radical views when young though his father was a Conservative MP), the transition to Labour rule seems to have been effected calmly, whatever the private doubts of individuals. It was Ernest Bevin, after 1945, who most captured Foreign Office hearts; hardly a political memoir exists which fails to sing the praises of this extraordinary foreign secretary.

How much authoritative information is conveyed by these memoirs? One learns a great deal about how work was done in the old Foreign Office and the effects of the 1905 reforms. Dreaming of being a modern Talleyrand, Vansittart was told to 'fag and decipher, to fill the Cabinet's pouches with papers, to copy out telegrams in violet ink and rub them into scores on stacks of decomposing "jellyfish", whose fragments were pervading.'[40] The 1905 reforms liberated the juniors from these often paralysing routine tasks by giving the purely clerical work to second division clerks employed in registries, as was done in other domestic departments. Admittedly, even after 1905, juniors spent most of their time ciphering and deciphering telegrams, registering, indexing and filing secret papers, filling the 'Cabinet pouches' and processing 'confidential' material. But men were soon given more interesting tasks, writing memoranda on special subjects or drafts of replies to dispatches from abroad, and were later encouraged to become 'specialists' on particular areas or problems. Strang is quite detailed in his description of both his own job and the way work was done in the pre- and post-1945 Foreign Office.

One gets a less detailed account of how overseas missions were run. There was no typical day in the life of a British diplomatist. Until the 1920s, the diplomatic staff did all the paper-work, including the ciphering, the copying and the registering of dispatches. Nevile Henderson claims the only job not done by the diplomats in the chancery was the stamping and posting of letters. By the mid-1920s, most missions employed archivists and typists. But the main function of the establishment remained the collection of information (most diplomats, with the notable exception of Vansittart were scathing about 'intelligence agents'), and this was done formally, through interviews and meetings, and informally, at dinners and balls, while playing tennis or shooting, or by trips outside the capital. Both before and after the Great War, there were reports of economic and financial matters as well as the whole range of subjects that came under the heading political instructions. Requests for information could range from the use of paperclips (cited above) and rules for the proper folding of dispatches to enquiries about the mating habits of birds of paradise. There were happy and unhappy posts as there were 'good' and 'bad' ambassadors and ministers. The efficiency of the mission depended on the head of chancery, usually a first secretary, and, in Paris, a diplomat with a considerable reputation at home.

The work in the chancery, though partly done by clerical staff after 1919, did not vary with time. As is clear from these accounts there was a basic similarity in the tasks to be done. Owen O'Malley, commenting on a visit to the legation at Tehran in 1925 where Sir Percy Loraine motored out 20 or 30 miles to greet him, comments on the physical appearance of overseas posts.

All Legations and Embassies have something in common. Outside, they may well differ; in one case the building may conform to local architecture; in another His Majesty's Government may have constructed a residence more appropriate to St. John's Wood or Woking. Inside, though, imitation Hepplewhite furniture from the Tottenham Court Road will certainly have been provided by the Office of Works for every room, the decoration will vary with the taste and income of the head of the Mission. But in all Missions the offices resemble each other closely; here are the same stationery, the same filing cabinets, the same pencils and punches and calendars and the same Foreign Office List and 'Who's Who' on the same tables and desks. In the residential part of the house too, though the servants may be white or black or yellow, there will be the same order and kindly discipline, the same Lux, Ronuk, chintz, potplants, water-colours, large bath towels and Bromo which the Englishman carries round the world like a snail its shell . . . In nearly but not quite all Missions, too, there will be the same welcome from the host for the visiting colleague, the same preliminary exchange of service news and scandal and, for the guest, the delightful relaxation from the fatigues of his journey.[41]

In almost every memoir there are brilliant portraits of chiefs and colleagues as well as often shrewd assessments of foreign diplomats (note the positive view of von Jagow, the pre-war German diplomat who was trusted and liked) whom one might well meet again at another post. There is a high degree of concurrence about the respective merits of those who had reached the top of the promotion ladder. Sir Mortimer Durand was found wanting in every respect even before his disasters in Washington; Sir George Graham was judged too concerned with his career and the techniques and mechanics of diplomacy to the exclusion of its substance. The brilliant and much admired Lord Dufferin, whose financial distress at the end of his Paris embassy evokes general sympathy, the prestigious 'Lord', Lord Cromer at Cairo, the patient, quiet, but effective Ronald Campbell, the well-read and good-humoured Esme Howard, the well-liked 'Ponderous' Percy Loraine, and the highly intelligent and eloquent Cecil Spring-Rice, move in and out of these pages along with a whole array of other diplomatic and Foreign Office names. The historian will find much here that gives a new dimension to the impersonal papers which are his daily diet.

The memoir material will not provide a full or even an authoritative view of the diplomacy of the pre-1914 period or a balanced account of the 1930s. *The Mist Procession* gives at least one man's overall impression of the long march of events; others tend to be more personal and less propagandistic. There are numerous reasons for the diplomatic thinness of some of the accounts, even where they describe actions in which the writer took part. Discretion was the cardinal virtue of the service; young diplomats were warned never to speak outside the Office of what they heard within its walls. Well before the passage of the Official Secrets Act, memoirists did not write about the debates which lay behind the foreign secretary's actions. As O'Malley wrote:

The efficient conduct of business in the Foreign Office depends almost more than anything else on complete frankness between the Secretary of State at the top and the latest joined member of the Service at the bottom. This would be shattered if any member of the brotherhood, high or low, had reason to fear that words spoken within this citadel of mutual trust and confidence might afterwards be made public.[42]

It was this sense of 'brotherhood' which protected Donald Maclean and the other members of the 'Cambridge Comintern' and which explains the terrible sense of shock which their defections caused throughout the service. There are exceptions to this general reserve on questions of policy, and many autobiographies contain some nugget of information not found in the official or even private papers. Some books, Sir George Buchanan's *My Mission to Russia and Other Diplomatic Memoirs* (London, 1923) and the whole group of writings, such as Nevile Henderson's *Failure of a Mission*, Walford Selby's *Diplomatic Twilight 1930–1940* (London, 1953), Vansittart's *Lessons of My Life* (London, 1943), as well as parts of *The Mist Procession*, composed to defend or attack the policy of appeasement, were written with that purpose specifically in mind. Traditionally, it was more common for politicians than for diplomats to take on the role of advocate. But before the Second World War ended, diplomats felt compelled to have their say about their own position on the vexed question of 'appeasement'. There are also scattered in the pages of even the more anodyne memoirs, accounts of incidents and meetings that can again enlarge the historian's mental maps. In Horace Rumbold's and Rennell Rodd's accounts there are references to disagreements with Lord Salisbury, and the latter is surprisingly critical of the Foreign Secretary's diplomacy during his last administration.[43] Hardinge writes not only of his role during the Dogger Bank incident but of his first-hand memory of the famous Poincaré–Curzon encounter in Paris in the summer of 1922, immortalized in Harold Nicolson's *Lord Curzon: The Last Phase*.[44] Owen O'Malley writes about his part in the settlement of the Hankow incident which fills gaps in the official record.[45] There is, though it relates to a later period, a brilliant reconstruction of John Balfour's encounter with Winston Churchill ('Greatly elated at this chance of seeing the PM in council') as they battled over the wording of the draft telegram to be sent to President Roosevelt in August 1940. After destroying the American department's draft and producing a far longer but also more stinging rejection of the president's demand that, in case of defeat, the British fleet should be moved across the Atlantic, Churchill turned on the thoroughly cowed Balfour: '"I blamed the length of your draft and now I have composed a longer one myself", he said with boyish pleasure at his handiwork. "I'm afraid I have rather mauled your draft." "I only did what I was told", I moaned. "I know, I know", was his benevolent answer . . .'. On Halifax's instructions, a new and far milder telegram was drafted and sent, but in Churchill's history of the war, the full text of his abortive telegram is given.[46] It would have been unlikely that any diplomat of the 'old school' would have recounted this conversation, though it confirmed all Eyre Crowe's prejudices about politicians mixing in diplomatic affairs.

This essay deals primarily with the first decades of the twentieth century but only three of the samples selected stop with the First World War. To the historian reading these memoirs, conventional historical divisions, such as the Great War, seem less important than the lines of continuity which linked the old and new diplomacy. The conventions and forms of the 'old order' persisted far longer than even the diplomats assumed. There are repeated references to the disappearance of 'good society' and the 'grand seigneurs' of the past, but the date of reference extends from 1880 to 1938. Lord Gladwyn refers to the curious fact that in 1939 'the entire Government machine on the foreign side, outside No. 10, was at the beginning of the war dominated by Old Etonians'. 'Take Foreign Affairs strictly speaking, Eden, Halifax, Cadogan, Vansittart, Nevile Henderson (regrettably), Ronnie Campbell, Percy Loraine, Harold Macmillan, Duff Cooper, almost all the tops, had been at Eton.'[47] The same comment about Eton is still being made in 1990 with little justification. Owen O'Malley's forthright reflections on becoming minister in Budapest in 1941 are unusual only in their published form:

There is no doubt that to be a British Ambassador or Minister can be highly enjoyable. In the first place it is good to travel the world in comfort at Her Majesty's expense; nice to have the best places in trains and ships and at the opera, big houses to live in, lots of good servants (in every country in the world being a servant in the British Embassy is a much sought-after job) and a staff which attends to all the boring time-wasting details of travel, house-keeping and social obligation; above all nice to be the cock on top of one's own little dunghill, master of one's time and movements and able to give instructions which will be punctually and thoroughly carried out.[48]

This is admittedly not the account which will be written by the recent ambassador to Kuwait who was chef to his remaining three-man team.

If there is a stereotyped picture of the diplomatic life in an earlier era, the diplomats contributed to its creation. The radical readjustments of the camera occur only in the 1950s and 1960s and, even then, just a hint of Marcel Proust's M. Norpois' world persists. The differences between those books published before and after 1939 lie more often in the pages and binding than in the tales which they tell.

NOTES

For a much more detailed, authoritative account of the background of clerks and diplomats, and descriptions of the Foreign Office and the British diplomatic service, see Raymond Jones, *The British: Diplomatic Service, 1815–1914* (London, 1983), and *The Nineteenth Century Foreign Office: An Administrative History* (London, 1971).

1. Lord Vansittart, *The Mist Procession* (London, 1958), pp. 98–9.
2. Owen O'Malley Ms, Undated memorandum, *Memoranda, 1928–1941.*
3. Vansittart, p. 408; Lord Strang, *Home and Abroad* (London, 1956), pp. 274–6 and 279.
4. Owen O'Malley, *The Phantom Caravan* (London, 1954), p. 36.
5. Sir Hughe Knatchbull-Hugessen, *Diplomat in Peace and War* (London, 1949), p. 244.
6. Quoted in Gordon Waterfield, *Professional Diplomat: Sir Percy Loraine* (London, 1973), p. 18.
7. Lord Hardinge of Penshurst, *Old Diplomacy* (London, 1947), pp. 28 and 62.
8. Knatchbull-Hugessen, p. 75.
9. Earl of Onslow, *Sixty-Three Years* (London, n.d.), p. 104.
10. Knatchbull-Hugessen, p. 232.
11. Nevile Henderson, *Water under the Bridges* (London, 1945), p. 53.
12. Nevile Henderson, *Failure of a Mission* (London, 1940); *Water under the Bridges*; *Hippy, in memoriam: the story of a dog* (London, 1943).
13. Strang, p. 49.
14. Lord Gladwyn, *The Memoirs of Lord Gladwyn* (London, 1972), pp. 58–9.
15. Strang, p. 275; see also Strang's *The Foreign Office* (London, 1952) and *The Diplomatic Career* (London, 1962).
16. George Rendel, *The Sword and the Olive, 1913–1945* (London, 1957), p. 50.
17. Hardinge, p. 49.
18. David Kelly, *The Ruling Few* (London, 1952), p. 151.
19. Quoted in Z. Steiner, *The Foreign Office and Foreign Policy, 1898–1914* (Cambridge, 1969), p. 19.
20. O'Malley, p. 26.
21. Francis Oppenheimer, *Stranger Within: Autobiographical Pages* (London, 1960); Andrew Ryan, *The Last of the Dragomans* (London, 1951). For further citations and information see D.C.M. Platt, *The Cinderella Service: British Consuls since 1825* (London, 1971).
22. Kelly, pp. 207–8.
23. Quoted in Alan Sharp, 'Lord Curzon and the Foreign Office', in Roger Bullen (ed.), *The Foreign Office 1782–1982* (Frederick, MD, 1984), p. 70.
24. Horace Rumbold, *Final Recollections of a Diplomatist* (London, 1905).
25. Onslow, p. 50.
26. Hardinge, p. 46.
27. Henderson, p. 30.
28. O'Malley, p. 60.
29. Vansittart, p. 334.
30. Ibid., p. 45.
31. O'Malley, p. 34.
32. See M. Dockrill and Z. Steiner, 'The Foreign Office Reforms, 1919–1921', *Historical Journal*, Vol. xvii (1974), pp. 131–56, for details of the changes made in 1919.

33. O'Malley, p. 51.
34. Gladwyn, p. 37.
35. Kelly, p. 260.
36. Rumbold, p. 303.
37. Knatchbull-Hugessen, p. 13.
38. Gladwyn, p. 57.
39. Strang, pp. 50–1.
40. Vansittart, pp. 43–4.
41. O'Malley, p. 77.
42. Ibid., p.157.
43. Rumbold, p. 66; Sir James Rennell Rodd, *Social and Diplomatic Memories, 1902–1919*, 3rd series (London, 1925), pp. 38–9.
44. Hardinge, pp. 272–3; Harold Nicolson, *Lord Curzon: The Last Phase* (London, 1934).
45. O'Malley, p. 157.
46. John Balfour, *Not too Correct an Aureole* (London, 1983), pp. 74–9.
47. Gladwyn, p. 106.
48. O'Malley, p. 247.

10
Shield of Memory: The Memoirs of the British Foreign Policy-Making Élite 1919–39

B.J.C. McKERCHER

The only guide to a man is his conscience, the only shield to his memory is the rectitude and sincerity of his actions.

(Winston Churchill, November 1940)[1]

Memoirs are like a shield that political leaders fashion to protect their reputations, and this is especially true of those produced by the small élite that controlled or sought to control British foreign policy in the period between 1919 and 1939. The Great War had ended on a note of optimism for most British diplomatists, who reckoned that they could use their country's leading position within the victorious Allied coalition to shape the peace settlement – and, consequently, international relations – in a way that would better protect British interests. Most important in this regard was to ensure that another war of 1914–18 proportions, with its enormous expenditure of blood and treasure, would never again threaten the safety and security of Britain and its Empire. During the peace conference period, and for almost two decades thereafter, the British foreign policy-making élite[2] endeavoured to ensure international peace and security as the best guarantee of Britain's continuing status as the world's only global power. Alas, the hopes of 1918–19 and the hard work of the succeeding 20 years turned to dust when Hitler's armies invaded Poland in September 1939. For the second time in a little more than a generation, general war in Europe erupted – to be followed two years later by additional hostilities in East Asia and the Pacific when Japanese leaders decided to resort to arms – with deadly consequences to British and Imperial security. By the end of the fighting, Britain found herself the junior member of the Allied alliance, while her Empire was in process of disintegration.

Little doubt exists, therefore, that the formation and implementation of British foreign policy in the 1920s and 1930s occurred at a critical juncture in the history of the state and its imperial presence in global politics. In this light the actions of the foreign policy-making élite are fundamentally important. Less than 12 months after the German attack on Poland, a small but prominent group within Britain's pre-1939 diplomatic establishment were indicted by critics as *Guilty Men* – responsible for the 'failures' of British diplomacy in the interwar period that led in aggregate to the rise of Hitler, the concomitant instability in Europe, the unpreparedness for war and the outbreak of hostilities.[3] Focusing on the supposed linchpin of British inter-war diplomacy – appeasement – this tract unleashed a bitter debate over culpability for the war. The purpose here, however, is not to rehash the debate on appeasement and the origins of the war which, over half a century, has not abated to any appreciable extent.[4] Finger-pointing has achieved little, because it is always easy to use hindsight to judge the past actions of diplomatists, to criticize them for what was not obvious a month, a year, or even 50 years before some débâcle. What is difficult, on the other hand, and less appealing therefore, is to understand how and why men acted as they did, how they perceived the situation at the time and how they responded to it.

The volume of books and articles relating to the course of British foreign policy in the inter-war period is staggering. Thanks to the opening of British public archives with the advent of the 30-year rule in 1968, as well as the wide availability of private manuscript collections and published documents, the empirical basis for secondary studies is rich and diverse. Memoirs are an integral part of this base. But, significantly, they have rarely been treated collectively as an important primary source in the study of inter-war British diplomacy. This is partly the case because the final musings written by the participants only appeared in the 1970s. Just as important, there is a suspicion that memoirs in and of themselves are simply the self-serving ruminations of men which darken rather than illuminate the historical record. Such a suspicion is ill-founded. Admittedly, an element of polemicism enters into memoir-writing; so, too, does a degree of disingenuousness. However, these are normal human reactions which historians should seek to understand rather than dismiss out of hand or deprecate what memoirists have recorded.[5]

Memoirs provide valuable insight into the human dimension of foreign policy-making and, flowing from this, two certainties exist about the British accounts relating to the 20 years after 1919. The first is that they were written not to cloud the historical record. With very few exceptions, each man who put pen to paper understood that if his observations and explanations were to stand the test of time, they would have to be as honest as possible. Nearly all members of the inter-war élite were appreciative of the subject of history, because they either read it in school and university or later consumed history books, or both.[6] They knew that eventually, once the archives were opened and historians and others entered them, their reputations would be tarnished irrevocably if they printed outright falsehoods. The second certainty is that these memoirs are the relatively honest reminiscences of individuals who sought to put on the public record their assessment of how the course of events proceeded. This does not suggest that errors of memory do not crop up. They do,[7] and historians must be wary of this. However, errors and deliberate falsifications are different entities, and the latter are extremely rare.

It is not surprising that memoirs, especially those of the British foreign policy-making élite of the inter-war period, have been written to shield the reputations of their authors. It *is* surprising that they should be considered in any other way. That is why Churchill's remark in November 1940 (quoted above), made in his eulogy of Neville Chamberlain, is apposite. Churchill had emerged by the time of the Munich agreement of 1938 as the embodiment of anti-appeasement sentiment in Britain. He rose to the premiership in May 1940, displacing Chamberlain, because of the abject failure of the latter's foreign policy. Both at the moment of his death and since, Chamberlain was and has been regarded as the arch-appeaser, the one leader who advocated this discredited policy from his central position in several governments in the eight years after 1931. But whether Chamberlain was a 'guilty man' is not the point. What Churchill was saying – all the more poignant given that he and Chamberlain had had strong disagreements on a range of domestic and foreign policy issues for at least a decade – was that Chamberlain's conscience about what he had done in the realm of external policy was clear. If criticism of this man's foreign policy was going to be made, his critics would also have to consider the sincerity and rectitude of his actions. And the same could be said for the other side of the ledger: what was it in leaders that caused them, for good or bad, to pursue what were ultimately successful policies? One might well decide to apportion culpability or sagacity to individuals occupying positions of influence, but mistakes and successes can be appreciated only by understanding the reasons underlying how and why men and women acted as they did. This is how leaders should be judged, and it is how the memoirs of the British foreign-policy-making élite for the period from 1919 to 1939 should be assessed.

A number of themes emerge in a reading of British diplomatic memoirs relating to the inter-war period, themes which illuminate the problems with which the elite wrestled and how they attempted to handle them. The challenges and dilemmas entailed: the choice between traditional support for the European balance or reliance on collective security through the League of Nations as the best protection of international peace and security; the quest for allies to maintain British interests in face of the manifold, simultaneous threats to those interests in Europe and Asia; the position of the Empire in foreign and defence policy, indeed the whole question of Imperial defence as a *sine qua non* of Britain's global status; the enigmatic diplomatic status of both Bolshevik Russia and isolationist America; and, fuelled by the powerful new ideological dimension of inter-war European diplomacy, the increasing significance of morality in the pursuit of foreign policy. All of these matters remained fundamental to Britain's leading role in international politics in the two decades after the Armistice of November 1918, as well as to its transition from pre-eminent world power to junior power by the mid-point of the Second World War.

Going further, these themes vary in emphasis depending on when the memoirs were written, before or after 1939 – the milieu in which they were written is important. Those men who wrote and published before the German invasion of Poland knew that their work was important, and that the work they had done at the Paris Peace Conference and throughout the 1920s and 1930s remained fundamental to Britain's continuing as a power of the first rank. They did not foresee the outbreak of the Second World War; hence, their writings are telling in this respect. Those moved to write after 1939, whether to justify their earlier endeavours, to criticize or meet the criticisms of adversaries, or to put some objectivity into the debate engendered by the 'guilty men' tract, are another matter. They knew the war had come. Moreover, as time passed and Britain slipped into the second rank of powers, their part in the policies and events of 1919–39 became part of a larger historical canvas on which other events – the rise of the superpowers, the advent of the cold war, and the loss of the Empire – came to the fore to rival the Second World War in importance in international history.

For the purpose of this analysis, only the memoirs produced between 1919 and 1939 will be considered. Since they were written before the Polish crisis of 1939 and remain untouched by the subsequent controversy over responsibility for the war, they provide added insight into how and why British foreign policy evolved as it did. The memoirs of these 20 years are divided into two subdivisions which tend to reflect the generational differences of the memoirists. Before Fascist Italy, Nazi Germany and militaristic Japan rose up to challenge British hegemony, memoirs show little concern about the erosion of British power and influence.[8] These were essentially the efforts of older men, whose careers began before 1914 and who published reminiscences before, say, 1935. Concern here revolved around the supposed crushing of German militarism, the importance of the Paris peace settlement and how the work done in the roughly 15 years thereafter respecting issues like reparations, European security and disarmament was undertaken to safeguard against another slaughter. Memoirs and other autobiographical writings appearing in the latter half of the 1930s, with the international horizon darkening, are different.[9] They looked more to the existing situation, speculating on how Britain arrived there and what policy alternatives were available to promote stability. The earlier tomes in this period were marked by a degree of optimism; the latter by a growing pessimism.

Although there is an abundance of inter-war memoirs produced by the lower levels of the élite, important lacunae exist at the three highest echelons: the prime ministers, foreign secretaries and permanent under-secretaries at the Foreign Office (the civil service heads of this ministry).[10] Death, languidness and a reluctance to write are the reasons for this. However, by stretching the definition of memoirs to include contemporary published speeches and other writings, the lacunae can be filled in to a degree.[11] Obvious limitations exist in using these sorts of autobiographical materials. For instance, as they were usually designed for calculated political and diplomatic purposes at the time of delivery, speeches need to be approached warily. Despite such difficulties, these additional selections provide insight into the generation and justification of particular policies of the inter-war period. They also provide a way of understanding better the themes which emerge in the corpus of British diplomatic memoirs relating to the two decades after 1919.

As had been the case for several centuries before, British foreign policy in the inter-war years pursued two traditional goals: maintaining the European balance of power and defending the Empire. Significantly, the former dominated the memoirs produced in the two decades before 1939 and reflected the overriding concern of the élite about Continental stability and the belief that, should another war break out there, Britain could not remain neutral. The memoirs from the optimistic first 15 years after the war share one similarity in their discussion of the European balance: the authors' intention to provide Britain with the deciding voice in Continental affairs. Beyond this, however, ideas naturally diverged about how this could be achieved in light of the differing personalities and the apparent latitude in policy alternatives.

David Lloyd George controlled British foreign policy, as he did most aspects of his government, from December 1916 to October 1922. By the time he left office, however, his peacetime policies had suffered several major reverses: the American Senate's refusal to ratify the Treaty of Versailles which led to the United States' withdrawal from European security questions; the consequent French hard line towards Germany over the enforcement of the Versailles treaty; and the increasing German resentment towards the Western powers. All of this was exacerbated by the crumbling of the German economy under the pressure of reparations forced on the Weimar Republic, coupled with the loss of economically important provinces to the successor states. Lloyd George's post-October 1922 writings emphasize that Franco-German relations in the three years after the signing of the Versailles treaty could only have stabilized had France been provided with a feeling of security which, to work, had to be offset by a reduction in German distaste for the treaty.[12] But his writings are also telling in that he pointed out that to achieve this effect British policy needed to avoid aligning too closely with either Paris or Berlin; success in maintaining the balance would come from not favouring one power over the other. An element of realism was injected into this, however, as, on one side, French antipathy towards Britain was fed by the refusal of Lloyd George's government unilaterally to guarantee France's security after the Americans reverted to isolation while, on the other, German resentment of the Versailles restrictions was enhanced by the memory of Lloyd George's 1918 electoral stance as the man who would punish Germany for its transgressions. But if Lloyd George had no desire or opportunity to find a European ally to maintain the balance, this could not be said of finding an extra-European one. Even after the Senate rejection of the Versailles treaty and the American demand that Britain honour its war debts, Lloyd George looked to the United States as the one potential ally on which Britain could rely to maintain the European balance.[13]

Of course, maintaining the balance did not involve concentration on
the Franco-German question to the exclusion of other issues. During
his tenure as prime minister and afterwards, Lloyd George showed his
courage by seeking an accommodation with Bolshevik Russia. His
political writings stress that if peace was to be secure, Britain could not
ignore Russia, despite the revolutionary bent and murderous reputation of Lenin and his cohorts, because of its size, contiguity with
eastern Europe, and potential economic and military strength. A
working relationship with Russia would benefit Britain because it
would both make the political situation in Europe more stable and
benefit British trade.[14] However, he was out of office before he could
normalize Anglo-Russian relations, so it fell to others to find solutions
to this and the other problems threatening Britain's diplomatic
position after 1922.

The memoirs penned by his successors and published before the
mid-1930s show that during these years a variety of solutions to the
questions plaguing European security and, hence, the balance of
power were still both available and attempted. The Labour Party,
containing a range of men and women opposed to the 'old diplomacy'
which in their minds had led to the crisis of 1914, formed two inter-war
governments: one for nine months in 1924 and a second from 1929 to
1931. During the First World War and the peace conference period, its
leaders embraced the idea of maintaining peace and security through
the League of Nations and the collective action of its members, large
and small. This created antipathy between Labour luminaries and the
Foreign Office, the bastion of 'old diplomacy'.[15] Once in office, men
like James Ramsay MacDonald, the prime minister, and Lord
Parmoor, the minister responsible for League affairs – convinced of
their moral purity – reckoned that the best way to attain Continental
stability was to work through the new international organization.[16]
Parmoor's memoirs demonstrate that Labour's intention was to have
Britain concert with other powers to guarantee French security and use
arbitration, rather than resort to arms, to settle territorial and other
disputes.[17] Moreover, reducing arms would give the Germans, already
disarmed to a degree via Versailles, their own feelings of security. The
point was that Britain must not act unilaterally; it could only work
by promoting a co-operative spirit. This can be seen in Labour
reminiscences about resolving the bugbear of reparations. MacDonald
and his Chancellor of the Exchequer, Philip Snowden, endeavoured to
work with other powers interested in this question, including even the
United States, and not to dictate to Berlin. At Versailles, the peace

treaty had been forced on Germany. 'A Labour Government', Snowden recorded about efforts made in 1924, 'could not follow the precedent of the Paris Peace Conference and decline to hear the views of the Germans upon a matter so vitally affecting them'.[18]

Relations with Bolshevik Russia held a fascination for Labour, especially for its trade union element, which saw the rise of a worker-controlled government in Russia as a positive result of the war. True, the Bolsheviks were brutal; but they had toppled a brutal regime. MacDonald sought to normalize relations by exchanging permanent diplomatic missions and, to sweeten the atmosphere, concluding a commercial agreement. Although all of this was handled badly by MacDonald – Snowden and others balked at giving the Russians open-ended loans, especially as the Bolsheviks proved reluctant to pay Tsarist debts[19] – and led to the fall of the first Labour government, Labour memoirs show that British foreign policy still had several options before it in 1924 to settle the matter of European security.

Led by Stanley Baldwin, the Conservative ministry which succeeded the first Labour government in November 1924 inherited an unsettled European situation. It also possessed a different view of how to come to grips with the problem of maintaining the balance. Normalizing relations with Russia proved not to be feasible since, for ideological reasons, the Conservative caucus refused to countenance any formal link with Moscow. But it was the Baldwin government's response to the Franco-German situation which proved its crowning diplomatic achievement. Austen Chamberlain, the foreign secretary and the dominant voice in British foreign policy from November 1924 to June 1929, came to endorse the by then accepted view that Britain would have to hold the balance between France and Germany. By early 1925, Chamberlain supported a proposal to enter into a regional agreement whereby Britain would guarantee the Franco-German border. Wanting to shore up the British position in the Mediterranean by strengthening Anglo-Italian relations, Chamberlain persuaded the Italian dictator, Benito Mussolini, to join in this guarantee. In October 1925, following months of complex negotiations, an Anglo-Italian guarantee of the Franco-German border was undertaken in a treaty signed in the Swiss town of Locarno. With this, Chamberlain accomplished what none of his predecessors since 1919 had done. More than this, he tied the Locarno treaty to the League by having Germany admitted to the League Council as a permanent member, an acknowledgement of great-power status and Germany's re-entry into the comity of nations.

Chamberlain's subsequent writings about Locarno argue that it was the only possible means of bringing stability to Europe by the mid-1920s.[20] Indeed, the Locarno system proved to be the basis for European stability over the next decade by giving Germany equality with the other great powers and by providing France with security. Most important, it gave Britain the leading role in Europe. After its success at Locarno, Baldwin's government opted to participate fully in the League, not as an end in itself but, instead, as a means of keeping the peace. As Chamberlain asked pointedly in 1935: 'Is it not better to recognize the danger in time and guard against its occurrence, rather than sit idly by until the world is in flames?'[21] Forcefully adumbrated in the autobiographical writings of men like Baldwin and Chamberlain, this attitude explains the basis of British foreign policy in the late 1920s.[22] Britain was not separate from Europe. 'Whether we like it or not', Baldwin observed, 'we are indissolubly bound to Europe, and we shall have to use, and continue to use, our best endeavours to bring to that Continent that peace in which we and millions of men up and down Europe have an equal belief and an equal faith.'

Until the threat posed to European stability by Hitler began in 1935 – when he announced the rearmament of Germany in violation of Versailles – the Locarno system existed as the basis of European great-power politics. When Labour returned to office in mid-1929, its European policy simply followed the path set out since 1924. Unfortunately, the second Labour government found itself increasingly preoccupied with the domestic ramifications of the major economic crisis precipitated by the Wall Street collapse in October 1929. Still, between June 1929 and August 1931, the life of this ministry, a range of actions were available to Labour in foreign policy: a new reparations agreement, international arms limitation, a reliance on the League and more. As in domestic politics, the idea held that something positive could be attained if only enough effort was directed in the right direction. Snowden's memoirs, completed in August 1934, suggest that the options for British diplomacy were shrinking,[23] while those of Parmoor are more positive. The last three sentences of Parmoor's musings encapsulate best the prevailing attitude of the second Labour ministry:

I see that the hope for the future is to be found in those lessons of Christian truth which I was taught in the days of my childhood. I realise that peace and righteousness are inseparable. In the words of St. James – 'The Fruit of righteousness is sown in peace of them that make peace'.[24]

This seems a fitting testament to the perception of the situation in the early 1930s just as the choices available to British diplomatists began to constrict.

The other goal of British foreign policy, Imperial defence, had not been ignored during the decade and a half after the Paris Peace Conference. Élite memoirs in this respect wax eloquent on the formal Empire, its position in the world, and its role in international affairs. Everyone from Arthur Balfour, a senior statesman, to Lloyd George took the public position that this polity of free nations and colonies constituted a force of good.[25] Putting such platitudes aside, the élite did work hard to keep the Empire strong and viable through two general policies: ensuring the primacy of the Royal Navy – the better to defend both the formal and informal empires – and seeking to reform the basis of intra-Imperial relations. Significantly, the question of the navy as a means of projecting national will is virtually ignored by memoirists in the period before the mid-1930s. On the other hand, maintaining good relations with the one power possessing the economic resources to outbuild Britain – the United States – was a different matter. Although Lloyd George's government agreed to formal naval parity in capital ships and aircraft carriers with the United States at the Washington conference of 1921–22, Lloyd George left no retrospective assessment on the importance of this to Imperial defence. Instead, he focused on the need to find a working relationship with the Americans; other prominent élite members followed suit, recognizing in their memoirs that naval strength formed the basis of Britain's claim to global power status, but tying it to the overall matter of good Anglo-American relations rather than specific mention of the ability to defend the Empire.[26] Although Anglo-American relations were unsettled from 1922 to 1930 because of the naval question – the London naval conference of 1930 saw complete Anglo-American naval parity formalized in a treaty – British élite memoirs do not reflect this.[27] The reason probably derives from the unspoken assumption that the Royal Navy would always be strong enough to protect the home islands, overseas colonies and markets and the routes linking them. The sense of optimism remained. Although their effectiveness in limiting naval arms proved to be minimal, a series of arms limitation conferences were held between 1922 and 1934. Britain always participated for mixed reasons, chiefly retrenchment, but the ultimate goal of achieving some sort of disarmament as a means of providing greater security remained at the fore. Élite memoirs do not equivocate on this.[28]

The second policy, Imperial reform, was a different matter. Empire contributions to the war in manpower, money and casualties led to post-war pressure from the dominions to have more independence in their external policy. Canada was prominent in this respect. Thus, when discussing the Empire between 1919 and 1939, British memoirists argue that Imperial policy entailed essentially conceding to the legitimate demands of the independent dominion governments for reform. They paint the Empire as an evolving organism, one that changed to meet new realities.[29]

But I do say that the experiment we are trying is a result of a natural development [Balfour noted in 1927] that it has that great security behind it; and I am confident that the patriotism, commonsense, the instinctive looking to the past, and working for the future which have been the characteristic of the English-speaking peoples, are going in the future to bring to a successful issue one of the noblest experiments mankind has ever tried.

British leaders were responsible for protecting the Empire they had inherited. Just as they were prepared to do everything possible to assure the continuation of the Empire by keeping the navy at strength and meeting legitimate calls for reform, they did not shy away from opposing with all the armed force they could muster those who would use violence to rip away their holdings. Austen Chamberlain put on record his government's determination to resist all attempts to force a British retreat in China by force of arms, and this was backed up by the dispatch of British forces to China in 1927 to shore up the British position. This sort of attitude, encased in a collection of the Foreign Secretary's speeches published in 1928,[30] demonstrated an optimism by the élite that British armed strength could be brought to bear successfully to maintain both the Imperial status quo and Britain's existence as a global power. Several alternatives were available to protect the Empire – naval agreements with the United States, the legal redress of dominion grievances and the application of armed force. One or another, or any combination, could be used to maintain British interests.

By the middle of the 1930s, however, the options in Europe and the wider world were narrowing as a result of the rise of Nazi Germany, the estrangement of Italy from Britain and the advent of militaristic Japan. On top of this, strains within the Empire, mainly in India and Palestine, involved the dispatch of increasing numbers of troops from the home islands to keep order. Élite memoirs reflect these changing international circumstances by showing concern about the implications this had for Britain. With the United States now strictly isolationist behind its newly passed neutrality laws, and with the naval and debt questions resolved so as not to beckon American initiatives, the problems confronting the élite were increasing. While London still possessed some latitude, its ability to bargain was limited by three factors. First, successive British governments had been disarming in degrees since the Washington conference, a trend which continued in the 1930s despite the growing arsenals of Germany, Italy and Japan. Second, the British could not rely heavily on other powers should they need assistance. The United States would probably hold back no matter how dire Britain's position became, and France was sandbagged behind the Maginot Line, its leaders preoccupied with domestic discord. Given the independence shown by Canada, which was coupled with an isolationism that mirrored that of its southern neighbour, full Imperial support could not be relied upon. Finally, the economic crisis engendered by the crash of 1929 had yet to be surmounted. Times had changed, and to Britain's disadvantage.

These changing times led to an erosion of optimism about how British policy should be pursued. Although the watershed between optimism and pessimism comes generally around 1935 in terms of written memoirs, some of the élite became disenchanted with the situation in which Britain found itself several years before. Harold Nicolson, a sensitive and urbane man and, by the judgement of his contemporaries, a gifted diplomat, resigned from the diplomatic service in 1929. Although family reasons and a desire to achieve more in his life contributed to this decision, he also became disillusioned with the work he had to do representing Britain abroad[31] – his last post being Berlin. Nicolson's disillusionment was given form three years after his return to private life with the publication of his memoir of the Paris Peace Conference. Although this is an excellent recounting of the monumental efforts made by the peace-makers to bring order to the chaos created by the war, his basic argument held that the peace imposed on Germany had been too harsh. 'Given the atmosphere of the time', he noted in his introductory chapter, 'given the passions aroused in all democracies by four years of war, it would have been impossible even for supermen to devise a peace of moderation and righteousness.'[32] Here lies the key to comprehending the growth of pessimism within the majority of the élite later on. Despite the best efforts of mortal men and all that had been done subsequently through the League, Locarno, refashioning the Empire and more, the basis of the new international order that had been hammered out by the peace-makers had been flawed from the outset. Pessimism need not have arisen from such an assessment. But it did, and this derived from there being fewer options available to maintain the balance of power in Europe, to keep the situation in the Mediterranean in equilibrium and to assure the safety of the Empire east of Suez. Those who published memoirs in the closing years of the inter-war period shared Nicolson's concern.

These memoirs generally contain two interwoven elements. The first, naturally, is a recounting of the careers of the individuals writing them, this to show the work they had done and the problems they had faced, along with some analysis to explain their achievements and failures. Following on from their experiences and the lessons they had learned, the second element entailed some argument about how best to pursue foreign policy. Not unexpectedly, given the re-emergence of German power and the alignment of Rome with Berlin, Europe dominates these books. Two men, Lord Howard of Penrith, a career diplomat, and Admiral Sir Barry Domvile, a senior naval officer for most of the inter-war period, are representative of élite memoirists in the late 1930s.

Howard retired from the diplomatic service in 1930 after capping his career with six extremely successful years as ambassador in Washington. Published in 1935 and 1936, his two-volume auto-biography relates that he had been schooled in the 'old diplomacy' that dominated British foreign policy prior to 1914.[33] Though he was wedded to traditional ways of thinking about the exercise of external power, his triumph as a diplomat came from skill in assessing events dispassionately and in adapting to new situations by recognizing that they required new responses. His memoirs emphasize that he accepted the rule of law in international politics, which he defined as the norms of international intercourse that sought to correct injustices without recourse to arms.[34] None the less, his autobiography also shows that he remained an arch-realist, advocating strong armed forces, the need to make no concessions without obtaining concessions in return, the imperative concern of maintaining the balance of power in Europe with or without the League and the preservation of the Empire.

Like Nicolson, Howard laid the blame for much of Europe's problems on the flawed Paris Peace Settlement. Unlike Nicolson, however, who reckoned that peace-making was too difficult even for supermen, Howard censured Lloyd George and his American and

French counterparts, respectively Woodrow Wilson and George Clemenceau.[35] The chance for long-term peace and stability had been present at Paris, but these men had squandered the chances for this by myopic policies and the arrogant belief that they, ignoring expert advice provided by Howard and others, could resolve the problems in peace-making by themselves. Howard's pessimism found graphic portrayal when he speculated on what a history lesson would be like in the year 2000 AD. The point was to emphasize an era of lost opportunities:

The teacher had passed rapidly in review the events leading up to the War of 1914–1918 (no longer spoken of as the Great War), of the destruction of life and of cities and villages. This, however, was nothing compared to the losses inflicted on the whole of Europe during the war that followed only twenty-five years later, which converted whole countries into shambles, and provinces and cities into areas of starvation and misery.[36]

While pessimistic about how events were unfolding, despite the fact that his embassy at Washington in the late 1920s had led to extremely cordial Anglo-American relations as a basis for future international co-operation, he considered that all was not lost. But it would take monumental efforts on behalf of his countrymen to avoid war. Howard put this in an open letter to his four sons – and by implication to those of their generation – in his memoirs.[37] What he was saying, based on the lessons he had learnt in a half-century career in diplomacy, was that the totalitarian regimes, including Russia, regimes which had little respect for law and justice, had to be opposed should the need arise with the weapons of 'old diplomacy'.

After more than 45 years in the Royal Navy, Domvile retired in 1936 ending a career which included sea commands, the directorship of naval intelligence, and the presidency of the Naval College at Greenwich.[38] Just as Howard embodied 'old diplomacy', Domvile can be thought of as being in the 'sea dog' tradition of Britain's senior armed service. His memoirs published in 1937 affirm this with comments like:

I have no patience with these schemes for making war kinder and more gentlemanly, so dear to the heart of the politician – gas, air, submarine – all have had their turn at being humanised. War is a cruel, beastly, inhuman thing, entirely unsuited to any regulations or laws other than the law of expediency, which is the only one that governs it.[39]

Domvile's memoirs make the essential argument that, by the 1930s, Britain and the Empire had nothing to fear in Europe, the Far East, or anywhere else as long as their ability to defend themselves remained unfettered. The problem resided with Britain's civilian political leaders – his career, including attendance at inter-war naval conferences, had given Domvile a firsthand view of high policy-making. Towards these men Domvile held strong prejudices, untempered by any realization that they had to juggle external commitments, the level of arms to maintain them and domestic political pressures.[40]

But Domvile's significance in the matter of what memoirs can relate about the debate over British foreign policy in the late 1930s comes from his suggestion that Britain had everything to gain by aligning with Nazi Germany. The concluding chapter of his autobiography relates a trip he took to Hitler's Germany just as he retired from the Royal Navy.[41] He admired the Nazi leaders he met while on this journey, particularly Heinrich Himmler, the head of the SS; he also made plain that he proudly shared the anti-Semitism of his hosts. But the importance of what he wrote is that he firmly came down on the side of those in Britain who were arguing that Britain should accommodate German territorial and other demands. Domvile argued that Nazi Germany, despite all that might be said of its domestic policies, stood as the sworn enemy of Bolshevik Russia. 'Himmler was genuinely concerned at the dangers of Communism to Germany and the rest of Europe', Domvile recounted, 'and described Germany as repeating history by being the bulwark of Western civilisation against this new peril from the East.' More than this, Domvile believed Nazi assurances that Germany looked on Britain as a friend and desired good Anglo-German relations above all else. Implicit in this stood the notion that readjustments to the 1919 territorial settlement in eastern Europe could only strengthen Germany against Bolshevik Russia, a course that would give Europe stability.

Domvile's ideas about aligning with Germany were more extreme than those held by the vast majority in Britain who favoured appeasing Germany; after all, alignment and appeasement were different propositions, the latter not necessarily resulting from Germanophilia. Additionally, his reasons for moving closer to Germany were based on having Hitler's regime in the front line against the spread of Bolshevism. Still, the juxtaposition of his memoirs with those of Howard shows the dynamics of the debate among the foreign-policy-making élite in the late 1930s. Nazi Germany and Fascist Italy were moving closer together. France seemed an uncertain friend upon which to rely. With the apparent determination of the United States to stay wrapped in the cocoon of isolationism, the position in the Far East had the appearance of danger. The willingness of the dominions, mainly Canada, to aid Britain in a moment of crisis presented a question which could not be answered with precision. Therefore, what should Britain do? Just as leaders of the time were divided, so, too, were those who wrote their memoirs. And, importantly, the memoirs show a pessimism about the options confronting British diplomacy. Though poles apart, Howard and Domvile agreed that the situation lacked sanguinity. The choices available had constricted: either pursue some accommodation with Germany, to allow a freer British hand in the Mediterranean and the Far East, or mount a sustained opposition to Hitler to convince him that a limit to British forbearance existed. Unlike the 1920s or early 1930s, the latter course was restricted because of the changing political constellation in Europe, German rearmament, the League's seeming weakness and a generally bleak strategic situation.

British diplomatic memoirs published between the two world wars need to be compared with other sources when used to study the development of British foreign policy during this pivotal time in Britain's history as a great power. Still, with all their imperfections, these books throw additional light on the problems that the élite sought to tackle and the solutions they recommended. The memoirs from the entire period show above all else the primacy of Europe in British diplomatic calculations. In varying degrees, they show the determination of the élite to have Britain play 'the honest broker' in Continental affairs. In the optimistic first 15 years, although some diplomatists might at particular times have been more sympathetic to one power or another, there was a tendency to argue in memoirs that Britain had not sided with any one power against any of the others. This explains why the spirit of optimism prevailed. No one European power in the first years of peace seemed capable of tipping the balance dangerously against Britain. Furthermore, at least as expressed in the autobiographical writings of the élite, British optimism stemmed from their having an array of options to create stability. From tampering with the Paris Peace settlement through to Locarno, British leaders explored a variety of methods for ensuring peace. While the memoirs emphazise that Britain could not do this alone, that it needed to concert with other powers to achieve stability, they also show that the élite had time and the luxury of being able to pursue one endeavour and then another.

Of course, the balance of power could not be ignored in this search for a condominium of interests with other powers – indeed, this was why a search was necessary. Élite memoirs expose the general belief that in the hard world of international politics after the Great War, maintaining the balance of power was the *raison d'être* of British foreign policy. After a number of false starts, the Locarno system became the tangible expression of this. Austen Chamberlain only did what Lloyd George, Labour leaders, and the rest tried to do without result for seven years. His political adversaries – Parmoor was one – might disagree with his means; they could not quarrel with his ends. The Locarno system became the basis for European security until the advent of Hitler and the events of the mid-1930s changed the dynamics of the balance of power. By then the chances to revise Locarno were bleak. Italy had become antagonistic towards Britain; Germany was arming to right the wrongs of Versailles; France had little desire to take the initiative or follow a British one; the League was weak; the United States trenchantly isolationist; Imperial support remained uncertain; and Bolshevik Russia stood as an unknown quantity. Suddenly, British options had diminished to just two: either oppose Nazi Germany with its Italian ally or appease them. Here lay the fountainhead of pessimism, a result of the breakdown of the new international order hammered out by Lloyd George and the other leaders after 1918. The peace was flawed, so that some remedial action was necessary. Howard and Domvile offered two different visions of how this could be arranged. Ultimately, appeasing Germany failed; deterring German aggressiveness was finally embraced because the balance of power had to be protected at all costs.

Élite memoirs bear witness to the fact that there were no 'guilty men' in control of British foreign policy in the 20 years after 1919. They were just men. They were guided by their consciences, and the preservation of their memories – the rectitude and sincerity of their actions – came when they used their memoirs to explain what they had done. As Neville Chamberlain wrote tellingly in the spring of 1939: 'I shall not abandon my efforts for this much longed for Peace, and I trust my readers, whoever and wherever they may be, if they shared my ideal, will give me their good wishes and, so far as they can, their help, in the cause to which I am devoting myself.'[42]

NOTES

1. C.R. Coote and P.D. Bunyan, *Sir Winston Churchill. A Self-Portrait. Constructed from his own sayings and writings and framed with an introduction* (London, 1954), p. 283.

2. This employs the narrow definition of the élite – those actually responsible for creating and implementing policy – outlined in D.C. Watt, 'The Nature of the Foreign-Policy-Making Elite in Britain', in his *Personalities and Policies. Studies in the Formulation of British Foreign Policy in the Twentieth Century* (London, 1965), pp. 1–15.

3. 'Cato' (Michael Foot, Frank Owen, Peter Howard), *Guilty Men* (London, 1940).

4. Compare W. Murray, *The Change in the European Balance of Power, 1938–1939: The Path to Ruin* (Princeton, NJ, 1984); and its review by D. Cameron Watt, 'How it ought to have been', *Times Literary Supplement*, No. 4, 301 (1984), p. 984. Then see D. Cameron Watt, *How War Came* (New York, 1989).

5. A.J.P. Taylor's acid-tipped pen was regularly employed to this end. For instance, 'Eden (Lord Avon) gave his prewar memoirs in *Facing the Dictators* (1962) . . . In any case, Eden did not face the dictators; he pulled faces at them'; in A.J.P. Taylor, *English History, 1914–1945* (Oxford, 1965), p. 627.

6. For example, C. Attlee, *As It Happened* (London, 1954), p. 14; R.A.B. Butler, *The Art of the Possible* (London, 1971), p. 10; A. Duff Cooper, *Old Men Forget* (London, 1953), p. 38; P.M. Gore-Booth, *With Great Truth and Respect* (London, 1974), pp. 28–9; 1st Earl of Halifax, *Fullness of Days* (London, 1957), p. 52; 14th Earl of Home, *The Way the Wind Blows* (London, 1976), p. 38; H.M. Knatchbull-Hugessen, *Diplomat in Peace and War* (London, 1949), p. 7; and on and on. Of course, there are exceptions, for instance, P.J. Grigg, *Prejudice and Judgement* (London, 1948) which, for a dozen pages, explains in detail his mathematical education.

7. For instance, there are several minor errors of fact in Lord Howard of Penrith, *Theatre of Life* (2 vols.) (London, 1935–36). This does not detract from the accuracy of the issues he discusses, nor does it suggest he deliberately distorted the truth. He wrote much of his memoirs from memory, a not unusual occurrence; see B.J.C. McKercher, *Esme Howard. A Diplomatic Biography* (Cambridge, 1989), pp. 20–1 and 305–6.

8. For example, R.H. Beadon, *Some Memories of the Peace Conference* (London, 1933); A. Chamberlain, *Down the Years* (London, 1935); Viscount D'Abernon, *An Ambassador of Peace: Pages from the Diary of Viscount D'Abernon* (3 vols.) (London, 1929–30); R.B. Haldane, *An Autobiography* (London, 1929); and F.O. Lindley, *A Diplomat Off Duty* (London, 1928).

9. For example, A. Eden, *Foreign Affairs* (London, 1939); G. Lansbury, *My Quest for Peace* (London, 1938); Marquess of Londonderry, *Ourselves and Germany* (London, 1938); and A.C. Temperley, *The Whispering Gallery of Europe* (London, 1938).

10. Of the five Prime Ministers – David Lloyd George, Andrew Bonar Law, James Ramsay MacDonald, Stanley Baldwin and Neville Chamberlain – only Lloyd George wrote memoirs; of the nine Foreign Secretaries – Arthur Balfour, Lord Curzon, MacDonald, Austen Chamberlain, Arthur Henderson, John Simon, Samuel Hoare, Anthony Eden and Lord Halifax – five published autobiographical sketches; and of the six permanent under-secretaries – Lord Hardinge, Eyre Crowe, William Tyrrell, Ronald Lindsay, Robert Vansittart and Alexander Cadogan – just two published records of their career.

11. For example, S. Baldwin, *On England* (London, 1926); S. Baldwin, *Service of Our Lives* (London, 1937); S. Baldwin, *An Interpreter of England* (London, 1939); Earl of Balfour, *Opinions and Argument from Speeches and Addresses of the Earl of Balfour, 1910–1927* (London, 1927); N. Chamberlain, *The Struggle for Peace* (London, 1939); and even Eden, *Foreign Affairs*.

12. See D. Lloyd George, *Slings and Arrows. Sayings Chosen From the Speeches of the Rt. Hon. David Lloyd George* (Toronto, 1929), pp. 283–92.

13. D. Lloyd George, *Where Are We Going?* (London, 1923), pp. 108–9.

14. D. Lloyd George, 'Should We Make Peace With Russia?', in ibid., pp. 301–11.

15. Lord Parmoor, *A Retrospect. Looking Back Over a Life of More than Eighty Years* (London, Toronto, 1936), p. 196.

16. See P.J. Noel Baker, *The Geneva Protocol for the Pacific Settlement of International Disputes* (London, 1925). Noel Baker was Parmoor's private secretary during the first Labour government.
17. Parmoor, *Retrospect*, pp. 213–64.
18. Viscount Snowden, *An Autobiography*, Vol. II: *1919–1934* (London, 1934), p. 672.
19. Ibid., pp. 681–3; and R.B. Haldane, *An Autobiography*, pp. 328–31.
20. For instance, A. Chamberlain, *Down the Years*, pp. 151–71.
21. Ibid., p. 167.
22. See Baldwin's ideas on disarmament in 1923 in his *On England*, pp. 227–35, from which the subsequent quote is taken: and Chamberlain's on the cultural unity of Europe, of which Britain was an integral part, in his *Seen In Passing* (London, 1937) which was published posthumously.
23. Snowden, *Autobiography*, Vol. II, pp. 1031–42.
24. Parmoor, *Retrospect*, p. 323.
25. For example, Balfour, *Opinions*, p. 171; and Lloyd George, *Slings and Arrows*.
26. See Lloyd George's remarks on the unveiling of Abraham Lincoln's statue at Westminster on 28 July 1920, in Lloyd George, *Slings and Arrows*, pp. 261–2.
27. For instance, Baldwin, *This Torch of Freedom: Speeches and Addresses* (London, 1935), pp. 57–75; Balfour, *Opinions*, pp. 241–7; and Chamberlain, *Down the Years*, pp. 321–8.
28. Even for those holding diametrically opposing political views on almost every other issue. Compare Baldwin, *On England*, pp. 227–36; and Parmoor, *Retrospect*, pp. 229–64 *passim*.
29. See S. Baldwin, 'Responsibilities of Empire', in S. Baldwin *et al.*, *Responsibilities of Empire* (London, 1937), pp. 9–13; and two of Balfour's speeches in *Opinions*, pp. 170–83. The next quotation is from the latter, p. 183.
30. Chamberlain, *Peace in Our Time*, pp. 255–65.
31. N. Nicolson, *Portrait of a Marriage* (London, 1973), pp. 211–15.
32. H. Nicolson, *Peacemaking 1919* (London, 1933), p. 7.
33. Howard, *Theatre of Life*, Vol. I, pp. 49–102, and Vol. II, pp. 13–186. See McKercher, *Esme Howard*, Chs. 1–3.
34. Howard, *Theatre of Life*, Vol. II, *passim*. Compare with his *Sanctions: Confidence: Disarmament; Recovery* (London, 1932).
35. Howard, *Theatre of Life*, Vol. II, pp. 277–82 and 297–8.
36. Ibid., pp. 631–3.
37. Howard to his sons, 5 July 1936, ibid., p. 639.
38. Domvile's biography is still to be written, but a quick outline of his career can be seen in *Who's Who 1937* (London, 1936), p. 919.
39. B.E. Domvile, *By and Large* (London, 1937), pp. 127–8.
40. For instance, ibid., pp. 104–5, 182 and 249.
41. The rest of this paragraph is based on ibid., pp. 233–49.
42. N. Chamberlain, *The Struggle for Peace*, p. 6.

11
'Married to Affairs of State': Memoirs of the Wives and Daughters of British Diplomats

VALERIE CROMWELL

On 5 November 1986, *The Times* carried a feature article which discussed the difficult situation facing an increasing number of British diplomatic wives in the 1980s. The author described the problems created for wives with careers both within and outside the diplomatic service. These are problems which have only surfaced in the British service since the late 1960s. At different levels in the service, wives have set out on careers alongside their husbands (and, of course, vice versa) and had to face hard choices at the time of an overseas posting. Occasionally these choices have led to the husband's transfer to the home civil service or to the wife's refusal to accompany her husband abroad: more often, the result has been the abandonment of the spouse's existing career and the acceptance of a domestic role with only the possibility of occasional local work. This is particularly hard at a time when more and more couples are pursuing parallel careers. The Foreign and Commonwealth Office concedes that it is losing 'good men' in their 30s as their wives press them to leave: it also recognizes the wife's role: 'Frankly', a spokesman admitted, 'if a wife chooses to be involved in the embassy work, it's unpaid benefit for us.'[1] And so it has been, somewhat paradoxically, for the 200 years of the Office's existence.

What was paradoxical and different, in the years before the 1950s, was that the world of diplomacy had offered women, both wives and daughters, the opportunity to participate in the world of politics and administration, an opportunity denied to the vast majority of middle- and upper-class women. The reluctance of the higher civil service in the early twentieth century to recruit women other than as clerks and typists threw into relief the unique situation of the women in diplomatic families. It was to be a particular irony that the diplomatic service was to be the last branch of the British civil service to admit women to its non-clerical ranks: even after 1945, when female first division members of the diplomatic service were being recruited, they had to resign on marriage. For diplomatic wives and daughters, the intermingling of family, social and diplomatic life created a political role. As the diplomatic world extended after the settlements of 1815, the increasing number of diplomatic wives and their children in embassies and legations abroad found themselves expected to move with ease in the network of international relationships associated with the great courts of Europe and the American continent. Although their social background was usually more than adequate for the lifestyle expected of them, their education certainly was not. For most of the nineteenth century and the early years of the twentieth century, the women who married young diplomats had, in the main, been born into families in which it was generally accepted that education for girls would and should be significantly different from and inferior to that of their brothers. Girls' education meant either teaching at home by an unqualified governess or away from home at inadequate schools, concerned to inculcate social graces rather than to train the mind. Only in the 1860s were the first moves being made to open up secondary and higher education and to force wider employment opportunities for middle- and upper-class women. In the main, the world of practical politics was unknown to them. Although, by 1900, women could serve on Poor Law and School Boards, until 1918 women could not vote in parliamentary elections or become Members of Parliament. That group of significant women which signed 'The Appeal Against Female Suffrage' in *The Nineteenth Century* in 1889 specifically identified the world of foreign policy as one totally unsuitable for women.[2] But the women were there, active, failing, and succeeding.

What gave these women their special position was the enduring concept of the embassy as a family. It was this concept which enabled the diplomatic service to persist for so long with its practice of recruiting unpaid diplomatic attachés for its junior ranks. If young men were to be received into the embassy as members of the household, then they must be of an appropriate social class to be acceptable at the ambassador's dining table and in his wife's drawing room. Similarly, the reception of a young man into an embassy was seen as a suitable training for the world of politics, and not necessarily as the introduction to an extended career in the diplomatic service. The social and political tone of an embassy depended on the skills – or lack of them – of the ambassador's family: in an obituary for Lady Sherfield, written in June 1985, a friend underlined the continuance of these assumptions in the British embassy at Washington in the 1950s when her husband was ambassador there: 'Under them, the embassy was a true diplomatic family.'[3]

In considering the place of political memoirs as a genre, and as a historical source, I would argue that the memoirs of diplomatic wives and daughters provide a very special source for the study of the role of a group of women placed, at the time, in a unique social and political position, and for an assessment of the attitudes of those women to that role. The style of discourse in these memoirs repays serious consideration. The very publication of them raises rather different questions from the publication of the other groups of memoirs under consideration here. They are not numerous. Publication of them must indicate courage, bravado or eccentricity. They were usually published after the death of husband or father. Unlike most male political memoirs, they are not, in the main, self-justificatory or self-praising. They tend not to be repetitive chronicles of social gossip. As with other published memoirs, they often derive from extensive diaries: in one case, reference is here made to an as yet unpublished diary. They contribute a wealth of social and political observation. They suggest clues to an understanding of the complex levels of social gradation and nuances in very different societies as they have altered over the last 200 years. Importantly, they are not written by women 'hidden from history', but by women whose position in the embassy and legation was recognized, in many ways, as the key to the successful tenure of an overseas posting. The memoirs of the diplomats themselves are often rich in personal detail and observation on their families and cannot be ignored in any consideration of the female contribution to embassy life: they cannot, however, do more than complement the commentaries of wives and daughters on their own particular social and political role. As with all memoirs, it must be remembered that the women who wrote them were a special, self-selected and unusual group. It is certainly worth mentioning that the publication of such memoirs has become much rarer as the twentieth century has progressed: this may be the result of changing social or official attitudes within the service or possibly an indicator of the changing style and function of the embassy. The social side of diplomatic life still looms large, but the diversification of embassy work with the growth of, in particular, commercial and economic, scientific and technological at the expense of political functions has transformed the image of the embassy as a family into that of an office, away from the official residence. That shift in the balance of work, while expanding the role of the diplomats, has marginalized that of diplomatic wives just as changing perceptions of women's working life have made their need for a positive role the greater. A diplomatic wife recalled her arrival in Santiago in the early 1980s:

Our very kind predecessor and his wife showed us round the house and made us welcome. Then he said to Robert, 'Now I'll take you home to the embassy and show you the offices.' . . . The wife showed me the local shops. It was one of the worst moments. I was very slow in coming to terms with the situation. It was probably worse for me than other working wives because I had worked for the Foreign Office.[4]

Perhaps the appearance of novels of frustration will replace the publication of memoirs by diplomatic women.

A focus on some of the main insights revealed in these memoirs indicates something of the range and variety of material in them. None of the writers considered here came from families other than of aristocratic, landed, professional or substantial business status. It must therefore be remembered that their attitudes were constrained not only by their sex, but also by their limited range of social experience.

There can be no doubt that the right or wrong choice of a wife was thought to and could affect a diplomatic career. Also, many of the requirements for a good diplomat were equally required for his wife. Discretion, charm, wit, elegance – but not too much of that – and liveliness were all to be hoped for in a future ambassadress. Until well into the twentieth century, social ease at the highest level was assumed: marriage to a girl with court connections was a particular bonus. The marriage of Augustus Paget, minister in Saxony, to (Wally) Walpurga, Countess of Hohental, a maid of honour to the Crown Princess of Prussia, Queen Victoria's eldest daughter, and well known in the English court, was commented on favourably by the Bloomfields: it was eventually to lead to the publication in the 1920s of an extensive and rich series of memoirs by Lady Paget on her diplomatic life.[5] Lady Bloomfield herself, daughter to the second Baron Ravensworth, sister to the Marchioness of Normanby who had been one of the Bedchamber ladies in the 1835 Bedchamber Crisis, had also, as a young girl, been a maid of honour to the Queen. She recounts in her memoirs that her mother's early advice to her to be pleasant and discreet at court was to pay dividends later in her husband's diplomatic career.[6] These were clearly the 'star' marriages. The ease with which both Bloomfield and

Paget married aristocratic girls with court connections (1845 and 1860) was not often matched as time progressed. The memoirs show that even the distant prospect of possible promotion to ambassador carried less and less of the social cachet it had had in the mid-nineteenth century. Meriel Buchanan describes Lord and Lady Bathurst's resistance to the idea of her father, George, marrying their daughter in 1883:

Lord Bathurst did not consider a penniless and very junior Secretary at the Embassy in Vienna, the youngest son of a Scottish Baronet, at all a suitable match for his lovely daughter. It was true, he conceded, that even a junior Secretary might one day become an Ambassador at some great European Court, but very many diplomats never got any further than being a Counsellor, or at best a Minister, in some far-way South American capital.[7]

Duff Cooper had to face similar entrenched opposition in 1918 when he tried to marry Lady Diana Manners, the celebrated beauty and daughter of the Duke of Rutland, but then his reputation was not of the best.[8]

Once married, the wife was under the microscope as the memoirs make clear. Lady Paget did not spare the second wife of Sir Andrew Buchanan, ambassador at Berlin: Lady Buchanan, she complained, had filled some of the rooms with her heavy early Victorian furniture, had shocking manners, dined at eight when everyone in Berlin dined at six, provided atrocious food, cooked by a female cook imported from Scotland, and used table silver which looked as if it had not been cleaned for weeks.[9] Lady Paget was hardly more charitable towards Lady Bertie at Rome.

I ended by dining at the Embassy, as I had refused the Berties' invitations once or twice before. It is all changed, and another spirit pervades the house. All the old romantic feeling is gone, and Louis XVI and Empire furniture and hangings of the most Londony type disguise what once hath been. . .
Sir Francis Bertie is a clever and agreeable man, and poor Lady Feo is now pathetically active and *prevenante*; but it is of no avail, the Romans do not care for them and persist in regretting us . . .[10]

Lady Bertie had other critics; during the First World War, when her husband was ambassador at Paris, it was noticed that she spent most of her time at Monte Carlo and that she was also extremely vague.

At one of the large parties at the Embassy a niece of hers made a bet as to how many times she would come in and go out and come in again without being recognised. I believe it was only at the sixth entry that Lady Bertie said, 'Haven't I seen you before?'[11]

Lady Tyrrell, at Paris, was also notorious for her vagueness in the late 1920s.[12] Lady Monson came in for criticism on rather different grounds, largely because she was half-South American, but that criticism tended to be charitable.

a pretty little woman, but not quite the style of an Ambassadress . . . she appears rather nervous and overcome by the grandeur of the position in which she is now placed . . . They were somewhat odd . . . and especially astonished the sober Viennese. She had no idea of her position and what to do, and one day, when her husband had a headache and could not accompany her to a reception at Princess Metternich's, she heard, as she was taking off her cloak, the sound of the shrill bell which is rung in every Viennese house to announce a visitor of importance. She at once, to the intense astonishment of all the footmen waiting in the anteroom with their masters' and mistresses' cloaks, turned tail and fled back to her carriage and drove home.[13]

Monson was not, however, to be handicapped: to some surprise, he was appointed to Paris in 1896. Paris was considered the most desirable post until well into the twentieth century. It is clear that, by contrast, for Constantinople, as early as the 1870s, social, class and personal qualities of the diplomatic wife did not weigh heavily in appointments: neither the low social origins of Lady White nor the existence of Sir Clare Ford's mistress was considered an insuperable obstacle. The memoirs, indeed, illustrate how far the diplomatic wives fell short of the ideal set out clearly by Meriel Buchanan:

her discretion, or indiscretions, could make or mar her husband's career. She had to be not only a gracious hostess, but a delightful guest, never showing boredom or lassitude. She had to have an inexhaustible patience in performing irksome duties, answering tiresome questions, and putting up with people whose company she found wearisome. She had to have consummate tact, and know when to hold her tongue, and, being very often in possession of secret information, she had to feign ignorance, and not betray her knowledge by the flicker of an eyelid.[14]

Much the most extensive memoirs by 'diplomatic women' as they are described here, in order to distinguish them from female diplomats, are those of Georgiana Bloomfield and 'Wally' Paget, both, as I have explained, aristocratic and not handicapped financially. They are followed by those of Meriel Buchanan, daughter of Sir George Buchanan and granddaughter of Sir Andrew Buchanan, both diplomats, whose mother had been forced to endure some of the discomforts feared by her father. 'Wally' Paget sharply noted:

Our present Embassy (Vienna) is composed of the Buchanans, who are very poor, with expensive tastes. He is the most good-natured, easy-going creature, but cannot refuse himself any amusement. Lady Georgie is Lord Bathurst's daughter, and though not brought up to it, she sweeps her rooms, washes the clothes and does everything herself. She always looks neat, and her room is so pretty. She has large blue eyes, which she uses.[15]

Neither of Meriel Buchanan's books appeared before the 1950s when she was in her 70s: *Ambassador's Daughter* (1958) is, in part, a defence of her father's role, as ambassador in St Petersburg, during the Russian revolutions. In the mid-twentieth century, after the publication of Roma Lister's *Reminiscences – Social and Political*, which appeared in 1926, the most substantial memoirs, after those of Meriel Buchanan, are those of Lady Gladwyn of the Paris embassy and, a rather special case, those of Sir William Hayter, which depend heavily on his wife's manuscript diary.[16] None of these memoirs of post-First World War diplomacy matched the range and perceptiveness of those of the pre-1914 years. That is in itself important for what it shows of the declining importance of diplomatic women. This change of approach is, as is made clear by Zara Steiner in Chapter 9 of this work, matched by the change in tone of the diplomatic memoirs by men, a change explained by very different factors, which were transforming the functions of the diplomats.

In all diplomatic memoirs, there is a pronounced tendency to underline the 'travel adventure' side of the diplomatic life: what, in the main, the memoirs by diplomatic women display is an emphasis on the resilience of the wives and families in the face of the demands of a peripatetic family life abroad. It was and is, after all, a life of packing and unpacking, the life of a somewhat well-heeled nomad, that a diplomatic bride had, and has, to face, at whatever level of the service. The best analysis of these demands is by Lady Paget:

Many people think, or thought, that Diplomacy was all fun, good dinners, dresses, balls, heaps of servants who did nothing onerous, etc., etc. It is nothing of the sort, at least for women who have a conscience, and as I was burdened with one, I will give some account of my trials . . . To me it was also a serious drawback to have no house of my own, which I could make beautiful . . . I could not have lived as Lord Lyons did at Paris when one day he said to me, pointing to a table cover, 'Not even that belongs to me', and wherever I went I dragged all my furniture about with me . . . I will now relate some of my worst trials which were adventures with the children. How the wives of the married Secretaries, who had families, managed in those days has always remained a mystery to me, as many were badly off . . .

It must be remembered that such a thing as a sleeping-carriage was unknown, also in the depths of a Northern winter they were not heated, and

only lit by a miserable little oil light. Also there was no food to be had except at
the most important stations, where there was an hour's stoppage. No papers
were sold at the station, and also there were no connections from other trains,
and it often happened that one had to wait many hours at a station or even pass
the night in a ghastly little inn . . .

I start on Thursday afternoon from Leipzig, take at Berlin the train which
starts at eleven o'clock at night, and arrive at Hamburg at seven in the morning,
and start again in the evening for Copenhagen . . .

This was a fearful journey. The cold was intense. I felt very ill and had to lie in
bed all day long at Hamburg. I noticed that V's cheeks were very red and his
eyes unnaturally bright when the nurses brought the children home from their
walk. We left Hamburg at eight o'clock in the evening. At Altona we had to
change, and then came the long, dreary, jolting, icy drive to Kiel, then the
change into the boat in the middle of the night, in Arctic temperature and with
small children. I took V. into my cabin, but after an hour he woke with an attack
of croup. I did what I could to relieve him, and then the cabin next to ours
caught fire. Every now and then I heard the ship sawing its way through the ice.
I was so unwell I could hardly stand, but needless to say that the maids and
nurses were quite useless. At last we arrived at Korsoer and had the usual three
hours in the ghastly waiting-room, and at noon we reached Copenhagen. This is
only one example of the many journeys to and from Copenhagen.[17]

Paget's posting to Lisbon was to offer his wife warmth of temperature
but also gruelling journeys by boat. She describes the long voyage, with
all the maids and nurses and the two small boys prostrate with sea-
sickness, and only the little girl able to come on deck. She arrived 'to find
that all our plate had been stolen in the custom house . . . I confess that I
always suspected . . . a certain impecunious Minister of having taken a
fancy to our spoons and forks'.[18]

Lady Bloomfield describes her equally terrible travel to St Petersburg, after her marriage in 1844: on the boat between Travemunde
and Cronstadt it had been necessary to take 'a horrid second class
cabin', where 'the dirt, discomfort, and wretchedness exceeded all
description'.[19] Stealing was a hazard also in St Petersburg. She recounts
a stair carpet being stolen during the night: 'the brass bars which
fastened it down were scattered about' and that Clanricarde, as ambassador, had all his silver mounted harness stolen.[20] Meriel Buchanan
repeats the complaints of a life of 'settling down in new surroundings
and being uprooted again, of long and sometimes uncomfortable
journeys, of difficulties of housekeeping'[21] and, of course, these remain
the continuing complaints of the diplomatic life.

What is always assumed is that the hardships and costs are compensated for by appropriate pay and allowances. The memoirs show

how important it was until after the First World War for diplomatic families to have substantial private means. There is not space here to discuss the complications and reforms in the diplomatic salary structure, but only to indicate how the memoirs contribute to an understanding of how family budgets came to terms with the social and diplomatic requirements placed on them. Even Lady Paget was prepared to complain in print. She describes the surprise they met on arrival in Lisbon:

we did not receive the usual outfit given to Ministers when they move from a second-class to a first-class mission, and upon A.'s enquiring the reason, he received the astounding answer that Lord Russell had raised Copenhagen to a first-class mission a few years ago on purpose for him, but neither he nor anybody else had imparted the fact to us, nor had we received any outfit as is usual on these occasions. Lord Clarendon was apparently equally ignorant of this fact, for I founded my request for Lisbon particularly upon our wish to go to a first-class mission. Had we been aware of the real state of things we might not have cared to incur the great expense of moving without promotion. The clerks who manage the finances of the F.O. were no doubt enchanted at this economy of several thousands which they made.[22]

The Office recognized the problem in a private memorandum to the Queen on 19 September 1867 after she had pressed for the promotion of Robert Morier from Frankfurt to the Berlin embassy:

It is a badly paid service in which promotion lags slower every year. Good men are only kept in it from the ambition of distinguishing themselves in its higher ranks and are willing to spend their private means for some years in the hope of being remunerated by the rank and emolument of Missions and Embassies.[23]

Meriel Buchanan's memoirs underline the continuing relative poverty of her parents noted by 'Wally' Paget in the 1880s. She explains that in Vienna her parents could not afford 'a regular nurse; a little Austrian maid was supposed to look after me and help with the work in the flat'. On the appointment of her father as first secretary to the legation at Berne in 1889, the situation was much the same:

Emily came to us, engaged primarily as my nurse, but becoming as time went on the invaluable support of the whole household. She acted as cook or house-maid whenever there was a crisis, valeted my father, mended and altered my mother's dresses, and cut some of them down to make clothes for me.[24]

When the lease of their Berne house came to an end in 1892, Buchanan tried to get another post, but was disappointed: 'he took a small flat in the centre of the town. My mother and Emily found that this entailed far less work and expense than a house, but . . . I missed the big garden and found the daily walks in the streets very boring.'[25] A sudden move to the post of secretary of legation and chargé d'affaires at Coburg brought the family some relief financially: Meriel's mother now had a maid and Meriel herself a daily governess. By the time her father was appointed British diplomatic agent to the Arbitration Convention called at Paris in 1898 to settle the dispute between Venezuela and the British colony in Guiana, her mother had no housekeeping duties and was finding time hanging heavily on her hands.[26] His appointment to Rome as counsellor in 1900 took the family to a flat in the elegant Palazzo Borghese but with a good many discomforts:

ours was on the top floor of one of the wings. In those days no lifts had been installed, and one had to climb a stone staircase of a hundred and twenty steps to reach it; and when, as happened frequently, the water supply failed and every drop had to be carried up from the courtyard, this became a serious drawback. The high rooms with their stone tessellated floors were magnificent, but almost impossible to heat in winter, and that year happened to be an exceptionally severe one. The painted ceilings were beautiful, but one of them had developed an ominous crack, and a temporary ceiling of stretched canvas had to be put up. The rats and mice, which inhabited the attics above us, used this canvas as a playground, scampering up and down it and making as much noise as a regiment of cavalry. And with the first warm days sandflies, which bred in the old walls, came out and made sleep impossible . . . the only sign of their presence being a prick like a small red-hot needle and in the morning face, neck and arms would be covered with red lumps, making one look as if one were sickening for smallpox.[27]

Promotion had brought a salary adequate for domestic help, but not the provision of suitable housing. Bright spots like the efficient domestic staff available for the newly married Hayters in Shanghai in 1938 remained equally rare: 'We thus started our married life with a degree of luxury, on the domestic front, that we were never to attain again except, passingly, in the Embassy in Moscow.'[28] For the Buchanans, the achievement of the first headship of a mission, in Sofia, meant their first official house but still no relief from a failed water supply in summer, frozen pipes in winter and insect life.[29] It was to be on the wives and families of diplomats that the more practical drawbacks of the diplomatic career fell particularly hard. As with the Buchanans, arrival at the top rank of the profession usually meant an inadequate and badly maintained house: settling into the legation at Tehran in 1894, for instance, 'sorely taxed Lady Durand, as the furniture and carpets were worn out, and the servants hopelessly inefficient'.[30] The kind of elegance and luxury represented by the British embassy in Paris remained extremely rare and beyond the experience of most diplomatic families.

For all these family and domestic matters, the memoirs are significant indicators of social expectations and attitudes. What of the political and diplomatic role that it can be argued was of a more 'public' or semi-official nature, and which was taken by these women? In general, these memoirs demonstrate an intelligent awareness of the political world in which the women moved. But that is hardly surprising, given that they are a self-selected group of extrovert and articulate women. Only rarely was this not so. Meriel Buchanan describes one such:

Lady Currie, who wrote books and poems under the name of Violet Fane, seemed always oppressed by the many social duties imposed on her as Ambassadress. Her dislike of entertaining, and her inability to distinguish between the Black and White families who adhered either to the Vatican or to the Quirinal, made her almost glad when the Court mourning occasioned by the death of Queen Victoria . . . put an end to all social gaieties.[31]

A young attaché, Thomas Hohler, had noticed similar behaviour on the Curries' earlier posting in Constantinople:

Lady Currie had great beauty, charm and intelligence, and had achieved marked success with her novels which appeared under the name of Violet Fane, but diplomatic duties wearied her sorely, and the sound of her tiara rattling against the mirror which hung behind her usual seat after dinner, as she gently sank into slumber, was the well-known signal to her guests that it was time for them to go home.[32]

Such behaviour was clearly eccentric and atypical enough to justify remarking on it. Those women with the interest in and awareness of the diplomatic implications of their husband's work, could, by their special involvement in that formal entertaining, which played and plays such an important part in diplomatic life, not only acquire a vast amount of information on the current state of international relations, but also play a constructive part.

'Wally' Paget's memoirs hold very little back in their portrayal of her diplomatic life. Because of her extensive and appropriate court connections, she played a significant 'go-between' role in the marriage negotiations between the Prince of Wales and Princess Alexandra of Denmark, while the Pagets were posted to Copenhagen.[33] Her own experience of German politics placed her in an unusually well-informed, but delicate, situation as the Schleswig-Holstein crisis developed:

When I returned to Copenhagen it was to find A. [her husband], Mr. Lytton and the whole of the Legation violently Danish. I had heard this question discussed all my life as it belonged intrinsically to German politics. As far back as 1848 I remembered my father travelled through the Duchies and came back with stories of Danish oppression and injustice. Though I did not think the German mode of procedure always quite correct, I knew that in the main they were right and it was painful to me to hear such terms as 'liars' and 'thieves' applied to them. However, I soon learnt that silence was my best and only safeguard, and I used to assist at the political discussions, trying to appear as if I did not listen. It was a sad and weary winter for me . . .[34]

As Paget's career progressed, the closeness of his wife to the Crown Princess of Prussia ensured a continuing flow of information from the Prussian and later German court: the appointment of Paget to Italy in 1867, where he stayed till 1883, diverted her interest into the complications of Italian politics in the significant period of unification and after. Her account of the volatile diplomatic world in Rome in its early days as state capital is vivid and perceptive.[35] Muttering again about the Treasury's meanness in refusing to pay for any part of the thousands of pounds required to do up the old house which was to become the new legation 'when, in reality, they ought to have given us an outfit sum, as is usual at every move',[36] she launches into a colourful description of the new-sprung *corps diplomatiques*: Fournier, the new French representative, 'a clever doctrinaire . . . Utopian, *cassant* and violent' was an old friend from The Hague; Count Wimpffen, from Austria, was 'a *routinier*, a quiet, sensible man' with a socially superior wife who 'was capricious and showed herself little'; the new Americans lived a very retired life: 'Mr. March was a book-worm and she was always ill and when she received she sat like a sibyl on her throne, quite immovable. Mr. Wurts, their secretary, made all the running.'[37] Social life was extremely difficult:

It was difficult to give a dinner party in Rome as there were so many people who were all bent upon having the highest rank. There were Ambassadors and Cardinals, Knights of the Annunziata and the Roman princes, not to mention the swarms of foreign royalties of every description, who descended upon Rome the first years it was a Capital.[38]

The streets of Rome were also extremely dangerous. While in Rome, Lady Paget involved herself deeply in social and cultural life: her memoirs for that period reflect that. Appointment to Vienna in 1884 restored her to the world of German politics, which she was only to leave in 1893. She indicates the level of her participation in political life in this description of a dinner at the Kalnokys:

I could not resist chaffing Foucher about the French elections . . . The only fear is that France, which, as a Republic, is a jelly fish, might, under a Monarchy, return to its sharkish proclivities. Grevy holds his post as President simply by virtue of his imbecility . . . Count Andrassy and Baron Huebner came to see me today. Count Albert Apponyi, the leader of the Hungarian Opposition, dined. These three certainly are the cleverest men in Austria. Count Andrassy, a man of inspiration and action, capable of sudden decisions; Count Huebner cultivated and full of knowledge of the world and wide experience; Count Apponyi dashing . . .[39]

That her participation was at more than a social level she indicates in her musings on their departure from Vienna on retirement:

During nearly all the time that we have been here the Balkan question has threatened to set Europe on fire. Vienna has been the point where all the threads converged. Ciphers were long and frequent and often came in the evening. A., who always was the most considerate of chiefs, and therefore rightly adored by all his staff, did not like to send for his secretaries when they were dining out and, consequently, often deciphered the telegraphs himself. I generally helped him and became quite an adept in this pursuit. I remember one occasion . . . A. was dining with the Emperor and I had some people to dinner too. I was in full dress with my tiara etc., because we were all going on to the *théâtre paré*, when a long cipher arrived. Ralph [her son and then a very junior diplomat] went at once to decipher it and I joined him as soon as our guests were gone. It was a very important telegram and it was most necessary for A. to have it at once. We, therefore, worked hard for more than an hour and were able to take it with us when we met A. at the theatre.[40]

It is interesting to note that when the legation in Rome was upgraded to an embassy in 1874, the Earl of Malmesbury, then Lord Privy Seal, troubled to send her a note from a Cabinet meeting: 'I have had a very happy quarter of an hour in being one of those to decide that you shall be an Ambassadress forthwith. My congratulations to Augustus.'[41] It may have been a kind politeness, but she certainly deserved the recognition.

Lady Bloomfield's memoirs lack the panache of Lady Paget's and are certainly less outspoken: she came from an older generation and her memoirs were published 40 years before those of Lady Paget, in 1883. They nevertheless convey an impression of careful observation and a keen awareness of the significance of her role. She was later to edit the memoirs of her diplomat father-in-law. Meriel Buchanan's memoirs indicate how far a daughter could participate in the official life. She described the rising tension in St Petersburg in the summer of 1914:

A Secretary of the Austrian Embassy came to say good-bye before leaving St. Petersburg with the rest of the staff, and was incredulous when I said that my sympathies were with Russia. 'But England will do nothing' he said. 'Her agreement with Russia is a purely nominal one. She will only act as a mediator and will not take an active part in this foolish quarrel.' . . .

I had been inclined to refuse to see him, to be angry with him for coming, but looking up into his nice grey eyes, which were so hurt and puzzled, I felt a sudden regret that our friendship should end in this way . . .[42]

A girl in her 20s, she found it hard

to bear the incessant questions with which one was bombarded. Difficult to find excuses and explanations for England's hesitation. Almost impossible to reply when people said sadly that there might not have been a war if England had, at the very beginning, announced her intention to fight with France and Russia.[43]

When war was declared, she volunteered for hospital work and describes extensively life in the embassy as the war progressed. She was even taken by her father on a visit to a British submarine. After the revolution in Russia and the war ended, Buchanan was posted to Rome. Meriel recounts the difficulties faced by a diplomat in the immediate post-war years:

The two Foreign Offices which now seemed to be operating in Downing Street also added to my father's difficulties, and although he was not opposed to the new diplomacy of conferences and meetings, he was hurt and humiliated when the Prime Minister refused to invite him to the Conference at Genoa, in spite of the Italians' special request for his presence there.[44]

Her description of her financial difficulties on the death of her father in 1924 adds to the weight of material now being published on the plight of 'surplus' middle-class women.

For the more recent period, the field is thin, but still important for what the memoirs tell of the changing role of the diplomatic wife.

Alongside the memoirs of her husband who was ambassador in Paris in the years 1954–60, which were published in 1972,[45] Cynthia Gladwyn published in 1976 a profile of previous British ambassadors to Paris: this depends heavily on other memoirs and reminiscences.[46] It charts the decline of the semi-official role for the diplomatic wife and, of course, also the decline in status of the great European embassies in the world of the superpowers and the emergence of the European Community. The inter-war period had seen some slightly odd appointments to Paris, not least that of Sir George Clerk (1934–37), who was barely on speaking terms with his eccentric wife. After the liberation of France, the choice of the Duff Coopers restored the elegance and style of the embassy. Diana Cooper's interests were cultural and artistic, and she was soon able to make the embassy the hospitable centre of French intellectual life in contrast with the deprivations being faced in French society. She was also careful in her reception of those who had not been particularly enthusiastic supporters of the Resistance, ensuring that they were acceptable to moderate Gaullists. Duff Cooper in his memoirs recounts their love for the embassy and his gift of his library to it.[47] The memoirs of Sir William Hayter, *A Double Life*,[48] owe much to the unpublished diary of his wife. He was appointed minister at Paris in 1949 and then ambassador at the highly sensitive post of Moscow in 1953. Iris Hayter's diary covers the period at Paris immediately after the retirement of the Duff Coopers and the spell in cold war Russia.[49] Oliver Harvey had succeeded the Coopers and set a rather less intimidating tone, employing an excellent chef and giving small dinners often including the Hayters with French cabinet ministers. Hayter himself admits that while in Paris French social life tended to squeeze out 'purely diplomatic entertainment'.[50] His wife's diary bears this out:

Usual round of flowers, hair & Hediard [a grand Paris grocer] – we had the Greenes & François & John Price & a new arrival Scott [on Ismay's staff] & Miss Locke to lunch. I was photographed for *Tatler* in ball dress after. David & Piers Rooke & a friend came to tea & Canasta with Teresa before dentist. Read a book by Eric Ambler till v. late . . . Went to Balmain a.m. & chose green alpaca suit & arranged to get short evening dress on approval.[51]

Her diary changes only slightly in tone with their appointment to the embassy in Moscow. There is much concentration on social arrangements, but occasionally, at moments of high tension such as the Suez Crisis, the political situation emerges:

2nd Walk with Aare a.m. Mr. & Mrs. Miles & Mr. Kirkwood & Miss Shaw &
Miss Gladwell (Miss S. & Miss G. are leavers) lunched. Tea with Cooper
Kleusch = Barbara was there v. nice gay flat in Sadovia. We are still bombing,
but the emphasis is on temporary police action. There are rumours that
Russian tanks etc. are being moved into Hungary again. We asked whether the
Syrians wanted us at their party for their president at the Sovietskaya & they
said they did so we went even though in the meantime the wireless said (we get
the BBC easily) S. has broken off relations with us. Everyone was v. polite. The
only expression of disapproval was from the Italian ambassador who shook
my hand instead of kissing it. I have been trying to achieve this for years & feel
he is the last person, both personally & because of Italy's role in the war, to
have any right to condemn anything so that we were amused & cheered up.[52]

There is little sense here of an ambassador's wife playing other than a
social and domestic role.

Material in the memoirs which relates to the specifically social side
of diplomatic life has been excluded here, important though that is in
the conduct of international relations. These memoirs are immensely
rich in evidence for that and also for the changing implications of court
and diplomatic protocol and procedure. There was no way that a
diplomatic wife could avoid the obligation to participate. On Sir
George Clerk's appointment as ambassador to Paris in 1934, the
Foreign Office stipulated that his wife must play her part as ambassadress to the full: it did, after all, have good reason to suspect that she
might not.[53] It is hardly surprising that many of these memoirs are
preoccupied with social matters for which their writers had been
responsible. Occasionally, a wife was presented with a particularly
pioneering and difficult social role. This was the case with Mary
Crawford Fraser, whose husband was appointed minister in Japan in
1888 and remained there till his death in 1894. Her memoirs are extensive and valuable for their picture of Japanese society as it reacted to
early Western contacts.[54]

Because of the significance of social entertaining in diplomatic life,
the memoirs of diplomatic women provide an important source.
Whereas the memoirs of diplomats concentrate on the diplomat's
political role and his impressions of the country to which he is posted,
those of his wife and daughters present a picture of a support service
without which it is not easy for a bachelor diplomat to succeed.
Current changes in the expectations of diplomatic wives may well
threaten many of the assumptions about diplomatic life. The emergence
of the Diplomatic Service Wives Association in 1965 to consider and
improve the position of diplomatic wives was an indication of signifi-

cantly changed attitudes.[55] For none of these memoirists did the diplomatic life appear a personal sacrifice: it may have meant much personal discomfort and disruption, but it also gave much satisfaction. It is hardly unexpected that the memoirs convey an impression of a job well done. What is perhaps surprising is the air of down-to-earth professionalism in even the most aristocratic of the writers: these were women with an officially recognized political role.

NOTES

1. *The Times*, 5 November 1986.
2. *The Nineteenth Century*, Vol. CXLVIII (June 1889), p. 781.
3. *The Times*, 1 June 1985.
4. *The Times*, 5 November 1986.
5. Walpurga, Lady Paget, *Scenes and Memories* (London, 1912); *Embassies of Other Days* (2 vols.) (London, 1923); *In my Tower* (2 vols.) (London, 1924); *The Linings of Life* (2 vols.) (London, 1928).
6. Georgiana, Lady Bloomfield, *Reminiscences of Court and Diplomatic Life* (2 vols.) (London, 1883) Vol. I, p. 21.
7. Meriel Buchanan, *Ambassador's Daughter* (London, 1958), p. 2.
8. Duff Cooper, *Old Men Forget: the Autobiography of Duff Cooper* (London, 1953), pp. 94–5.
9. Buchanan, *Daughter*, p. 50.
10. Paget, *Tower*, Vol. II, pp. 454–5.
11. Sir Nevile Henderson, *Water Under the Bridges* (London, 1945), p. 83.
12. Sir William Hayter, *A Double Life* (London, 1974), p. 20.
13. Paget, *Tower*, Vol. I, pp. 43 and 52.
14. Meriel Buchanan, *Victorian Gallery* (London, 1956), pp. 196–7.
15. Paget, *Linings*, Vol. II, p. 444.
16. Buchanan, *Daughter*; *Gallery*; Cynthia, Lady Gladwyn, *The Paris Embassy* (London, 1976); Hayter, *Double Life*; Roma Lister, *Reminiscences – Social and Political* (London, 1926).
17. Paget, *Linings*, Vol. I, pp. 85–6.
18. Paget, *Embassies*, Vol. I, p. 211.
19. Bloomfield, *Reminiscences*, Vol. I, pp. 135–43.
20. *Reminiscences*, Vol. I, p. 154.
21. Buchanan, *Gallery*, p. 197.
22. Paget, *Embassies*, Vol. I, pp. 210–11.
23. Royal Archives I 48/54. Private Memorandum, Foreign Office, 19 September 1867 cited in R.A. Jones, *The British Diplomatic Service, 1815–1914* (Gerrards Cross, 1983), p. 176.
24. Buchanan, *Daughter*, pp. 4–5.
25. *Daughter*, p. 13.
26. *Daughter*, p. 29.
27. *Daughter*, pp. 31–2.
28. Hayter, *Double Life*, pp. 47–8.
29. Buchanan, *Daughter*, p. 55.
30. Percy Sykes, *Sir Mortimer Durand* (London, 1926), p. 227.
31. Buchanan, *Daughter*, p. 33.
32. Thomas Hohler, *Diplomatic Petrel* (London, 1942), p. 3.
33. Paget, *Embassies*, Vol. I, pp. 138–67.
34. *Embassies*, Vol. I, p. 180.
35. *Embassies*, Vol. I, pp. 270–8.
36. *Embassies*, Vol. I, p. 270.
37. *Embassies*, Vol. I, pp. 271–2.

38. *Embassies*, Vol. I, p. 275.
39. *Embassies*, Vol. II, p. 392.
40. *Embassies*, Vol. II, p. 555.
41. *Embassies*, Vol. I, p. 288.
42. Buchanan, *Daughter*, p. 121.
43. *Daughter*, p. 123.
44. *Daughter*, p. 217.
45. Gladwyn Jebb, Lord Gladwyn, *Memoirs of Lord Gladwyn* (London, 1972).
46. Gladwyn, *Paris Embassy*.
47. Cooper, *Old Men*, pp. 382–3.
48. Hayter, *Double Life*. See also his *The Kremlin and the Embassy* (London, 1966).
49. Iris, Lady Hayter, unpublished diary in her private possession.
50. Hayter, *Double Life*, p. 88.
51. Iris Hayter, MS, 22 and 23 April 1952.
52. Hayter, MS, 2 November 1956.
53. Gladwyn, *Paris Embassy*, pp. 214–15.
54. Hugh Cortazzi (ed.), Mary Crawford Fraser, *A Diplomat's Wife in Japan* (New York, 1982), abridged from Mary Crawford Fraser, *A Diplomatist's Wife in Japan* (London, 1899). See also her *Diplomatist's Wife in Many Lands* (New York, 1911) and *Further Reminiscences of a Diplomatist's Wife* (London, 1912).
55. The Association was formed from an amalgamation of the Commonwealth Relations Office Wives Society (formed in 1955) and the Foreign Service Wives Association (formed 1960) on the merger of the two offices.

12

The Published Political Memoirs of Leading Nazis, 1933–45

LEONIDAS E. HILL

The era of the Third Reich generated a vast corpus of memoirs, both published and unpublished. No one has attempted an overview of the published ones for decades,[1] and some of the unpublished collections are scarcely known. For example, I have read 256 autobiographies written in the period 1939–40, of which only a few have been published in their entirety or in part.[2] All were submitted for a competition conducted by three Harvard University professors offering prize money for accounts of 'My Life in Germany Before and After Hitler'.[3] Most of the authors were German and Austrian Jews who had fled before the outbreak of the war and wrote their autobiographies in exile, a few in Sweden and Australia, in Paris and Shanghai, a considerable number in London, many more in the United States.

Such non-Nazi autobiographies contrast starkly with the 581 auto-biographies of stormtroopers collected by the sociologist Theodore Abel at Columbia in 1934 and used by Peter Merkl for his studies of political violence and stormtroopers.[4] These two collections may possibly provide a composite profile of the persecutors as well as the persecuted. But these committed Nazi memoirists, like the entrants in the Harvard contest, were not entirely political in the sense addressed by the present collection of essays on the political memoir, and they stopped their accounts early in the Nazi era.

Mention of the stormtroopers and their victims nevertheless suggests important questions about the memoirs of leading Nazis. Did they resemble the stormtroopers in being prototypical Nazis? How did they claim to have viewed the political process in the Third Reich before and during the war? Did they grasp and confront the evil nature of the regime or honestly describe their own complicity? What were their purposes in writing their memoirs? Are these memoirs still valuable to historians and of interest to the general reader?

The answers to these questions will be sought in a number of the *published* political memoirs of leading servants of the Nazi regime or those who were well-placed to observe them from the beginning to the end of the Third Reich. Yet there are also many unpublished memoirs by, for example, Field-Marshals von Weichs and Milch, Generals Blomberg, Adam,[5] and von Falkenhausen in the Koblenz and Freiburg branches of the Bundesarchiv of the Federal Republic of Germany, or the Institut für Zeitgeschichte in Munich. These were not published for various reasons. A few authors themselves placed restrictions on their memoirs in the archives, and did not want their publication then. They wrote them for their families, or for historians, rather than for the public. Some had scruples about damaging the reputations of colleagues through critical evaluations or recollections of them. The money that they might have obtained by publication was not their first interest. Widows did not attempt to clear their husbands' reputations as was the case with Ribbentrop, Keitel and Jodl. The existence of these unpublished memoirs suggests that in some countries during particular periods a tradition of writing memoirs without necessarily intending publication became established. Prominent Germans have apparently long considered such authorship a normal occupation in retirement.[6] The generals had first to overcome whatever inhibitions endured because of Constantin von Alvensleben's rule that 'a Prussian general dies but does not leave any memoirs'.[7] The tradition in Germany was no doubt first strengthened greatly by the triumphs of the wars of unification, then by the exculpatory purposes that have motivated the recent generations of leading Germans who managed their country's affairs before, during and after the two world wars. Most other countries have not had the same or so powerful a tradition; they have also not had to explain so many misjudgements and profound defeat in two disastrous world wars.

A reminder is necessary of the circumstances in which most of these memoirs of Nazi Germany were written or conceived. With the exception of Weizsäcker the authors were taken into Allied custody at the end of the war. Many of the military relinquished their swords and, at the command, demand or request of their captors, picked up their pens. Allied interrogations jogged their memories.[8] While incarcerated together in rooms with listening devices to record their conversations, they examined their mistakes and speculated on the nature of the flawless third world war their successors would fight.[9] Asked to write about their experiences they were eventually provided with war diaries and documents. The result was a series of accounts of the war by those who had conducted it on the German side and presumably knew it best.[10]

These interrogations, conversations and studies were the basis or the substance of the memoirs that they wrote before or during their trials, while in prison or after release. The memoir was sometimes a product of a relatively short imprisonment, before execution, as with Ribbentrop and Keitel, whose widows published their work, Hans Frank, or the commandant of Auschwitz, Höss, whose executioners printed his recollections.[11] Jodl's widow in effect wrote and pasted together his memoirs after his execution.[12] Diels had already written a manuscript by 1935 and Gisevius one by 1941. In the Vatican, Albrecht von Kessel and Weizsäcker were both at work: Kessel on a single draft in 1944–45;[13] Weizsäcker on two in that period and a third in 1947. The most important transition was from the second to the third version, which he wrote after his return from the Vatican with the help of letters, diaries and notes in his home in Lindau during 1947, before he was indicted and taken into custody for his trial.[14] Papen and Schacht could only write after escaping conviction in years of trials, first by the Allies, then by denazification courts.[15] Kesselring and Speer wrote in prison with the permission of their captors, but Speer smuggled his manuscript and diaries outside. In a British internment camp in 1946 Otto Dietrich described Hitler and his milieu with anecdotal memoir touches. Raeder and Dönitz penned their accounts after release from Allied, the Austrian Neubacher from Yugoslav, imprisonment.[16] The record, if that is what it is, of Halder's conversations constitutes a quasi-memoir.[17] Memoirs of the Nazi era still appear but at a diminishing rate, such as, recently, Walter Bargatzky, Christa Schroeder and three Austrians who served the Nazis, Reinhard Spitzy, Franz von Sonnleithner and Glaise von Horstenau.[18] It would be interesting and perhaps important to know the development of every one of these memoirs from first to last draft, to know what was introduced and what was deleted, to examine this in conjunction with their interrogations, testimony and the available documentation, but this will be the task of many historians and biographers if the drafts are available.[19]

These memoirs can be considered as little more than the justifications of party, political, administrative, judicial, diplomatic, military (army, navy, air force) and intelligence[20] élites, if not others. Some scholars have asserted the existence of an alliance between these élites and the Nazis and, almost without naming any individuals, have described the bonds between them.[21] In the abstract as well as concretely these were numerous, strong and clear, but not unexpectedly the memoirists obscure them. The historian's simpler abstraction and descriptions of the concrete aspects of the symbiotic relationship appear more convincing than the memoirist's account of his motives, but the elusive discrepancy between the two accounts still deserves close examination. Biographers writing with access to other documentation concerning their subjects can frequently clarify their views and allegiances at the time and may confirm their accounts rather than the model and our suspicions.

This is not the place to scrutinize their accounts of their childhoods, adolescence, and early adulthood. An older generation fought in the First World War while a younger one experienced the war in other ways.[22] Few of these memoirists describe their views on German responsibility for the outbreak of the First World War, on war aims or on the reasons for Germany's defeat, and their biographers rarely have much evidence. Such material is available for Weizsäcker, who was an exception in providing a reasonably accurate account of his views: his moderation was unusual in the navy and few in the military had a comparable outlook. Unlike Weizsäcker, most of them had grandiose ambitions for Germany during the First World War, opposed a compromise peace, rejected domestic reform, inclined to accept the thesis that Germany had been defeated by a stab in the back and rejected or only reluctantly accepted the republican regime.[23] But Schacht and Schwerin von Krosigk were anomalous as elected representatives in the revolutionary council movement, the first favouring the Democratic Party, the second the DNVP and still a monarchist. Schacht distinguished himself in 1923 as well as afterwards in the service of the Republic; Schwerin von Krosigk rose to prominence after 1929.[24]

Accounts of the early Weimar Republic frequently conceal their authors' true attitude to counter-revolutionary and anti-republican forces. Manstein, Guderian and Höss joined Freikorps units; Senger und Etterlin volunteered to fight against the 'Bolsheviks' in Saxony.[25] Some of them sympathized with Kapp and his Putsch; Raeder's disingenuous remarks about the role of the navy in the Kapp Putsch are exemplary in this regard. However, Manstein approved military action against Kapp, and Weizsäcker at the time ridiculed Kapp for his nearly ruinous stupidity, although the language of his memoirs is restrained.[26] No doubt a few of them wished success to right-wing revolutionaries like Hitler in 1923. Baldur von Schirach,[27] whose parents invited Hitler to tea in 1925, has acknowledged his early and enduring anti-Semitism. Schirach joined a paramilitary organization in 1924, the SA in 1927, and after 1928 helped subvert the Weimar Republic as a National Socialist student leader, while nationalistic conservatives such as Papen, Schacht and Meissner[28] played a notable part in helping Hitler to power and serving him afterwards. Without being actively disloyal most of the memoirists were disaffected, and even when, like Weizsäcker and Schwerin von Krosigk, they had not voted for Hitler and were reassured by his dim prospects at the end of 1932, they rather easily rationalized further service after his appointment. The military memoirists assert that they remained apolitical throughout their careers, but that at the deepest level the Allies were responsible through the Versailles Treaty.

Their denials of having supported Hitler and the Nazi party are partial grounds for their rejection of the popular thesis that their élite concluded an alliance with the Nazis. Others made such an alliance; they simply followed or collaborated. Few acknowledged that they welcomed Hitler's destruction of parliamentary democracy, and with the exception of Gisevius and Papen most barely mention the Reichstag Fire and the Enabling Act. None discusses the book burnings; the arrests of Weimar politicians from the KPD, SPD, Center, Democrats, trade unions and so on; the Nazi murders of a number of them; the system of concentration camps. There is usually very little on the Gestapo and SS as domestic instruments of control and terror, except by Gisevius and Diels who were employed in the former. Gisevius recounts the events of 30 June 1934 at length; he subsequently passed incriminating documents about the Gestapo to Oster. The other memoirists note the murder of Roehm and his SA associates – whose suppression as putschists and a challenge to the army, generals such as Keitel approved – and express distress over the fate of Schleicher and Bredow. Papen mourned his associates Bose and Jung. The memoirists had obviously not taken Hitler seriously when he said that 'heads would roll'. A number of them strike a note of genuine concern about Nazi persecution of the Protestant and Catholic churches, compared by Papen to 'the methods of the Bolsheviks'.

They claim that they were not anti-Semitic and deplored the treatment of Jews when it came to their attention with the pogrom of 10 November 1938. Schwerin von Krosigk's and Schacht's claims about protecting Jews and condemning the pogrom have been doubted.[29] Although Speer claimed that he was never an anti-Semite and was chiefly offended by the mess on 10 November 1938, he only mentioned this at his publisher's urging.[30] The self-confessed anti-Semites Schirach and Spitzy also both deplored the violence and destruction of the pogrom, which Sonnleithner did not notice. The dry and factual language of most of the military memoirs hides their authors' earlier ideological commitments, their ambitions, their social-Darwinistic contempt for other peoples, their arrogance and toughness. However, Weizsäcker's private language in his diaries and hundreds of private letters was usually as spare as that of his memoirs and as bereft of anti-Semitism, while some affidavits from his trial show he was horrified by the pogrom.[31]

The memoirists failed to grasp Hitler's larger intentions: they seem never to have heard the word *Lebensraum*. Even those at the top never admit awareness of the wild and distant hegemonical visions of Hitler, and certainly not of his plans for *Weltherrschaft*. Hitler's translator Paul Schmidt of course only witnessed his restrained language to visitors.[32] The military personnel who heard Hitler in February 1933 talk about his most grandiose ambitions appear not to have taken them seriously. Instead they focused on the next short-range steps in their own sphere, whether political, economic, diplomatic or military, so as to contribute to the resurrection of a Germany at least capable of defending itself against Polish aggression, the possibility obviously chosen to emphasize Germany's humiliating weakness.

They applauded Germany's departure from the Disarmament Conference and the League of Nations (though Papen opposed this), as well as its introduction of conscription. Most were equally enthusiastic about its enormously accelerated rearmament and the escape from the 'fetters' of Versailles, although some qualified this approval because their own service did not benefit as much as the other services, or could hardly cope with the pace of the increases. Others, such as Schacht, worried about the deleterious effects of these increases on the economy, especially with the Four Year Plan, and foresaw that rearmament on such a scale would upset the balance of power in Europe and bring war nearer. Some military leaders deplored Himmler's expansion of armed SS units before the war, and even more their vast growth during it.

All took the return of the Saar as their due, but they were unnerved and impressed by the risks taken with the reoccupation of the Rhineland. Manstein's role in the planning is absent from his memoirs.[33] The diplomats (Weizsäcker) and army were dubious about Germany's engagement in Spain (reported by Warlimont,[34] who does not mention his own presence there), the navy and air force (Raeder and Kesselring) approving, but with reservations because of the danger to ships and the limited number of planes, even while uniformly labelling the Republican side the 'Reds' and perceiving a Bolshevik menace there. A number of those who were present at or informed about the 5 November 1937 'Hoßbach' conference became convinced that Hitler was only spurring the reluctant military to greater effort. They therefore appear not to have seen the cloud of war on the distant horizon. Nevertheless Hoßbach himself recorded the strong reaction of those who rightly saw such a cloud.[35] Weizsäcker was not informed of the conference but had long been worried about war.

Papen and Weizsäcker put an innocent face on their work in or regarding Austria. After their worries about the reactions of Great Britain and France, and the deficiencies of Germany's improvised (on which, see Warlimont) military entry, partly designed by Manstein but again unrecorded by him, they welcomed Anschluss, as did Kordt and his younger Austrian associate, Reinhard Spitzy. Some diplomats and military feared war over Czechoslovakia and argued against it, instances of which are mentioned by numerous memoirists, particularly Weizsäcker and Schwerin von Krosigk; all of them were already convinced that expression of moral objections to Hitler was counterproductive. As then, so in retrospect Kesselring believed his air power would have facilitated an easy conquest of flimsy Czech defences. Better qualified observers, such as Hitler, as recalled by Speer, were more impressed. Weizsäcker and Kordt describe warnings to Great Britain and the plot against Hitler, headed by Halder, in which Kordt participated.[36] Kordt's friend Spitzy admits admiration for Hitler but also manages to claim an oppositional role.

Albert Speer tells a very different story. The first large part of his memoir is about his architectural efforts and Hitler, who is practically supine much of the time unless excitedly planning buildings. This is the Führer of the faddish polycratic state, if one can believe in that. Speer himself drew and planned and hardly knew about the nature of the regime. He could not recollect any new insights after the pogrom of 10 November 1938.

The military memoirists are not candid about their desire after Munich for Prague because of the strategic advantage occupation of Bohemia and Moravia gave them against Poland, long prominent on their wish-list because of the Corridor. Weizsäcker had promoted an alternative programme and foresaw the deleterious political effects of the Ides of March; but the military found the operation so easy that, as authors, they looked back with disinterest. The large territorial and material gains of 1938–39 made an enormous difference and only a few congenital pessimists such as Weizsäcker amongst these high-level memoirists opposed almost all the subsequent territorial aggrandizements – the invasion and conquest of Poland, Denmark and Norway, western Europe, the Balkans and Russia – at first with some energy, later with formal, written arguments.

This is not to say that any of them by their own account supported aggression. The memoirists are careful about these matters. Only Hitler, Ribbentrop and a few others who did not survive actually wanted to occupy Czechoslovakia and then invade Poland. The military planned strictly under orders, although their memoirs do not conceal their outrage at the post-war treaty boundaries for Czechoslovakia and Poland and their conceits. The recent volume by Spitzy is exemplary in this regard. Yet Guderian affirms the need for a Polish buffer between Germany and the dangerous Soviet Union. The memoirists thought Hitler was bluffing as he had done in the summer of 1938, or that Poland and its guarantors would sensibly capitulate when faced with the freshly consummated Nazi-Soviet Pact, believed impossible that summer by diplomats such as Weizsäcker, Hilger, and Herwarth,[37] but not Ribbentrop. Weizsäcker and Kordt warned the British and Herwarth warned the Americans. Nicholas von Below even recalled conversations with Hitler in 1939 about an eventual invasion of Russia.[38] While acknowledging the dangers of a two-front war, Hitler and Ribbentrop had guaranteed that Great Britain and France would stay out of the war. But they removed ambassador Dirksen[39] from London and frustrated all efforts to resolve the crisis through diplomacy.

Some of the memoirists were deeply shaken by the outbreak of war. Weizsäcker almost immediately lost a son and predicted defeat for Germany. Kordt wanted to forestall a premature 1939 campaign in the west by the assassination of Hitler, which was nearly achieved by Elser, an unwilling autobiographer.[40] From the life of the Abwehr officer Josef Müller comes an account of a bizarre oppositional diplomatic effort in the Vatican with the same aim.[41] Much more modest attempts were made in 1940 to prevent the Scandinavian campaign. However, the conquest of Denmark and Norway was pre-emptive; Great Britain had already violated Norwegian neutrality and the next step was obviously the seizure of bases there. Raeder concealed his important role and his reasons. Germany was barely in time as Churchill's memoirs supposedly demonstrate. Belgium collaborated with France, already at war with Germany, so had to be conquered at the same time.

Holland was in the way, would have been used by Great Britain or France and had to be denied the neutral status it enjoyed during the First World War. These were necessities of war, as was the bombing of Rotterdam according to Kesselring, whose memoirs exude the pride of his force's role in the conquest of France and excuse their failure at Dunkirk. Other authors pin the blame for restraint at Dunkirk firmly on Hitler and Rundstedt. Raeder was pessimistic about Operation Sealion, the invasion of Great Britain, and stalled, whereas Kesselring explained why he thought it was feasible and should have been attempted. The navy wanted a Mediterranean strategy rather than the invasion of Russia, and Kesselring regretted his ignorance of Raeder's designs: together they might have persuaded Hitler.

Weizsäcker wanted Germany to restrain Italy from attack on Greece; Italy's difficulties and the presence of British forces in Greece would have necessitated Germany's descent into the Balkans even without a coup in Yugoslavia, which was decisive. Despite Weizsäcker's evidence that Hitler talked of the conquest of Russia immediately after crushing France, and Loßberg's that planning commenced then,[42] and with the exception of Warlimont who put his unalterable decision in July 1940 and attributed it to his hatred of Bolshevism, they agree that he decided only in December 1940 and then because of the USSR's obviously expansionist intentions in the north as well as the south. Nevertheless, Weizsäcker, Schwerin von Krosigk, Keitel and Raeder record various objections on their part and by others against the undertaking. After the invasion a number found confirmation of Hitler's good judgement in the massing of Russian troops, which supposedly indicated aggressive intentions; thus 'Barbarossa' was a preventive war. At least Weizsäcker knew otherwise and did not share the widespread confidence on the eve of the fatal venture.

Barbarossa constituted a caesura in the history of the Third Reich which is reflected in many of the military memoirs. Those engaged on the eastern front dissect the mistakes, mainly Hitler's, such as dispersing instead of concentrating their forces on Moscow, sacrificing Paulus at Stalingrad and failing to withdraw and concentrate more intelligently thereafter. Kesselring believed a Mediterranean strategy might have succeeded if Germany had invaded Malta, sent Rommel west to thwart the Allied invasion of North Africa rather than allowing him his last desert campaign, and prevented the capture of the armies in Tunisia. But Kesselring's optimism suffers scathing criticism in the pages of Senger und Etterlin. Diplomatic ties with Italy to the end are described by Rintelen, Rahn and Dollmann.[43] Raeder and

Dönitz emphasize the misplaced priorities in the Atlantic naval war. With more submarines, which they had sought, what they might have wrought!

Virtually all of the authors were deeply and genuinely anti-Communist during the Weimar Republic and Third Reich, but their manipulation of this theme in their memoirs is probably related to publication during the cold war. Thus some mention the dangers of Bolshevism after the First World War or after 1929 in Germany, in Spain after 1936 and from the USSR after 1939. Many emphasize the danger in 1940 and the massive preparations discovered upon invasion in 1941. This theme leaps into high relief in 1944–45: the Allies should have recognized the Soviet threat to Europe and joined Germany, thus sparing it territorially by preventing the westward advance of Bolshevism. This argument is central to Dönitz's account of his brief successor government, which attempted to manipulate the menace to Germany's advantage, but many of the other memoirists constitute a muted and suggestive chorus. If only the Allies had not been so superficial and had been able to see as deeply as Germans, who possessed a historically grounded wisdom because of their perilous geographical position!

The military memoirists claim that they conducted themselves according to the laws of war and did not control the party forces which committed the atrocities. Or they call the atrocities reprisals, and claim they accord with international law. None of them describes at length, and some do not even mention, the ruthless occupation policies, the exploitation and murder of populations, the deportation and extermination of Jews, the mistreatment and high death rate of Soviet prisoners of war and their employment and that of civilians from all over Europe as slave labour, although the documents and their actions implicate or incriminate many of them.[44] Schwerin von Krosigk claims that he opposed evacuations and slave labour; Weizsäcker refers to more modest ameliorative efforts; from criticism of Hitler's murderous *Kommando* order in Russia Werner Otto von Hentig moved to opposition;[45] Senger und Etterlin refused to circulate Hitler's order to kill women and children in the war against partisans in Russia, and later in Italy would not execute captured Italian officers. Two generals connected with the attempted coup against Hitler, Heusinger and Speidel, subsequently served with distinction in the Bundeswehr and NATO.[46]

No more than Weizsäcker did Speer admit to knowing about extermination camps. Yet Speer, Dönitz and Schirach heard Himmler describe the policy of extermination. It seems clear that Speer did know and that he assumed responsibility at his trial for less than he actually did.[47] Schirach confessed in his book that he had learned about the death camps but only after the deportations from Vienna for which he was convicted. He dated his knowledge later than he should have, apparently still attempting to escape full responsibility.[48] Weizsäcker read reports about the operations of the Einsatzgruppen but it has not been proved that he knew deported Jews would be murdered.[49] He eschewed examination of incriminating documents and the historical background in his memoirs, as did most of the other authors.

Kesselring, Schwerin von Krosigk, Dönitz and Raeder use the *tu quoque* argument stubbornly and at length about their trials. Most of them were tried in some court, if not by the Allies then in German denazification trials, were treated like criminals, often but not always convicted, sometimes executed, more often imprisoned for a few years and released early. Many memoirs deny that the courts were competent, that the law was applicable, that access to documents was equal for prosecution and defence, that translations were accurate, that their affidavits were credited, that justice was done and that their mean treatment was merited. A few end with Germany's surrender or barely mention their trials. Speer admitted guilt and accepted the verdict, but probably as part of a strategy to win acceptance of his claim that he had not known about extermination in Auschwitz and had parted from Hitler to save as much as he could at the end. He still engaged in deception and strove to set his own stamp on his guilty reputation.

Certainly if we return to the questions posed at the beginning of this essay it can be said that the memoirists do not resemble the stormtroopers and few appear in their own memoirs as prototypical Nazis. Some of them were never and others were at best reluctant members of the Nazi Party. Most committed to Nazi ideology and especially to Hitler personally were Ribbentrop, Speer and Höss. Ribbentrop learned nothing and Speer much about himself at his trial and in writing memoirs. Höss is exceptionally revealing but hardly understood his own revelations. Most of them served the Nazis loyally as professionals, a few with another fundamental loyalty (Senger und Etterlin as a Christian), while others opposed Hitler, committed treason or considered assassinating Hitler (Weizsäcker, Kordt, Gisevius, Schlabrendorff).[50] Their memoirs help us understand how they continued serving the Third Reich.

How did they view the political process in the Third Reich? Almost all of them had forsaken the Weimar Republic and wanted a more authoritarian government emancipated from the constraints of democracy and parliamentary government. Their goals were in the realms of foreign policy, armaments and soldiers, ships and sailors, internal 'order' and eventually territorial gains. Many hoped the war aims of Imperial Germany would be achieved by the Nazis. However much they deplored the way the political process functioned, most of them approved some of the major results for their arm of the state and for Germany's position in Europe. Only during the war, indeed after the invasion of Russia, did more of them finally perceive the deeper flaws in the political system, above all the fatal concentration of power in Hitler's hands.

The evil nature of the regime should have been evident early, but few of them saw it before 1939, and all too many missed it afterwards too. In contrast, when they wrote in 1939–40 almost all the entrants in the 'My Life in Germany' contest already knew better than the later published Nazi authors the effects of Nazi rule on the state and society and on themselves. Mostly Jews but also some political opponents of Nazism, they saw what few of the highly placed servants of Nazism glimpsed: its fanaticism, viciousness, murderousness, ideological devotion, destructiveness, cynicism, inhumanity, corruption, greed and warlike nature. To justify the use of every one of these words their memoirs provide massive evidence. They burned their own letters, diaries and books before the Nazis did, tried to become anonymous, innocent of their pasts; they were hunted and beaten, tormented in the concentration camps of 1933 and after; they were boycotted, robbed, extorted; they were banned from their professions, then from parks, theatres, shops, restaurants, from whole towns; they were spied upon and insidiously controlled; their children were taunted and humiliated, eventually turned out of the schools. All of this was diabolical. These observers could see that war was approaching and prayed that Great Britain and France would stop Hitler, or that some German general, or anyone else would. The chief characteristics of this appalling police state were injustice and bristling potential aggressions, which the published memoirists largely missed; after the war a few admitted the heinous wartime fulfilment of those inhumane pre-war preliminaries.

What were their purposes in writing? Comparison of these memoirs makes clear a number of purposes of most of the authors: to establish the ignorance and innocence of the author as a non-political professional by writing hundreds of pages of diplomatic or military history with recollections of encounters and conversations with famous men in the course of extensive travels; to demonstrate that he was not an ideological 'Nazi', even when formally a member of the Party or the SS; to argue that his branch of the government only followed orders, encouraged moderation and maintained as best it could its traditional standards rather than having become a criminal, aggressive organization as the Allies charged at Nuremberg; to preserve his honour and reputation, whether diplomat, soldier or sailor, and pin the blame for many major mistakes on Hitler, Ribbentrop and Göring; to claim that the diplomats had reported honestly and the military fought cleanly, had been ignorant of and not participated in the Holocaust, in contrast to their opponents' terror bombing and despoliation of property; to assert that Germany was driven to Hitler by the Versailles treaty, undertook the Second World War in the estimable cause of revision, would not have expanded the war if it had been allowed its justifiable gains, and then could have been a bulwark against Bolshevism, so mistakenly allowed by the Allies into Eastern Europe at the end. Speer is a prime example of the many who concealed their driving ambition, Dönitz of those who distanced themselves from a close relationship of reciprocal respect with Hitler.[51]

Are these memoirs valuable to historians or of interest to the general reader? A problem for historians is that even a few years after the war the memoirists have read one another, the historians available at the time they wrote, plus published and unpublished documents. The books before us are not the simple products of the author's recollections and reflections, and a few were probably at least partially ghost-written, as has been so often the case with commercially valuable memoirs in recent decades. Speer had the advice of his publisher and Joachim Fest may have polished his prose.[52] Schirach's recording of his memoirs was reworked by Jochen von Lang.[53] Nevertheless, memoirs are an indispensable source of atmosphere, individual perspective, analysis of situation and evaluation of character, of anecdote and quotation. Historians must scrutinize and weigh these carefully; some historians accept what others reject. This process is simplified when the content of the memoirs can be corroborated by letters, diaries and notes, and the manuscript of memoirs not originally intended for publication can be checked against the volume in print. These conditions have been met only in the case of Weizsäcker.

Historians have learned much from these memoirs about the rivalries of branches of government and agencies in the Third Reich, and have found confirmation that Hitler encouraged or tolerated their struggles, which facilitated his domination. The descriptions of the participants make it easier to understand and interpret a vast amount of other personal and official material; the stages, relations, methods, pettiness, alliances and hostilities would not be so sharply defined and vivid without the memoirs.

These writings almost automatically raise their authors into a different position in history, which they sought. But few of them can have anticipated that they would be subjected to such scrutiny and scathing criticism, that their writings would fuel such keen analysis. The anticipated result, a profile of Nazi-man, however, eludes us, and we are left with a rich if not very inspiring collection of human beings. Indeed, Höss represents the nadir of autobiographical reflection about heinous acts.

The general reader presumably applies less stringent criteria and reads in the belief that the memoirist's report is more immediate and personal than any other, except diaries and letters. Many of them seek first-hand evidence about Hitler. If the comments written in the margins of Nazi memoirs in university libraries are admissible evidence, some readers are anything but credulous. Furthermore, the number of these memoirs apparently stolen from these libraries might make one suspect a high value placed on them by Neo-Nazis. Their opponents are not likely to have taken them because they probably agree that there is not a genuinely great political memoir among them.

NOTES

I thank The Social Sciences Humanities Research Council of Canada for grants facilitating this study and my wife Nancy for wordprocessing many versions.

1. Walther Hubatsch, *Deutsche Memoiren 1945–1953. Ein kritischer Überblick*, in Helmet Dahms (ed.), *Geschichte und Politik*, Heft 8 (Laupheim, n.d.); Gotthard Breit, *Das Staats- und Gesellschaftsbild deutscher Generale beider Weltkriege im Spiegel ihrer Memoiren*, in Militärgeschichtliche Studien, Vol. 17 (Boppard am Rhein, 1973).
2. Käte Frankenthal, *Der dreifache Flucht: Jüdin, Intellektuelle, Sozialistin. Lebenserinnerungen einer Ärztin in Deutschland und im Exil* (New York, 1981); Karl Löwith, *Mein Leben in Deutschland vor und nach 1933: Ein Bericht* (Stuttgart, 1986); Andreas Lixl-Purcell (ed.), *Women of Exile. German-Jewish Autobiographies Since 1933* (New York, 1988).
3. The main collection is in the Houghton Library, Harvard University, but some are in the Leo Baeck Institute, New York.
4. *Early Nazis* (Princeton, NJ, 1975).
5. On his memoirs, which I read in the Institut für Zeitgeschichte, see Anton Hoch and Hermann Weiß, 'Die Erinnerungen des Generalobersten Wilhelm Adam', in Wolfgang Benz (ed.), *Miscellanea. Festschrift für Helmut Krausnick zum 75.Geburtstag* (Stuttgart, 1980).
6. Ernst von Weizsäcker encouraged his father to commence his memoirs in retirement after the First World War, and toward the end of the Second World War he wrote two drafts of his own autobiography.
7. Alfred Vagts, *A History of Militarism. Civilian and Military* (New York, 1959), p. 25.
8. The records of many of these interrogations are in the National Archives, Washington, DC.

9. Related to the author by Prof. W. Stull Holt, History Department, University of Washington (Seattle), who worked in intelligence in England.
10. Charles B. Burdick, 'Vom Schwert zur Feder. Deutsche Kriegsgefangene im Dienst der Vorbereitung der amerikanischen Kriegsgeschichtsschreibung über den Zweiten Weltkrieg. Die organisatorische Entwicklung der Operational History (German) Section', *Militärgeschichtliche Mitteilungen*, Vol. 10, No. 2 (1971), pp. 69–80; see also Albert Kesselring, *Soldat bis zum letzten Tag* (Bonn, 1953), *Kesselring: A Soldier's Record*, Lynton Hudson (trans.) (New York, 1954).
11. Joachim von Ribbentrop, *Zwischen London und Moskau, Erinnerungen und letzte Aufzeichnungen* (Leoni am Starnberger See, 1953), *The Ribbentrop Memoirs*, Oliver Watson (trans.) (London, 1954); Wilhelm Keitel, Walter Görlitz (ed.), *Generalfeldmarschall Keitel, Verbrecher oder Offizier? Erinnerungen, Briefe, Dokumente, des Chefs OKW* (Göttingen, 1961), Walter Görlitz (ed.), *The Memoirs of Field Marshal Keitel* (London, 1965); Hans Frank, *Im Angesicht des Galgens: Deutung Hitlers und seiner Zeit auf Grund eigener Erlebnisse und Erkenntnisse* (Neuhaus, 1955); Rudolf Höss, Martin Broszat (ed.), *Kommandant in Auschwitz: Autobiographische Aufzeichnungen* (Stuttgart, 1958), *Commandant of Auschwitz, The Autobiography of Rudolf Höss*, Lord Russell (intro.), Constantine Fitzgibbon (trans.) (London, 1959).
12. Luise Jodl, *Jenseits des Endes. Leben und Sterben des Generaloberst Alfred Jodl* (Vienna, Munich, Zurich, 1976). See also Bodo Scheurig, *Alfred Jodl: Gehorsam und Verhängnis* (Berlin, Frankfurt am Main, 1991).
13. Rudolf Diels, *Lucifer ante Portas. Zwischen Severing und Heydrich* (Zurich, n.d. [1949]); Hans Bernd Gisevius, *Bis zum bittern Ende* (Zurich, 1946) and *To the Bitter End*, Richard and Clara Winston (trans.) (Boston, 1947). Kessel's manuscript was finally published almost 50 years later: Albrecht von Kessel, Peter Steinbach (ed.), *Verborgene Saat: Aufzeichnungen aus dem Widerstand 1933 bis 1945* (Berlin, Frankfurt am Main, 1992).
14. See L.E. Hill, 'The Genesis and Interpretation of the Memoirs of Ernst von Weizsäcker', *German Studies Review*, Vol. X, No. 3 (October 1987), pp. 443–80; Ernst von Weizsäcker, *Erinnerungen* (Munich, 1950), *Memoirs*, John Andrews (trans.) (Chicago, 1951).
15. Franz von Papen, *Der Wahrheit eine Gasse* (Munich, 1952), *Memoirs*, Brian Connell (trans.) (London, 1952); Hjalmar Horace Greeley Schacht, *Abrechnung mit Hitler* (Hamburg, 1948), *Account Settled*, F. Fitzgerald (trans.) (London, 1949).
16. Albert Speer, *Erinnerungen* (Berlin, 1969), *Inside the Third Reich: Memoirs*, Richard and Clara Winston (trans.) (New York, 1970), *Spandau. The Secret Diaries* (New York, 1976); Otto Dietrich, *Zwölf Jahre mit Hitler* (Munich, 1955), *Hitler*, Richard and Clara Winston (trans.) (Chicago, 1955); Erich Raeder, *Mein Leben* (Tübingen, 1956), *My Life*, Henry W. Drexel (trans.) (Annapolis, 1960); Admiral Karl Dönitz, *Zehn Jahre und Zwanzig Tage* (Bonn, 1958), *Memoirs: Ten Years and Twenty Days*, R.H. Stevens and David Woodward (trans.) (Cleveland, 1959), *Mein wechselvolles Leben* (Göttingen, 1968), *40 Fragen an Karl Dönitz* (Munich, 1970); Hermann Neubacher, *Sonderauftrag Südost 1940–1945* (Göttingen, Berlin, Frankfurt, 1956).
17. Peter Bor, *Gespräche mit Halder* (Wiesbaden, 1950).
18. Walter Bargatzky, *Hotel Majestic. Ein Deutscher in besetzten Frankreich* (Freiburg, 1987); Christa Schroeder, *Er war mein Chef* (Munich, 1985); Reinhard Spitzy, *So haben wir das Reich verspielt. Bekenntnisse eines Illegalen* (Munich, Vienna, 1987); Franz von Sonnleithner, *Als Diplomat im 'Führerhauptquartier'* (Munich, Vienna, 1989); Peter Broucek (ed.), *Ein General im Zwielicht. Die Erinnerungen Edmund Glaises von Horstenau* (3 vols.) (Vienna, Cologne, Graz, 1983, 1988).
19. The original versions of the Hoßbach memorandum have been examined by Jonathan Wright and Paul Stafford, 'Hitler, Britain and the Hoßbach Memorandum,' *Militärgeschichtliche Mitteilungen*, Vol. 43, No. 2 (1987). Schirach's tape-recorded memoirs have been compared with the printed version by Michael Wortmann. See note 53 below.
20. Walter Schellenberg, *The Labyrinth*, Louis Hagen (trans.) (New York, 1956).
21. J. Dülffer, 'Die Machtergreifung und die Rolle der alten Eliten im Dritten Reich', in W. Michalka (ed.), *Die nationalsozialistische Machtergreifung* (Munich, Vienna, Zurich, 1984), pp. 182–94. My article cited in note 22, especially p. 238, casts doubt on Dülffer's thesis.

22. For analysis emphasizing differences between generations see L.E. Hill, 'The National-Conservatives and Opposition to the Third Reich before the Second World War', in Francis R. Nicosia and Lawrence D. Stokes (eds.), *Germans Against Nazism. Nonconformity, Opposition and Resistance in the Third Reich. Essays in Honour of Peter Hoffmann* (New York, Oxford, 1990), pp. 221–51.
23. See L.E. Hill (ed.), *Die Weizsäcker Papiere 1900–1932* (Berlin, 1982).
24. Lutz Graf Schwerin von Krosigk, *Memoiren* (Stuttgart, 1977).
25. Erich von Manstein, *Verlorene Siege* (Bonn, 1955), *Lost Victories*; Anthony G. Powell (trans.) (Chicago, 1958); Heinz Guderian, *Erinnerungen eines Soldaten* (Heidelberg, 1951), *Panzer Leader*, Constantine Fitzgibbon (trans.) (London, 1952); Frido von Senger und Etterlin, *Krieg in Europa* (Cologne and Berlin, 1960), *Neither Fear nor Hope. The Wartime Career of General Frido von Senger und Etterlin, Defender of Cassino*, George Malcolm (trans.) (New York, 1964).
26. See *Die Weizsäcker Papiere 1900–1932*, p. 345, 15 March 1920.
27. Baldur von Schirach, *Ich glaubte an Hitler* (Hamburg, 1964).
28. Otto Meissner, *Staatssekretär unter Ebert, Hindenburg, Hitler* (Hamburg, 1950).
29. See Marlis G. Steinert, *23 Days. The Final Collapse of Nazi Germany*, Richard Barry (trans.) (New York, 1969), pp. 100–9; R. Rürup, 'Das Ende der Emanzipation: Die antijüdische Politik in Deutschland von der "Machtergreifung" bis zum Zweiten Weltkrieg', in A. Paucker (ed.), *Die Juden in Nazionalsozialistischen Deutschland/The Jews in Nazi Germany 1933–1943* (Tübingen, 1986), pp. 102, 110 n. 54.
30. Albert Speer, *Inside the Third Reich*, pp. 51 and 169–71; Matthias Schmidt, *Albert Speer. The End of A Myth*, Joachim Neugroschel (trans.) (New York, 1984), p. 194.
31. *Die Weizsäcker Papiere 1933–1950*, p. 509 n. 149 and 'The National-Conservatives', p. 235, and n. 110.
32. Paul Schmidt, *Statist auf diplomatischer Bühne, 1923–45. Erlebnisse des Chefdolmetschers im Auswärtigen Amt mit den Staatsmännern Europas* (Bonn, 1949).
33. See Field Marshal Lord Carver, 'Manstein', in Correlli Barnett (ed.), *Hitler's Generals* (New York, 1989).
34. Walter Warlimont, *Im Hauptquartier der deutschen Wehrmacht, 1939–1945* (Frankfurt am Main, 1962), *Inside Hitler's Headquarters, 1939–1945*, R.H. Barry (trans.) (New York, 1964).
35. Friedrich Hoßbach, *Zwischen Wehrmacht und Hitler, 1934–1938* (Wolfenbüttel, 1949).
36. Bor, *Gespräche mit Halder*; Erich Kordt, *Wahn und Wirklichkeit* (Stuttgart, 1947), *Nicht aus den Akten . . . Die Wilhelmstrasse in Frieden und Krieg; Erlebnisse, Begegnungen und Eindrücke, 1928–1945* (Stuttgart, 1950).
37. Gustav Hilger, *The Incompatible Allies; A Memoir-History of German–Soviet Relations, 1918-1941*, Alfred G. Meyer (co-author) (New York, 1953), *Wir und der Kreml*, Roland Schacht (trans.) (Frankfurt/M, 1955); Hans-Heinrich Herwarth von Bittenfeld, *Zwischen Stalin und Hitler. Erlebte Zeitgeschichte 1931 bis 1945* (Frankfurt, Berlin, Vienna, 1982), *Against Two Evils* (New York, 1981).
38. Nicolaus von Below, *Als Hitlers Adjutant 1937–45* (Mainz, 1980). Various historians find such recollections contrary to their interpretation. See H.W. Koch, 'Operation Barbarossa – the Current State of the Debate', *The Historical Journal* Vol. 31, No. 2 (1988), pp. 377–90. Sceptical about a similar record is Paul Stauffer, *Zwischen Hofmannsthal und Hitler. Carl J. Burckhardt. Facetten einer aussergewöhnlichen Existenz* (Zurich, 1991).
39. Herbert von Dirksen, *Moskau, Tokio, London; Erinnerungen und Betrachtungen zu 20 Jahren deutscher Aussenpolitik, 1919–1939* (Stuttgart, 1949), *Moscow, Tokyo, London. Twenty Years of German Foreign Policy* (Norman, 1952).
40. *Autobiographie eines Attentäters Johann Georg Elser. Aussage zum Sprengstoffanschlag im Bürgerbräukeller, München am 8. November 1939*, Lothar Gruchmann (ed. and intro.) (Stuttgart, 1970); see also Schellenberg, *The Labyrinth*.
41. Josef Müller, *Bis zur letzten Konsequenz. Ein Leben für Frieden und Freiheit* (Munich, 1975).
42. Bernhard von Loßberg, *Im Wehrmacht Führungsstab* (Hamburg, 1949).
43. Enno von Rintelen, *Mussolini als Bundesgenosse; Erinnerungen des deutschen Militärattachés in Rom, 1936–1943* (Tübingen, 1951); Rudolf Rahn, *Ruheloses Leben; Aufzeichnungen und Erinnerungen eines deutschen Diplomaten* (Düsseldorf, 1949); Eugen Dollmann, *Dolmetscher der Diktatoren* (Bayreuth, 1963).

44. See Yehuda L. Wallach, 'Feldmarschall Erich von Manstein und die deutsche Judenaus-rottung in Russland', in *Jahrbuch des Instituts für deutsche Geschichte*, Vol. 4 (1975), pp. 457–72; Christian Streit, *Keine Kameraden. Die Wehrmacht und die sowjetischen Kriegsgefangenen 1941–1945* (Studien zur Zeitgeschichte, Vol. 13) (Stuttgart, 1978); and Omer Barton, *Hitler's Army. Soldiers, Nazis and War in the Third Reich* (New York, 1991).
45. Werner Otto von Hentig, *Mein Leben – eine Dienstreise* (Göttingen, 1962, 1963), p. 353 ff.
46. Adolf Heusinger, *Befehl im Widerstreit. Schicksalsstunden der deutschen Armee 1923–1945* (Tübingen, 1950); Hans Speidel, *Aus unserer Zeit. Erinnerungen* (Berlin, Frankfurt a.M., Vienna, 1977).
47. See Schmidt, *Albert Speer*; Peter Padfield, *Dönitz. The Last Führer. Portrait of a Nazi War Leader* (London, 1984), pp. 322–6.
48. Bradley F. Smith, *Reaching Judgment at Nuremberg* (New York, 1979), p. 240.
49. See L.E. Hill, 'The Conviction of Ernst von Weizsäcker on Count V at Nuremberg', in George Kent (ed.), *Archives, Archivists and Historians. Essays in German History in Honour of John Mendelsohn and Robert Wolfe* (Fairfax, Virginia, 1991).
50. Fabian von Schlabrendorff, *Offizieren gegen Hitler*(Zurich, 1946), *They Almost Killed Hitler* (New York, 1947).
51. Schmidt, *Albert Speer*; on Dönitz see Speer, *Spandau. The Secret Diaries*, pp. 333–4.
52. See Schmidt, *Albert Speer*, p. 12.
53. See Michael Wortmann, *Baldur von Schirach: Hitlers Jugendführer* (Cologne, 1982), p. 231 n. 22.

13
Trials and Tribulations: The Making of the Diefenbaker and Pearson Memoirs

JOHN A. MUNRO

Over the past 20 years I have been associated with two major and several minor Canadian political memoirs projects. Variously have I functioned as researcher, editor, amanuensis, clear medium, advocate, keeper and custodian. My work has involved both print and film and, in my capacity as founding director of Canada's first prime ministerial library, exhibition. It is probably safe to say that I know as much as anyone needs to know about the production of political memoirs. A dispassionate observer of my life's work, however, I am not. Nevertheless, I am prepared to examine it, share such lessons as I have learned and perhaps, in consequence, learn something more.

Although I would not advise a career as a political ghost-writer-cum-literary hack to anyone, I admit that I would do it all over again! I have been used, abused, vilified, threatened, shunned, slighted, denied work and too often reduced to impecuniosity, but I have also been privileged in my close association with two of Canada's former Prime Ministers, have enjoyed their trust and justified it far beyond the grave. This and the sure knowledge that the six volumes of the Pearson and Diefenbaker memoirs are important sustain me still.

There are in circulation in English-speaking Canada nearly a quarter of a million hardback copies of these volumes plus a far larger number in paperback editions. (None has ever been translated into French.) And millions of Canadians, again mainly English-speaking, watched the 26 half-hours of prime time television involved in the Canadian Broadcasting Corporation (CBC) film version of the same. From an historiographical point of view, this makes the tenth decade of Canadian politics unique. Its two protagonists remain its most influential chroniclers. And it is they who have set the agenda for debate. For the time being at least, historians and others who ignore this challenge or attempt for other reasons to sanitize this period do so at the risk of rendering their works irrelevant or at best marginal. In this regard, let me cite York University historian J.L. Granatstein's *Canada 1957–1967*.

It is my intention in what follows to be as blunt as possible in the hope of reducing some degree of inevitable misinterpretation. For example, four years after I had spoken critically about some of my ghost-writing in 1979 at the University of Manitoba, one of the professors who had been present expressed his continuing gratitude for my exposition, exclaiming, 'I just tell my students not even to bother looking at the Diefenbaker memoirs, that they're nothing but a pack of lies and that I was told this by the man who actually wrote them!'

Unfortunately, I had rather brought this upon myself by writing a less than laudatory obituary of Diefenbaker. It all, however, seemed such a good idea at the time. A year or so before Mr Diefenbaker's death, the journalist Alan Rogers (the son of Norman Rogers, Canada's Minister of Labour, 1935–39, and of national defence, 1939–40), who had been updating the Diefenbaker file at the Ottawa *Journal*, asked if I might be interested in doing something that had never before been attempted in Canada: a critical obituary of a national political figure. I accepted a commission to do this and wrote an eight-column, finely balanced assessment of Diefenbaker's life and career in which, in passing, I cast aspersions on his veracity as a memoirist. All this the *Journal* stored in its computer bank, awaiting the fateful day. In the meantime, it sold rights to my piece to the Toronto *Star*, the Winnipeg *Free Press* and the Vancouver *Sun* (the Montreal *Star* chose to plagiarize it). The combined circulation of these five newspapers was enormous. I was taking a considerable chance in doing this and, in the event, the plan backfired. Rogers had guaranteed that the *Journal* would print every word I had written and use its influence to ensure that the other papers did the same, but he was on holiday when Diefenbaker died in August 1979 and much of my material was jettisoned by editors to accommodate extra photographs. The Vancouver *Sun* went even further. My second-last sentence read, 'He seemed a politician destined never to fade away'. The *Sun* left out 'never'. They then chose this as their headline! So much for my declaration of professional/personal independence.

Naturally, when I addressed interested faculty members in Winnipeg a month or so later, I handed out copies of the uncut obituary. Everyone, however, was more interested in the very public dispute being conducted daily in the press and on television over the Diefenbaker trust fund and the high drama (or farce) of the Diefenbaker funeral train, which had carried the bodies of Canada's thirteenth prime minister and his disinterred second wife from the old Chief's state funeral, and her grave, in Ottawa to their final resting place outside the Rt. Hon. John G. Diefenbaker Centre at the University of Saskatchewan in Saskatoon, with stops at every village, town and city *en route*. Ottawa columnist Charles Lynch compared the vicious quarrel that broke out on the train between myself and several others in the late prime minister's funeral party to *Murder on the Orient Express*. At issue was whether the Progressive Conservative Party of Canada was obliged to pay into the Diefenbaker estate a hitherto secret trust fund, and whether, in fact, this fund actually existed. Eventually, I won the day, but at no small cost to myself and to my friend and fellow pall-bearer, Keith Martin (Diefenbaker's executive assistant). I have often asked myself if I would have broken the story on the trust fund to the press if the Diefenbaker executors had not promised to have me dismissed as director of the Diefenbaker Centre because of the obituary. I would like to think that I would have done so. Diefenbaker had been deceived into thinking that he had over half a million dollars to leave to the University of Saskatchewan and the city of Prince Albert. I resented the fact that he had been made to appear a fool.

Be that as it may, apparently no one in my audience at the University of Manitoba heard my suggestion that there was much of value in the Diefenbaker memoirs, but that one had to proceed with caution when using them. This was hardly a declaration that they were a pack of lies!

In 1982, I again published an assessment of Diefenbaker's life and career, this time in the 'Introduction' to *The Wit & Wisdom of John Diefenbaker*. And again I issued a warning about his memoirs, 'So far as one is aware, there has never been any coherent expression of Diefenbaker's political philosophy. The reflections, reminiscences, revelations, recriminations and adinventions which make up his three-volume *One Canada* memoirs are, in many ways, political state-ments . . .'. Quite apart from this, however, I was surprised to discover how poorly John Diefenbaker's words fared on close examination, being neither funny nor profound. Mr Diefenbaker was a presence. And that presence was now departed. His voice – that voice saying those words – no longer rang in my ears. Nor does it now.

In 1990 the University of Saskatchewan's Diefenbaker Centre released certain documents dealing with Mr Diefenbaker's illness during the first week of the 1979 election campaign in Prince Albert. I was not present for his bouts of delirium, but I was there for the five weeks that followed. My original purpose was neither to look after Mr Diefenbaker nor to take any part in his campaign. It was to attempt to begin a fourth volume of Diefenbaker memoirs, to be called 'The Last Campaign'. I was going to create an election diary, primarily as a vehicle for his reflections on post-1967 Canada. Instead, when I appeared on the scene, Diefenbaker's local staff somehow determined to leave him in my charge, and it became my job to keep him out of mischief and to help get him re-elected. I suppose I can claim a modest success in all of this, although I am certain that Joe Clark and his supporters were not pleased when Mr Diefenbaker told a reporter from *La Presse* that Clark proved that 'anyone' could now become leader of the Conservative Party in Canada. No boundaries were ever possible between the professional and personal when one dealt with John Diefenbaker. (Perhaps this is a general condition for ghost-writers?) Of course, no self-respecting historian would ever have allowed himself to be caught in such a situation. But then again I am not one.

In the four and a half years of my association with him, Mr Diefenbaker had always been difficult and often downright impossible. I cannot count the times I despaired of ever finishing the first volume of his memoirs, never mind the second, third or fourth. He would lose the manuscript and telephone the project administrator, John Archer (then president of the University of Regina), complaining that I had failed to provide him with Chapters 1–6 of whatever volume was in preparation at the time. Archer would fly to Ottawa to placate him. The missing manuscript would be discovered in his study.

Or I would prepare a file of documents for discussion: for example on his meetings with the British Prime Minister, Harold Macmillan (and briefly with President Kennedy), at Nassau in December 1962. For amusement, because they were all classified 'Secret' or 'Top Secret' and 'Canadian Eyes Only', I put them in a Department of External Affairs red file folder, stamped 'Top Secret', and gave them to Mr Diefenbaker so that he might refresh his memory. A week or so later, I asked him if he had had a chance to examine this file. A puzzled look came over his face. He opened the centre drawer of his desk and rummaged about, finally producing the file. He scanned its contents and then announced, 'I can't let you see any of this, it's top secret'.

Or one or other of his colleagues would create gratuitous problems. For example, it was obvious to me from the outset that he was unable or unwilling to discuss with much sense or detail the period of his national stewardship as Canada's prime minister (1957–63). Bernard Ostry had interviewed him at length for the CBC TV series, 'The Tenth Decade'. Every time Ostry attempted to go beyond 21 June 1957, however, Mr Diefenbaker would drop back to the safety of the 1926 federal election. Peter Stursberg suffered a similar fate when he was doing interviews for the Public Archives. So did everyone else, with the possible exception of CBC TV producer Cameron Graham who managed at the eleventh hour to obtain just enough material to complete his series on politics in the tenth decade of Canadian confederation: the Diefenbaker–Pearson years, 1957–68. Consequently, when I began doing preliminary interviews (as opposed to the later filmed ones), I tried to be as unstructured as possible in the hope that I might thereby elicit something of value. (Obviously I thought it mad that I should have to develop stratagems to get him to provide me with the information I needed to write his memoirs for him.) In any event, his friends convinced him that he should give me no more interviews without prior written notice of the questions to be asked. This I did once and once only. There I sat beside his desk in his Centre Block office, microphone in hand. There he sat studying my list of questions. Finally, he was ready to reply, and for posterity I recorded these immortal words, 'Ah, yes, now let me see, question 5, hmm: yes'.

Invariably, I would get so frustrated, so angry that I would disappear for days, in search of my sanity. This of course would irritate him very much. On several occasions, he had my drinking habits investigated, but to no avail. (Even he seemed able eventually to understand that anyone who produced as much work as I did could not spend much time drunk.) Ultimately, he simply accepted my 'curious' behaviour, explaining to his cronies, 'This Munro, he's always late. He's Finnish, you know.' They would all nod in agreement as if he actually had made some sense. (My mother was Finnish, whatever that may explain.) It all reminds me of Mr Diefenbaker's impromptu press conference at the Château Laurier in Ottawa the day following Dalton Camp's re-election as president of the Progressive Conservative Party in November 1966. Pointing his finger and shaking his jowls, he declaimed, 'It's a long road that has no ash cans.' Those present, including many prominent members of the press, said, 'How profound!' No one said, 'Silly old b—'s got it wrong. It's a short road that has no ash cans.'

Mr Diefenbaker, as I intimated above, had that ability to make almost anything he chose to say sound impressive. But what was worse, he was able to convince himself that once he had pronounced upon something, nothing more need ever be said. Thus he created yet another obstacle for me in writing his memoirs. For example, he said: 'The Bill of Rights epitomizes my personal and political philosophy.' That was it. The subject was obviously important and it would be a strange volume of Diefenbaker memoirs without some considerable mention of it. So what was I to do? I can hear someone saying, 'Nothing. Should have let him stew in it.' However potentially satisfying, such a response would have been self-defeating. If I could produce a draft on the subject, he might respond. The only other legitimate narrative source available to me was *Hansard* (his papers yielded nothing very valuable). While his earlier speeches proved useful, I simply took his 1960 Bill of Rights speech and treated it as contemporary reflection. This in fact proved fair; his thinking 15 years later had progressed no further. Indeed, I can recall feeling rather pleased with my efforts which, when combined with some War Measures Act material, produced 12 pages of text. I was rather chagrined, however, to be roundly criticized in reviews for including too many excerpts from old speeches!

It was a crazy business. To begin with, the production schedule for the memoirs agreed to by Mr Diefenbaker and the late Hugh Kane, then president of Macmillan of Canada, called for a volume a year for the three years 1975–77. In addition, CBC TV proposed to produce a 13-part Diefenbaker memoirs series, for which I would do the research and interviews. Obviously, these projects were complementary. At the same time, Volume 3 of *Mike*, the Pearson memoirs, was still in process. (Although the manuscript was complete by July 1974, and the University of Toronto Press was primed to achieve autumn publication, the Pearson estate and its advisers opted to delay a full year so that this final volume dealing with Mr Pearson's terms as leader of the opposition (1958–63) and prime minister (1963–68) might be further 'refined'.) Needless to say, 1975 was one of those years! Indeed, that October both of 'my' books were on the national best-seller list at the same time.

Volume 1 of the Diefenbaker memoirs, which reconstructs his life and career to his election as national leader of the Progressive

Conservative Party in 1956, was largely based on interview materials, mine and everyone else's, plus such documentation as Mr Diefenbaker had in his House of Commons office and at home, including his own abortive attempts at memoir-writing. There was a large container of relevant papers in the Diefenbaker collection in storage at the Public Archives of Canada, but I did not discover them until long after I had completed writing. They were not listed in the inventory and, having accepted Mr Diefenbaker's story of the destruction of his legal and other files in Prince Albert, I had no reason to search.

If I recall correctly, I was not allowed (for whatever reason) to begin writing Volume 1 until February 1975, and this may be accepted as an excuse for its main structural fault. The story reaches its natural climax in Chapter 11 and, consequently, has to fight to sustain the reader's interest for Chapters 12 and 13. I should have rewritten the last half of this volume, but I did not have time to do so. As to the rather grievous errors (not lies) of this part, such as the confusion of dates which would have made him a bigamist, I was not present to correct the final pages or to influence Mr Diefenbaker's final revisions. I had been fired for refusing to write and sign an introduction lauding the high achievement of the Diefenbaker government, a document subsequently written and signed by Tommy Van Dusen and Greg Guthrie and included as an appendix. Volume 1, after all, stops before the period 1957–63. Readers interested in further detail on these matters should consult *Saturday Night*, November 1976.

Canadian journalist and popular historian Peter Newman once suggested that John Diefenbaker's success lay in the invention of John Diefenbaker. Volume 1 may well be about this apocryphal man. For example, some of Mr Diefenbaker's legal stories bear more than a passing resemblance to those told by Bob Edwards, editor of the *Calgary Eye Opener*, about Paddy Nowlan who, during his years at the bar (1890–1913), became western Canada's most famous trial lawyer. But what are we to make of this? If these stories represent a serious departure from reality, they may reflect a medical problem that I lack the professional competence to address, but if they are told merely to illustrate the limitations of frontier justice or simply to amuse, where is the harm? 'Adinvention' is the term I would use. The novelist's truth is usually infinitely more powerful than the historian's. Also one should bear in mind that this 'Canadian Book of the Century', as Macmillan with more enthusiasm than good sense advertised it, set all-time sales records in Canada – 60,000 hardback cover copies were sold in shops without the additional benefit of Book-of-the-Month Club sales.

The novelist Mordecai Richler, the book club's Canadian director, had offered *One Canada* the totally unacceptable status of 'alternative selection' to whatever Peter C. Newman had published in 1975. Richler and his friends may have found this amusing. Mr Diefenbaker did not: he considered Newman anathema, a Liberal Party agent who through *Renegade in Power*, Newman's 1963 book on Diefenbaker, had undermined Dief's leadership of the Progressive Conservative Party. This episode aside, only Jean Chretien (in two languages) has since surpassed the sales for Volume 1 of *One Canada*. Obviously, there is in Canada a great market for political hokum.

While Mr Diefenbaker was enjoying the life of a best-selling author, my co-editor on the Pearson memoirs, Alex Inglis, and I were extremely grateful to be given 'alternative selection' status by the Book-of-the-Month Club for Volume 3 of *Mike*! So far as I remember, the combined retail and book-club sales for Volume 3 were in the neighbourhood of 16,000, roughly two-thirds of the sales of Volume 2, the sales of which bore the same proportional relation to those of Volume 1 of *Mike*. I am told that this ratio applies to all multi-volume memoirs; it certainly did in the case of the Diefenbaker volumes.

Volume 3 of the Pearson memoirs has never stood very high on my list of personal achievements. It contains some very useful material, but its judgements, as I have mentioned, were 'refined' at the insistence of Mr Pearson's son, Geoffrey, to protect the interests of Canada's Liberal Party establishment. Let me take as an example the story of the dismissal of Yvon Dupuis from the Cabinet in January 1965. Our manuscript contained a fascinating exposition of the constitutional considerations involved when a minister of the crown refuses to accede to a prime minister's request for his resignation. Inglis and I were forced to edit out all of this because, in the opinion of Geoffrey and his party advisers, it made Mr Pearson look indecisive and bumbling. In my judgement, Mr Pearson never took himself as seriously as his son did. In the Dupuis case and in every other such instance, my recollection is that either the editors could agree to these changes or the Pearson estate would refuse to publish the book. Basically, we are talking about sins of omission. Thus derives the very pale truth of the editors' statement in their 'Introduction' that they 'have considered it their duty . . . to protect the integrity of the volume against any advice . . . that would have made it untrue to the materials from which it was derived'. It is important for readers to know that my erstwhile colleague, Inglis, disagrees with me in all this; his memory of this process is entirely different from my own. However, my copies of the drafts of the chapter containing the Dupuis story ('Politics in Disrepute') are on deposit as part of the John Munro Research Collection in the Special Collections Division of the University of British Columbia Library.

I am not suggesting that Volume 3 of the Pearson memoirs is worse than Volumes 2 and 3 of the Diefenbaker memoirs. Anything but. I am simply saying that it could have been better. *The Concise Oxford Dictionary* defines 'lie' as 'intentional false statement' and as 'things that deceive'. Ultimately, no one gains when the truth is deliberately distorted, however that is accomplished.

Speaking about lies, John Diefenbaker told some whoppers in his day. One that he told for fully 30 years was that he had been a member of the Canadian delegation to the San Francisco conference in 1945 and that during the opening ceremonies he had observed Field Marshal Jan Christian Smuts, a few seats in front of him, scribbling notes on the back of a cigarette packet. This he managed to retrieve when the meeting adjourned and the South African delegation moved on. What he discovered written on that cigarette packet was the Preamble to the Charter of the United Nations! Two points must be made in relation to this claim: Mr Diefenbaker was at the conference, but not as a member of the Canadian delegation. He was an adviser to Gordon Graydon, the Conservative house leader, who was a member of the Canadian delegation. Second, Field Marshal Smuts did not smoke. Is this more 'adinvention' or a lie by another name? I managed to have this story dropped from Volume 1.

I did not fare so well with his tale about Nikita Khrushchev at the United Nations in September 1960. Mr Diefenbaker had given a major address to the UN General Assembly condemning Soviet imperialism. He later claimed that Khrushchev had become so incensed as to bang one of his shoes on his desk to protest at the Canadian Prime Minister's remarks. The fact is that Khrushchev did bang his shoe, but not until some days after Mr Diefenbaker spoke. The version that appears in Volume 2 is a compromise, but still untrue. In this version we have Khrushchev banging his shoe during the speech of Senator Sumulong of the Philippines, who is recapitulating Mr Diefenbaker's arguments, as well as during the speech of the British Prime Minister, Macmillan, earlier the same day. It would appear that Senator Sumulong did condemn Soviet imperialism in terms similar to those used by Mr Diefenbaker, but that Mr Khrushchev did not bang his shoe in response, etc., etc. 'Oh, what a tangled web we weave,/When first we practise to deceive!' Because I could not completely prevent him from recapitulating this story everything else in Volume 2 is brought into question. Of course, for those predisposed to be hostile, any excuse will do. I remember one reviewer who discovered an error in arithmetic (originating with me, but missed by half a dozen readers). His conclusion was that if we could not get something so simple right, how could we be trusted to do anything else correctly?

Interestingly, the only criticisms Mr Diefenbaker seemed to take to heart were those attacking his claim in Volume 1 that he publicly opposed the internment of Japanese Canadians during the Second World War. Indeed, he was so upset at being pilloried by the New Democratic Party leader David Lewis and others over this that he insisted on repeating his claim in Volume 2. For the record, there is nothing to support Mr Diefenbaker's position either in his papers or in *Hansard*. Despite this, I have never doubted his word on this point. There is a consistency in his position on human rights issues over the years that cries out in his defence. Besides, I have now actually met someone who heard him speak on this subject to a Toronto civil rights group during the war.

The success of the first volume of *One Canada* quite convinced Mr Diefenbaker that he had written every word of it and that obviously he did not need me. (I suppose that the mark of a good ghost is his invisibility.) And we were into another new year before the call for help came. Consequently, the second volume was written under pressures of time quite comparable to those afflicting the first. On this occasion, however, I at least had a research base for my work. The Diefenbaker papers, 1957–63, run to some three million pages. My research assistant and I had been burrowing away since 1974. And in the summer of 1975, with a team of researchers, we launched a frontal assault on this mountain of paper. The reader will be surprised by nothing at this stage, not even that the filing system in the Prime Minister's office during Mr Diefenbaker's full tenure was dysfunctional. Only the man who had run it at the time knew how it worked and he was not forthcoming. And because we could not proceed in a normal way, I had to accept that I might well miss any number of essential papers. As it turned out, what I lacked was not documentation but the context for its employment. My criterion for the inclusion of any subject in the memoirs obviously had to be Mr Diefenbaker's interest in it. Thus, if readers have wondered why Volume 2 did not devote a single word to the subject of two-price wheat, this is the answer. I should mention that I also had a research assistant working on the files of the Department of External Affairs for this period, and paid for by the Department (thanks to Paddy Reid, the then director-general of the department's Bureau of Public Affairs). My function now was to argue Mr Diefenbaker's case before the court of history, and I chose my evidence accordingly. Mr Diefenbaker believed I had also an obligation to fight his enemies. He insisted that I write a 'Foreword' to Volume 2 for my signature and John Archer's attacking Peter Newman. This I did, but the word got out (the word always got out), and we heard that Newman had threatened to sue. I have never seen such a retreat! All that remains of my attack on Newman is some vague reference to acid pens and purple prose. My original draft may be found in the Munro Papers at the University of Saskatchewan's Rt. Hon. John G. Diefenbaker Centre.

A further comment on the 'Forewords' to the Diefenbaker memoirs may be in order, as others apparently have taken them a great deal more seriously than I ever have, my dismissal over that to Volume 1 to the contrary. John Archer and I signed those for Volumes 1 and 2. I signed the 'Foreword' for Volume 3. So far as I can recall, Dr Archer and I collaborated on the drafting of that to Volume 1, which established the nature of the exercise. This was merely intellectual fluff – it had no critical edge, nor could it have: Mr Diefenbaker demanded the right to approve every word. Indeed, when we showed him our draft, he insisted we take out a reference to his 'foibles'. 'I don't have foibles', he said.

On a more serious note, I have been upbraided often for a statement in the 'Foreword' to Volume 2: 'Hereafter, the initiates of the cult of quiet diplomacy will have to do more than indulge in liturgical cant to convert students of Canadian external policy to their point of view.' *Id est*: make your case, no one is obliged to accept the tenets of Pearsonian diplomacy on faith: a perfectly reasonable proposition. However, I never cease to be amazed by the anti-intellectualism of the Canadian foreign policy community. For example, in early 1989 I reviewed the volume by former Under Secretary of State for External Affairs Basil Robinson, *Diefenbaker's World*, for the Vancouver *Sun*. I was critical of it, as it deserved. It was not long before I received a telephone call expressing the displeasure of the External Affairs 'old boys' and assuring me that I had again 'shot myself in the foot'. I mention this for two reasons. First, Mr Diefenbaker, it would appear, remains a *bête noire* at senior levels in the Department of External Affairs. Second, for many years and at whatever personal cost, I appeared to be the only independent scholar prepared to defend him.

This latter situation seems at last to be improving, as a new generation of political analysts brings a perspective uncluttered by the biases of personal involvement to bear on the Diefenbaker period.

Volume 3 of *One Canada* was initially intended to deal exclusively with Mr Diefenbaker's opposition years (1963–67), until I discovered there was not enough material for it. Consequently, I held over the chapters on defence and the 1962 and 1963 elections from Volume 2. The result is the most important of the three Diefenbaker volumes. Some of the defence policy arguments represent the extreme of the thesis, but that was my job. It was, however, most irritating to have Mr Diefenbaker decide to inject gratuitous comparisons of himself to Lincoln and Churchill in the midst of rationalizations that barely hold water. The issue that pervades the first two-thirds of this volume is Canadian sovereignty *vis-a-vis* the United States. (Although Mr Diefenbaker never saw it this way, one can observe his betrayal of the myth of Canadian middle power and perhaps understand his continuing unpopularity in certain official circles in Ottawa.) Mr Diefenbaker's participation in the creation of this volume was mixed. Much of the defence material he virtually accepted as presented in draft, as he did the 1962 financial crisis chapter. Not so with the Cuban missile crisis or the events leading up to the defeat of his government in the House of Commons on 5 February 1963, or the later opposition and party chapters. The small chapter of excerpts from letters to his brother, Elmer, allowed me to bridge the book's two sections.

Personally, I am surprised at how well Volume 3 reads, especially after the way it was decimated by the libel lawyers of Macmillan of Canada. I would estimate that I made nearly 200 changes to accommodate them. It is my firm belief that we could have escaped suit in over 90 per cent of these instances. The newspapers define and redefine 'fair comment' every day. Were they to endure the sort of legal scrutiny Volumes 2 and 3 of the Diefenbaker memoirs were subjected to, they would cease to function. The real victim here was Volume 2 which could not afford, given its content, to lose any of its spark. Mr Diefenbaker, as may well be imagined, was not referred to in any of this. The publishers communicated with their lawyers and then directly with me. I made the required changes. To have proceeded otherwise would have involved histrionics, delays and endless complications for which neither the publishers nor I had the heart. Given the tightest of publishing schedules, 1976 could easily have become 1977 or 1978. Indeed, contract cancellation might have resulted had we not been able to wrest the completed manuscripts from Mr Diefenbaker's death-like grip.

The difference between the Diefenbaker memoirs project and the Pearson memoirs (including Volume 3) was as night is to day. The atmosphere on the latter was civilized and professional and, when Mr Pearson was alive, one worked for a man with whom one could actually converse. Certainly, he understood what my job as a research associate was all about, as opposed to Mr Diefenbaker who always claimed he could read his entire collection of papers in a week.

I first met Mr Pearson at the Learned Societies meetings in June 1970. He was the commentator on papers which my colleague, Alex Inglis, and I presented to an overflow joint meeting of historians and political scientists. At the time, Inglis and I were contract resident historians with the Department of External Affairs in Ottawa, respectively responsible for editing Volumes 4/5 and 6 of *Documents on Canadian External Relations*. In due course, we helped Mr Pearson turn his commentary into an article, which was published as a companion to Inglis' and my papers in the *Journal of Canadian Studies* (May 1972). This was after we *three* had suffered a most curious collective rejection by the committee responsible for publishing the Canadian Historical Association's annual proceedings and selected papers for 1970. Mr Pearson's piece also found publication in edited form in Volume 1 of his memoirs. But I digress.

So far as I am aware, it was my initial encounter with Mr Pearson at the University of Manitoba that led him some four months later to invite me to assist him with the research for his memoirs. I believe I had that balance of qualifications he was looking for in a research assistant: demonstrated competence without any challenging prominence. In other words, I would do what he wanted and not attempt to tell him what to do. This is not to say that he was not amenable to advice. I have always thought it significant that, at the suggestion of our late good friend, Archie Day, he began the 'Preface' to Volume 1 of his memoirs by quoting Benvenuto Cellini:

All men of whatsoever quality they be who have done anything of excellence or which may properly resemble excellence ought, if they are persons of truth and honesty, to describe their life with their own hand . . .

It was Mr Pearson's intention to do just that. Unfortunately, death intervened shortly after the publication of Volume 1, leaving Volume 2 unfinished and Volume 3 barely begun.

The consequence, to labour the obvious, as Geoffrey Pearson does in his 'Foreword' to Volume 2, is that the final versions of the last two volumes of *Mike* are not as L.B. Pearson would have written them: particularly so in the case of Volume 3. What one has here is the *formal* introduction of a third-person factor in 'edited' memoirs.

The Oxford English Dictionary defines an editor as 'one who prepares the literary work of another . . . for publication, by selecting, revising and arranging the material . . .'. This is as opposed to a ghost-writer, an 'artistic or literary hack doing the work for which his employer takes credit'. I have described at some length my trials and tribulations as a ghost-writer, information that has not been previously in the public domain. My role and that of my co-editor, Alex Inglis, in the making of the Pearson memoirs has long been public; it is merely expanded upon here. Perhaps because Inglis and I were breaking new literary and historical ground, we were scrupulous (well, fairly scrupulous) in setting forth in our 'Introductions' to Volumes 2 and 3 of *Mike* what we had done and why we had done it. For example, in describing our sources for Volume 2, we wrote:

Chapter 1 was written entirely by Mr Pearson. Chapter 2 was prepared in draft form by him but considerably reorganized by the editors. Chapters 3 and 4 were written by him but altered in accordance with his instructions. Chapter 5 was compiled from Mr Pearson's diaries, lecture material, correspondence, and transcripts. Chapter 6 was based on Mr Pearson's early draft with excerpts from diary entries and some transcript material added. Chapters 7 and 8 were based on a research paper, diary entries, speeches, CBC transcripts and correspondence. Chapter 9 was from his diary and transcripts in accordance with his instructions. Chapters 10 and 11 were from his own preliminary draft on Palestine, extensive instructions in the form of marginal comments on a research paper, plus diary entries, correspondence, lecture material, official documents, and transcripts. The two appendices are from Mr Pearson's diary. An attempt was made to incorporate this material into the text of the Korean chapters, but it proved too unwieldy. At the same time, the detail of diplomatic negotiations and of Mr Pearson's role at the United Nations made it important, at least for the more specialized reader, that the material be published.

In bringing these sources together the editors have freely transferred contemporary descriptive material into the past tense. They have, however, been careful not to allow contemporary opinions and judgements to appear as though they were later reflections. Wherever such judgements occur they are indeed later reflections.

When Volumes 1 and 2 of *Mike, the Memoirs of the Right Honourable Lester B. Pearson, PC, CC, OM, OBE, MA, LL D* won the 1973 Albert B. Corey Prize, awarded jointly by the Canadian and American

Historical Associations, the editors, not unexpectedly, received short shrift. We were told to be grateful for such recognition as our efforts received, which was obviously more than they were worth. Maryon Pearson, who received the award in the name of her late husband and the handsome cheque that went with it, had a less prejudiced view of our work. She gave us half the money.

Once in 1976, when I had accompanied Mr Diefenbaker to a book-signing session in Vancouver, a young reporter came up to me and querulously demanded, 'Why did both Pearson and Diefenbaker have to have you to write their memoirs?' I replied, 'Canada's a small country. I'm all we can afford.'

14
Harry S. Truman:
The Writing of his Memoirs

FRANCIS H. HELLER

Even before President Truman had announced his decision not to be a candidate for re-election in 1952, he had been approached by publishers eager to acquire the rights to his memoirs. This was, given his own interest in history, something he wanted to do although he had originally thought of it as a labour of love, something he would do for his daughter Margaret.[1] Once his plan to leave the White House had been made public, he was intensively pursued by publishers seeking to sign a contract with him. He was receptive to these overtures not only because he wanted to tell his own story but probably because he recognized that writing might be one way open to him to acquire an income. There was no provision for a pension (or any other benefits) for former presidents in those days,[2] and Mr Truman felt very strongly that a former president should not lend his name to any profit-making venture.[3] The sale of his memoirs made eminently good sense.

He asked a good friend, the journalist William Hillman,[4] to be his literary agent and it was Hillman who, with the legal advice of former presidential counsel Samuel Rosenman, dealt with the publishers and eventually negotiated a contract with Time-Life, Inc. In return for the sum of $600,000, the company was to receive from the President, no later than 30 June 1955, a publishable manuscript of 300,000 words and exclusive rights to it.[5]

Mr Truman also relied on Hillman and another friend, David Noyes,[6] to provide the assistance he knew he would need in the preparation of the memoirs. Both these men, however, had interests of their own – and on opposite coasts – which they could not relinquish, and therefore they could not commit themselves to the project on a full-time basis. It was apparently understood from the beginning that there would be a need for one or more writers and researchers to work on the memoirs full-time. Mr Truman apparently tried to interest Richard Neustadt,[7] a former White House aide, in the assignment but Neustadt declined, probably on the ground that it was essential for him to establish himself in the academic world. David Noyes then recruited Robert E.G. Harris,[8] a professor of journalism at the University of California at Los Angeles who had occasionally helped with speech-writing in the White House, and two younger men, Robert Goe and Dean L. Schedler, whose background was in writing and editing for government agencies.

Time, Inc. supplied a (gold-plated) recording machine. Tapes, of course, were not then in commercial use and this machine was essentially the recording equivalent of a 45 r.p.m. record player. Mr Truman hated it. Harris would come into his office in the morning and proceed to interview him. Then he would have Goe and Schedler check the recorded stories in the *New York Times* and other publications before he himself wrote a first draft.

There is little evidence in the chapters Harris wrote that he (or his two assistants) made much use of the documents in the numerous filing cabinets that lined the large office where Rose Conway (Mr Truman's secretary throughout his vice-presidential, presidential and post-presidential years) worked, as well as one wall of the reception area and one wall of the office Harris himself used (and which later on would be my office). These files remained in Miss Conway's custody until after Truman had died. They were then turned over to the Truman Library where they were identified as 'PSF', the President's Secretary's File. Although they constituted only a fraction of the papers that had been transferred to Kansas City for safekeeping until they could be placed in the library that Mr Truman hoped to see built somewhere near his home, they were the documents that actually had received the President's attention and thus represented the most important part of the 'Truman Papers'.

In having the papers that had come to his office moved to his home area Mr Truman followed a precedent established by George Washington himself. When the first President prepared to leave office in March 1797 he had all the papers in the White House taken to his home, Mount Vernon, in Virginia. From that time on (until the resignation from office of Richard Nixon in 1974), it was commonly assumed that a President's papers were his personal property and that he was free to do with them whatever he wanted.[9]

Some of the eighteenth- and nineteenth-century Presidents (the two

Adamses and Rutherford B. Hayes in particular) had a strong sense of history and of the importance which their papers might have for history. They saw to it that their records were properly stored and cared for. Others hoped that their heirs would look after the papers they left behind, but the heirs allowed them to be dispersed and sometimes even destroyed or lost. The papers of two Presidents, John Tyler and Zachary Taylor, were lost during the Civil War.

The Library of Congress did not begin to collect papers of American statesmen until the last quarter of the nineteenth century. It devoted a good deal of time and effort to the task but lacked the resources and often the qualified personnel to give them the kind of attention that an archive would provide. The National Archives, however, were not established until 1934 and initially also were short of staff and space to accommodate what came to be increasingly large accumulations of documents.

Franklin Roosevelt therefore decided that his papers should be placed in a repository of their own. He donated the land on his estate in Hyde Park, New York, and asked some of his friends to make plans to raise funds to build a combination library and museum to house his papers and memorabilia. This was the first of the so-called presidential libraries and the model for Mr Truman's plan for a library for his papers.[10]

Mr Truman's successors have all followed his (and Roosevelt's) example. Like all Presidents since George Washington, they took it for granted that the papers they wished to preserve were their property. An Act of Congress[11] authorized the General Services Administrator (under whose jurisdiction the National Archives then fell) to accept both the library buildings erected with private funds and the papers in them on behalf of the government of the United States, thus – at least by implication – recognizing the claim that the papers were private, rather then public property. Then, following the Watergate crisis and Nixon's resignation, Congress asserted the primacy of the public interest in presidential papers, first by a makeshift arrangement to cover the specific problem of the Nixon papers, and a few years later by a legislative declaration that Presidential papers are the property of the government.[12] The law was to go into effect with the first President to be newly elected after the law's passage. Ronald Reagan was therefore the first President whose papers were, by law, not his personal property.

The bulk of Mr Truman's papers were placed in storage in Kansas City where the National Archives soon assigned two professional archivists to undertake the task of preparing this accumulation for transfer to the Truman Library, whenever that building would be ready to receive them. Only the files directly under Miss Conway's eyes were moved to the office Mr Truman had rented in Kansas City.

There, shortly after he had returned from a Hawaiian vacation following the end of his presidential term, he began the task of writing, with Harris as his principal helper. By November 1953, approximately 150,000 words had been written. But Mr Truman did not like the product. Rather than write 'history' – as Mr Truman wanted it – Harris had, so Mr Truman came to believe, concocted a series of pleasant tales. On one occasion the former President said to me that the Harris manuscript reminded him of a typical *Saturday Evening Post* story: 'My Life and Happy Times in the White House, by Harry S. Truman as told to Robert E.G. Harris'.[13]

There may also have been some indiscretions by members of the Harris team but specific instances are hazy and unconfirmed. What mattered most was that Mr Truman did not like the product. So he told Hillman and Noyes to find somebody else, somebody who would 'write the history'.

Now it was Hillman's turn to find help and he came up with Morton Royce, an adjunct professor of history at Georgetown University.[14] Unfortunately, Hillman's lack of familiarity with the academic world misled him in his choice. Professor Royce had, for most of his life, been at work on a monumental project, a multi-volume history of the world. But, except for his doctoral dissertation, he had published only minor pieces, mainly in obscure, non-scholarly outlets. He was the kind of scholar who cannot put pen to paper until every last question is answered. Therefore, when he began to work on Mr Truman's papers and with the former President himself, he could not bring himself to start writing on any particular topic until, as far as he was concerned, every 'i' had been dotted and every 't' had been crossed. If Mr Truman's responses to his queries did not satisfy him, he would keep coming back at him. Eventually his insistence began to annoy Mr Truman.

Hillman and Noyes were more concerned over the slowness of Royce's progress. By March 1954, Royce, having started with the events of April 1945, had barely reached the Potsdam conference. The contract deadline was 30 June 1955. Earlier, following an assessment of the scope the memoirs might take, the contract had been revised to call for a total of 650,000 words to be turned over to Time, Inc. on that date.[15] Hillman and Noyes concluded that it was unlikely that Royce could complete the job in time.

In his book *Mr. Citizen*, Mr Truman, after alluding to press reports that 'while I was in the White House, and even afterwards . . . some people betrayed my trust' and denying that there were more than 'very few' such betrayals, wrote what is probably the only public comment he ever made about the writing of the memoirs:

I had to keep my past experience in mind when I began writing my Memoirs, and I had to select a staff of researchers who were not only competent but trustworthy. I soon found out that 'Potomac Fever' is not peculiar to Washington, and that even researchers assigned to simple and temporary duties, such as checking data, can soon develop surprising airs. I should not have been surprised at what some people will do when they get into proximity with the person of even a former President. However, it all worked out for the best.[16]

Obviously, this somewhat cryptic passage leaves it open to speculation as to whom and about what he was talking. But there can be little question that the two false starts were a considerable annoyance to him – and that they were costly. Mr Truman had not received any advance on the memoirs. He paid the salaries of his staff and of the researchers working on his memoirs and the rent for the offices they occupied. He bought his own stationery and postage stamps – and his correspondence was huge. He drove his own car. His only regular income was the pension to which he was entitled as a retired colonel in the army reserve. For the year 1955 that amounted to a little over $1,550.[17]

Thus the protracted problems with the memoirs caused him not only frustration but also financial difficulties. But it was Royce's slow rate of production, more than anything else, that finally led to the decision to let him go. According to Rose Conway (who told me that she was in the room when this was discussed) Mr Truman, half in jest and half serious, told Hillman and Noyes that they had each had their turn at trying to line up help and now he would see what he could do.

What he did was to telephone the president of the University of Missouri (Lloyd Middlebush) and the chancellor of the University of Kansas (Franklin D. Murphy). Dr Middlebush recommended a young journalism instructor, Herbert Lee Williams;[18] Dr Murphy nominated me, at that time a very junior associate professor of political science who had, however, three published books to his credit.

Williams was on leave from his university at the time, presumably to work on his dissertation though he was actually teaching at another college in Columbia, Missouri; but he was able to start almost at once.

Because Royce was still there, Williams was asked to work in the makeshift library (consisting mainly of a collection of bound volumes of the *New York Times*, the *Washington Post*, *Time*, the *Congressional Record* and Mr Truman's speeches and public statements, plus an array of standard reference works) that had been set up on the floor below Mr Truman's office.

I had to finish my spring semester classes before I could come to work in Kansas City and thus I inherited the office Royce had used. It was immediately adjacent to the former President's own. In fact, Mr Truman used a rack in my office on which to hang his hat and coat.

When, earlier in the spring, Hillman and Noyes had come to my campus for an initial interview, they had struck me at once as a rather incongruous pair. Hillman reminded me, both in appearance and in his voice, of a slightly smaller edition of the film actor Sidney Greenstreet. He was deliberate in his ways, always observing and assessing. He had been a correspondent abroad for one of the news services (where he claimed to have been the first newspaperman to have reported King Edward VIII's involvement with Mrs Wallis Simpson) and had later become the Washington representative for *Collier's* magazine and the Mutual Broadcasting System. It was at that time that he came to know Mr Truman.[19]

Noyes was short and wiry, given to lengthy rhetoric which often seemed to wax into the emotional. Originally in advertising and public relations, he had come to know the then Senator Truman during the Second World War service with the War Production Board.[20] On later occasions Noyes spoke at length about the key role he said he had played in any number of decisions made in the White House during the Truman years. Except for the fact that he apparently originated the (promptly aborted) plan in 1948 to send Chief Justice Vinson to Moscow,[21] I have not found – and I do not know of anyone else who has found – any evidence to support his claim that he had been the *éminence grise* of the Truman administration.

Hillman and Noyes played major roles in the process of producing the Truman memoirs but they had very little to do with the day-by-day work on the project. In practice, the two came to Kansas City about once a month, usually for three to five days. Although they lived on opposite coasts, I recall only two occasions when only one of them was in Kansas City – each time the other member of the duo was ill. When they were in town, they were inseparable but I always felt that there was an element of jealousy in their relationship – that they were united in their loyalty and commitment to Truman but that they also wanted to make certain that neither one nor the other would get ahead in the affection of 'the boss'. Hillman, as the former President's literary agent, handled all contacts with Time, Inc. and Doubleday & Company, the company that had acquired the domestic book rights from Time-Life, Inc. Noyes, on the other hand, had perhaps a better understanding of the task; certainly, of the two, he was the one with the better political antennae.

The two of them had prepared what journalists would call a 'story line': Noyes took the credit for the decision to begin with the succession to the presidency and to follow that by a retrospective account, going from childhood to the brief period of the vice-presidency. (For this 'flashback' there was a lengthy autobiographical sketch available which Truman had written out in longhand while he was vice-president.)[22] By the time I went to work for Mr Truman in late May 1954, that much had been written – once by Harris, a second time by Royce and a third time by Williams. But Harris' work (the 'Good God' script) then skipped around with little regard for the sequence of topics laid out by Hillman and Noyes. Royce had managed to do a fairly complete story on the first two months in the White House but had stalled when he came to the discussion of the use of the atomic bomb where he tried, unsuccessfully, to shake Mr Truman's long-established and never-wavering explanation that his only thought about the new weapon was that it might shorten the war and thereby save lives on both sides.

Hillman and Noyes very soon discovered that they could not expect Williams and me to work as a team. Not only did we work on different floors but I was almost a chain-smoker and Williams was the first person I ever encountered – they are legion now – who was not even polite about his dislike of tobacco smoke. (He also disapproved of drinking and thus declined the occasional invitations to join Mr Truman for lunch – which invariably started with bourbon and water.) So the duo of Hillman and Noyce dealt with us individually, giving us assignments from their list of topics. That list was, initially, virtually all-encompassing, far exceeding the 300,000 words envisaged in the original contract. This had led to the already mentioned renegotiation of the contract. Time, Inc. agreed to an increase in the number of words to 650,000 while Mr Truman consented to a limitation of the topics to be included.

Actually Time, Inc. was not too concerned about the contractual limit on the number of pages, especially since Mr Truman did not ask for an increase in the fee. Time's own plans were, all along, to publish selected passages, with appropriate photographs, in the weekly picture magazine, *Life*. Nor did it affect the *New York Times* which had acquired the rights to newspaper serialization without any commitment to print the entirety. But Time had sold the domestic book rights to Doubleday & Co. and the foreign rights to Allen & Unwin of London. For the book publishers the proposal to enlarge the memoirs meant that they would have to publish more than one volume, with all the added expense that involved. In the end, Doubleday agreed to the new figure of 650,000 words, to be marketed in two volumes. The British publisher remained adamant and published a shorter version, in only one volume.

While these negotiations were going on – and I knew very little about them, finding the evidence of them only much later in the files of the Truman Library – Hillman and Noyes re-examined their list of topics over and over again. It seemed to be a regular feature of their conversations with Mr Truman whenever they were in Kansas City. I recall, for instance, that I had done a considerable amount of research on a chapter that was to deal with Latin America and would highlight Mr Truman's visit to Mexico and his tribute, widely acclaimed by the Mexicans at the time, to 'Los Niños', when Hillman came to me to tell me that it had been decided to omit the Latin America chapter. The trip to Mexico received just one sentence in the memoir.[23]

Another recurrent part of the schedule of their visits was a review of what Williams and I had written. In effect, this was a first editing. But they came to this task with rather different perspectives: Hillman's experience tended to make him check mainly for completeness and accuracy of the account; Noyes' emotional commitment to Mr Truman (he often referred to him as 'the Lincoln of the twentieth century') caused him to look for ways to make his hero look good.

The principal editors of Time, Inc. and Doubleday & Co. came to Kansas City on separate visits in the autumn of 1954 to assure themselves that, in spite of the two false starts, the job was moving ahead and the schedule was likely to be met. Each of them was eager to provide additional help – an offer that did not particularly appeal to the Hillman–Noyes team since, of course, it would have meant at least partial loss of control for them.

In the end, Ernest Havemann of Time spent several weeks in Kansas City in the autumn of 1954 and carefully read through everything that had been written by that time. I found him a delightful companion whose suggestions were most constructive. He gave me, in effect, a first-hand insight into what the editors were expecting and were likely to do with 'our' manuscript. He did not, however, prepare any original copy. Neither did Hawthorne Daniel, an experienced writer with Doubleday who spent about six weeks in Kansas City in the spring of 1955. By this time, Lee Williams had left and I was the only person working on the project. Again I found the visitor to be a congenial mentor and a highly able critic; unfortunately, he suffered a relapse of an earlier illness and had to cut short his stay in Kansas City.

Williams, with whom I was never able to develop any close relationship, left Mr Truman's employ in early December 1954 to accept the directorship of the journalism programme at a Big Ten university. Considering that he was a rather junior member of the academic profession and had not yet completed his doctorate, this was a remarkable opportunity, and Mr Truman agreed that he should not miss this chance. I recall that Mr Truman came into my office and asked if I had heard about the offer that Williams had received and what I thought about it. After I had expressed the opinion that this was indeed an exceptional chance for so young a man, Mr Truman asked if I thought that I could finish the job by myself. By that time I had come to feel quite comfortable with the materials I had to use, and even more comfortable about my relationship with Mr Truman, so I assured him that I could do it. He had not consulted Hillman and Noyes and overrode their objections when they voiced them to him on their next visit to Kansas City.

In retrospect, Mr Truman was an almost ideal person to work for – and, more specifically, to work for on this kind of a project. On the one hand, he appeared to have complete confidence in Williams and me: Hillman and Noyes would give us the order in which each of us was to work on the chapters of the book; Mr Truman left us to develop our assignments without interfering. On the other hand, he was a reliable and careful editor of everything we put on paper. We soon learned that, if he had no commitments for the evening, he wanted to take our most recent output home with him; it would be returned to us promptly the next morning, carefully proofread and annotated, sometimes with notes indicating that such and such a comment had come from 'the boss', this is, Mrs Truman.

On occasions, Mr Truman would produce a handwritten memorandum that would reflect a personal recollection that we had not gleaned from the voluminous records we had been able to examine. The example that stands out in my mind concerns the account of the Democratic national convention in 1948. He brought me a sheaf of notepaper covered with his recall of the thoughts that went through his mind as he sat on a balcony overlooking the Chicago stockyards, waiting for the convention to complete the process of selecting him as its nominee. The theme was that every President, from Washington to himself, had been the subject of harsh criticism, often without good cause. On that hot summer night in 1948, Harry Truman had let his mind wander through history, considering every one of his predecessors and the major problems he had faced.

Although no one had given me any instruction to this effect, I always operated on the premise that anything that came to me in the former President's own words should, if at all possible, be incorporated into the memoirs. Whenever that occurred, my responsibility should be limited to assuring that all verifiable items (mainly names and dates) were correct. The pages he had handed me that morning were, as one might expect, full of such items. I checked every one of them. There was only one error: he had mistaken the date of the treaty of San Guadalupe Hidalgo by one year.[24]

I followed the same procedure with the transcripts of the interviews which Hillman and Noyes conducted with several of Mr Truman's former associates. The Secretary of State, Dean Acheson, the Secretary of Agriculture, Charles Brannan, the former Chairman of the Joint Chiefs of Staff and General of the Army, Omar Bradley, the Solicitor General, Philip Perlman, and the Secretary of the Treasury, John Snyder, were just a few of those who came to Kansas City at Mr Truman's request to be interviewed by Hillman and Noyes. I sat in on most of these sessions which Gene Bailey, a skilful and intelligent stenographer, took down in shorthand. (Mr Truman had hired Bailey after it had become obvious that the typing of the book manuscript was too much of an added load for his regular secretary, Rose Conway, and the receptionist, Frances Williams, the only two clerical employees he had.)

Miss Conway had been Mr Truman's personal secretary throughout his years as Vice-President and President. She had handled and seen practically every piece of paper that had crossed his desk in those years. Her knowledge of the files in his office was unsurpassed – as was her desire to protect them against any possible misuse. She and I got along well but there were occasions when she could be adamantly defensive about the papers in her custody.

Thus there was the time when, while I was looking through a file that was clearly identified as holding classified information,[25] I encountered a file folder that bore the notation 'Eyes Only' and a classification symbol that I knew existed but had never seen before. The continuing legend indicated that there were only eight copies, one for the President, one for the Secretary of Defence, one for the Chairman of the Joint Chiefs of Staff, one for the Chairman of the Atomic Energy Commission, the others for the corresponding officials in the British government. I decided not to turn the page. The next file was also 'Eyes Only' but with an identification symbol totally unknown to me; there were only four copies of this document, again evenly divided between Washington and London.

I asked Miss Conway how these documents happened to be in Kansas City. She bristled: 'They are the President's papers.' That was all she had to say – it settled the matter for her. I took it upon myself to speak to Mr Truman about it. He came into Miss Conway's office, took one look at the files and agreed with me; these were indeed papers that should not have been taken to Kansas City.

What ought he to do? I suggested that he call Dean Acheson in Washington, which he did. Half an hour later Acheson called back. Could Mr Truman arrange for a police escort from the airport to his office and back? One of the three members of the Atomic Energy Commission would leave Washington within the hour on a special Air Force plane to retrieve the documents. When the commissioner arrived, he was accompanied by a two-star general and two military policemen; a leather dispatch case was chained to his wrist; after he had placed the documents in the case, the general locked it and took charge of the key. I did not ask Mr Truman what these papers were.

Although Mr Truman took occasional trips out of town, mainly for speaking engagements, he generally observed regular hours and was in the office from about 8.30 in the morning until about 4 p.m., except for a usually rather extended lunch hour. Habitually, he would come into my office in the morning, returning what he had read the preceding evening and enquiring about the progress of the work. He was freely accessible throughout the day, responding to questions and, if requested, reviewing draft passages or pages. But he expected Williams (as long as he was with us) and me to compose the narratives we were working on, based mainly on the papers at our disposal.

By February 1955, approximately two million words had been written. This was, of course, far more than the publishers wanted and the task now came to be one of deleting and compressing. Hillman and Noyes now spent somewhat longer periods in Kansas City and worked mostly on the identification of material that could be left out or shortened. When Hawthorne Daniel joined us, he turned to the same task although from the stylistic rather than the subject-matter perspective. Copies of the manuscript were now sent out to a few of Mr Truman's closest associates. Samuel Rosenman and Dean Acheson each went through the entire accumulation. Others were asked only to look at particular chapters or sections.

Toward the middle of May the comments of these readers had been returned and we now turned to the final phase, a close, word-for-word reading. This was done in Mr Truman's office. Mr Truman, Hillman, Noyes, and I each had a copy before us and we would take turns reading the manuscript out loud. Gene Bailey, the stenographer, took notes.

This process took up the morning hours. Bailey and I were by that time in the habit of going to lunch together and would use that period to review his notes. I would then spend the afternoon making whatever changes had been indicated in the morning session while Bailey transcribed what I had worked on the day before.

Fortunately, the people at Time, Inc. had told Mr Truman that, while for the purpose of the contract they had to have 650,000 words on 30 June, only the first half had to be ready for publication. The second half, we were told, could be refined over the summer. Even so, the last two weeks before the deadline were hectic and both Bailey and I worked long hours, on one or two occasions around the clock. On 30 June 1955, the editor-in-chief of Time, Inc. was in Kansas City to take possession of the manuscript and to hand Mr Truman a cheque for $110,000 and seven promissory notes for $70,000 each, payable at annual intervals. This arrangement had been worked out by Samuel Rosenman so as to minimize Mr Truman's tax liability.[26]

The final work on the second half of the memoirs was completed by 1 September. *Life* published the first extracts from the manuscript, beautifully illustrated, later that month. The first volume of the book version was released by Doubleday & Co. in November.

Anyone placing the memoirs beside some of Truman's personal memoranda and letters[27] will very quickly recognize that the memoirs were 'staff-written', that only small parts of the work came from Truman's pen. He was clearly deeply involved in the process of producing the memoirs; but his nearly eight years in the White House had conditioned him to the preparation by others of the words he spoke and (most of) the letters he wrote. One may also assume that he had learned, over the years, that many of the memoirs of statesmen and politicians had been written with the help, whether acknowledged or not, of others. I do not recall that I ever heard him refer to the work in progress as 'memoirs'; he spoke of 'my history', and what this apparently meant to him was of almost Rankean simplicity: '*wie es wirklich geschehen ist*' – an unadorned recital of events.

The most concrete and at the same time the most revealing example of his perception of the task at hand occurred when I made an attempt to reconcile his account of an event with the conflicting version given by the other principal participant, James F. Byrnes. As Secretary of State, Byrnes had attended a critical foreign ministers' conference in Moscow in late December 1945. As related by Averell Harriman,[28] who, as the American ambassador in Moscow, was not only in attendance at the meetings but also Byrnes' personal host, Byrnes decided that it was not necessary for him to advise President Truman of the day-by-day progress of the negotiations which, in fact, involved some notable concessions to the Russians. Truman learned of these developments from the newspapers. Then Byrnes, from the aeroplane bringing him back to the United States, asked the State Department to arrange for radio time on all networks to allow him to make a direct report to the American people. The President, plainly annoyed by the Secretary's slighting of him, directed that he first report to him and that, to this end, he join the President forthwith aboard the presidential yacht *Williamsburg*, then on a recreational cruise on the Potomac river.

According to Truman, when Byrnes joined him, the President read him a strongly worded memorandum that made it clear that the Secretary's actions, both in Moscow and in seeking, on his return, to bypass the President, displeased him. The handwritten memorandum was reproduced in William Hillman's authorized publication of selected presidential memoranda, published in 1952 under the title *Mr. President*,[29] and it was among the papers I had before me as I set out to write up this particular episode. I knew that Byrnes, following the publication of the Hillman volume, had vigorously denied that such a memorandum had been read to him or that there was anything acrimonious about the session aboard the *Williamsburg*. If he had been confronted in the manner described by the Truman memorandum, he stated, he would have resigned from his office on the spot.[30] That seemed to me to be a rather plausible reaction. Was it possible to reconcile the conflicting accounts?

By this time I had come to believe that Mr Truman trusted me and, indeed, liked me a good deal. I decided to approach him – as tactfully as I could, remembering what I had learned about his reaction to my predecessor Royce's insistent questioning – and suggest that, perhaps, there might be a middle ground between the two accounts of the event.

Truman looked at me, almost unbelieving that I should have asked the question. Then came this telling reply: 'Jimmy Byrnes', he said, 'is entitled to his memory and I am entitled to mine – it's that simple.'

Another demonstration of his perception of what he was doing occurred after the publication of the extracts in *Life*. Someone at Time-Life, Inc. – Hillman asserted that it was Henry Luce himself – decided that General MacArthur should be given the opportunity to reply to the Truman version of the conflict between the two men. An advance copy of the general's article, bristling with derogatory comments on the former President and his account, was sent to Truman whose first reaction was to dash off a testy rejoinder. I do not know whether it was his idea to consult me or whether it was suggested to him by someone else (Rose Conway would be my prime candidate) but he sent the MacArthur text and his proposed reply to me and asked for my advice on the latter. I reminded him of the comment he had made to me in connection with the Byrnes matter; that seemed to settle it for him: he informed *Life* that he would have no comment.

Lastly, there is an episode that occurred after the writing of the memoirs had been completed but which is , I believe, part of the story. When I finished my work with him in late August 1955, he asked me whether I would like to have a few copies of the book. I opined that I would be honoured if he would inscribe three copies for me. In early December, after the first volume had appeared, Rose Conway telephoned me to say that, if I would come to the office in Kansas City, I could have my three copies and that Mr Truman would inscribe them for me. I told her that I would come in a few days later.

When I arrived at Mr Truman's office in the Federal Reserve Bank building, I discovered that the room I had worked in had become a storage area for large stacks, literally hundreds, of copies of the book. Miss Conway told me that these had been mailed in by people from all over the country, with the request that Truman autograph them. Always concerned about Mr Truman's financial condition, she bemoaned the fact that most of the senders had not even bothered to enclose return postage.

When, a few minutes later, I walked into Mr Truman's office, I commented on the accumulation of books. He observed that it had come as a surprise to him, that he had really not expected that there would be much interest in his memoirs. I said that it did not surprise me at all. He had, after all, presided over some of the most remarkable developments in the nation's policies and it seemed to me that even people who disagreed with what he had done would be interested in how these events looked from his vantage point. After a thoughtful pause Truman gave this reply (which I wrote down immediately after leaving his office):

You know, if it turns out, after some years have passed, that some of the decisions I made [and he ticked off about half a dozen, from the decision to use the atomic bomb to the creation of NATO] have been for the good of the country, then people will say that I did a good job. But if it turns out that, in the long run, they were not in the best interest of the country, then all that people will talk about will be mink coats and deep freezers [items that featured in the scandals that some of his staff members had become involved in] and they are going make me look worse than Ulysses S. Grant.[31]

Here, it seems to me, he recognized that history is not as simple a matter as he had often expressed – that it was not merely a matter of 'how things really happened' but how events are perceived in later light.

NOTES

Some of the material in this chapter was presented to the Jackson County (Missouri) Historical Society on 18 May 1958, at a meeting at which former President Truman introduced the author. The text is on file at the Harry S. Truman Library, Independence, Missouri. A similar version was published under the title 'The Writing of the Truman Memoirs', in *Presidential Studies Quarterly*, Vol. 13 (1983), pp. 81–4. The present essay is more comprehensive than either of the two earlier versions.

1. Harry S. Truman, letter to Nellie Noland, 5 August 1951. Harry S. Truman Library (HSTL), President's Secretary's File (PSF), Noland Papers, Box 2; printed in Robert H. Ferrell (ed.), *Off the Record: The Private Papers of Harry S. Truman* (New York, 1980), p. 215.
2. Public Law 745, 85th Congress, the first enactment providing a pension for former presidents (initially $25,000 a year), was not approved until 25 August 1958. United States Code (USC) Title 3, s. 102, note.
3. Harry S. Truman, *Mr. Citizen* (New York, 1960), pp. 57–8.
4. William Hillman (1895–1962). See the text below, at note 18.
5. Information on the contract (and subsequent modifications) is to be found in HSTL, Post-Presidential Files (PPF), files 'Arthur Mag' (Mr Truman's Kansas City lawyer) and 'Samuel Rosenman'.
6. David M. Noyes (1898–1981). Mr Noyes' obituary in the *New York Times*, 11 August 1981, presumably prepared by himself, states that he was appointed 'counselor to Mr Truman at the President's swearing-in on April 12, 1945' and that he had been 'involved in decisions on the atom bomb, the firing of Gen. Douglas MacArthur, recognition of Israel, creation of the Central Intelligence Agency, the Potsdam conference and the Marshall Plan'. No documentation for any of these statements is to be found in the files at the Truman Library. There is no doubt, however, that Noyes was a frequent visitor to the White House and an unofficial adviser to the President. See also the text below, at notes 20 and 21.
7. Richard E. Neustadt (born 1919) served first in the Bureau of the Budget and then on Truman's White House staff. After January 1953, he taught first at Cornell and Columbia Universities, then, since 1964, at Harvard University. His *Presidential Power* (New York, 1960; most recently revised as *Presidential Power and the Modern Presidents: From Roosevelt*

to Reagan (New York, 1990) is generally regarded as a major contribution to the under-standing of the presidential office.

8. Robert E.G. Harris (1903–77) taught journalism at Los Angeles City College from 1929 to 1942, served in the navy in the Second World War, was chief editorial writer for the *Los Angeles Daily News* from 1945 to 1949 and editorial columnist for the *Los Angeles Times* from 1949 to 1952. He joined the faculty of the University of California at Los Angeles in 1952 as a professor of journalism.

9. 'By custom and tradition the files of the White House Office belong to the President in whose Administration they are accumulated. It has been the invariable practice, at the end of an Administration, for the outgoing President or his estate to authorize the depository or disposition to be made of such files.' Memorandum from William J. Hopkins, Executive Clerk, the White House, 29 November 1963, to the White House staff, instructing staff members to maintain a clear separation between papers of the Kennedy administration and those of the new President. An identical memorandum was issued the day after the resignation of Richard Nixon. Copies of both documents are in the possession of the author. See also William Howard Taft (President 1909–13), *Our Chief Executive and His Powers* (New York, 1916), p. 34: 'The retiring President takes with him all the correspondence, original and copies, which he carried on during his administration'.

10. A complete enumeration of the fate and present location of the papers of the Presidents from Washington to Reagan is in Frank L. Schick, Renee Schick and Mark Carroll, *Records of the Presidency: Presidential Papers and Libraries from Washington to Reagan* (Phoenix, 1989). For an excellent and informative overview, see Raymond Geselbrecht, 'The Four Eras in the History of Presidential Papers', *Prologue* (quarterly publication of the National Archives), Vol. 13, No. 1 (1983), pp. 37–42.

11. Presidential Libraries Act, Public Law 373, 85th Congress, 69 Stat. 695 (1955).

12. Presidential Records Act of 1978, Public Law 591, 95th Congress; USC, Title 44, ss. 2107, 2108 and 2201 *et seq.*

13. The roughly 150 pages produced by Harris were put on a shelf in the large room used by Rose Conway. On top of the stack was one of Mr Truman's memorandum sheets, on which he had written, 'Good God, what crap'. In the days when I worked on the memoirs it was referred to in the office as 'the Good God manuscript'.

14. I have been unable to locate biographical information on Morton Royce. Since his status at Georgetown University was that of an 'adjunct' the university maintained no file on him. The slim file under his name at HSTL contains no personal data.

15. See note 5 above. The sum Mr Truman was to receive for the manuscript remained unchanged.

16. *Mr. Citizen*, pp. 88–9.

17. In a handwritten memorandum dated 6 April 1963, and found in his desk after his death, Truman lists his monthly pay as a retired colonel of the army reserve that year as $129.45 (that is, $1,553.40 on an annual basis). HSTL, PPF, Desk File, Box 2, 'Financial Notes'. That figure applied until 1 June 1958, when the first of several increases in the pay of retired military personnel went into effect. 72 Stat. 128, USC, Title 10, s. 1401, notes.

18. See Herbert Lee Williams, *The Newspaperman's President* (Chicago, 1984), pp. v–xi. These pages were previously published under the title, 'I Was Truman's Ghost', *Presidential Studies Quarterly*, Vol. 12 (Spring 1982), pp. 256–9. Williams makes no reference to anyone else having worked on the Truman memoirs.

19. See also above, note 4.

20. At our first encounter, Noyes told me that he had been assistant director of WPB. My departmental chairman who had served with WPB in Washington through most of the war years could not recall that he had ever heard the name. See also note 6 above.

21. Robert J. Donovan, *Conflict and Crisis: The Presidency of Harry S. Truman 1945–1948* (New York, 1977), pp. 423–35. Donovan's source for this attribution is a telephone interview with Noyes, ibid., p. 458, n. 33. Harold F. Gosnell, who makes the same attribution, traces it to Clark Clifford, in an interview with Jonathan Daniels: *Truman's Crises* (Westport, 1980), pp. 401 and 601, n. 45.

22. See Robert H. Ferrell's chapter in this volume.

23. Harry S. Truman, *Memoirs*, Vol. 2 (*Years of Trial and Hope*) (Garden City, NY, 1956), p. 104.

24. The passage in question was sharply cut down in the course of the final review of the manuscript. It may be found in Vol. 2 of the memoirs (*Years of Trial and Hope*), pp. 191–204. The reference to the treaty of San Guadalupe Hidalgo was among the material that was deleted.

25. Williams, in his account of the writing of the Truman memoirs (see note 18 above), complains about his inability to see classified materials. I do not recall that he mentioned this problem – if indeed there was one – at the time. In any case, I never encountered any objection on the part of Miss Conway, perhaps because she knew that my active duty assignment in the army during the Korean War had required a rather high-level security clearance that I still retained and that allowed me to see material marked 'top secret'.

26. Initially, Samuel Rosenman had sought to obtain a ruling from the Internal Revenue Service that, following the precedent set in the case of Dwight D. Eisenhower's Second World War memoirs (*Crusade in Europe*), would have acknowledged that, since the author of the book was not a writer by profession, the transaction was the purchase of a property he owned and hence subject to capital gains tax (at the rate of 25 per cent) and not income taxable at much higher rates. In Eisenhower's case the White House had intervened; in Truman's case the (Eisenhower) White House declined to become involved. The only alternative, therefore, was to spread the payments over a period of years. Information from files listed in note 5 above.

27. Mainly his autobiography and his private letters, both edited by Robert H. Ferrell and discussed in his chapter in this volume.

28. Walter Isaacson and Evan Thomas, *The Wise Men: Six Friends and the World They Made* (New York, 1986), pp. 345 and 781.

29. William Hillman, *Mr. President* (New York, 1952), pp. 21–3.

30. The same statement appears in his memoirs, published after the Truman memoirs had come out. James F. Byrnes, *All in One Lifetime* (New York, 1958), pp. 400–3.

31. I have previously reported this conversation in *The Presidency: A Modern Perspective* (New York, 1960), pp. 73–5, and in 'Truman', a chapter in Lord Longford and Sir John Wheeler-Bennett (eds.), *The History Makers: Leaders and Statesmen of the 20th Century* (London, 1973), pp. 325–7.

15
Truman: On and Off the Record

ROBERT H. FERRELL

The Truman memoirs came out in the mid-1950s, heralded by excerpts in *Life* magazine and whatever other displays of importance the publishers, Doubleday, could persuade the media (which in those days meant newspapers, magazines and radio) to promote. Thereafter, so an onlooker might have thought, the thirty-third President of the United States had done his bit for history. To use one of his favourite expressions as he grew older, 'That was all there was to it'.

The President was too wise an individual to take much pride in the memoirs, and having finished them he probably was glad to turn to other pursuits. He was an honest man and knew the memoirs were not his composition. He was the author of an autobiographical account inserted, virtually pushed, into the first volume, beginning at page 112, which opened in straightforward fashion with his birth in Lamar, Missouri, in 1884, and took his life through its stages until he reached the presidency. The several editors and writers of the memoirs did what they could with this account, taking out colloquialisms and sometimes a story or two, but they may have recognized that Truman needed some part of the memoirs that he could call his own and thus let him have his descriptive pages, his really personal pages, after which they could go back to the footslogging, mechanical detailing of the Potsdam conference and successive events of the first year of the presidency. It was only through the chance intervention of Francis Heller that this saga of minutiae was brought to an end with the first volume, entitled *Year of Decisions*, and the rest of the kaleidoscopic Truman presidential years were encapsulated, seven of them, in a second volume entitled *Years of Trial and Hope*.

Truman was out of his depth in the writing of his memoirs. Composing those two large volumes was not what he really liked to do.

Every evening when he took home another heavy chapter in his brief-case, to read during the after-dinner hours and pencil a few changes of wording or punctuation, he must have regretted that he had signed the contract and become involved with the writing of something that was not his own work.

The truth is that Harry Truman had a way with words. The man of Independence knew a good phrase when he saw it. He delighted in a well-turned sentence, a noun or verb that made sense. Certainly, and throughout his life, he was a poor speller; he kept a pocket dictionary on the presidential desk, and did his best, but all sorts of words eluded him, perhaps the most puzzling being 'sacrilegious', for which he tried several versions before passing the problem to Cousin Nellie Noland, to whom he was writing. He never could spell the name of Dean Acheson, which came out as Atchison or Atcheson. Beyond this delinquency he was a near master of prose, when he had a chance to write on a theme he enjoyed.

Truman's interest in words may, without question, be traced back to his years in the Independence public schools, where he studied under a succession of dedicated teachers. Of these individuals we know very little. A few were still alive when he became President, and he had kept in touch with them. Once in a while he would say something publicly about how they had helped him.

The principal teacher who interested him in recording his thoughts for the use of later historians was his history teacher, Miss Maggie Phelps, of whom he was exceedingly fond. In the autobiographical portion of the memoirs he devotes several paragraphs to his teachers but mentions Miss Phelps especially. And she it was who taught him the importance of history, on which subject the memoir section is loquacious. It required two and a half pages for Mr Truman to relate his debt to history, to tell his readers how important history is. History, he wrote, was the veritable school of statesmen, the fountainhead of experience – for with experience of the past the statesman could direct his own acts and look to the future. Miss Phelps, interestingly, seems to have taught history in paragraphs. 'In school, history was taught by paragraphs. Each great event in history was written up in one paragraph.'[1] When he was learning about history he memorized it by the paragraphing.

At the same time that the Independence high school teachers were inculcating in him whatever knowledge they had of the past, and of writing, and the general importance of learning, the young man was doing a great deal of reading, in the main because his spectacles made it impossible for him to engage in youthful sports other than as a virtual bystander, through the umpiring of baseball games. Expensive glasses forced him into reading. He had been 'fineprinted', as he described the process, when he was barely six years old, and unlike most youngsters of the time, fitted not merely with glasses but with proper glasses, so that a whole new world of print, not to mention vision of the outdoors and indoors, opened to him. Thereafter he was accustomed to spend time reading the Bible or else a large four-volume work on famous men and women of history that his mother had bought from a door-to-door salesman.[2] In high school he went through the books in the little two-room library, which served also as the public library of the town, and claimed afterwards to have read them all, even the encyclopaedias – a claim that was physically impossible, as there were nearly 4,000 books, by his own count, and that would have meant reading a book a day for 10 years. But the enforced reading during those high school years constituted one of the two periods in his life when he read systematically – the other being the years after 1964 when his health was failing and when, old and feeble, he ensconced himself in the little library room of the house at 219 North Delaware in Independence and again took up reading, sitting behind a little desk, slumped in a chair, books piled round him, usually reading biographies and other volumes about history, mainly American history.

This, then, was the background of the man who became President at one of the most crucial times in the history of the world, and who had read enough about the distant past, and took a large interest in writing, in composition, so that he could express himself very well indeed. This fact was not evident in the memoirs, nor did it become evident until his private papers were opened in the late 1970s and historians began to sense not merely his interest in but his fascination with expressing himself, and his concern for history that was so deep that he felt he needed to record, if possible even at the moment of decision, his thoughts on the highest matters of state.

In preparation for what lay ahead, and without the slightest sense of what was to lie ahead, the future President began to practise his writing in the year 1910 when he opened an enormous correspondence with a young woman in Independence, Elizabeth Virginia (Bess) Wallace, whom he married in 1919. These so-called 'Dear Bess' letters, which became available to historians in 1983, constitute the most remarkable presidential letters that have become available during the two centuries of the American presidency. To make such a claim might seem unsupportable, and this is not to deny the importance of other presidential letters. Certain it is that Thomas Jefferson's loquacious correspondence still rewards close reading, and that few statesmen, American or European, have been authors of comparable letters. The Jefferson letters, however, are often difficult to fathom, as the writer could write one thing, remark a second in conversation, and in his mind hold a third. In the annals of presidential prose the diary of John Quincy Adams comes to mind, but it contains enormous passages of testimony to Adamsonian crotchets of doubtful value to anyone but Adams himself. The diary of James K. Polk constitutes a presidential memoir of great historical value, and yet like that of his predecessor diarist it shows limitations – Polk was dour, taciturn, a calculating Methodist who at the outset of his presidency decided what he was going to do to Great Britain and Mexico and thereupon did it. The diary so testifies; it lacks the rumination one might have hoped for. But then maybe Polk's life was mostly on the surface, where the diary seems to lie. In looking to presidential writing one thinks also of the letters of Woodrow Wilson, remarkable testimonies to Victorian thoughts, sometimes too well turned and thereby unrevealing of their author. Beyond the era of Truman's presidency there are also the letters of Eisenhower, quite unexpectedly good in detail and careful in writing; Eisenhower was no fool, and had spent years as an army speech-writer, for such individuals as Douglas MacArthur, whom he disliked and sometimes detested. But the Eisenhower letters for all their qualities are often a little mechanical, slightly overblown, lacking the down-to-earth similes and thoughts of Truman's letters to Bess Wallace.

This is not the place to celebrate the 'Dear Bess' letters, save to remark that they are full of droll description, stories generated from farm life of the time – Truman was living on the family farm from 1906 to 1917 – or small-town experience in Grandview, Missouri, the locality near which Truman was writing. And the writer did not hesitate to talk about hopes and fears, thoughts on this and that; the letters often are quite personal – exactly the sort of thing that a historian, looking to what a prominent person may have had in mind, would desire. Of the hundreds of letters that Truman wrote to Bess before and during their marriage (and he wrote to her regularly whenever he was away from her, which from 1935, the beginning of his first Senate term, was frequent because of her dislike of Washington and her desire to return to the house in Independence), 1,268 survive. All but one are handwritten. Perhaps from his high school days, maybe from instruction from his mother, he felt that a typewritten letter was not a proper sign of respect or, in the case of Bess, of affection. Suffice to say that no corpus of presidential letters now known compares with the 'Dear Bess' letters.

That the 'Dear Bess' letters survived, incidentally, was not because their author was thinking about history, for he sent them to Bess through the post and seems not to have seen them thereafter. They survived because in 1904 she had moved, together with her mother and three brothers, into the house of her maternal grandfather and grandmother, because of her father's suicide the preceding year, and she remained in the same house for 78 years until her death in 1982 at the age of 97. A poor housekeeper in a house with 17 rooms, she literally stored the letters everywhere in the house – drawers, cupboards, under sofa cushions. Others went up into the attic where a leaky roof and the ministrations of pigeons, and of a raccoon which devoted its time to eating the pigeons, constantly threatened them – it was a wonder that they survived. Some letters she burned; her husband once found her doing that. Only to the letters written by Harry Truman in the years 1917–19, when he was in the army in Oklahoma and overseas for a year in France, did she devote special care, placing them in a box and tying it with ribbon.

The 'Dear Bess' letters constituted Truman's first large literary venture, and there were three others during his long life, albeit not of equal importance. Never again, to be sure, did he write in such detail of what he was doing, or of what he wished to do.

The second corpus of Truman memoirs, so to speak, has been described, because of the hotel in which he wrote, as the 'Pickwick papers'. These are a series of ruminative accounts composed over the years when their author was presiding judge, that is, presiding county commissioner, of Jackson County, the county containing both Independence to the east and, in the west, Kansas City. The task of judge was difficult, even harrowing, during the years in which Truman occasionally repaired to a room in the Pickwick Hotel to get away from office-seekers and think over his problems. The Great Depression of the 1930s affected life everywhere in the United States, not least in urban areas like Jackson County. The judge's problems increased because of the need to co-operate with the Pendergast political machine in the city, and also because of the heritage of local corruption that enveloped many Missouri county offices at that time, affecting some of his fellow judges in the three-man court. A very moral man, Truman had to square personal honesty with the requirements of county politics, and the task was so perplexing that on occasion he had to concede, notably when he allowed $1 million in county money to be paid out in bribes in order to save $10 million or more in road money that he had obtained in two large bond issues. For a future President of the United States the shattering compromises of county politics were excruciating, and he wrote about them frankly. The 'Pickwick papers', one must conclude, are themselves far better than the later formal memoirs both in their stark statement of the realities of American politics and in their commentaries on how their author proposed to meet his problems.

Some historians have chosen to cite the 'Pickwick papers' as proof of Truman's essential dishonesty. As he had learned to cut and paste morality in the Jackson County of the early 1930s, so they believe, he took his strictly bounded morality – that separated private from public behaviour – into the national arena, and the result was what Adlai Stevenson in 1952, running for the presidency, flatfootedly responding to a reporter's question, agreed was a mess in Washington. The designated epithet was 'the Truman scandals'. To those commentaries one can only respond that each individual, once he meets realities, must make his own equations, and historians can make theirs. The Truman scandals in long retrospect do not look so scandalous, and indeed appear to have been the ordinary confusions of any administration necessarily composed of a great many people, some of whom may be lacking in honesty or propriety.[3]

A third body of Truman memoirs, not much better known than the two mentioned above, is the autobiographical fragments that Truman composed over several years, beginning with the short-lived vice-presidency. When he was nominated and elected Vice-President in 1944, on the ticket with Franklin D. Roosevelt, it all happened so quickly that he was hardly able to realize what was going on. During much of that hectic period from July to November he was on the hustings, attempting to electioneer, as Roosevelt preferred to stay out of campaigning, and was in poor health. In this respect Truman knew immediately, upon his choice by the Chicago convention, that fate held a large task in store for him – for like all other insiders at Chicago he knew that Roosevelt would be elected and could not survive a fourth term. Truman knew that the Chicago convention had chosen him for President. As soon as he could find the time, and this turned out to be early the next year when as Vice-President he had to preside over the Senate, a chore that involved much sitting through humdrum debates, he undertook to set out his life, from graduation from high school in 1901 down to the remarkable days in which he was writing.

The result was an essay of 12,000 words, all handwritten, done at the presiding officer's desk in the Upper House, that was nothing less than an autobiography itself. This he combined over the next few years with other autobiographical writings, and together they form a small book.[4]

The autobiographical fragments – the bulk of them being the essay of 1945 – are quite revealing. As he had learned from Maggie Phelps, the President did it all by paragraphs, not bad advice if one thinks of it, for if it made for rotundity it certainly made for order. Several of the autobiographical pieces were composed for a book that Truman's journalist friend William Hillman published in 1952.[5] On several successive mornings, according to Hillman, the President gave him sheaves of manuscript in which he had written first of all an account of his life, which roughly paralleled the Senate composition, and then, interestingly, he had drawn up an essay about his association with Thomas J. Pendergast, the quondam boss of Kansas City who had gone to Leavenworth prison in 1939 and died early in 1945. The Pendergast explanation, several thousand words of it, omitted nothing and simply told how any Democrat who aspired to elective office in Jackson County in the 1920s and early 1930s, or aspired to state or even national office, had to make peace with the boss. The latter, Truman wrote, respected people who respected themselves; in his own case, as eastern and then presiding judge, he had refused to act dishonestly, and Pendergast went along with that – the boss could obtain money from the obliging city manager of Kansas City, Henry F. McElroy. And behind the boss's behaviour, the President averred, lay the confusions of dealing with an unruly city in a formative era. Moreover, the boss was personally honest, and fell from grace only when ill health and an insatiable habit of betting on the horses, and losing, so turned his judgement that he could not keep away from the money thrust upon him by the local light company and ultimately took the gift that brought about his downfall, a bribe from several dozen national insurance companies doing business in the state of Missouri.

The 'Dear Bess' letters, the 'Pickwick papers', and the autobiographical fragments form in themselves a memoir of a presidential life, but there is a fourth group of materials, known as the private papers, that were opened, as mentioned above, in the late 1970s – and these, even more than the other memoir sources, make up a truly remarkable set of materials from which to judge the public and private life of Harry S. Truman. No president of the present century, none of the preceding century nor of the few presidential years of the eighteenth century produced such papers. They deal with an enormous variety of subjects, and the President composed them partly by writing by hand, as with his earlier materials, but mainly through dictation.

For many years the private papers stayed under lock and key in the presidential wing of the Truman Library, and as long as he lived Truman denied them to anyone who enquired. One biographer followed him around during a morning walk and asked to see the papers, and the President curtly refused. Another enquired about the papers, was told he could see them, went to Independence for that purpose and discovered they were not for his eyes.

They were opened only after Truman's death, and it was with enormous pleasure that the present writer, who by chance came into the library to obtain a few quotations for a book about the First World War, managed to see the private papers before other historians.[6] Even today, long after the event, it is possible to savour the excitement of a late Friday afternoon in mid-December 1978, when, after I had been looking at postcards and a few letters of *circa* 1917–19, the next piece of business proved to be two boxes that a young archivist had placed on my library trolley, explaining that he thought their contents were interesting. I had thought that Erwin J. Mueller was enamoured of the handwriting in boxes 333 and 334 of the President's Secretary's Files. But when I took out the first box, almost in boredom, and removed a folder, it was to see within seconds that this material formed the richest presidential material I had ever seen. That first folder revealed diary entries – scrawled commentaries, dated, about what the President had just said to someone in the Oval Office. It showed memoranda about this and that, such as the Federal Bureau of Investigation, which the President asserted was interfering in his business; he was not going to stand for it, he said. Then there were the letters marked in the President's hand or that of his private secretary, Rose A. Conway, as 'Unsent'. These were letters, such as a missive to the editor of the Kansas City *Star*, Roy Roberts, which began on a note of equanimity, but then turned toward tempered explanations and soon the President, taking pen in hand, was tearing his correspondents into infinitesimal pieces.

What a wonderful body of material is the fourth memoir category, the private papers of President Truman! The diary entries, for such they are (his daughter Margaret wrote years ago that her father had never kept a diary, but changed her mind when she saw what lay in his papers), number over 400, and range from a few lines, scribbled after some 'customer', as the President described office visitors, departed, to thoughtful little essays composed early in the morning when his wife and daughter, late risers, were still in bed. As for the memoranda, they were casual pieces, on what struck the presidential fancy – often on what one might describe as political science, for the President considered himself a professional man of politics and liked to write about politics as a profession. The letters were of even more interest, for when Truman dictated to Miss Conway, who was adept at taking down what he said and seldom if ever allowed herself the luxury of changing it, he often let himself go. There was no telling when he would say something quite interesting, not so much about himself, though like any letter-writer he could get easily on to that subject, but upon matters of public business. The letters almost always had a personal touch. If answers were prosaic, as may have been the case when for less important letters answers were composed for him, the President liked to close with a penned postscript (which Miss Conway always copied on the carbon) that might convey a personal wish or refer to a wife or relative but often added what he may have considered spice, a sort of poke at the heathen, or a piece of humour. In no sense were Truman's letters like those of, say, President Calvin Coolidge, who liked to write 'yes' or 'no' or 'maybe' across the tops of letters he received, which notations his secretaries translated, nor those of Herbert Hoover who was a master of the two-sentence response: 'Thank you for your letter. I enjoyed it very much.' The Roosevelt letters, as enigmatic as the man, were often not merely written by secretaries but signed by them, and hence as expressions of presidential ideas were meaningless.

A special note should be made of Truman's post-presidential period, a decade or so, until 1964 when the president suffered an accident at home as a result of which he spent a period of time in hospital. Thereafter he began to succumb to a variety of afflictions of old age, and letter-writing was much reduced. He rapidly became a very old man, his weight dropping, his energy flagging and his eyes watery. He gave up public appearances, even visits to his Truman Library office nearby, and spent his days at home. The Missouri artist Thomas Hart Benton painted his portrait in 1971 – the year before he died – showing him in the little library room of the house, slumped behind the desk, holding a book and resting his arms on books stacked by his side and on the desk. But prior to his accident he wrote several dozen letters each day, with the assistance of Miss Conway, and because he was out of office he had time to go into detail on all sorts of subjects that he would have found it impossible to deal with during the presidential years. The post-presidential letters, not yet given attention by historians, are voluminous.

Something should be said not merely about the formal memoirs, published in 1955–56, but about two other books that the former President produced after he left Washington. The first, *Truman Speaks*, was simply a transcript of episodic lectures delivered at Columbia University in 1959 by Professor Truman, who spoke to a class of 1,200 scholars and after each lecture entertained questions. The material is vintage Truman, although the occasion allowed of no rewriting or rethinking. It was in these lectures that the former chief executive admitted he had not bothered himself over the decision to drop nuclear bombs on Hiroshima and Nagasaki and indeed had slept soundly the night after the Hiroshima decision. A generation of critics pounced on that remark. The other of these books was published in 1960, entitled *Mr. Citizen*, and was based on interviews by William Hillman, who, together with his friend David Noyes, a public relations man, during the presidency had persuaded Truman to publish *Mr. President*, the overstuffed, appallingly bad-taste picturebook that contains some of his autobiographical fragments. They persuaded Truman to bring out *Mr. Citizen* perhaps because the Eisenhower Republican years were coming to an end, and a Democratic decade was about to begin. The resultant volume was better than its predecessor but *Mr. Citizen* was no more revealing of the Truman presidency than Truman's other books.

One must therefore conclude that the Truman years and the great personality that lay behind them do not stand out in Truman's books. Such a literary form was not to be his. To write a good book he needed help, and all that fortune gave him was a series of less than able writers. With the help of a professional writer of ability, and plenty of time (Francis Heller had almost no time), he might have achieved something of considerable importance. The Truman era instead has its measure in papers the President created: the 'Dear Bess' letters, the 'Pickwick papers', the autobiographical fragments and the private papers including the diary entries, memoranda and especially the letters, presidential and post-presidential. Writers yet to come – Truman biographies thus far have been thin and insubstantial, no definitive volume based on the papers having yet appeared – will surely turn to this much more intimate and authoritative record to draw the lines of his life including, as we now recognize, the most crucial presidency in the nation's history.

NOTES

1. *Year of Decisions* (Garden City, NY, 1955), p. 119.
2. Charles F. Horne, *Great Men and Famous Women: A Series of Pen and Pencil Sketches of the Lives of More than Two Hundred of the Most Prominent Personages in History* (4 vols.) (New York, 1894).
3. Andrew J. Dunar, *The Truman Scandals* (Columbia, MO, 1984).
4. R.H. Ferrell (ed.), *The Autobiography of Harry S. Truman* (Boulder, CO, 1980).
5. *Mr. President* (New York, 1952).
6. *Off the Record: The Private Papers of Harry S. Truman* (New York, 1980).

16
Nixon and his Memoirs

STEPHEN AMBROSE

George Orwell wrote, 'To control the present is to control the past. To control the past is to control the future.' Politicians in retirement do not control the present, but they do their best to control the future's perception of the past. The motive, if not laudable, is understandable. The goal, at least in a free society, cannot be reached. Nevertheless, the way in which politicians-turned-writers go about striving for that goal is as revealing of their character as are their actions when they are in power.

Richard Nixon is not the most prolific American presidential author. Both Woodrow Wilson and Theodore Roosevelt have more words in print than he. But Nixon is easily the ex-President who has done the most writing about his experiences. He continues to produce books and articles at a pace professional writers cannot equal. The most recent volume, *In the Arena: A Memoir of Victory, Defeat and Renewal*,[1] published in the spring of 1990, will not be the last. It is not immediately clear, however, in what ways this work differs from the formal Nixon memoirs published in 1978.[2]

This highlights a problem with Nixon as memoirist – he keeps writing the same book, under new titles. Like the Ancient Mariner, he keeps tugging at our sleeve, anxious to tell us his story one more time, no matter how eager we are to move on. Still, the sheer volume of what he has written, along with the contents, make for special problems in dealing with Nixon as memoirist.

In the Liars' Club in Burlington, Wisconsin, three presidents' portraits hang on the wall. The first is George Washington, because he never told a lie. The second is Lyndon Johnson, who never told the truth. The third is Dick Nixon, who did not know the difference.

This is not quite accurate; it is more correct to say that he did not care about the difference, or – even more exactly – that he had a Soviet mentality with regard to historical truth. He believed that the past should serve the needs of the present.

On 21 March 1973, John Dean went into the Oval Office to warn Nixon about a cancer on the presidency and to discuss specific problem areas. One was the $350,000 in cash that Nixon's Chief of Staff, Bob Haldeman, had given to Howard Hunt and the other Watergate burglars, to buy their silence. Nixon was not worried. He said the 'Cuban committee' provided a cover for that; that is, that Dean could explain it away by saying the $350,000 had been raised by Cubans in Miami to cover legal expenses for the burglars.

'Well, yeah', Dean said, 'we can put that together. That isn't, of course, quite the way it happened.'

'I know', Nixon replied, 'but it's the way it's going to have to happen.'

This was the same man who encouraged Chuck Colson to direct Howard Hunt to write fake cables in order to implicate Jack Kennedy in the assassination of Ngo Dinh Diem, the South Vietnamese leader. In other words, one goes into Nixon's memoirs suspecting that the author's commitment to the truth is less than his commitment to making the author look good.

Not that he is alone in that. And indeed Nixon's motives in writing his memoirs are similar to those of nearly all other politicians – to make money, for catharsis, to influence later historians, to get back at his enemies, to justify his own actions. But because Nixon was unique, he also had a unique motive – to continue the cover-up.

Watergate and Vietnam dominate Nixon's memoirs of his presidency, but despite the outpouring of words on those subjects, there are no revelations, no new information, no insights, only defences. And he makes it impossible to check on or assess the accuracy of his claims, because the struggle that began in July 1973, when Alex Butterfield revealed the taping system, continues to this day – the struggle for access to the tapes. Through an aggressive use of the legal system, Nixon has managed to prevent scholars from using all but a dozen or so of the tapes; he has kept more than 150,000 written documents under seal; he has not allowed any scholar to examine his diary. He uses all three sources extensively in his memoirs; whether he uses them accurately and honestly or not simply cannot be judged. This situation, of course, arouses suspicions.

So does Nixon's attitude towards the public. In June 1973, after John Dean had turned against him, Nixon worried about the possibility that Dean might have made a tape recording of their conversation on 21 March (this was before Butterfield had revealed Nixon's own taping system). Still, Nixon told Haldeman, even if Dean did have a tape, 'we'll survive. You'll even find half a dozen people that will be for the President, down in Mississippi if nowhere else.'

Haldeman thought there would be 'a lot more than that'.

Nixon agreed. 'There's still a hell of a lot of people out there, you know, they, they want to believe, that's the point, isn't it?'

Nixon counted on that when he wrote his memoirs. Thus he commented on the conversation of 21 March: 'I had not finally ordered any payments be made to defendants, and I had ruled out clemency.'

The tape of the conversation on 21 March is one of those the Supreme Court ordered Nixon to produce, and it is available to scholars, and on it Nixon four times orders Dean to see to it that John Mitchell should get the blackmail money to Hunt, which Mitchell did the next morning. What Nixon must have been counting on in writing such self-serving and untrue words in his memoirs was that 'there's still a hell of a lot of people out there, you know, they, they want to believe'.

To cite another example: on 23 June 1972, less than a week after the break-in, Nixon told Haldeman to tell the CIA: 'Don't lie to them to the extent to say there is no involvement, but just say this is sort of a comedy of errors, bizarre, without getting into it. They should call the FBI in and say that we wish for the country, don't go any further into the case, period.'

In his memoirs, he quotes himself as having written in his diary, that evening, 'I emphasized to Haldeman, we must do nothing to indicate to Pat Gray or to the CIA that the White House is trying to suppress the investigation'. When he published that supposed diary entry, he knew the tape of his conversation in which he ordered the opposite was public.

He is indeed a bold and brazen man. He goes on in his memoirs simply to deny the truth – he asserts that no one from the White House approached the CIA to request that it cancel the FBI investigation, except John Dean, who acted on his own without Nixon's knowledge!

What are we to make of such material? Nixon's assertions that black is white, that lies are true, that what he said he did not say and that what he did not say he said, are part of a piece: the contempt he feels towards those who report on his activities and actions, and the contempt he feels for the public at large.

'I could see no reason whatever for trying to bug the Democratic national committee', Nixon wrote in his memoirs. He claims that the comment was a diary entry made a day after the burglars were caught. He called the break-in a 'bizarre business, some sort of a prank'.

Thus did the cover-up begin, and to this day these words constitute Nixon's basic defence. *He* knew nothing about it and he could not for the life of him work out *why* anyone would want to break into the Democratic National Committee (DNC).

In a lifetime of bold and brazen acts, this was the boldest and most brazen, as well as the most successful. That students, scholars and the general public continue to ask these questions, as if they were legitimate, as if there were some unsolved mystery, constitutes a triumph for Nixon.

He had been after Larry O'Brien, chairman of the DNC, for 12 years. O'Brien had close connections to Howard Hughes; Nixon was desperate to know what O'Brien knew about the Hughes–Nixon relationship. Yet Nixon pretended, at the time, in his memoirs and ever since, that he could not understand why his people bugged the DNC.

On the subject of the break-in at Daniel Ellsberg's psychiatrist's office, Nixon gives a wonderfully convoluted explanation of his own role: 'I do not believe I was told about the break-in at the time . . . Ehrlichman says that . . . he told me about it after the fact in 1972. I do not recall this, and the tapes of the June–July 1972 period indicate that I was not conscious of it then, but I cannot rule it out.'

In so writing, Nixon was taking his own advice. Frequently he told aides who were about to face the grand jury, 'just tell them you can't recall'.

Another problem with Nixon's memoirs is that, for all their length, he leaves out so much. Thus we are spared the details of what promises he made to the Chinese in 1972 about Formosa (Taiwan), while we are all but overwhelmed with the details of the small talk he exchanged with Mao Tse-tung. He uses the same technique in describing his meetings with Leonid Brezhnev. The theme is best summed up in an order Nixon gave to Dean on 20 March 1973: 'Make a complete statement, but make it very incomplete.'

Another problem with Nixon's memoirs is that he was a man so full of contradictions that he did not even recognize them when he made them. Thus he quotes himself as telling Colson that his surrogate speakers in the 1972 campaign were 'reacting in their usual stupid way, by defending rather than attacking'. Then in the next paragraph, without any attempt at explanation or justification, he wrote, 'Ted Agnew, Clark MacGregor, Bob Dole and their teams were doing a magnificent job. They were not only effective spokesmen for the administration but kept McGovern on the defensive with sharp thrusts against his far-left views.'

It is a strength of Nixon's memoirs that much of the material is pure Nixon – the resentments, the hatreds, the flashing insights, the boldness and risk-taking, the world statesman – they are all here.

Nixonian cynicism: 'Most people are your friends only as long as you can do something for them or something to them.'

Nixonian self-pity: in 1958, Nixon campaigned hard for the Republican Party, which nevertheless took a frightful pounding in the congressional elections. Nixon summed it up: 'My campaigning had had little visible effect, had gained me little thanks or credit, and had tarred me with the brush of partisan defeat . . . I should have sat it out.' What he failed to note was that the Party regulars never forgot that Dick was there when no one else was.

Nixonian pretence: at every major point in his life, Nixon had to have a crisis. He simply could not make a decision without putting himself – and those around him – through a crisis. By the end of 1967, Nixon had been running full-time for the Republican nomination since the morning after Goldwater's defeat in 1964. Yet he tells us that he was tortured by indecision, and that late on the night of 22 December 1967, he committed his doubts to his yellow legal pad.

He begins, 'I have decided personally against becoming a candidate.' He listed a dozen reasons for that all-but-unbelievable decision; for example, he had decided not to run because he no longer relished the combat and lacked the zeal. He builds this drama through five full pages of his memoirs. Eventually he asks his daughters for advice, and his friends, and ultimately, at a family dinner, he asks his maid, 'Why must I do this terrible thing?' She replied, 'You are the man to lead the country! This was determined before you were born!' He then agreed to run. Who knows what he would have decided had she replied, 'Don't do it'.

Nixon's view of the press was that it ran the country. He writes, 'The media are far more powerful than the President in creating public awareness and shaping public opinion.' For a contrasting view, recall what Eisenhower said at his last press conference, when asked if he thought the media had been fair to him over the years. 'When you get right down to it', Eisenhower replied, 'I don't see much that a reporter can do to a President, do you?'

For all his evasions and ducking and dodging and squirming, Nixon could sometimes be brutally direct and correct. In June 1969, he announced that he was beginning to withdraw American troops from Vietnam. He comments in his memoirs, 'Thus began an irreversible process, the conclusion of which could be the departure of all Americans from Vietnam.'

Nixon could also be brutally direct in describing his aides and associates. Kissinger, he writes, was 'Machiavellian, deceitful, egotistical, arrogant, and insulting'. Secretary of State William Rogers was 'vain, uninformed, unable to keep a secret, and hopelessly dominated by the State Department bureaucracy'. As for himself, Nixon goes on, 'I valued both men for their different views and qualities'.

Sometimes Nixon could accurately express the feelings of millions of his fellow citizens. Here he is on the Congress: 'By 1973 I had concluded that Congress had become cumbersome, undisciplined, isolationist, fiscally irresponsible, overly vulnerable to pressures from the organized minorities, and too dominated by the media.'

Nixon had even more contempt for the press and television. He personalized all criticism; he could not believe that commentators were disagreeing with the policy. Thus when a storm of protest erupted after he launched the bombing of Hanoi at Christmas 1972, he wrote about 'the disgraceful record of the media' on Vietnam and assessed the motives of his critics as follows:

The media simply cannot bear the thought of this administration under my leadership bringing off the peace on an honorable basis which they have so long predicted would be impossible. The election was a terrible blow to them and this is their first opportunity to recover from the election and to strike back.

A month later, the day after the cease-fire was finally signed, Nixon met Kissinger. He quotes in his memoirs from his diary: 'I told him that I didn't want us to have any hatred or anything of that sort toward our enemies.' Among other things, what is remarkable about that statement is that when Nixon said 'our enemies', he meant the American doves, not the North Vietnamese Communists. He went on, 'They are disturbed, distressed, and really discouraged because we succeeded, and now we have to start to play to those who are willing to give us somewhat of a break in writing the history of these times.'

Nixon's method of playing to those who are writing the history of his times is to be very selective in granting interviews, and to do all he can to keep his tapes, his documents and his diary under seal.

And yet this contradictory man will do the most surprising things. He has always guarded his own privacy jealously and fiercely; he is strongly and quite rightly critical of reporters who invade it. Yet he quotes extensively from his daughters' diaries written at times of great emotional stress. His account of his last days in the White House draws heavily on Tricia's and Julie's diaries and memories; it is a painful subject, yet there it is, all laid bare, and by their father. His account of how he and Kissinger spent his final night in the White House is too embarrassing to repeat.

There are many positive features to Nixon's memoirs. As might be expected, he is eloquent and convincing in defending *détente* and in explaining the need to recognize China in 1972. His assessments of foreign leaders are usually good and sometimes brilliant. He is especially worth reading on Mao, Khrushchev and Brezhnev.

The great virtue of Nixon's memoirs is that they are authentic. They reflect and illuminate the many sides of this most complex of men, not least his astonishing ability to come back. Driven from office in disgrace, he has resurrected himself, thanks in large part to his writing efforts. In his memoirs, he explains the source of the strength that keeps him going. His mother, he relates, was on her death bed. He said to her, 'Mother, don't give up.' She pulled herself up in the bed, and in her last words said, 'Richard, don't you give up. Don't let anybody tell you you are through.' He comments, 'What a marvellous legacy.'

He has been drawing on it since, and is still drawing on it. He will never give up. He will never let anyone tell him he is through. He will be there for ever, tugging on our sleeves, eager to tell us his side of the story.

NOTES

1. Richard Nixon, *In the Arena: A Memoir of Victory, Defeat and Renewal* (New York, 1990).
2. Richard Nixon, *RN: The Memoirs of Richard Nixon* (New York, 1978).

17
Political Biography and Memoir in Totalitarian Eastern Europe

JÁNOS BAK

As a medievalist I am usually not professionally concerned with contemporary politics, but I lived in Hungary until 1956 with the good or bad fortune of knowing a number of political figures; also, I have kept a watchful eye on the historical and political writings of my country of birth, including political memoirs – essentially out of personal interest. In this essay I shall argue that to be a student of medieval sources is not so far away from the topic of political biography and memoir as it may appear.

Medias in res: it seems that political memoirs were as rare, almost heretical, among Bolsheviks and their latter-day followers as auto-biographies were in the Middle Ages. (Fewer than a dozen such writings are known from the centuries between St Augustine's *Confessions* and the *Mémoires* of Philippe Commynes.) The reason for this is, I propose, a parallel belief in the paramount importance of the community – there that of all Christians, here the Party – as opposed to the individual. Of course, I do not want to repeat the obsolete commonplace that the Middle Ages knew no individuals, just as the communist movement never denied the role of personalities, but it was in both cases something out of the ordinary and regarded as unseemly immodesty to write down one's own life and thoughts, be they orthodox or less so. Neither do I want to deny the existence of writings about outstanding persons of the church, of kingdoms or of the Party; however, these were usually written by others about great men – the different types of *gesta regum, gesta pontificum* and so on, and the parallel genres of semi- or truly official lives of martyrs and leaders of the workers' movement or red generals; or they were outright glorifications of cultural heroes: saints and miracle-workers in the former, secular saints – from Marx and Engels to Lenin, Stalin and Mao Tse-tung – in the latter. One major difference may be that no saint, as far as I know, ever added to his or her own life story what Stalin personally added to his: 'Although he led the party and the people with consummate skill and had the unqualified support of all the Soviet people, Stalin was free of any vanity, pretension or personal glorification.'

Without wishing to appear flippant, I believe that in systems with a closed and collectivistic outlook (which may be said grosso modo of both periods under review) the exemplary biography of the cultural hero is a significant tool of education, socialization or, if you are cynical, indoctrination. The core theories (theologies) of such systems are so complicated that the average member of the community (and many of them were illiterate both in medieval Europe and in post-revolutionary Soviet Russia or Soviet Asia) cannot comprehend them; hence it appears futile to the mandarins to try teaching them. However, the life story of the hero is a familiar, one might say folkloric, pre-Christian and pre-revolutionary tradition, well known and loved by the audiences. Such texts are, therefore, much more successful vehicles for conveying the core values of the system – by presenting the model behaviour of martyrs, saints or great men of the movement – than any treatise. The secular saints' lives and martyrologies (the Russian versions of *acta martyrum* were the several volumes on exile and forced labour under the Tsarist regime: *Katorga i silka*) were semi-recreational corollaries to the highbrow texts prescribed for study, such as the *Short Course* on the history of the Party (blasphemously perhaps comparable to the Scriptures and the works of the Church Fathers), or the theoretical pieces, the treatises of Marx, Engels, Lenin, Stalin and so on (comparable to theological works or commentaries on the Bible). Scriptures – communist and other kinds alike – make heavy reading, accessible only to the initiated, while narrative examples, sometimes based on terse scriptural references, are usually much more popular. That medieval hagiography made extensive use of folkloric material has often been emphasized, most recently by the Russian medievalist Aron Iakovlevich Gurevich and the authors of the French *Annales* school. It would be easy to show that the different hagiographical genres of the communist movement were built on the very same narrative folk tradition, or, more precisely, on the different levels of such traditions. For example, there were sober (sombre) official readings at Party seminars and schools for cadres, comparable to the more or less learned Latin *Lives* read to monks in the refectory.

There were also more popular genres, innumerable versions, usually anonymous, with titles like 'Tales about Lenin' and 'Anecdotes from Stalin's Life', with mild humour, events illustrating the 'human touch', encounters of the heroes with children, and the like; very similar to vernacular saints' lives. And there were even some rhymed ones, which also had their Old English and Old French forerunners 500 or 600 years earlier.

Of course, these stories were formulaic. Any trained medievalist or Kremlinologist can generate at his own fireside a saint's or a Soviet hero's life respectively, for it will invariably begin with humble origin (in medieval lives there was some variation on this theme) followed by early signs of conversion or rebellion against evil demands, confrontation with the enemy, heroic acts in word or deed, preferably both, participation in the main events of the movements, acquaintance with the chief heroes, probably some kind of temptation (in the modern ones of Menshevik deviation or something similar) successfully overcome with the help of self-criticism, and so on (only the miracles at the grave are missing in the Bolshevik formula). The repetitive nature of such tales may bother the outsider, but ethnographers assure us that – and, as all of us who have read tales to children have experienced – it does not disturb the folkloric audience, but rather delights it by offering recognition.

And now the last parallel. I believe that it is correct to date the spread of the heretical practice of writing – or at least of dictating (in best medieval fashion) – a personal and more or less genuine autobiography with the beginning of the end of the communist system, just as one could, *mutatis mutandis*, point to the first stirrings of the Reformation and secularization in early modern times. In our times, in the eastern European systems, the emergence of the genres we are interested in began with the decline of the closed hierocratic system of Leninist–Stalinist communism, and to be precise, with the secret political memoirs of Nikita Sergeyevich Khrushchev, the first major leader of a communist power who lived to look back at his years in office – at leisure, out of office. We should perhaps note – however pedestrian this observation may sound – that a practical reason for the lack of political memoirs in the communist world was the fact that important leaders usually served to the natural or – more frequently violent – end of their lives and had no physical chance to write in retrospect about their time in office. However, I believe that the theological attitude – if I may put it thus – was the more significant one.

As is well known, Khrushchev's memoirs were soon smuggled back into the USSR and circulated in *samizdat* selections, as powerful weapons in the hands of the still very much persecuted opponents of the regime in the post-Khrushchev era. Revelations about Stalin and Stalinists reached Russia earlier through other underground publications, but these were written by lesser protagonists: policemen or diplomats who had defected to the West. The authenticity of Khrushchev's writing and, of course, the high-level information he was able to divulge was unique. Some memoirs have been published since, such as Brezhnev's – which was merely a variation on the hagiographic genre – and more recently Gromyko's. The former bore the mark of the previous types also in so far as it was taken out of circulation once the hero became an 'un-hero'. The latter belongs, as far as I can see from reviews, in the 'usual' category of reminiscences of western diplomats, and only seems to be more crudely selective than most others in leaving out unflattering aspects of the writer's life. I believe, however, that the attempt at presenting a 'western'-style memoir is also a sign of abandoning the traditional Bolshevik-collectivist model.

I do not know whether a much earlier and very important political memoir – once again written by a heretic – that of Milovan Djilas, was available, even if only in limited numbers, in the USSR until recently. As is well known, Djilas wrote about his wartime experience in Stalin's headquarters, from the point of view of the self-sacrificing puritan communists of the guerrilla underground in wartime Yugoslavia, very much put off by the lifestyle of Stalin and his entourage. That book was published in Tito's Yugoslavia at a time when the Soviet denunciations and pressures on the country threatened all but war: clearly, censors from the Yugoslav state security, the UDBA, allowed such a personal tone to appear only because it did not touch on any of their hallowed heroes. However, when later Djilas and his friend Dedijer went so far as to write in their memoirs about Josip Broz (Tito) – even though not in unflattering, merely not hagiographical – terms, they found themselves in jail or in exile.

Apart from the few successors of Khrushchev, mentioned above, the recent changes in the USSR have not yet triggered the extensive publication of political memoirs. But there has been peculiar use – or, from the point of view of the officials, abuse – made of some official biographies. Some years ago, when the press was still quite strictly controlled a book was published in Hungary reproducing not a smuggled-in western text, but a collection of Bolshevik biographies from the volumes of the 1928–30 biographical dictionary *Granat* and older editions of the *Great Soviet Encyclopedia*. It contained, without any commentary, a series of originally official biographies of people who had become 'un-persons' (some of whom had subsequently been reinstated) conveying, merely by the repeated closing line or lines 'executed in 1937 (or 1938 or 1939) during the trespasses against Socialist legality', the mass murder of communists by their Stalinist comrades. The number of people with impressive revolutionary backgrounds, the conspicuous presence of persons from minorities, Jews, Latvians, Georgians, Hungarians and so on, and the total lack of any indication that any of them would have been other than devoted fighters for the 'Great Cause' made this collection a powerful indictment against the system.

It may also be worth noting that among the followers of Khrushchev there were some important military leaders. In fact, the memoirs of generals had already begun to appear in professional journals under Khrushchev, but they remained within the purview of military science. However, even these were stopped under Brezhnev. The memoirs of Generals Zhukov and Konev, the heroes of the battle for Berlin, published in the 1960s, also broke the barrier of silence; while still resembling the older official writings which gave mainly factual information, they did add their bit to the anti-Stalin ideological campaign by revealing the inner workings of the high command during the Second World War, not only debunking the 'Great Generalissimo's' military genius, but also shedding light on a number of political issues, such as the decisions about the Warsaw uprising, the true story of the Slovak uprising and the like. But, of course, these cannot fully count as political memoirs, being largely written for general military staff readers and concentrating on technical matters of command and troop deployment. However, Zhukov's reminiscences were so 'hot' that parts were originally expurgated and only later, with the progress of glasnost, were they published – in no less important an organ than *Pravda*.

It is interesting to note that in the USSR it was the soldiers who were among the first to open a crack in the wall of official misinformation – because that is exactly what happened in Hungary.

Strictly speaking, one should omit from this discussion the memoirs and biographies written in the first post-war years, before the communist take-over, and those written and published in western exile, for they do not fit the title of this essay nor did they, at the time of their publication, play the same role as the ones written and published in the 1960s or later. However, since some of them became in reprint – first semi-legally then openly in 1988–89 – 'best-sellers' and, I propose, also served as models for others, let us quickly take note of them. The first group, published in 1946–48, comprised memoirs by old demo-crats of the 1918 revolution (such as one of Károlyi's ministers) and by social democrats (such as Vilmos Böhm). They aimed at denouncing the communists of 1919, thus more or less explicitly warning against a new attempt at a 'proletarian dictatorship' in post-war Hungary – to no avail. The communists were represented by one widely read and widely advertised book: Zoltán Vas, who is considered further below, wrote *Sixteen Years in Jail* about his predicament under the Horthy regime. Since Vas was a co-defendant of the post-1945 leader of the Hungarian Communist Party, Mátyás Rákosi, in their trials in the 1920s and 1930s, this book already foreshadowed the hagiography of the 'personality cult'. The other group of memoirists, though small, was important for the future: this comprised military leaders from both sides of the fence. From one side came the memoirs of Vilmos Nagybaczoni Nagy, minister of war under Horthy, written as early as 1946. In these he denounced his pro-German comrades-in-arms and the German high command that had sacrificed an entire Hungarian army at the Don, and tried to justify both Horthy's attempt to leave Hitler's camp and his own change of sides. I do not believe this book had much political impact, for the communist take-over which made all these topics taboo for decades, came too soon after its publication. While not a great piece of writing, it deserves mention as it was among the first to be reprinted in the late 1960s and was followed by a series of memoirs with similar content. I shall return to these shortly. The other side was represented in the form of memoirs by partisan leaders and resistance heroes. Some of these belong more to the official type of Bolshevik biographies, yet they still contain relevant personal and political information. The publication of these memoirs stopped soon, too, partly because their authors – for example if they were fighters in the Spanish Civil War – vanished into Rákosi's jails.

For almost 20 years no personal memoirs or political biographies were published, except, of course, the hagiography mentioned above, from translations of the *Lives of Stalin* and so on to local versions of the life of Rákosi. The latter faced the same problems as the Russian Bolshevik ones, for they had to skirt all the taboo issues of inner-party struggles and avoid mentioning, unless in deprecatory terms, all the 'un-persons' who had vanished during the purges of Stalinism. Moreover, Rákosi, a young man in entirely secondary positions during the 1918–19 revolution, had to be given a revolutionary pedigree; this was achieved by means of fictional accounts of his inclusion among the original members of the Hungarian Communist Party and as one of the heroes of the 1919 war. A battle – the 'Battle of Salgótarján' against the Czecho-Slovak bourgeois interventionists – was invented, and photographs were even manufactured which showed not Béla Kun or Vilmos Böhm, but Rákosi marching in front of the troops in that sole victorious campaign of the Hungarian Red Army. What a sad commentary on the mores of the hired writers of tyrants! For Rákosi happened to have quite a respectable heroic record as a courageous defendant in semi-fascist inter-war Hungary, where he twice faced the gallows and was rescued by genuine international protest from French, German and English intellectuals.

Meanwhile, a fair number of Hungarian politicians and statesmen either were clever enough or were forced to emigrate. They in turn began to publish their memoirs in exile, from Michael Károlyi of 1918 fame through the wartime premier Miklos Kállai to the non-communist politicians of the coalition era, such as Ferenc Nagy, Imre Kovács, Béla Sulyok, and last but not least Admiral and Regent Nicholas Horthy himself. While some of these accounts might have found their way into Hungary, especially after the early 1960s, when travel was once again permitted, even with strict customs censorship at the borders, their readership was western, Hungarian or otherwise (for most of them were soon translated into English or German), and thus of no immediate concern in the present context. This was true – though somewhat less so – of the memoirs published by those who left Hungary in 1956 or later, such as the author of what I believe is still the best book on a fabricated show-trial, Béla Szász, and the important, though controversial, Cardinal Mindszenty.

With these names we have reached the late 1960s, the golden age of post-revolutionary consolidation, the Kádár regime in Hungary. It appears that by the end of the 1960s, a good 10 years after the revolution, some editors and historians found it possible to risk a revisionist stance – not on 1956, for that would have cost at least their jobs, but on some other taboos, first of all the country's history during the Second World War. In the space available, I cannot go into details of how the assessment – or lack thereof – of Hungary's participation in the war was dovetailed into the entire post-war communist ideology, other than to say that the short formula of 'treacherous fascist leaders having joined the anti-Soviet war' was all that could be said about it. True, among professional historians judgements on the inter-war period became more differentiated after 1960, and writers of fiction – or semi-fiction – risked addressing the national trauma of many hundreds of thousands of casualties at the Don (as well as of the

Hungarian atrocities in occupied Yugoslavia); but the breakthrough came with the publication of memoirs by politician-soldiers. The life histories of two generals of the General Staff, both briefly junior Cabinet members, one dead, one still alive at the time of publication, were published as a 'pilot project', and, having been successful in the bookshops and not censored by the Party, became the leaders of a series entitled 'Ages and Witnesses'. The series now comprises some 40 volumes, and includes memoirs of varied value and significance.

What was the function of these trial balloons? Clearly, the editor-in-chief of a literary publishing house (ironically, formerly a high officer of the political police himself) was given authority to revise the post-1945 image of the pre-war and wartime period, though not in authoritative history texts – that might have been seen as too dangerous – merely in the guise of 'personal stories'. (Incidentally, a more serious biography of Béla Kun, written by a researcher in the Party History Institute, and published by its press encountered opposition from no less a quarter than the Russian Embassy in Budapest; the book had to be withdrawn 24 hours before it was due to be promoted as Book of the Week. But that is another story.)

The series 'Ages and Witnesses', although it included some volumes sufficiently lightweight to pass Party censorship, soon contained the memoirs of an old communist (Zoltán Vas) and a former social democrat turned slightly critical Kádárist (György Marosán). Details began to emerge about the introduction of the communist dictatorship, or such previously unmentionable topics as the deportation of thousands of Hungarian citizens in the 1950s under the pretext of ridding the towns of 'class enemies' (a category that included virtually all the pre-war civil servants and higher-ranking officers of the old army, whether they had joined the anti-fascist resistance or not). Many more forbidden subjects were first mentioned in the series – within limits. Zoltán Vas, a communist of 1919 pedigree, who had been jailed for 16 years together with Rákosi and belonged to the Muscovite leadership that took over the country in 1945–48, but who in 1955–56 joined the side of Imre Nagy and the other so-called counter-revolutionaries, managed to have the first two volumes of his memoirs, covering the period 1918–48 published. He achieved this by telling the authorities that they were already available in the West; however, this blackmail did not help him to get the last volume into print. Vas died a few years ago and, as far as I know, Volume 3 is available in Canada only in manuscript form. (Times are changing so quickly in Hungary that the insights he offered are by now commonplace and probably no publisher will risk money on an old communist's ramblings.)

My last section begins with the Marosán memoirs, with the lively titles *Hot Oven* (which is only partly metaphorical, for the author started out as a baker) and *The Road Has to Be Marched to the End*. While Vas wrote his book several years after having been smoothly ousted from every political post, Marosán wrote in what might be called western fashion, still in the midst of political life, though no longer holding state office. His book was not merely an opening of windows – true or false – on a secret and secretive cabal of communist leadership, but also an attempt to win friends and denounce enemies still in power. I said 'true or false'. It is believed (and can be proved in a few cases, where documents have come to light) that he was the author of a number of historical legends about his enemies in the Central Committee of the Communist Party. Still, it is his word – which he promises to back up with documents – against that of all others that maintains that there was in fact a Central Committee meeting about the judicial murder of Imre Nagy and his friends in 1958, a matter of some symbolic importance for the survival of communist politics in Hungary.

Memoirs of this sort, containing a good measure of whitewashing the self and of blaming others, are now emerging in some numbers. The most peculiar of these are perhaps the reminiscences of Vladimir Farkas, son of one of the leading figures of the Stalinist Rákosi era, himself a highly placed officer of the political police, who had served time for 'trespasses against socialist legality' in the period of Kádárian de-Stalinization. In long interviews (a form now very much in vogue in Hungary, where a whole archive of oral history has been set up containing such tapes and texts, though few of them have yet been published in printed form), Farkas argues that he has been made a scapegoat for many others and charged – out of court, to be sure – with atrocities with which he had nothing to do. While his words about regretting not having died during the war (most of his family was murdered in Auschwitz or in Stalin's camps) may sound moving, experts are convinced that he was one of the most vicious torturers during his years of office and that both he and his father were in fact the pillars of the dictatorial regime that they are reputed to have been. Of course, and this is an aspect worth noting, the documents of the inner-party power struggle are not and may never become accessible for detached historical research, hence historians and laymen alike are condemned to working out the truth in a series of lies. If memoirs always – and necessarily – contain a mixture of fact and fancy, this will be even more so with the writings that emerge from collapsed autocracies, where historians will have less chance to separate the wheat from the chaff than elsewhere.

In conclusion while memoirs of the true sort – whatever that definition may mean – were not written in the Bolshevik world, so long as it stood as a monolithic structure, political biography of the hagiographic type played an important role in the indoctrination of the population, more or less for the same reasons that memoirs elsewhere become 'best-sellers'. Easy to read and personal in tone (true, in this context the personal touch was often false) biographies can convey the political message more successfully than any history book or political treatise.

Memoirs resembling those of the western (and, of course, non-communist eastern) European tradition have emerged in the last few decades as both symptoms and – in a minor way – catalysts of totalitarianism's decline, by having served as popular and widely read denunciations of the dictatorial regimes of the past. They were pioneers in the treatment of taboo subjects, just because they were not seen as official and 'learned' statements, and they had a significant impact because of their accessibility. Partly fulfilling the same purpose as in the West, that is, the *ex post facto* justification of a politician's actions and the exposition of political creeds by narrative treatment, political memoirs are now in the forefront of that intellectual movement which is commonly referred to as glasnost. However, there are still too few public personalities who have managed to survive their time in office long enough to present well-researched and reflected-upon memoirs. And if there are only a few personal statements, they may be easily dismissed as exceptional and unique, too weak to demonstrate the true nature of the system (as with the collection of Bolshevik lives from official sources). However, considering the speed with which governments – and now ruling parties – rise and fall, as, for example, in Poland, we may expect to read a good number of interesting memoirs in the near future.

NOTE

Professor Bak's chapter was written in 1989, before the demise of the Soviet Union and the communist regimes of Eastern Europe.

18
Struggle in the Spy House: Memoirs of US Intelligence

WESLEY K. WARK

The spy memoir offers an undoubtedly beguiling and popular formula of non-fictive revelation, a window on 'clandestinity'.[1] Modern fantasies spun around the imagining of a covert life and the flourishing of romantic and conspiratorial views of politics in which espionage is frequently seen as a source of succour or a threat to civilization help fuel the fascination. Widespread curiosity and concern about the burgeoning influence of intelligence agencies, whose place in the structure of government has been revolutionized during the twentieth century, also guarantee the spy memoir a ready contemporary audience. Spy memoirs, in turn, frequently promise to reveal what intelligence service is 'really like'.

Dust-jacket advertising tends to suggest that just such a contract between writer and reader, both intent on an expert guided tour of the *sub rosa* world, is about to be fulfilled. One mass-market publisher beckons the reader into the literature of intelligence memoirs with the following appeal: 'The books delve deeply into the people, events and techniques of modern espionage – the puzzles, wiles, ruthlessness, romance, and secrets of this endlessly fascinating world. Written by eyewitnesses or experts, they read "like fiction". But they are undeniably more powerful, because they are true . . .'.[2] Clearly Ballantine Books, at least, sees the formulaic success of such memoirs as a product of a popular appetite for spy stories, allied with the competitive advantages of the 'truthful' memoir over the fictive tale of espionage. There is no reason to doubt the soundness of Ballantine's market research, or sensibilities. The frequency with which intelligence memoirs enter the best-seller lists is proof enough.[3] Yet as a recipe for orienting the memoir of intelligence within the wider categories of political memoir and the genre of autobiography, the Ballantine blurb is potentially misleading.

It would be natural to suppose that the intelligence memoir is but a branch of the larger industry of the political memoir, distinguished within this enterprise merely by its special subject matter and occasionally sensational nature. There is no doubt that espionage memoirs can be conceived to fit the formalist model proposed by Roy Pascal of outwardly directed narratives of observation and action within the political world. They would largely fail, as does political memoir literature, Pascal's test of 'true autobiography', because of their lack of attention to the development of the individual personality, a canonical intention first established, according to Pascal, by Rousseau's *Confessions* (1782).[4] Pathos and pride mark the intelligence memoir as distinctly as they do the political memoir, in what G.P. Gooch saw as the memoirist's effort to surmount mortality. Gooch's rather old-fashioned strictures about the mendacity of political memoirs and their limited usefulness as source material for the historian are equally applicable to the spy literature.[5] Archetypal structures, of the sort that interest Susanna Egan, can be unearthed in the narratives of spy memoirs to prove them akin to the patterns of autobiography; the youthful 'quest', the moment of crisis in maturity and the confessional impulse of old age (or at least retirement) can be seen to shape these stories.[6] Spy memoirs reveal the same traditional authorial intentions as do political memoirs and autobiography at large: confession, apologia and the desire to repossess one's past are variously featured.[7] Put another way, memoirs of intelligence all partake of what William Spengemann identified as the three formal strategies available in the literature: historical self-explanation, philosophical self-scrutiny and poetic self-expression.[8] St Augustine's *Confessions* is, therefore, their common if distant root. There may even be an 'autogynography' lurking in the heart of the rare intelligence memoir written by a woman.[9]

But for all this generic likeness and critical fit, it can be argued that the spy memoir has some very distinctive features, a product not simply, as one might imagine, of the unique nature of its subject matter, but rather of the larger phenomenon of this literature's struggle for survival. The memoirs of what the unfortunate early American spy, Nathan Hale, called 'peculiar service' have their peculiar qualities.[10] The voices that emerge from the spy house tell the story of conflict – of a struggle to imagine, create, sell and sustain the inherently contradictory form of an individual account of a secret organization. Political memoirs, essentially tales of public conduct, face no such contradictions. The authorial strategies used to wage these battles mark out the distinctive terrain of the intelligence memoir. They all address, in their variety, the fundamental problem of constructing a narrative that will meet the special needs of the genre. This construction is made difficult by the fact that authors typically have aims that range far beyond the relating of their careers and experience and because the requirements for a narrative 'I' are so much at odds with the secrecy, the collective nature of work and the culture of intelligence.

A notable feature of intelligence memoirs is a vigorous, sometimes violent, effort to clear a space for the truth of the genre within a crowded literature dominated by spy fiction, media reporting and popular history. The brashness of the Ballantine claim, quoted above, is frequently echoed in authorial statements in the opening sections of spy memoirs. The superiority of the intelligence memoir is established through its greater claims to realism, while competing genres are denounced for their lack of authenticity. Spy-fiction writers are the villains most frequently assaulted by the memoirists for distorting the realities of intelligence, but the list usually also includes academics, journalists, 'exposé merchants' and sometimes 'paranoid liberals'. Ray Cline, a former senior intelligence official, in *Secrets, Spies and Scholars*, promises to avoid, by writing from experience, 'the romantic myth-making and the gossipy pseudo-exposures that make most of the literature of US intelligence nearly worthless'.[11] Russell Jack Smith, also from the same senior realm of US intelligence, makes the accusation that spy fiction has 'fastened a grossly distorted, frivolous image upon a highly serious, highly professional activity'.[12] He ranks memoir above documented history, by arguing that such writing as his has a greater appeal for the general reader, 'who wants mostly to know what it was like'.[13] More crudely, the author of *The Essential CIA*, Thomas Bell Smith, promises to acquaint people better with the 'grass-roots' realities of US intelligence, 'so that they can live with it and respect its problems. So that the fantasies of James Bond on the one hand, and the paranoid attacks of the liberal left on the other, won't continue to obscure the true face of this essential arm of our government.'[14]

An emphasis on authenticity is designed to achieve more than shelf-space for the intelligence memoir. It is also a strategy designed to overcome a basic problem confronting the memoir writer – namely how to convince the reader of the value of memoir itself. Why, after all, should anyone believe a spy, accept a spy's concept of reality or pay attention to a spy's version of covert events? A frequent narrative recourse is the hyperbolic suggestion that intelligence memoirs have a monopoly of truth-telling. But the main narrative device of the traditional memoir, the first-person account of experiences, is often viewed, by spy memoirists, as a hindrance to the task of convincing the reader. The privileged position of the author, who was once inside the secret walls of the intelligence community, is crafted into monopolistic wisdom, often by remaking the memoir into a hybrid, borrowing from history, fiction and other narrative forms. Denunciation of these competing voices often masks take-over bids.

While the confident assertion of authenticity in the spy memoir suggests a literature that knows itself, in fact a confusion of identity exists at the heart of most such texts. Paradoxically, one of the narrative strategies adopted by spy memoirs rests on efforts to resist some of the key demands of memoir, and reveals uncertainty and anxiety about the genre. Frequently, either overtly or in the construction of their works, authors deny that they are engaged in writing a memoir. The denial is usually contradicted if not by the form, then by the contents of these works. The most sterile expression of an authorial rejection of the memoir formula is contained in Archie Roosevelt's *For Lust of Knowing: Memoirs of an Intelligence Officer.* Roosevelt states his position thus:

In the true tradition of an intelligence officer, I have confined my narrative to what I saw and let you form your own opinions, rarely giving any of my own. I have viewed my role as one of telling facts for others to study and use to make policy decisions. I make observations and try, not always successfully, not to say what action, if any, should be based on my findings. I've always been a reporter, not an editorialist.[15]

Two things stand out about this rationale. One is the statement of the intelligence officer's code – the separation of facts from opinions, information from policy decisions; another is the presumption that the purpose of an intelligence memoir is to contribute to a policy debate. Neither undertaking is particularly upheld by the flow of Roosevelt's narrative, which becomes a kind of extended travelogue and ultimately loses sight even of the florid promise of the book's title.

Other revealing examples of a fundamental confusion about what constitutes a memoir, and an effort to camouflage and shape a narrative to other ends, exist in the literature. Stansfield Turner boldly proclaims in his *Secrecy and Democracy: The CIA in Transition*: 'It [his book] is not a memoir or a chronicle of my stewardship as Director of Central Intelligence. Above all it is not an apology for errors I may have made. It is also not intended to titillate the curious with accounts of spying and intelligence. I'll leave that to the novelists.'[16] Yet, on the very next page, the reader confronts the following statement: 'This book, then, is about my experiences from 1977 to 1981 guiding American intelligence through change . . .'.[17] Turner's book, whatever his authorial denials, is a memoir and it is an apology, especially with respect to his mishandling of the Cuban brigade issue (which he calls 'the most serious intelligence failure of my tenure') and public attacks on his fascination with the technology of automated intelligence collection at the expense of the more traditional agent system.[18] Readers might even find aspects of his account titillating, not least his attacks on certain personalities in the US Central Intelligence Agency (CIA) and on such CIA rivals as the National Security Agency (NSA) and the Defence Intelligence Agency.

Other authors have chosen to distance themselves from the memoir format not just by disclaimer but in the structure of their narratives. Ray Cline states in his foreword that 'this book about intelligence is in a limited sense a memoir, though not a full or systematic one; it draws in depth on my recollections of activities'.[19] Much later in the text we read: 'My aim is not to tell a personal story but the story of an institution and a political process.'[20] Cline resolves his difficulties with the memoir by providing two separate narratives: one a historical account of the evolution of the CIA; the other a personal account of his experiences, introduced in trailing sections of chapters under the heading 'Perspectives'. The strategy is not very successful. Philip Agee, the most radical of CIA memoirists, and a man accused by his detractors of having become a Soviet or Cuban agent in the process of writing his account (Turner talks of his having been 'brainwashed'), adopts the most extreme strategy for the memoir in his *Inside the Company*.[21] Here he avoids the memoir format altogether by casting his recollections in the shape of a 'diary' constructed at the time of writing, rather than kept during his career. He does not have much to say about this decision except that he chose a 'diary format . . . in order to show the progressive development of different activities and to convey a sense of actuality'.[22] Actuality, in this instance, would appear to be a codeword for the inscribing of 'authenticity'. Agee clearly did not invoke the diary format in order to write a personal story; instead his diary is strangely devoid of intimacy and remains a device for narrating a documentary history. Twelve years after *Inside the Company*, Agee wrote a second book, this time cast as a memoir, prompted in part by his new publisher and by the demands of his audience for a more personal recounting of his experiences, an appetite that Agee confesses he found puzzling.[23] Once launched into memoir writing, Agee clearly found it a liberating form. He produces in *On the Run* a long, obsessive and garrulous but highly personal account of the tribulations he experienced as an author and political radical at the hands of the CIA and a variety of European governments. However, few authors have had Agee's opportunity, or desire, to experiment with a second volume, and to benefit from the observed evolution of the genre. Individual authors rarely have the chance to reassess their sceptical views of memoir, or to augment an institutional account with a personal history.[24]

What seems common to the narrative strategies of Roosevelt, Cline, Turner and (the early) Agee, is their collective distrust of the memoir format. None of these authors confronts this issue openly, so we are left to speculate on its root. That root seems to be the assumption that the memoir cannot adequately serve to bear historical witness or convince the reader. No doubt it also has to do with the 'clandestine mentality' shared by these otherwise disparate writers and the difficulties that a lifetime in the culture of intelligence, with its emphasis on secrecy, cover-names, compartmentalization and the 'need to know' principle, creates for the writer suddenly experiencing the desire to describe and explain a career. In this sense intelligence veterans are the most unlikely of memoirists and their struggles with the genre are scarcely surprising. Few of these writers attempt to use the memoir format to achieve or relate any degree of self-knowledge. The character of the narrator is frequently absent.

There are notable exceptions to the practice of avoiding the formal requirements of memoir. Yet even in those texts where memoir is acknowledged as the intent and where it is allowed to dominate some part of the narrative, the temptation to use the same structure for other purposes is irresistible. Former CIA Director William Colby's memoirs, though composed with the aid of a ghost-writer, are forthright in embracing the goals of memoir. This is a first-person narrative, which attempts to give a full account of the author's life, with a traditional emphasis on apologia. 'It is the purpose of this book', Colby tells us, 'to show why I believe what I believe'.[25] Yet that stated purpose, in fact, blends with polemic and the author's defence not of his own career but of the organization he served. Shortly after his summary dismissal by President Ford in 1975, Colby tells us he 'decided to write this book to try to present a real picture of American intelligence to contest the sensational and hostile images that domi-

nated the media . . . '.[26] Ralph McGehee attempts to resolve the contending pressures of the genre early in his narrative by admitting that
he was driven by two different motives: to reveal the true (and to
him illegitimate) nature of the CIA as the 'covert action arm of the
Presidency' and to 'understand my own life'.[27] Inevitably, the former
motive comes to dominate the narrative and the character, thoughts
and personality of McGehee remain shadowy. A sort of shorthand is
used to describe complex states of mind and feeling: thus McGehee
tells us that he arrived in Saigon in October 1968 greatly doubting the
CIA's role and competence in that conflict; he left Vietnam 'full of
anger' and determined to 'expose' the Agency's part in the war.[28]

The nature of the basic struggle that spy memoirists have with the
genre has had the effect of precluding much in the way of formal
experimentation. The spy memoir remains mostly locked in a conservative mode, with only the occasional use of reconstructed dialogue
or chronological disruption to authenticate or dramatize a linear
narrative. It is significant that reconstructed dialogue is sometimes
used to display ethical thinking (as in David Atlee Phillips, *The Night
Watch*) or to project a picture of divided counsels (as in Bruce Jones,
War Without Windows).[29] In both cases it seems a strategy to avoid a
degree of personal retrospection and insight. Here again, the spy
memoir signals its close and safe affinities to history and its distrust of
experimental modes of fiction or psychological devices.

Notable, too, in the spy memoir literature is the absence of what is,
to autobiography, a vital element of the story. These texts are normally
devoid of any identification of a moment of revelation about the nature
of one's life and identity. Instead, the progress of self-knowledge is
often hinted at, but remains blurred. Philip Agee, for example, never
fully manages to convey what spurred him from the position of loyal
covert operations warrior to anti-capitalist activist. Sometimes authors
portray themselves as holding on to tattered convictions over a long
period, as in the case of John Stockwell, whose loyalty to the CIA was
badly damaged by his experience of the retreat from Vietnam but who
stayed on to conduct one last covert operation for the Agency, in
Angola, before resigning.[30] Joseph Burkholder Smith conveys a similar
sense of slowly declining faith in the CIA over a long career spent in
Asia and Latin America.[31] Those who write their memoirs with the
avowed intention of defending the reputation and importance of the
CIA also tend to skirt crises, shock or doubt; their narratives reveal
equanimity or steadfastness. Only David Atlee Phillips, with his
frequent, if sometimes unconvincing, displays of emotional and ethical

introspection, is an exception. There is, in general in these spy memoirs, a failure of candour. Once again, the dominant rules of the genre at large are broken by these peculiar memoirs.

The emphasis on authenticity and the avoidance of the formal demands of first-person narrative are structural conditions that affect the way in which the spy memoir is narrated. Both the contract of 'realism' and the effort to establish a more 'objective' position for the narrator serve to feed a third strategy present in the genre, one which profoundly affects its contents. This strategy looks for ways to support the polemical thrust of the spy memoir, often its central construct. When the critic Roy Pascal spoke of the 'polemics of memory', he was calling attention to the ways in which reconstructing the past required a shaping vision and both conscious and unconscious selectivity.[32] The polemical battles engaged in by intelligence memoirists greatly extend this principle, almost to the point at which the memoir ceases to be memoir at all.

The polemics of memory in these works speaks to the very origins and *raison d'être* of the spy genre. For virtually every such memoir is required to escape from the constraints of official secrecy. The motive for this frequently difficult enterprise usually transcends the need of the author to recapture his/her own past, and becomes to establish the truth about the intelligence community within which he/she worked. Intelligence memoirs often become the story not of a single individual, but of a powerful organization. In doing so, they take on the shape of a story couched in the voice of a personal narrator but driven by the exculpation or denunciation of an institution.

Polemical arguments provide the intelligence memoir with a resolved and sometimes reductive narrative, in which the portrait of a career is sacrificed to conclusions about the rights and wrongs of the espionage state. The writer's vision of the historical process therefore often takes precedence over the personal experience, bending the nature of memoir in the direction of partisan history. The boundary between memoir and history text becomes blurred, especially when the personality and individual experience of the author are submerged in a general historical narrative. The frequently expressed desire to tell 'what it was really like' in the corridors of intelligence is rarely achieved. Often it is simply abandoned somewhere in the midst of a text, as the argument from history takes command.

The polemics of intelligence memoirs are targeted not only on the general public but also on competing visions. In the process, what was an internal debate within an intelligence community becomes a public issue, with the memoir as a weapon. Peter Wright's *Spycatcher* provides the single most famous example of such a phenomenon, with its public airing of a contentious battle within Britain's MI5 regarding mole-hunting, but the motive is endemic in American memoirs.[33] Here the battle lines are easily drawn, featuring what might be called defenders of the intelligence faith versus dissidents, with the core of the faith being, in recent times, the CIA's role in covert operations.

Naturally, polemic has stimulated counter-polemic; in this way the US memoir literature has become almost self-sustaining. Authors from opposing camps occasionally credit each other with providing a stimulus to reflection and writing. Thus Joseph Burkholder Smith acknowledges that it was, in part, the revelations contained in Philip Agee's denunciatory account of his CIA career that made him rethink his vocation and ultimately write critically about the political covert operations in which he had been engaged.[34] More fundamentally, the appearance of individual spy memoirs has served to alert others to the very possibility of such an undertaking. The encouragement thus provided should not be underestimated. Ralph McGehee provides a poignant illustration of the ways in which a single published text can overcome the alienation of secrecy in his account of the liberating impact that the discovery of Sam Adams' article for *Harper's* magazine in 1975, on the corruption of intelligence in Vietnam, had on his own thinking.[35] More direct contacts and networks between dissident CIA memoirists have sustained their individual efforts, as the support given by Victor Marchetti to Philip Agee, in the early days of anti-CIA exposés, makes clear.[36] Spy-memoir writing has thus become not an individual, but a collective enterprise, well in keeping with its polemical and narrative strategies.

Few of the strategies of survival enumerated above suggest the potential power of the spy memoir. This power derives not from privileged insight into a significant profession or historic moment, not from revelation of individual character and psychology, not from the tapping of archetypal forms of expression, certainly not, as Hart contends, from its experimental confrontation with allied modes of fiction, and not from the fusion, as Pascal would have it, of individual and historical experience.[37] What sustains the power of the memoir of intelligence, what probably sells the memoir in the eyes of both writer and reader, is its fascinating expression of the code of the intelligence officer, of the clandestine mentality. In their polemical assaults on, and defences of, the US intelligence community, and in their multitudinous versions of its history, American spy memoirs convey the logic of intelligence service in haunting and tragic ways. That logic, in its simplest form, suggests that good intelligence might have saved the day. What is meant by good intelligence varies enormously, of course. For those memoirists like Frank Snepp, John Stockwell, Joseph Burkholder Smith and Bruce Jones who served in Vietnam, a climacteric for the intelligence community as it was for the nation at large, it is often equated with political wisdom, with a more insightful and in-depth understanding of the Vietcong and the North Vietnamese. For others, like Philip Agee and Victor Marchetti, good intelligence takes on ethical overtones, and comes to mean an intelligence service that should have operated according to some different moral and operational code – less committed to covert operations; less intrusive and manipulative in its foreign intelligence operations; more respectful of the legal limits of conduct; devoted more to analysis than to action. For others still, good intelligence is reduced to a nostalgic argument about what might have happened if a single event had been altered and a different action taken in the light of available information. William Colby provides a prime example of this tendency in his highlighting of the US-supported but ill-fated Diem coup in Vietnam as the point from which history turned sour.[38]

The varieties of meaning attached to the idea of good intelligence are perhaps less significant than the nature of the conceit itself, and its consequences for the shape of the intelligence memoir. The conceit has romantic overtones; it suggests that intelligence services and the officers who serve these institutions enjoy a very special power to influence events and to shape history. Conversely, when history fails to turn out for the best, there looms the shadow of an imagined intelligence failure. In the magnificently obsessive memoir by Frank Snepp of his service in Vietnam, this conceit becomes the stuff of an unusually evocative and powerful account. The slow-motion, agonizing fall of Saigon becomes a metaphor for the retreat of the CIA from grace, of America from power, and of individual wise men from their potentialities.[39]

The conceit of intelligence's special status in history is at the heart of the clandestine mentality. It forces the memoirist into a struggle with the genre formula. The result is a literature of polemic (designed to save intelligence), in which historical narrative displaces personal insight and revelation of the self. Despite the common disclaimers of spy memoirists against their spy-fiction brethren, the conceit of intelligence in fact aligns these works with the historical motifs present in much of the fictional literature.[40] In spy fiction history is made by clandestine 'Great Men'; in the memoirs history is made, or unmade, by 'Great' intelligence organizations, with individuals the privileged and 'objective' witnesses of secret events.

The internal strategies present in the spy memoir are not autonomous but were shaped by an external history of production. The creation of a tradition of spy memoirs to help sustain production, the emergence of a set of exemplary models for the genre, and the constant struggle against official and self-imposed censorship, were as responsible for the peculiar nature of this branch of the literature as was the effort to accommodate the clandestine conceit to the formulaic rules of memoir.

The production chart of US intelligence memoirs is marked by outbursts of writing followed, at least historically, by periods of quiet. It also marks the US literature, since 1945, as outproducing its national competitors by an ever-widening margin. This latter circumstance is in keeping with a number of vital factors: the exponential growth of the American intelligence community since the end of the Second World War; the attendant rise in public interest and concern about espionage; the relatively free environment in which intelligence matters are debated in the US; the degree of constitutional protection afforded freedom of speech; and the presence of a strong investigative or whistle-blowing tradition in journalism and publishing.[41] In contrast to the situation even in other western democracies, a critical mass exists of writers, publishers, readers and, above all, tolerant laws. While legislation does exist to control and monitor the production of intelligence memoirs in the US, essentially by requiring that all serving and former intelligence officers submit manuscripts for review by a CIA panel prior to publication, there is no suggestion, as in Britain, that the object is to prevent the existence of the intelligence memoir.[42] Quite the contrary, for a considerable part of the memoir literature functions in its polemic cast to defend the record of US intelligence and to argue for the necessity of espionage as an instrument of American policy.

A starting point for a quantitative assessment of the literature is provided by a pioneering bibliography published in 1986 by the Congressional Research Service. While some of the methodology employed may be suspect, especially the decision to differentiate intelligence memoirs and 'exposés', this bibliography paints a graphic picture of literary output. It counted only six memoirs and no exposés published in the 25 years between 1949 and 1974. The years 1974–75 stand out as a watershed, not only for the general production of books about US intelligence, but especially for memoirs and exposés. In the 10-year period between 1975 and 1985 (when the survey ends), the Library of Congress counted 17 exposés and four memoirs, for a total of 21 personal narratives on intelligence, a considerable increase in production.[43] This trend shows every sign of continuing.

Yet the time frame chosen by the Library of Congress fails to tell the whole story, especially if one is seeking the modern roots of this genre. These can be traced to the remarkable publication on 1 June 1931 of Herbert Yardley's *The American Black Chamber*.[44] Yardley's memoirs told the story of MI8, the code-breaking bureau which he headed from its inception in 1917 until its demise in 1929. Secrets haemorrhaged from the book, among them that American signals intelligence had been able to read Japanese diplomatic communications during the negotiations at the Washington disarmament conference of 1921–22, giving the US a distinct advantage in the difficult bargaining over naval ratios that was a feature of the conference. More sweepingly, Yardley revealed that his American 'Black Chamber' had during the span of its existence broken over 45,000 coded messages from some 21 countries, including Britain, France, Germany, Mexico and the Soviet Union.[45] The US government, which learned of the book's existence before publication, concluded that it could do nothing to stop its appearance. The Japanese press denounced this evidence of American espionage in peacetime.[46]

In its contents, the memoir was a 'grab-bag', containing stories that ranged from the highly technical (for example, an account of the methods used for breaking the 'Waberski cipher') to those verging on the style of the dime novel, especially where Yardley recounted the adventures of elusive female German spies (Madame Maria de Victorica); from stunning revelations of American intelligence successes and failures to minor anecdotes. This pioneering memoir was essentially shapeless, following no obvious literary precedent. Yet the Yardley memoir showed signs of an embryonic narrative method that would eventually incorporate the devices of authenticity, quasi-historical narrative and polemic.

Herbert Yardley was perfectly conscious of the pioneering status of his book and he devised a style to fit. In the preface to the first edition, Yardley wrote:

In the written history of the world, there is not so much as a glimpse behind the heavy curtains that enshroud the background of secret diplomacy. The background? The Black Chamber. The Cryptographic Bureau, where specialists pore over cipher telegrams of foreign governments, where chemists forge diplomatic seals and photograph letters of foreign plenipotentiaries.[47]

This melodramatic note was one which Yardley was to call on several times in his text. The specific theatrical flourish of the curtains suddenly drawn back on secrets of state would itself be repeated more than once in the text.[48] To sustain the effect, Yardley sometimes addressed the reader directly, emphasizing for his audience the magnitude of some achievement and, on one occasion, begging putative Soviet spies not to assassinate him in revenge for his printing some copies of decrypted Soviet documents in his text.[49] But for the most part, the melodrama was restricted to external events rather than to depictions of Yardley's own life. Reference to a nervous breakdown that he suffered in the summer of 1918, at the peak of MI8's work, is mentioned, for example, only in passing. A second breakdown in 1922 (following the success of MI8's work for the Washington conference) and the kinds of nightmares that accompanied it, are also given cursory treatment.[50] Yardley laid the foundations, in this way, for the intelligence memoir's emphasis on dramatic institutional history at the expense of personal or psychological insight. The curtains were to be drawn back on an organization and on *sub rosa* events, but not on the individual.

Yardley's memoir also set the genre in motion by his use of his text as a vehicle for a polemical attack on the US government's naivety about code-breaking, arguing that it was, prior to 1917, 'attempting to conduct successful diplomacy and warfare with schoolboy codes and ciphers' and lamenting, later in the book, that the US had failed to live up to the standards of the Soviet Union or Great Britain in its post-war employment of espionage and code-breaking.[51] The polemic is linked to apologia. Yardley's implicit justification for his memoir and its revelations was that it would call attention to the need for American vigilance and modernization in the world of international espionage. He used his text to urge the State Department to adopt a system of machine encipherment. The story of the closing down of his 'Black Chamber' in 1929 at the behest of a new, moralistic Secretary of State (Henry Stimson), who is alleged to have stated 'Gentlemen do not read each other's mail', is related in tones of funereal sadness. The folly of the act, according to Yardley, was felt immediately. The US was badly outmanoeuvred by Great Britain and Japan in the London naval treaty talks of 1930.[52] The bitterness that undoubtedly fuelled Yardley's decision to write his memoirs breaks through the surface only at the close of his account, when he reflects on his career: 'Sixteen years of drudgery, illness, espionage, brain-wearying science, flowery letters and honours. Why? To what purpose?'³³

Yardley provides no answer to this singular reverie. His account ends abruptly with the termination of Yardley's official career; yet the very fact of the memoir itself suggests the answer. Yardley, like his successors, would take up the pen to complete in public the unfinished business of a career in espionage.

Whatever Yardley's own motives, he proved that there were readers who wanted a glimpse behind the curtains. Sales of *The American Black Chamber* were respectable – 17,931 copies in the US alone in 1931 – though nowhere near best-seller levels. Translations appeared in French, Swedish, Chinese and Japanese. The Japanese version sold out at 33,119 copies to an indignant populace.⁵⁴

It was not the modest sales figures of the book, but rather its very existence in the market-place, especially internationally, that made the US government furious. After 1931, it moved to impound two further volumes of memoirs by Yardley, carefully studied the pot-boiler novels that he wrote for scraps of further intelligence leaks, refused his services during the Second World War, and kept him under flat-footed surveillance to discover whether his restaurant in New York was a centre for Axis intrigue.⁵⁵ Congress passed an act, inspired by Yardley's book, to prevent the publication of further revelations of America's code-breaking and cipher communications.

The circumstances of the production of *The American Black Chamber*, as much as its narrative structure, helped to define the nascent genre of the US spy memoir. Yardley's influence was both creative and constraining. He bequeathed a melodramatic style, a heady dose of spy revelations, a linked polemic and apologia and an emphasis on the history of an institution rather than of an individual. His book uncovered the existence of an audience enthusiastic for insights into the clandestine world, long before such tastes could be tapped by an indigenous spy fiction. The treatment meted out to Yardley by the authorities was a warning of the likely pitfalls for any writer desirous of following his lead.

Yardley's book had no immediate successors, perhaps because the constraints outweighed the creative possibilities of the spy memoir, and it was only after the Second World War that a new generation of American authors with knowledge of intelligence and a story to tell came forward. *The American Black Chamber* emerged as one model for such writing in an altered political climate, and in circumstances that reversed Yardley's own experience of publication. In the immediate post-1945 years, the retired head of the Office of Strategic Services (OSS), General 'Wild Bill' Donovan, led a crusade to protect the legacy of his wartime intelligence service, cherish its history and ensure that the US possessed an adequate intelligence service to protect it from the perils of the atomic age, Soviet expansionism and communist fifth-column political tactics. As part of his crusade, Donovan encouraged former officers of the OSS to write up their stories of wartime service.[56] The result was a small amount of literature that replicated important aspects of the Yardley formula, including the melodramatic style, revelations of clandestine events and the polemical thrust – this time about the lessons that war taught concerning the need for a powerful intelligence system to perform as the country's 'first line of defence' and prevent an 'atomic Pearl Harbor'.[57] With the creation of the CIA in 1947, and its rapid expansion after the onset of the Korean War in 1950, the need for a Donovan-style publishing crusade passed, and the US intelligence community settled down to a largely untroubled *sub rosa* existence, founded on a consensus about the need for intelligence in the cold war that stilled fears about the rise of an American 'gestapo'. When this quiet was troubled, the occasion tended to be not a flamboyant Yardleyesque memoir, but some débâcle followed by a blue-ribbon committee of investigation (such as that conducted by General Maxwell Taylor after the CIA's disaster at the Bay of Pigs). The Yardley model went into abeyance.

But all was not entirely quiet on the memoir front. In 1953 a former OSS agent, Donald Downes, published an account of his wartime experiences, *The Scarlet Thread*.[58] Downes' memoir represented a significant departure from the loyal and hearty tales of the first wave of sponsored post-war memoirs; nor did Downes' work owe much to the Yardley precedent. It was, in fact, a book written against the grain of the day. Conceived by Downes from his home in exile in Rome, and published in London, *The Scarlet Thread* was a bitter-sweet reminiscence of intelligence.

Downes described himself as a 'small fry Admiral Canaris from the sticks', and his memoirs describe a journey from innocence to sordid and disillusioning experience both of himself as an intelligence officer and of the US, which entered the war, as Downes put it, a 'secret intelligence virgin'.[59] Downes was an early enthusiast for the concept of intelligence, and understood by it something more than the adventures of spies. Indeed he, like his wartime boss, General Donovan, was greatly impressed by the threat of Fascist 'fifth column' tactics, and was convinced of the need for the US to engage in espionage to counter this danger. After considerable persistence, the use of family connections, and journeyman work for a variety of intelligence organizations, Downes joined the newly created OSS in 1942. His subsequent career was traumatic, culminating with the failure of 'Operation Banana', in which Downes witnessed the decimation of a select band of anti-Franco guerrillas that he attempted to infiltrate into Spain, and insubordination in Italy, where Downes refused to serve under incompetent officers and attempted to protest against an American policy that he thought pro-Fascist. After this experience of the secret war in the Mediterranean, Downes' career sped downhill. An intelligence mission to the Middle East in the spring of 1944 led him to characterize matters there as a combination of 'unlovely British scheming and American ignorance'.[60] His last OSS post, as an officer attached to the White House staff to write special reports for the president, lasted a scant three months. Downes resigned in frustration at the end of 1944, when he found that his warnings about British policy in the near east and American rightist proclivities in Italy were failing to have any effect.

There are two persistent themes that run in parallel in Downes' memoir. One concerns the amorality of almost all intelligence work; the other concerns the failure of the US to live up to its own particular moral standards in the war. The charting of a 'fall from grace' takes the intelligence memoir in directions never conceived of by either Yardley or the post-war publicists. In establishing the potential evils of engagement in international espionage, Downes' work was, simply, ahead of its time. His text would ultimately be a precursor for the dissident, anti-CIA works that poured forth in the 1970s, many written by men who had experienced similar falls from grace and come to question the rightness and utility of American intelligence practice.

In other respects, in finding intelligence a metaphor for an individual state of sin and suggesting, even in outline, the conscious exploration of character through the device of recounting a career, Downes' memoir provided a model that few subsequent writers would be willing, or able, to emulate. Downes had in fact found a way for the spy memoir to achieve both its own peculiar aims and those of more traditional autobiography. But most of his successors were unable to conjoin personal and historical narratives and opted, especially as the polemical wars grew stronger, for the latter.

Yet another experiment that occurred in the period between Yardley, the Second World War and the expansion of memoir writing from the mid-1970s would also prove to be largely without progeny. In

1947 Elizabeth MacDonald published the first modern American memoir of intelligence written by a woman.[61] MacDonald had served in psychological warfare with the OSS in the Second World War and her book appeared in the midst of that small stream of post-war literature about OSS life and work. It even carried the imprimatur of General Donovan himself. But from the preface onwards, MacDonald's memoir was at some cross-purposes with its contemporaries, because it was written by a woman, designed to relate a woman's experience of intelligence, and took on the task not of extolling or denouncing the virtues of intelligence, but of proving the virtues of women in intelligence to a sceptical audience.

This is not to suggest that *Undercover Girl* was a straightforwardly crusading book. In fact, an uneasiness with its own purpose sits at the very heart of the book. Even the preface, written in stern tones by MacDonald's former chief, hints at the struggle that is to come in the narrative. Donovan wrote:

Reading her book should give a better understanding of the way in which a strategy of disunity and confusion can be carried out against us in time of peace and yet how it can be guarded against by an alert and informed American public. *This is the message behind the lively good humour of this book.* [emphasis added][62]

For much of the text that follows, MacDonald advances a picture of the serious contribution of women to intelligence in war, denounces attitudes that hindered such an achievement, but just as quickly retreats from her argument, often by calling attention to the clichéd and silly ideas that she held about spying. There is much talk of MacDonald's dreams of becoming a *femme fatale*, of the Mata Hari legend (seemingly inspired by the 1920s Fritz Lang film version starring Greta Garbo), and of such tools of the trade as 'black satin décolleté evening gowns'.[63] These were self-images, but they were also foisted by the author on other female agents that she met during the war.[64] It may be that this was the narrator's true voice; it may be that MacDonald was writing to expectations about what an audience in 1947 would anticipate from a romance-struck female agent in a male world. In any case, this voice clashes with the passages in the text where MacDonald remembers, with great anger and frustration, the many obstacles placed in her path as a female intelligence officer – mildly expressed in a phrase about 'the inconvenience of being a woman'.[65]

Not until the very close of the book are these contending voices in any way harmonized. Here, MacDonald recreates (or invents) what she calls a 'Scheherazade social', a long evening's conversation, in which MacDonald took part between a group of American army officers and OSS agents confined to a house in China at the end of the war. The conversation was stimulated by the remarks of a 'recalcitrant' paratrooper, who grumbled out loud about the uselessness of women in war. This is the springboard for a 15-page discussion of 'OSS heroines', clearly designed to put their history on record.[66] Yet MacDonald, even for this purpose, places herself in the background, as a merely interested listener and recorder to a discussion offered by her male companions.

MacDonald left the OSS at the end of the war, and she brings her story to a close at this point. The conclusion of the memoir is pure anticlimax, avoiding as it does any overt summing up of the text's debate on the role of women. Yet there is something typical in the way in which she portrays the nature of her final task for OSS (to write a *post mortem* on morale operations) as both significant and inconsequential. The book ends with a jingle which MacDonald says she substituted for the report she felt unable to complete. Her 'singing commercial' for psychological warfare is introduced quite jauntily, but by this time the reader is on guard for the tensions in much that MacDonald has to relate. The 'Man' with the 'A Bomb' does stand out:

> When asked what to do with MO [morale operations]
> The girl who had tried it said: 'Oh,
> I would file it away
> Until some future day
> When the Man with the A Bomb says, "Go!"'[67]

MacDonald's memoir reveals many of the characteristics that critics have found unique to women's autobiography: the lack of an assertive voice, the uncertainty about achievement, the sense of alienation and the fragmented portrait of personality.[68] Yet no 'autogynography' has emerged in intelligence memoirs. MacDonald's book has remained a solitary creation, despite the growing numbers of female officers in the American intelligence community after 1945.[69] The polemical thrust of the spy memoir remained wedded to battles over institutional history and ethics in the style first propounded by Yardley and Downes and the genre has continued as a male monopoly.

The cold war silence that wrapped the American intelligence community was only occasionally disturbed during the 1950s and 1960s.[70] Yet as the foreign policy consensus of these decades finally broke down and as the dogma of national security began to erode, silence was replaced by the raucous noise of public disorder and debate in the mid-1970s. Memoirs played their part in establishing 1975, in particular, as the 'year of intelligence'. On the eve of the 'year', Victor Marchetti, a former CIA officer, and John Marks, formerly of the State Department, published a path-breaking account of their careers in post-war American intelligence.[71] Marchetti, the authorial driving force in the combination, had been searching for some time for an appropriate form in which to publicize his critical review of US intelligence. He had tried his hand, first, at a spy novel, published in 1971 as *The Rope Dancer*. This is a crude and violent piece of fiction. The hero, Paul Franklin, 'Special Assistant to the Deputy Director of National Intelligence' (whose career is modelled on that of the author), is revealed as a casual traitor, a murderer and a man whose political views border on the fascist. If Franklin, the protagonist, is far from being a sympathetic figure, neither is the world he inhabits – revealed as full of Soviet moles in high places and ultimately ineffectual mole-hunters, who pay a mortal price for their failure. Scattered through the text are fragments of more studied commentary on the CIA, of the sort that would be featured subsequently in *The CIA and the Cult of Intelligence*. One heartfelt speech by Paul Franklin reminds the reader that 'This Agency was set up to keep our government informed on the intentions and actions of our enemies and potential enemies, not to screw around with creating and maintaining ridiculous governments that are oblivious to the real world and the needs of their own peoples.'[72] But for the most part, Marchetti early loses polemical control of his novel to the routine action that he puts in motion in the plot.

    The CIA and the Cult of Intelligence is a different matter. In this work, a memoir almost wholly given over to polemic, Marchetti and the less obtrusive Marks attack the CIA for having betrayed its original mission as a centralized office for intelligence assessment, and charge it with having become, instead, a secretive and dangerous covert action weapon for successive American Presidents.[73] Marchetti and Marks explain this historical development by various means, including the need for the fledgling CIA to find tasks it could conduct in the face of bureaucratic opposition from other government departments, the failure of the CIA to maintain a hold on the new technologies of intelligence and the Agency's burgeoning anti-communism. But at the heart of their argument stands a description of what they understand as the 'clandestine mentality', to the pervasiveness of which the authors attribute the CIA's fixation on covert operations. Such a mentality operates to distance the CIA from any moral reflection and from the changing political sentiments of the nation. It is described as 'a separation of personal morality and conduct from actions, no matter how debased, which are taken in the name of the United States government and, more specifically, the CIA'.[74] Marchetti and Marks end their account with an appeal that confirms the centrality of the theme of the evils of the 'clandestine mentality': 'The United States is surely strong enough as a nation', they write, 'to be able to climb out of the gutter and conduct its foreign policy in accordance with the ideals that the country was founded upon'.[75]

The idea that America's secret foreign policy was indeed being waged in 'the gutter' was given a further sensational boost in 1975, with the appearance of Philip Agee's *Inside the Company*. Like Marchetti, Agee had been searching for the right literary form to hold his passionate account of life and times in the CIA. As with Marchetti, memoir was not his first choice.

Agee's 1975 account plotted a descent similar to that of Downes, from high-minded idealism (or at least ideological smugness) and commitment to disillusionment. For Agee, his own and the Agency's failure to use covert operations in Latin America to any purpose except to sustain in power a network of pro-American, anti-communist military dictatorships was the key to understanding. At the age of 33, Agee discovered himself to be but a 'secret policeman of capitalism'.[76] He resigned from the CIA in Mexico City in 1969, then spent a controversial period in Cuba, allegedly to do 'research' for his memoirs, which emerged in diary format, published in London, six years later. More than any other single work, Agee's *Inside the Company* functioned as the polemical point of reference for subsequent debate in the memoir literature.

Along with the surfacing of Marchetti and Agee, the action in the 'year of intelligence' was stimulated by the high-flying investigative journalism of Seymour Hersh (who had previously won a Pulitzer Prize for his reporting of the My Lai atrocity in Vietnam) and the subsequent chain of government commissions convened to explore Hersh's allegations about the nature of CIA involvement in domestic politics and in covert operations abroad. The first of these commissions, chaired by Nelson Rockefeller, failed to 'contain' the debate on the CIA, and the focus of attention quickly passed to special committees of the House and Senate established by Congress to get to the bottom of these matters. The better-organized Senate committee, chaired by Frank Church, soon put the CIA under an uncomfortable spotlight, holding televised hearings into such dramatic issues as CIA assassination attempts and the weaponry employed. Even congressional inquiries, it seemed, were capable of imitating aspects of the newly revived formulas of the intelligence memoir.[77]

The long-term impact of these public investigations was to open the way for a further outpouring of memoir literature, often after an interval of shocked, delayed reaction. Polemic and counter-polemic issued forth. One senior official of the CIA, a director of the western hemisphere (or Latin American) division, was so shaken by public criticism of the Agency that he took early retirement in order to launch a campaign to restore popular faith in the CIA and to educate the nation in its realities. The weapons that David Atlee Phillips chose were the memoir and the lecture circuit. Phillips' *The Night Watch*, first published in 1977, was a memoir with an undoubted polemical thrust, but it had other qualities which were to help establish the hitherto weak literary credentials of the genre. Phillips, a former journalist and amateur dramatist, wrote with style and wit and brought a degree of unwonted political sophistication to the intelligence memoir. The author's habits of reflection, of a certain humility about past mistakes and of at least a show of moral perplexity about the limits and legitimacy of covert operations all served to advance the Downes formula for treating the ethics of intelligence and personal experience. Moreover, Phillips' work embraced the memoir format more fully than many of its predecessors, treating the reader to some display of the author's personality and character development, as well as to an account of a dramatic life. Historically, the work is of sufficient stature as a source to be at the centre of some vigorous disputes.[78]

Similar qualities were displayed in William Colby's memoirs, *Honorable Men*, the first such work to be published by a CIA Director. Other works of this period, written from the same angle of argument as Phillips and Colby, tend to eschew the memoir format and embrace instead a historical narrative, leavened with personal anecdote. Ray Cline's *Secrets, Spies and Scholars* (1976) was an example; others would follow in writing, as Mark Lowenthal put it, 'from experience, but not of experience'.[79]

Both pro- and anti-CIA memoirists used the memoir form and often took similar approaches. Writers from both camps used story-lines that resembled historical narratives and which benefited from the legitimizing function of history. More personal narratives sought to convey authenticity in the force of experience, sometimes in the touchstone of Vietnam. The most expressive of these texts was Frank Snepp's *Decent Interval*, published in 1977. An account of intelligence and policy as experienced by Snepp while serving in the CIA station in Saigon between 1972 and 1975, *Decent Interval* is a sophisticated exercise in history, memoir, polemic and, unusually, portraiture. Many of the characteristics of this work – its great length, obsession with details, repetitiveness and forensic curiosity about the individuals for whom he worked – seem to derive from a conceit of clandestinity to which Snepp gave conscious expression. At the close of his book he writes: 'As a former intelligence officer I must believe, perhaps naively, that right decisions taken at appropriate moments on the basis of accurate information might have averted the outcome, or at least modified it.'[80] Ironically, this most literate of memoirs, which Snepp wrote, in part, to illustrate the inadequacies of American intelligence in Vietnam, profited the author not at all. The author's revenues from the sale of the book were sequestered by the CIA, as a result of Snepp's failure to submit his manuscript to the Agency for review and security deletions prior to publication.

The conjuncture of congressional investigations into the CIA and the fall of Saigon in 1975 subsequently provided the memoir literature on intelligence with a ready audience and three inexhaustible themes: the morality of covert operations, the utility of secret intelligence and the Vietnam experience. After the initial searching for literary precedents that characterized the work of Marchetti and Marks and Philip Agee, the historical evolution of the intelligence memoir literature does begin to appear to have a determinative influence. The books by Yardley and Downes provided models for the spy memoir to imitate and enlarge upon, and would begin to be recycled as the battle between anti-CIA and Agency loyalists was engaged.

The commodity value of the post-1975 spy memoir was exemplified by one further development. Spy-fiction writers soon intruded into the expanding memoir scene, borrowing from the available formulas for their own purposes and gesturing towards authenticity, often by the suggestion that these texts are really undercover memoirs forced to operate as novel. In the preface to James Grady's novel, *Six Days of the Condor* (conflated by Hollywood to three days and spiced up by the presence of Robert Redford and Faye Dunaway), we learn that:

The events described in this novel are fictitious, at least to the author's best knowledge. Whether these events might take place is another question, for the structure and operation of the intelligence community are based on fact. Malcolm's [the protagonist's] branch of the CIA and the 54/12 Group do indeed exist, though perhaps no longer under the designations given them here.[81]

Slightly less convoluted is the foreword to Robert Littell's *The Amateur*, which tells the reader that the hero, Heller, is a real character who cannot write his own story owing to CIA censorship. Littell is doing this for the unfortunate Heller, using, so he tells us, secret information pieced together from a variety of sources into a fictional framework.[82]

Such fictional memoirs, curiously, have little better success in delineating personality than do their real-life counterparts. Their imitative manner, in fact, is so thorough that the fictional spy memoir ends up recreating the quasi-historical documentary typical of its factual cousins.

After an impressive debut, but a slow and painful evolution, the American memoir of intelligence has now, it is safe to say, arrived as a distinctive genre with its own literary models, formulas, agendas and potentially best-selling status. It is shaped by internal struggles as authors attempt to find a voice and a narrative method to convey their experiences and polemics. It is also shaped by external struggles, as writers vie with each other in pursuit of a portrait, typically, of what the CIA was really like, and as dissidents and loyalists alike wrestle with the requirements of official secrecy and the ingrained habits of clandestinity.

The value of this literature rests with readers' expectations. An official audience monitors spy memoirs for their discretion and polemical content, and presumably rates the authenticity of such works according to their security-mindedness and polemical thrust. Such a reading has been going on since the first anxious scrutiny of Herbert Yardley's *American Black Chamber*. The CIA's in-house, confidential journal, *Studies in Intelligence*, now regularly provides reviews of recently published memoirs.

Among a general readership, studies of best-sellers suggest a probable range of analogous responses to intelligence memoirs, from the desire for pure 'escapism' to the opportunities provided by popular work for individual and collective self-empowerment.[83] Such studies also suggest that historical accuracy is not a prime expectation of readers. In the future, general readers will imbibe the standard diet of documentary and polemic and probably, as with the case of Agee, wish for more individual characterization.

Historians comprise but a small and peripheral readership of intelligence memoirs and their traditional scepticism about the genre is peculiar to themselves. This scepticism is rooted in concerns about the lack of documentary support within the memoir, the frequent impossibility of providing verification through archival research, and the doubtful 'objectivity' of the narrator.[84] Most of these objections are of dubious theoretical worth and tend to miss the point of the spy memoir's real value and real limitations. To return to our beginning: spy memoirs provide a potentially valuable window on clandestinity, valuable both because they exist in an otherwise strongly rationed world of information and because they illuminate not history directly but the changing and pluralistic mentality of the intelligence world itself. The limits on the value of the intelligence memoir are defined not by the criteria of evidence supplied, verification and objectivity (criteria that historians would wish to apply to their own work), but by the size and shape of each narrator's 'window'. Spy memoirs would appear to be invincibly anecdotal, inevitably garrulous and often impersonal – conditions created by the narrator's experience of espionage. Retirement or dissent, both forms of escape from the intelligence community, release pent-up streams of narration; but the author can rarely surmount the operating conditions of intelligence work itself. The window is often deep, but usually narrow. Graham Greene explained the phenomenon in *The Human Factor*, where he describes in the most elegant and chilling way the nature of the 'need to know' principle in espionage. The sinister figure of the MI6 doctor, Percival, explains to a bewildered and innocent-minded Colonel Daintry 'how we all live in boxes – you know – boxes'. The lesson proceeds with Percival trying to make his point to the even more bewildered Daintry by lecturing him on the analogy between intelligence compartmentalization and the perfectly constructed, geometrical abstract paintings of Ben Nicholson. 'Just try to understand that picture', Percival urges. 'Particularly the yellow square. If you could see it with my eyes, you would sleep well tonight.'[85] Most intelligence careers, while not, thankfully, like that of the fictional Dr Percival, are constrained by limited experience, the internal rules of secrecy and the rather rigid hierarchical structure of the intelligence community, all of which prevent the acquisition of any synoptic knowledge of the doings of American intelligence. Even when a degree of synoptic understanding is achieved, usually by the possession of high office, there still remains the perennial difficulty of translating the restrictive, clandestine experience into an overt narrative.

It is the essential paradox of the spy memoir that it goes in disguise, using the cover of historical documentary and personal narrative as the case requires. The case is usually conceived as a difficult mission to repudiate or legitimize the institution of intelligence; but sometimes it is also an assessment of a character, the author's own. Historians should perhaps borrow the vision of Dr Percival in order to reflect on what intelligence memoirs are, and how to value them. The clandestine mentality may be fundamental to our age; understanding it may be vital to the perception of government and national security policy.

For students of autobiography, the changing face and fortunes of the spy memoir suggest both the plasticity of the genre and the ways in which its structure and intent are largely shaped by writers. The nature of their pre-literary vocation inevitably shapes the voices that emerge. Translating clandestine silence into public address defines the peculiar problems and appeal of the spy memoir.

NOTES

1. John G. Cawelti and Bruce A. Rosenberg, *The Spy Story* (Chicago, 1987), on pp. 2–3 discuss the nature of what they call 'patterns of clandestinity' in American popular culture. They acknowledge that their discussion is stimulated in part by the memoir of Victor Marchetti and John Marks, *The CIA and the Cult of Intelligence* (New York, 1974).
2. Frontispiece to 'The Ballantine Espionage/Intelligence Library', quoted from Herbert O. Yardley, *The American Black Chamber* (reprint edition, New York, 1981).
3. At the time of writing, the memoirs of a junior Mossad (Israeli intelligence) officer had been on the *New York Times Best Sellers* list for 10 weeks. Victor Ostovsky and Claire Hoy, *By Way of Deception* (New York, 1990). The same year also saw the publication of memoirs of US intelligence in the Second World War and Vietnam.
4. Roy Pascal, *Design and Truth in Autobiography* (London, 1960).
5. G.P. Gooch, 'Political Autobiography', in Gooch, *Studies in Diplomacy and Statecraft* (New York, 1942), pp. 227–90.
6. Susanna Egan, *Patterns of Experience in Autobiography* (Chapel Hill, NC, 1984).
7. Francis R. Hart, 'Notes for an Anatomy of Modern Autobiography', *New Literary History*, Vol. 1 (1970), pp. 485–511.
8. William C. Spengemann, *The Forms of Autobiography: Episodes in the History of a Literary Genre* (New Haven, 1980).
9. Donna C. Stanton, 'Autogynography: Is the Subject Different?' in Donna C. Stanton (ed.), *The Female Autograph: Theory and Practice of Autobiography from the Tenth to the Twentieth Century* (Chicago, 1984).
10. Hale was an amateur American spy who was captured and executed by the British during the American Revolutionary Wars. His dying words became famous: 'I only regret that I have but one life to lose for my country'. A statue of him stands in the grounds of the CIA headquarters complex at Langley, Virginia.
11. Ray S. Cline, *Secrets, Spies and Scholars* (Washington, 1976), p. v.
12. Russell Jack Smith, *The Unknown CIA: My Three Decades with the Agency* (New York, 1989,) p. 3.
13. Ibid., p. 14.
14. Thomas Bell Smith, *The Essential CIA* (privately printed, 1975), p. 199.
15. Archie Roosevelt, *For Lust of Knowing: Memoirs of an Intelligence Officer* (Boston, 1988), p. xiii.
16. Stansfield Turner, *Secrecy and Democracy: The CIA in Transition* (New York, 1985), p. 3.
17. Ibid., p. 4.
18. Ibid., see p. 229 ff. for the CIA's role in the rediscovery of a Soviet combat brigade in Cuba;

p. 95 for a typical defence of his handling of technical matters.
19. Cline, p. xi.
20. Ibid., p. 216.
21. Philip Agee, *Inside the Company: CIA Diary* (Harmondsworth, 1975). For the 'brain-washing' comment, see Turner, p. 62.
22. Ibid., p. 9.
23. Philip Agee, *On the Run* (Secaucus, NJ, 1987), p. 12.
24. William Colby's second volume of memoirs (with James McCargar), *Lost Victory: A First-hand Account of America's Sixteen Year Involvement in Vietnam* (Chicago, 1989) proceeds in the opposite direction from Agee, containing rather less of a personal narrative than there is in *Honorable Men* (see note 25).
25. William Colby and Peter Forbath, *Honorable Men: My Life in the CIA* (New York, 1978), p. 21.
26. Ibid., pp. 445–6.
27. Ralph W. McGehee, *Deadly Deceits: My 25 Years in the CIA* (New York, 1983), p. xi.
28. Ibid., p. 124 and 159.
29. David Atlee Phillips, *The Night Watch* (New York, 1982); Bruce E. Jones, *War Without Windows* (New York, 1990).
30. John Stockwell, *In Search of Enemies: A CIA Story* (New York, 1978).
31. Joseph Burkholder Smith, *Portrait of a Cold Warrior* (New York, 1976).
32. Pascal, p. 19.
33. Peter Wright, *Spycatcher* (New York, 1987); for a critical review of this book, see D. Cameron Watt, 'Fall-out from Treachery: Peter Wright and the Spycatcher Case', *Political Quarterly*, Vol. 59, No. 2 (April–June 1988), pp. 206–18.
34. Joseph Burkholder Smith, p. 15.
35. McGehee, p. 184.
36. Agee, *On the Run*, p. 84.
37. Hart, p. 490; Pascal, pp. 11 and 83.
38. Colby, *Honorable Men*, pp. 203–18 discusses the fall of the Diem regime, with which Colby had intimate relations; he returns to the theme of the disastrous nature of the US decision to depose Diem in *Lost Victory*.
39. Frank Snepp, *Decent Interval* (New York, 1977).
40. For a discussion of the uses of history in spy fiction, see Wesley K. Wark, 'Introduction: Fictions of History', in Wesley K. Wark (ed.), *Spy Fiction, Spy Films and Real Intelligence* (London, 1991).
41. Useful histories of the post-war US intelligence community include Rhodri Jeffreys-Jones, *The CIA and American Democracy* (New Haven, 1989); Loch Johnson, *America's Secret Power: The CIA in a Democratic Society* (New York, 1989); John Ranelagh, *The Agency: The Rise and Decline of the CIA* (New York, 1986); Harry Howe Ransom, *The Intelligence Establishment* (Cambridge, MA, 1970).
42. Many American memoirists, including former directors of the CIA, have complained about the nature of the CIA review process. See, *inter alia*, Colby, *Honorable Men*, p. 474; McGehee, 'Appendix: This Book and the Secrecy Agreement', in *Deadly Deceits*; Marchetti and Marks, especially 'Publisher's Note', 'Authors' Prefaces' and 'Introduction', by Melvin L. Wulf; Turner, 'Appendix: A Word on Censorship', in *Secrecy and Democracy*. For a succinct account of British official secrecy, see Clive Ponting, *Secrecy in Britain* (Oxford, 1990). Passage of the revised Official Secrets Act of 1989 (CM 408), making 'unauthorized' publication a criminal offence, seems destined to prevent the publication of future British intelligence memoirs.
43. The Library of Congress bibliography is the basis of the article by Mark Lowenthal, 'The Intelligence Library: Quantity vs. Quality', *Intelligence and National Security*, Vol. 2, No. 2 (April 1987), pp. 368–73.
44. Herbert O. Yardley, *The American Black Chamber* (first edition, 1931, reprinted New York, 1981).
45. Ibid., p. 222.
46. Information on official responses to Yardley's book is taken from the introduction by David Kahn to the 1981 reprint of *The American Black Chamber*, and from the Yardley papers at

the National Archives, Washington, DC, RG 165, Military Intelligence Directorate (MID) file 10039–299 and RG 457, National Security Agency (NSA), file SRH 038. The relevant British Foreign Office files on this matter have been 'weeded'.

47. Yardley, p. xvii.
48. Ibid., p. 20.
49. Ibid., pp. 164–5 and 162.
50. Ibid.; the descriptions of Yardley's breakdowns are on pp. 132 and 212.
51. Ibid., pp. 20, 161 and 246.
52. Ibid., Ch. xx.
53. Ibid., p. 250.
54. Sales figures come from David Kahn's introduction to the reprint edition of *The American Black Chamber*, p. xiii.
55. The government's watch over Yardley can be followed in the MID and NSA files, see note 46; surveillance during the Second World War is reported in Yardley's FBI file, FBI archives, Washington, DC.
56. For Donovan's efforts see Thomas Troy, *Donovan and the CIA* (Frederick, MD, 1981), pp. 291–2; and Bradley F. Smith, *The Shadow Warriors: OSS and the Origins of the CIA* (London, 1983), pp. 406–7.
57. Wesley K. Wark, '"Great Investigations": The Public Debate on Intelligence in the US after 1945', *Defence Analysis*, Vol. 3, No. 2 (June 1987), pp. 119 –32.
58. Donald Downes, *The Scarlet Thread: Adventures in Wartime Espionage* (London, 1953); Robin Winks devotes an excellent chapter to Downes' career in *Cloak and Dagger: Scholars in the Secret War* (New York, 1987).
59. Ibid., pp. 205 and 151.
60. Ibid., p. 168.
61. Elizabeth P. MacDonald, *Undercover Girl* (New York, 1947).
62. Ibid., p. viii.
63. Ibid., pp. 39, 117 and 184.
64. Ibid., p. 108.
65. Ibid., p. 76.
66. Ibid., pp. 246–61.
67. Ibid., p. 305.
68. See, for example, Estelle C. Jelinek, *The Tradition of Women's Autobiography: From Antiquity to the Present* (Boston, 1986); Patricia Meyer Spacks, 'Selves in History', in Estelle C. Jelinek (ed.) *Women's Autobiography: Essays in Criticism* (Bloomington, Indiana, 1980); Donna C. Stanton, 'Autogynography: Is the Subject Different?' (see note 9 above).
69. A colleague of MacDonald's in OSS, Jane Foster, published a memoir in 1980, *An Unamerican Lady* (London, 1980), but it says very little about her wartime career in intelligence and is given over, instead, to a harrowing account of her tribulations with McCarthyism. In 1966 a former CIA officer, Sylvia Press, published a *roman-à-clef* entitled *The Care of Devils* (New York, 1966), again about McCarthyite persecution. Malcolm Muggeridge claimed in *Esquire* magazine that the book had been sabotaged by the CIA.
70. One such disturbance was caused by the publication of a critical review of the CIA by journalists David Wise and Thomas Ross, *The Invisible Government* (New York, 1964).
71. Victor Marchetti and John D. Marks, *The CIA and the Cult of Intelligence* (New York, 1974).
72. Victor Marchetti, *The Rope Dancer* (New York, 1971), p. 49.
73. Marchetti and Marks, pp. 4, 12 and 104.
74. Ibid., p. 248.
75. Ibid., p. 377.
76. Agee, *Inside the Company*, entry for 28 Oct. 1968.
77. For an account of the Senate investigation see Loch Johnson, *A Season of Inquiry: The Senate Intelligence Investigation* (Lexington, KY, 1985).
78. Phillips' memoir has emerged as a prime, but controversial, source for an understanding of the CIA covert operations against Guatemala in 1954, see Stephen G. Rabe, 'The Clues Didn't Check Out: Commentary on "The CIA and Castillo Armas"', *Diplomatic History*, Vol. 14, No. 1 (Winter 1990), pp. 87–96.
79. Mark M. Lowenthal, 'The Intelligence Library: Quantity vs. Quality', *Intelligence and*

National Security, Vol. 2, No. 2 (April 1987), p. 368.

80. Snepp, pp. 578–9.
81. James Grady, *Six Days of the Condor* (New York, 1975), preface.
82. Robert Littell, *The Amateur* (New York, 1980), foreword.
83. One such study is John G. Cawelti, *Adventure, Mystery, Romance: Formula Stories as Art and Popular Culture* (Chicago, 1976).
84. For a traditional expression of the historian's approach to memoir, see Gooch, op. cit.; and the more clever appraisal by Robert Young in Chapter 3 above.
85. Graham Greene, *The Human Factor* (Harmondsworth, 1978), pp. 38–9.

19
British Memoirs and Official Secrecy: From Crossman to Thatcher

JOHN F. NAYLOR

A seismic tremor briefly shook the fortress of official secrecy in Britain in 1975, when Her Majesty's Government failed to obtain a legal injunction which would have prevented the publication of the first volume of Richard Crossman's *The Diaries of a Cabinet Minister*.[1] The controversy had already been joined, as the *Sunday Times* had serialized this 'insider' account of contemporary Cabinet government: Crossman provided not only a record of actual Cabinet proceedings, but also a detailed description of the minister–civil servant relationship. What was not so well understood was that the former Labour minister had more than the present-day functioning of Cabinet government in his sights; he was also much concerned with the way in which that process came to be viewed historically. In the apt description of Hugo Young, whose book, *The Crossman Affair*,[2] is itself an 'insider' account, Dick Crossman intended 'to destroy the conventions which had rendered innocuous or misleading, or both, the writings of most former Cabinet Ministers about their time in office'.[3] In place of this time-honoured genre of officially informed retrospective memoirs, Crossman meant to forge a more accurate genre which we can conveniently describe as the 'Cabinet diary'; the approach, however, is open to others as well, for example, ministers outside the Cabinet or senior civil servants. In fact, some ministerial accounts operate above Cabinet level, in the rarified precincts of an 'inner Cabinet', discussing matters in a fashion which will dictate or even preclude Cabinet discussion; portions, but not all, of Crossman's volumes illustrate this point.

Why did Crossman, in opting for a new approach, reject the traditional, officially sanctioned memoir, in the preparation of which the former minister could secure the assistance of the Cabinet Office? Here, in my view, is the nub of Crossman's rejection of the traditional memoir:

Memory is a terrible improver – even with a diary to check the tendency. And it is this which makes a politician's autobiography (even when he claims his rights and uses the official Cabinet papers) so wildly unreliable . . . If I could publish a diary of my years as Minister without any editorial improvements, as a true record of how one Minister thought and felt, I would have done something towards lighting up the secret places of British politics . . . Of course the record is not complete, it never could be. But it is vastly fuller than the kinds of jottings on which most politicians base their memoirs.[4]

Thus the case for the 'Cabinet diary', although Crossman himself has been widely, indeed near-universally, criticized by his colleagues of the Wilson era for an egocentric and subjective product. Such a criticism seems to me unfair, because Crossman did not deceive himself or his readers:

Of course the picture which this diary provides is neither objective nor fair – although as a lifelong political scientist I have tried to discipline myself to objectivity . . . A day-to-day account of a Government at work, as seen by one participant, is bound to be one-sided and immensely partisan. If it isn't, it too would fail to be true to life.[5]

So much then for Crossman's methodology. Whether a new genre results, standing independent from the memoir, is open to discussion: one can acknowledge Crossman's case for independence, but counter that with the proposition that the two styles exist in a continuum. What Crossman calls 'memory' might better be characterized as 'hindsight', and an able memoirist can guard against this bias in his account. While offering no binding settlement of this dispute, I will opt for separation of the two, pleading constraints of space; in the present essay, I will forgo the pleasures of engaging with the multi-volume 'Cabinet diaries' of Crossman and his Labour colleagues, Barbara Castle and Tony Benn; also sacrificed for the present are the recently published political diaries of Hugh Gaitskell and Hugh Dalton, although I am unable to resist recording the astonished reaction of Dalton's colleague but not close friend, Herbert Morrison, upon reading unfavourable references to himself in the first volume of Dalton's memoirs, which drew heavily upon that very record: 'I didn't know the b— kept a diary like that.'[6] This must be one point in favour of the diarists.

Returning to the theme of political memoirs, I referred above to the British government's failure to prevent the publication of Crossman's first volume; the reversal came from the Lord Chief Justice, Widgery, and was all the more surprising because the Attorney-General had decided not to proceed under the catch-all provisions of the Official Secrets Act, 1911 but had, instead, tailored his case to the modish and evolving common law precept of 'confidentiality'. The strategy succeeded, as Widgery's opinion testifies: 'The expression of individual opinions by Cabinet ministers in the course of Cabinet discussion are matters of confidence, the publication of which can be restrained by the Court when this is clearly necessary in the public interest.'[7] Yet in a tactical sense, in this case amounting to a matter of timing, the Attorney-General came up short, for Widgery ruled that 'there must . . . be a limit in time after which the confidential character of the information . . . will lapse'. The Lord Chief Justice found that such 'a limit in time' had passed: 10 years and three general elections ensured that publication would not 'inhibit free and open discussion in Cabinet hereafter'. Crossman had in the meantime died, but his 'Cabinet diaries' were alive and well. In due course the second and third volumes appeared, without governmental intervention, the final volume only eight years after his very last words, etched in irony, had recalled a farewell meeting with the Queen after Labour's loss in the 1970 general election: 'She doesn't make all that difference between Labour and Conservative and, for her, all this simply means that, just when she has begun to know us, she has to meet another terrible lot of politicans.'[8]

What the judicial process had potentially yielded to would-be memoirists was quickly reclaimed by those whom I have elsewhere called 'the custodians of Cabinet secrecy', namely the present-day Cabinet Office. In fact, a second front had been opened – even before the conclusion of court proceedings – with the appointment of a Committee of Privy Councillors on Ministerial Memoirs, chaired by Lord Radcliffe. Their work was both completed and accepted by the Wilson government with unusual dispatch, suggesting a close relationship. Briefly summarized – and these are the present guidelines – the Radcliffe Committee recommended that a special standing be given to ministerial memoirs, subject to certain conditions, to which I shall refer below; they concluded that diaries of public affairs served legitimate purposes, although the timing of their publication mattered a great deal; and they insisted that any such ministerial accounts ought not to impair the confidential relationships among ministers and between them and their advisers. In no case ought national security to be endangered, nor should Britain's relations with other countries be damaged. The Cabinet Secretary, as had been the case before Crossman, would exercise oversight; the official 'vetting' which Crossman and his executors had avoided was restored to the administrative process whereby ministerial memoirs could be published, although ministers could claim a right of appeal to the Prime Minister of the day. In specific terms, the Radcliffe Committee freed the Cabinet Secretary to approve ministerial memoirs at any time, provided that national security, diplomatic relations and 'confidentiality' were not breached. If confidential relations were exposed, a period of 15 years would have to pass before publication, but concern for security and diplomacy might in some cases mandate non-publication for an even longer period. 'Confidentiality' would lapse after 15 years, except with regard to individuals – civil servants – still in the public service. Generally speaking, the Radcliffe report was not at great variance with Widgery's opinion regarding 'the limits of time', and this ministerial period stands in considerable contrast to the '30-year rule' which separates historians from access to official materials. Obviously, memoirs and 'Cabinet diaries' were to be treated alike, but one could hardly ask for official demarcation.

Such are the official parameters within which memoirists were asked to operate, but the sanction came as something of a surprise: the Privy Councillors concluded that legal mechanisms were inappropriate for purposes of enforcement. Instead, they cast the obligation in moral terms, as a 'public duty' binding upon all former ministers. The Privy Councillors went so far as to grant that if the undertaking were not universally honoured, it could none the less withstand an occasional breach. It has sustained at least one such assault, as Barbara Castle published her first volume of *Cabinet Diaries, 1974–76*, in 1980;[9] her account clearly lifts the veil of 'confidentiality' from her dealings with both civil servants and fellow ministers, although she is by no means as critical of the former as Crossman, self-appointed scourge of the mandarins, had been.

From the first, Mrs Castle had viewed the Radcliffe report with scorn, but she failed to respond to my enquiries about the submission of her manuscript prior to publication. I am inclined to think that if she had submitted her manuscript, the Cabinet Office would informally have written off the Wilson years, and probably the remaining Labour years under Callaghan, to 1979, an opinion confirmed by the latitude accorded the publication of Tony Benn's diaries. I am even more confident that no one in Downing Street or in the Cabinet Office – the sequence is deliberate, for other events demonstrated that Sir Robert Armstrong deferred to Margaret Thatcher – is prepared to write off the Thatcher years in anything like a similar fashion.

In turning to recent political memoirs, I must reluctantly exclude a number of accounts of compelling interest which are centred elsewhere than in the Cabinet room or were contributed mainly by civil servants, permanent and temporary. A number of these – by Sir Roderick Barclay, Nicholas Henderson and Evelyn Shuckburgh (in diary format) – stem from the Foreign Office, and I select only one item from the first as a reminder that memoirs can be written for reasons other than to set the record straight. Barclay reported a piece of advice given him by a prospective publisher: 'I have been told that if I want to appeal to a wider public I should be indiscreet, emphasise the personal weaknesses of the great, and in general adopt a strident tone.'[10] Crossman had commercial considerations in mind in remarking about retired ministers 'feathering their own nests', but Sir Roderick chose to maintain his probity and published his memoirs privately; the fact that he moved on to the family banking firm of Barclays no doubt afforded him a freedom from commercial concerns.

Certainly the most important accounts by a civil servant in the last decade are the No. 10 Downing Street diaries, 1939–55, which Sir John Colville published in 1985 under the title, *The Fringes of Power*;[11] I treat his diaries here only because of their importance and general interest. Several times seconded by the Foreign Office to No. 10, Colville served as Winston Churchill's principal private secretary in his peacetime administration. On occasion troubled by the propriety of maintaining a diary,[12] Colville settled for ensuring its safety; as a result, he kept a record of policies and personalities in war and peace which rival the analogous efforts of Sir Maurice Hankey and Tom Jones. During the war, he was not privy to Cabinet proceedings, save at a remove, but his proximity to Churchill then and later rivalled that of Hankey to Lloyd George. Very much sympathetic to Churchill after some initial Chamberlainite scepticism, Sir John's account is a 'warts and all' depiction of the great leader in strength and decline; and as for Churchill's last two years in office, following his stroke in May 1953, the seriousness of which was masked from his own Cabinet as well as Parliament and public, Colville retrospectively remarks: 'The distance between the fringes and the centre was far shorter than it had once been.'[13] Readers of Martin Gilbert's biography will recognize that Colville's work is an essential source, ironically keeping close company with a memoir which the Churchill family and associates have long lamented, namely Lord Moran's *Churchill Diaries, 1940– 1965*.[14]

Notwithstanding the publication of Colville's diaries at a remove of 30 years, the volume provoked some controversy; the former Prime Minister Edward Heath recently addressed the question of whether Colville was entitled to keep a diary, remarking, 'it was always understood that Sir John gave an undertaking to the other private secretaries that diaries would not be published'.[15] This is yet another twist in the publication of officially informed diaries, it appears, but I find it difficult to think that official objection would be taken to Colville's diaries, given the long-time wide latitude afforded works about the war, not least to Churchill's own memoirs. And likely to be of some import are Sir John's impeccable 'establishment' credentials: most historians would need to use a 'social register' in sorting through his characters and connections, not least of which are his wife's close ties to the Queen. Viewed realistically if possibly cynically, Buckingham Palace is surely pleased to have this volume to balance the petulant criticisms of the monarchy found in Tony Benn's 'Cabinet diaries'. As an added inducement to his royalist readers, Colville assures them that the diary of George VI's private secretary, Sir Alan Lascelles, will be 'a document of unusual interest',[16] when someday published. And this will probably be well before official documents relating to the abdication of Edward VIII see the light of day!

What about the memoirs of those charged by the electorate with the exercise of power? At its pinnacle, we have witnessed the completion of Harold Wilson's memoirs, involving a near-contemporary account, *Final Term: The Labour Government 1974–1976*, and a retrospective one, *The Making of a Prime Minister, 1916–64*.[17] In the former, the Labour leader wrote a political history of the frustrating final last years of office, in fewer pages (242 pages) than his predecessors Eden and Macmillan. My impression is that Wilson was more economical in his description of Cabinet proceedings here than in his account of 1964– 70; details of Cabinet discussion seem to be given only where the public were already acquainted with them, one example being the unorthodox referendum on Common Market membership in 1975. Whether the former prime minister consciously set a good example within the Radcliffe guidelines – he was working well within the 15- year parameters – or whether he decided that he could not beat his indefatigable Cabinet diarists, Barbara Castle and Tony Benn, at their own game is mere speculation. What we do know is that there is not a word of a putative MI5 conspiracy mounted against his government in the memoir; yet during the preparation of this volume, he acted rather bizarrely in lodging such allegations with the investigative reporters Barry Penrose and Roger Courtiour. Their book, *The Pencourt File*,[18] incorporates an astonishing account of what Wilson convinced them had been going on within the security service. Needless to add, the story hardly ends there, but it is for others to relate. Little need be said of Wilson's memoirs of youth, education, the civil service and his political maturation. His attitude towards the monarchy has somewhere been described as 'mawkish', and in that vein I am inclined to label this memoir cloying. Yet genuine humour is found in a jibe directed young Harold's way by Nye Bevan:

'I thought . . . that you were a Yorkshireman but your Dad has been telling me all about Manchester. Where were you born, boy?' With a Yorkshireman's natural pride, I said, thinking of Sheffield's steel, 'Yorkshiremen are not born; they are forged.' 'Forged were you?' said Nye in that musical Welsh lilt of his, 'I always thought there was something counterfeit about you!'[19]

Did the mature Lord Wilson reflect that some might think the joke was on him, after his long years of government service? I doubt it, but in accord with doctrines of equal time, let me leave the final word to him, as he reacted to the criticism that his leadership reflected a kind of political Houdiniism meant to keep the party together at all costs:

The highest aim of leadership is to secure policies adequate to deal with any situation, including the production of acceptable new solutions and policies, without major confrontations, splits and resignations . . . It may be bad for the headlines and news placards, but it has been sought and achieved by our greatest leaders . . . It is sometimes galling to be criticized for achieving it.[20]

His Labour successor as Prime Minister, James Callaghan, has written his memoirs, *Time and Chance*,[21] without the benefit of a diary, although he made occasional notes of interesting conversations. An experienced politician, Callaghan was aware that several diarists were looking over his shoulder; Crossman had died, but the new Prime Minister moved to reduce the diarists' numbers by one in excluding Barbara Castle from his regime. Tony Benn remained, and he has published his diaries for the period;[22] possibly others will emerge as well. As for Callaghan's recollections, one finds a few breaches of the doctrine of Cabinet collective responsibility in the Wilson years, but those matters were already revealed. Yet Callaghan's description of his dealings as Foreign Secretary with Argentina over the Falkland Islands is well worth the attention of those interested in the roots of the 1982 conflict, concerning which he concludes with justified irritation: 'The verdict of history must be that the Labour Government kept the peace and the Conservative Government won the war.'[23] He is also critical of certain findings of the Franks report on the conflict, remarking that they are 'perverse in the light of the evidence the committee heard'.[24] For no apparent reason, he reports individual ministerial views at a Cabinet meeting he chaired on 18 November 1976 and on the government's strategy at a subsequent Chequers conclave, which was not a formal Cabinet meeting. On the whole, however, his memoirs are quite restrained; they do not reveal too many Cabinet secrets. Tony Benn recently remarked that Callaghan was 'passionately opposed' to a Freedom of Information Act: 'He loathed the idea of anybody knowing anything.'[25] Callaghan's readers will not be much surprised by Benn's partisan judgement.

Space does not permit much consideration of other retrospective memoirs derived from the Labour regimes, written by Douglas Jay, Michael Stewart, Edward Short and Joel Barnett; there may be others. Jay's is a full-sized review of his lengthy involvement in Labour politics; I will note only his depiction of strong opposition to Britain's entry into Europe and his difficult dealings over that issue with Harold Wilson, whom he accuses at one point of 'a direct doublecross'.[26] It is likely that most relevant here is the implication that the prospect of memoirs may influence political behaviour, as Jay reports very slow progress at a late-evening meeting of leading ministers and civil servants in July 1965, 'largely because George Brown marched up and down the room in eloquent dissent, and finally remarked that the scene would not look well in either his or Wilson's memoirs' (p. 323). Michael Stewart, who was twice Foreign Secretary, produced a memoir, *Life and Labour*,[27] that leads nowhere, in good part because he refuses either to disclose Cabinet proceedings – on the grounds that the Privy Councillor's oath precluded any such disclosures (though ironically, Widgery had five years earlier placed no stock in that oath) – or to discuss minister–civil servant relations. No former minister has so embraced and even exceeded the Radcliffe guidelines, and Stewart's distaste for Crossman's efforts is palpable: 'Crossman was not always able to distinguish between what he thought had happened (or wished had happened) and what had actually occurred.'[28] The criticism, however, is shared by many of Crossman's colleagues, and it warns us to tread warily. To cite Crossman's sometime close ally Barbara Castle, doing battle with him: 'Thank God I've kept a diary, Dick, so there will be someone to challenge the Crossman version of history. And, by heavens, I will!'[29]

On the other side of the House of Commons, the only Tory Prime Minister falling under the Radcliffe restrictions is Ted Heath, voted out of office in 1974 and from the party leadership soon thereafter. Active in the Commons as an 'elder statesman' to this day, Heath has yet to publish his memoirs. In lieu of what could prove his informative account, two major Conservative leaders, and two lesser, have written memoirs of the traditional sort. Chancellor under Macmillan and Home Secretary in Heath's regime, Reginald Maudling wrote a literate and even amusing account of no particular depth.[30] As a keeper of records, Maudling can be placed at the opposite end of the spectrum from Labour's diarists: he preserved one conversation only, 'about the only detailed record I ever kept. Alas, I kept it in pencil and when I came to look at it a year or two later, it had faded beyond reading.' With the insouciance that marked his public career, Maudling added: 'Anyway, the details do not matter all that much'.[31] Maudling chose to keep civil servants' advice in confidence, and he reported little of conversations with colleagues or adversaries. In fact, the best Maudling story comes from his Labour successor as Chancellor, Callaghan, who reports the 1964 exchange of portfolio, residence and financial crisis in these terms: 'Sorry, old cock, to leave it in this shape. I suggested to Alec Douglas-Home this morning that we should put up the bank rate but he thought he ought to leave it all to you. Good luck.'[32] Maudling's amiability, which is disputed nowhere, did not endear him to Margaret Thatcher, with whom he parted company soon after she became party leader. No doubt protective of her public standing, Maudling took memoirist's aim at one policy only, remarking that her monetarist theory was 'totally divorced from reality' (p. 208). Few words, but ahead of his time.

His Tory colleague, Lord Carrington, stayed the Thatcherite course a few years longer, and several government crises as well. The best-written and I think the most engaging of the post-Crossman memoirs, Carrington's account, *Reflect on Things Past*,[33] spells out his resignation as Foreign Secretary in the wake of the Falklands invasion in a moving way: 'The anger of the British people and Parliament at the Argentine invasion of the Falklands was a righteous anger, and it was my duty and fate to do something to assuage it; the rest was done by brave sailors, soldiers and airmen, too many of whom laid down not office but their lives.'[34] His sentiment impresses as genuine, but the memoir is neither controversial nor revealing. Of course the Falklands come to the fore, although Carrington does not go beyond the Franks report in commenting on intelligence estimates prior to the invasion; most substantive may be his treatment of British relations with black and white Africa. Given the power of his feelings and the grace of his pen, Carrington may more than any of his contemporaries sustain historians' hopes for a truly significant memoir in years to come, if he follows Harold Wilson's 1967 scenario for a sequence of such accounts:

One . . . I will write immediately we leave office and that will be an absolutely factual record of the Administration. Later, when I retire, I shall publish a much fuller account in which I will give far greater detail . . . Thirdly . . . I shall write a book about what really happened with instructions that it should not be published until after my death.[35]

I suggest that any such final version by Peter Carrington could be worth the wait.

Less promising in such terms is the timid foray of the present Conservative Foreign Secretary, Douglas Hurd, the longest survivor in office of those who transferred allegiance from Heath to Thatcher. His memoir, *An End to Promises*,[36] was based upon diaries although Hurd next asserted that they were not to be trusted: 'Either they are written for effect, or else they are a safe deposit where the writer only stores those thoughts which he would not express at the time in public' (p. 7). I do not agree that diaries can be reduced to such an 'either-or' proposition, because motivations are far more complex. Despite his lack of confidence in his source, Hurd's is a genuine political memoir, critical of the Heath government but decidedly not of the man whom he served as political secretary. Cast along similar lines but devoid of 'insider' details, despite his ministerial service under Heath and Thatcher, is the memoir of Jim Prior, *A Balance of Power*.[37] Prior contrasts their styles of leading the Cabinet, not necessarily to Mrs Thatcher's benefit: 'If Ministers were never quite sure in Ted's day what Cabinet had decided until we saw the Cabinet Minutes the next day [a familiar complaint over the years], with Margaret it generally seemed that everyone in the country knew as soon as they opened their Friday morning paper.'[38] Even under-nourished memoirs afford moments of insight.

In contrast to these useful Conservative accounts, others who have failed to meet the political loyalty oath of Thatcherism – 'is he one of us?' – have chosen to publish but not perish in their public careers, not yet anyway. Typical of those who want to write something about the present and future rather than the past is the present Secretary for the Environment, Michael Heseltine, who acknowledges that his *Where There's A Will*[39] is neither a history of recent events nor a volume of memoirs; the latter, he remarks, comes only with retirement, and other temporarily retired Tory ministers seem to couple that notion with a desire to explicate the ideas and policies which sustain their interest in politics. For lack of a better term, I would characterize such efforts as 'tracts for the time' and attribute them also to Sir Ian Gilmour and Francis Pym, the latter of whom leaves us with one historical vignette in reporting his dismissal at Thatcher's hands in 1983: '"Francis", she said, "I want a new Foreign Secretary."'[40] While lacking in such dramatic moments, the polemical approach is echoed in the ranks of the political opposition, albeit a stage removed from Labour ranks. Both David Owen and William Rodgers, founder of the now defunct Social Democratic Party, have written such accounts of recent history to serve partisan ends: Owen's book, *A United Kingdom*,[41] is an engaging review of the misdirected and ineffective efforts of Conservative and Labour regimes alike over the past 30 years. By no means a memoirist, Owen brings an unusual perspective to his polemic; his craft leaves little doubt that this former Foreign Secretary could produce an engaging memoir.

A word or two in conclusion: after 13 years, the Radcliffe guidelines remain effective; with the exceptions of Barbara Castle and Tony Benn, former ministers have heeded them. Even Tony Benn's 'Cabinet diaries' of the Callaghan years emerged at a remove of over a decade, and the Cabinet Office chose not to challenge them. Besides, the Radcliffe report accepted the risk of an occasional transgression. The Thatcher administration may well have proscribed the keeping of a 'Cabinet diary' for its ministers, but – judging by Cabinet conventions over the years – any such decision would be restricted to her administrations; a future government could decide to alter those arrangements. Ministerial memoirs are no longer linked to section 2 of the Official Secrets Act. In 1989 that piece of onerous legislation, dating back to 1911, was revised: there were only a handful of references to ministerial memoirs in the extensive debate in the House of Commons, and government spokesmen accepted or inferred no connection whatsoever. Whatever form they may take in years to come, whatever their strengths and limitations, ministerial memoirs stand independently as a valuable source for the student of modern British politics and government.

NOTES

1. Richard Crossman, *The Diaries of a Cabinet Minister* (hereafter *Diaries*) (London, 1975).
2. Hugo Young, *The Crossman Affair* (London, 1976).
3. Ibid., p. 11.
4. *Diaries*, Vol. I, pp. 12–13.
5. *Diaries*, Vol. I, p. 13. With regard to his attempt to achieve objectivity, I would submit that he failed to attain this.
6. Quoted, *Political Diary of Hugh Dalton, 1918–1940, 1945–1960* (London, 1986), p. 612.
7. John Naylor, *A Man and an Institution* (Cambridge, 1984), p. 308.
8. *Diaries*, Vol. III, p. 953.
9. Barbara Castle, *Cabinet Diaries, 1974–76* (London, 1980).
10. Roderick Barclay, *Ernest Bevin and the Foreign Office* (London, 1975), pp. xi–xii.
11. John Colville, *The Fringes of Power* (London, 1985).
12. For example see the entry for 1 Jan. 1941, p. 326.
13. Ibid., p. 670.
14. Lord Moran, *Churchill Diaries, 1940–1965* (London, 1966).
15. House of Commons, *Debates*, Vol. 125, 15 Jan. 1988; col. 612.
16. Ibid., p. 292.
17. Harold Wilson, *Final Term: The Labour Government 1974–1976* (London, 1979) and *The Making of a Prime Minister, 1916–64* (London, 1986).
18. Barry Penrose and Roger Courtiour, *The Pencourt File* (London, 1978).
19. Wilson, *The Making of a Prime Minister*, p. 10.
20. Wilson, *Final Term*, p. 121.
21. James Callaghan, *Time and Chance* (London, 1987).
22. Tony Benn, *Against the Tide: Diaries, 1973–76* and *Conflicts of Interest: Diaries, 1977–80* (London, 1989–90).
23. Callaghan, *Time and Chance*, p. 377.
24. Ibid., p. 377.
25. House of Commons, *Debates*, Vol. 125, 15 Jan. 1988, col. 606.
26. Douglas Jay, *Change and Fortune* (London, 1980), p. 406.
27. Michael Stewart, *Life and Labour* (London, 1980).
28. Ibid., p. 133.
29. Barbara Castle, *Castle Diaries, 1964–70* (London, 1984), p. 660.
30. Reginald Maudling, *Memoirs* (London, 1978).
31. Ibid., p. 130.
32. Callaghan, *Time and Chance*, p. 162.
33. Lord Carrington, *Reflect on Things Past* (London, 1988).
34. Ibid., p. 372.
35. Quoted by Tony Benn, *Out of the Wilderness* (London, 1987), p. 487.
36. Douglas Hurd, *An End to Promises* (London, 1979).
37. Jim Prior, *A Balance of Power* (London, 1986).
38. Ibid., p. 66.
39. Michael Heseltine, *Where There's A Will* (London, 1987).
40. Francis Pym, *The Politics of Consent* (London, 1984), p. ix.
41. David Owen, *A United Kingdom* (London, 1980).

The Anatomy of Political Memoir: Findings and Conclusions

GEORGE EGERTON

At a stage in the proceedings of the Conference on Political Memoirs when participants were wrestling with multiple definitions of political memoir, Zara Steiner captured a common sentiment in suggesting that we were dealing with 'a very messy genre'. The term 'polygenre' expresses this truth somewhat more decorously; but there is no denying the polymorphous nature of 'this monster in literature'. The difficulty of classifying memoir in tidy categories, however, should not stand as an argument for diminishing its significance or impeding the development of a helpful body of criticism. Most genres, not least historical, are messy around the edges.[1] Moreover, political memoir has functioned in some form as a recognized category of historical writing in the development of all literate cultures, and at present shows no sign of attenuating. However problematic this genre may be, participants in the Political Memoirs Project are agreed that without such records of their deeds by political leaders or their scribes, knowledge of vast tracts of the past, as well as many facets of contemporary history, would be inaccessible to historians.

The term 'polygenre' has been proposed to categorize our subject in the hope that this would prove heuristic in opening it to more critical understanding. The term is apposite to both the genre's polymorphous internal constitution and its propensity to take on the forms of related external genres, as well as its diverse socio-political functions. Our review of the findings of the Conference on Political Memoirs and the essays included in this volume will proceed by addressing the principal elements and forms presented by the genre over the course of its development, appraising its particular attractions and vulnerabilities, and assessing functions it has come to exercise in modern political cultures. It is hoped that the collaborative findings herein presented will be useful in serving as a first critical exploration in the anatomy of political memoir.

The early Greek and Roman usages of the term memoir identified its essential attribute as a simple, unadorned personal record of an action, event or experience which could serve as a prompt to memory. Here the vital element is the descriptive recording of data. In the development of the genre over many centuries, this element has remained central: describing personal experiences, deeds – *res gestae*. Since the seminal changes in human cultures have regularly been effected and signified in political processes and related military engagements, personal narratives written by the political and military élites of antiquity and pre-modern cultures have presented one of the most valuable forms of historical records. The production of such contemporary narratives, based on personal participation and observation, has preserved a datum of the human past usually more vivid and accurate, for all its distortions, than the annals, chronicles and other forms of pre-modern historiography. Historians have, from the earliest times, recognized that the closer such records were to the phenomena described in both time and place, the greater their potential value as reliable sources of information.

In its unadorned form of recording political phenomena such a memoir would now be termed a political diary or journal. Modern political diarists such as Richard Crossman and Tony Benn emphasize the virtues of the diary/journal form in terms of the immediacy and accuracy of the record and therefore the credibility of the messages conveyed.[2] Diary in this sense is compared favourably to political memoir, composed retrospectively in the modern usage of the term, and marred, it is alleged, by faulty or selective memory and the tendency to 'neaten things up'. No doubt political memoir invites retrojection of personal and political interests held by the memoirist at the time of writing into the narration of the past, in the attempt to persuade contemporary or future readers. This temptation is endemic, but it is neither wholly irresistible nor uncontrollable. It might be added that not dissimilar temptations face the diarist who writes with a constant eye on publication and the messages to convey thereby, as well as the editor who often has great selective latitude, and may not be averse to neatening things up as well. Clearly, with their respective distinctions, political diary and memoir both constitute closely related forms of contemporary historiography: by nature they each address a past which lies within the personal memory of the writer; the content therefore reflects the limitations of perspective as well as the immediacy of experience which are the respective defects and virtues of contemporary recording. For the historian or political analyst, moreover, the well-placed political diarist or memoirist can offer invaluable sources of privileged information on contemporary history long before the official documentation becomes accessible. This consideration places most historians firmly in the camp of those opposing attempts by governments to restrain diarists and memoirists from early disclosure of privileged records and information. At the same time, and somewhat ironically, both politicians and historians perhaps share some aversion to a regime of completely unrestrained disclosure; aside from the virtues of confidentiality in the promotion of candid discourse in Cabinets, uncontrolled disclosure would soon devalue the worth of published political diaries and memoirs, while also diverting central elements of political discussion and decision-making – and the attendant official documentation – out of the usual institutions and into subterranean channels.

In any event, political memoirists usually wish to do much more than record political engagements or provide early access to historians. If the diarist can claim advantages of immediacy and descriptive accuracy, the memoirist can point to the capacity for retrospection, reflection and the application of literary style in crafting a unified narrative out of personal political experiences. It is recognized at once that this element invites reductionism, bias, the creation of a persona, special pleading and outright dishonesty in promoting or defending personal interests. The intentional and, even more insidious, the unconscious element of personal interest operating in political memoir represents its most distinct and endemic defect as a form of historiography. This feature, however, has been well scrutinized by the critics of memoir since antiquity, and modern historians are not only prepared to control narrative sources for this factor but also to exploit the evidence of personal interest as a vital datum itself. However cunning, the memoirist is almost invariably self-betrayed into the hands of the later historian. Hence: 'The book is the man', or, more provocative, Job's 'Oh that mine enemy would write a book'.

The explanatory and interpretive functions of political memoir often tempt the author into the paths of vindication, exculpation and the byways of personal interest. Equally they hold the potentially rich promise of reflection on the exercise of leadership and the operation of a political system. With the experience of office, and knowledge of 'the inner springs of power', political memoirists have regularly claimed to be uniquely positioned to offer lessons in political statecraft. Few of the essayists in this volume have found their subjects rich in political wisdom or prescriptions capable of direct application to present politics. Indeed, when dealing with the likes of Frederick, Napoleon, Talleyrand, Bismarck, Lloyd George, Nixon, to name but a few, the precept might well be: read their deeds, not their books! Nevertheless, where memoir addresses the challenges of political leadership with candour and integrity, there is wisdom to be gained; and if the store of available political guidance from practitioners is a rare commodity, it is, for this reason, that much more precious. From the memoirists featured in this study, wisdom is to be found in such passages as Bismarck's explication of the necessity for preserving European peace in the period after 1870; the policy dilemmas portrayed by British naval, military and diplomatic élites in face of the menace to peace prior to each of the world wars; the laments of Weizsäcker on the destructive course of Nazi aggression, the reflections of Gandhi and Nehru on the politics of resistance to British imperial power; even the proud rehearsals by Nixon of the opening of relations with China. Instruction is to be found also in the evasions and omissions which feature all too prominently in most memoirs. Here one thinks of Truman's aversion to public reflection on the most consequential of all his decisions as President – sanctioning the use of atomic bombs – despite his prolixity on almost every other subject. Even the outright distortions and lies can be didactic, as with the moral revulsion induced by Nazi memoirs of exculpation.

Much more usual and valuable than the direct translation of political precepts from memoirs is the stimulus that this genre regularly gives to reflection and public discourse on the enduring challenges of political leadership. The engagement of the reader with the memoirist in the political dramas of the past provides a potentially rich fund of experience and schooling for the willing student. Of course other forms of historiography and political science can put forward similar didactic claims and offer a more sophisticated schooling. But the memoirist has major advantages over the academic competition; these advantages relate to the readership targeted and engaged. Scholarly political analysis and historiography, with few exceptions, seldom reaches much beyond the confines of academia and the mandarinate. Political memoirs, by contrast, regularly reach both the political leadership and a popular readership in modern political cultures. Political leaders are drawn to contemporary memoir out of curiosity about what judgements are being passed on themselves and their political cohorts. Concurrently, the appeal of political memoir to mass readerships is apparent from the commercial demand from publishers, the mass media and the data from book sales and readership surveys.[3]

In discussing the popularity of political memoir, our study touches upon a field now attracting major critical attention – reception. Historical criticism has traditionally concentrated on the production of historiography; the side of consumption, impact and reception now invites overdue treatment. In this regard, the comparative attractions of political memoir appear to derive from its capacity to personalize and dramatize political and historical phenomena, while often offering up a fare of sophisticated entertainment. Political memoir is by nature personal; it records personal political engagement and experience, or what has been witnessed. The personal linkage between the author and the past in memoir transforms the description of events, behaviour and circumstances into the narration of personal experience. The resulting memoir has the potential to appeal with greater immediacy and drama to a readership, whose own categories of recognition, empathy and reception are powerfully predisposed to the personal, than other forms of historiography where the style is more abstract and impersonal. Indeed the seminal personal referent of memoir provides a constant resource for ordering information and unifying narration which equally serves both writer and reader.

The personal element inherent in political memoir represents the feature it shares most closely with the genres of biography and autobiography. Political biographies drawing heavily on personal knowledge and relationships have often been entitled a 'memoir of' the subject. Equally, political memoir is, in common usage, regularly termed 'political autobiography'. While biography, and especially autobiography, have received intensive critical attention of late, little of this criticism has addressed the subject of political memoir. This lacuna no doubt reflects both the disinterest in literary sensibility and style on the part of most political memoirists and, equally, the disengagement from 'realism' of much contemporary literary criticism. As the editor's essay notes, Roy Pascal's classic study of autobiography does make helpful distinctions between autobiography and memoir according to whether the focus is primarily inward, on the development of the self, as in the case of autobiography, or more external, on others, on events and deeds, as with memoir. This delineation is useful and indicates why few politicians, their lives largely dominated by externalities, are candidates for autobiography in this sense. Pascal nevertheless concedes that when a politician's career represents a distinct development of the self, and expresses deeply a personal outlook, as with Gandhi, then political autobiography in the true sense is possible.[4] Another exception suggested by Pascal occurs when the character of a leader stamps itself so powerfully on the political development of a period as to suggest the domination of personality over circumstance – as with a Napoleon, Bismarck or Churchill. But even when the autobiography takes on the story of a political calling, Pascal argues that 'the very massiveness of political and social events makes it almost impossible to review them from an individual standpoint . . .', and if the political autobiographer persists in putting himself at the centre, he courts falling into 'rank vanity'.[5]

No doubt, memoir usually presents a more appropriate venue for the politician in reviewing and reflecting on political engagements. But this does not mean that the personal dimension of memoir need be muted; this can be narrated with due proportion by the political actor if proper care and honesty are brought to the writing. The principal temptation is not so much to exaggerate one's personal credit for political successes, although this motive is always powerful, as to depict past behaviour and experience from the interpretive perspective of the author *at the time of writing*, with retrospective knowledge of the consequences of past engagements. The tendency to retroject perspectives and motives, to rationalize behaviour, to attribute present meaning to past experience, whether done consciously or unconsciously, for Pascal represents 'the original sin of autobiography'. So too with political memoir, the urge 'to neaten things up', to exaggerate intentionality in treating past success, to rationalize failures, and particularly to find a unity and pattern in the disorder of past political strife – all present seductive attractions. Much of modern critical theory on autobiography, in the light of such considerations, rejects the possibility of the autobiographer narrating accurate information about past events and experiences. Instead the genre should be appraised in literary and psychological terms with the development of identity and the presentation of personality serving rightfully as its principal function. As Pascal puts it, more is demanded from the autobiographer than an account of events and circumstances: 'one must be set free from them as historical facts, and from the concern with their accuracy as historical documents, in order to savour the quality of the central personality'.[6] Still more radical criticism would appraise autobiography under the categories of poetics and fiction – metaphors of self, novels of self-exploration.[7]

If Nixon's conception of truth as depicted by Stephen Ambrose would suggest the appropriateness of fictional categories when dealing with some political autobiographers, generally historians are reluctant to follow literary critics down this path. While political memoir shares much with autobiography in its personal focus and features, for historical critics it must be appraised equally as historical literature as it purports to describe political events and experiences. With all the distortions to which this type of personal historiography is prey, the potential for honesty, accuracy and insight remains; for historians 'truthfulness', however old-fashioned, ultimately stands as a fundamental critical concern in the evaluation of memoirs.[8] In this regard, the credibility of political memoir as historiography is enhanced very substantially when the memoirist supplements memory with careful resort to documentation. The collection and preservation of personal papers, as well as the maintenance of a regular diary, will pay rich dividends to the intending political memoirist. Conversely, political memoirs composed largely from reminiscence, without the assistance and control of supplementary documentation, are unlikely to stand as credible or substantial records. Finally, the integrity of a political memoir is strengthened if the memoirist conscientiously preserves personal documents for future researchers.

Political memoir, it can be concluded then, finds its most apposite critical location within the broad camp of historiography. Memoirists, for all their inherent focus on the personal, emulate the principal functions of historiography in attempting to describe past events and conditions, to explain the causes of these events and to interpret their meaning. Since the rise of modern historiography in the eighteenth century, memoirists have forgone the claim to be uniquely qualified to write the general history of their times. Nevertheless, in certain circumstances the political memoirist can aspire to produce a history of a major episode in which he or she was centrally engaged. When the talent for historiography is present, where the documentation produced in the course of the events has been collected and if assistance and time for writing are available, then the political memoirist has the potential to produce a first history of the episode based on both unique remembrance and privileged documentation. Here one thinks of the war memoirs of both Lloyd George and Churchill, who wrote with truly historical compass, and heavily influenced subsequent historiography of the two world wars of the twentieth century.

Few memoirists can aspire to this scope of writing, or hope to put an enduring stamp on the historiography of their era. Political memoir in modern cultures functions primarily in that interval between the contemporary discourse of journalists and political scientists, and the operation, a generation or so later, of professional historiography as it begins to reconstruct the past from accessible sources. It is the potency of political memoir in thereby shaping the popular, living generational memory of a culture which adds particular importance to promoting a critical understanding of its political and historical functions. Our study suggests that political memoir functions in modern cultures to conceptualize popular understanding of historical processes largely in terms of the dramas of political leadership. In this it joins with other popular media in performing an essentially conservative function by enhancing and legitimating the status and role of leaders. Harold Laski, in reviewing the *War Memoirs* of Lloyd George, lamented the very brilliance of the wartime prime minister's dramatization of his political struggles; this obliterated any sense in the reader's mind of the larger socio-economic forces driving history.[9] It is the élites – political, military and diplomatic – who have dominated the genre; their constant motif of vindication and rationalization cannot but serve to persuade, conservatively, that things could not have turned out differently or, alternatively, that only different leadership – theirs – would have brought improvement.

The essays in these volumes do provide some counter-evidence of a potentially radical function for political memoir: the literature of challenge that Milton Israel has identified in Indian nationalist memoirs, the repression of memoirs by communist totalitarian regimes as portrayed by János Bak, and the efforts made by the British government to prevent publication of the Crossman diaries as reviewed in John Naylor's essay, and later the revelations of Peter Wright in *Spycatcher*. A few other well-known memoirists who wrote with radical intent could be mentioned: Madame Roland, Garibaldi, Hitler (a special case), Trotsky, Khrushchev, Solzhenitsyn. The list is not long, however; the Left has generally failed to rival the political Centre and Right in the production of political memoir, and very few revolutionaries or political radicals find inclination or leisure (apart from imprisonment or exile) to compose memoirs. In France the revolution absorbed and then consumed most of its leaders. János Bak has shown how memoir literature was denigrated by the Bolsheviks. None of the Chinese communist leadership has produced memoirs. In Britain, the diaries of Crossman and Tony Benn perhaps best illustrate the influential didactic functions memoir and diary can perform in

promoting political discourse and criticism from the Left; they show
little evidence, however, of advancing radical mobilization, and the
authorities have so far left Mr Benn free to do his worst.

Most modern political memoirs have but a brief flowering in the
attention of the public and the popular media; then they wither and
die, finding resurrection, if ever, only as sources in the hands of curious
historians. The historian is grateful for such sources, whatever their
shelf-life, and can infer from them much that eludes other types of
documentation. Only a small and select company of political memoirs
endure to form part of the permanent literary store of human wisdom
and fascination. Entry to the pantheon of political memoirists goes to
those few who have not only lived in and made 'interesting times', but
exploited the elements of this polygenre with genius: as wilful recorder
of prodigious *res gestae* (Caesar); as penetrating political observer
(Saint-Simon, Tocqueville); as revealing political autobiographer
(Babur, Chateaubriand, Gandhi); as encompassing historian of epic
political engagement (Clarendon, Lloyd George, Churchill). These
memoirists have accomplished what their predecessors in antiquity
yearned for: their names will enjoy 'everlasting existence on the lips of
the living'.[10]

NOTES

1. Philip Guedalla defined biography as 'a region bounded on the north by history, on the south by fiction, on the east by obituary, and on the west by tedium'. Cited in Lord Butler, *The Difficult Art of Autobiography* (Oxford, 1968), p. 3.
2. R.H.S. Crossman, *The Diaries of a Cabinet Minister* (3 vols), (London, 1975–77); Tony Benn, *Against the Tide: Diaries, 1973–76* (London, 1989), p. xi.
3. The extravagant bidding by publishers for political memoirs is reviewed by Otto Friedrichs in *Time*, 2 September 1985, p. 66. Evidence on comparative sales of political memoirs and biography can be found in book trade journals – *Publishers Weekly* in the United States, and the *Bookseller* and *Publishing News* in Britain; see particularly the annual *Publishers Weekly Yearbook*, and also the *Gallup Annual Report on Book Buying*. For readership surveys and analyses see the many reports of the Publishers Association (Britain) and The Book Industry Study Group (United States). Biography and autobiography regularly top the sales and readership listings in the non-fiction category, nearly always outperforming history proper.
4. Roy Pascal, *Design and Truth in Autobiography* (Cambridge, 1960), p. 6.
5. Pascal, pp. 10 and 120. A quip by Balfour on Churchill's *The World Crisis* captures this point: 'I am immersed in Winston's brilliant autobiography disguised as a history of the Universe.' Cited in Butler, p. 12.
6. Pascal, p. 20.
7. For recent critical theory on autobiography see James Olney, *Metaphors of the Self: The Meaning of Autobiography* (Princeton, 1972), and two symposia he has edited, *Autobiography: Essays Theoretical and Critical* (Princeton, 1980), and *Studies in Autobiography* (New York, 1988); and Susanna Egan, *Patterns of Experience in Autobiography* (Chapel Hill, 1984). Similar critical themes are addressed with regard to biography in Ira Nadel's *Biography:*

Fiction, Fact, and Form (London, 1984).

8. The applicability and utility of post-structuralist literary theory to historiography is thoroughly addressed in the *American Historical Review*, Vol. 94, No. 3 (June 1989). The resistance of historians and biographers to theory which would deny or diminish the possibility of accurate reconstruction of past lives and their cultural contexts is powerfully presented by Anne Twaite and others in Eric Homberger and John Charmley (eds.), *The Troubled Face of Biography* (New York, 1988).

9. George Egerton, 'The Lloyd George *War Memoirs*: A Study in the Politics of Memory', *Journal of Modern History*, Vol. 60 (March 1988), p. 84.

10. An expression used commonly in ancient Egyptian epitaphs.